The new aestheticism

MANCHESTER
UNIVERSITY PRESS

The new aestheticism

edited by
John J. Joughin and Simon Malpas

Manchester University Press
Manchester and New York

distributed exclusively in the USA by Palgrave

Published by Manchester University Press
Oxford Road, Manchester M13 9NR, UK
and Room 400, 175 Fifth Avenue, New York, NY 10010, USA
www.manchesteruniversitypress.co.uk

Distributed exclusively in the USA by
Palgrave, 175 Fifth Avenue, New York,
NY 10010, USA

Distributed exclusively in Canada by
UBC Press, University of British Columbia, 2029 West Mall,
Vancouver, BC, Canada V6T 1Z2

British Library Cataloguing-in-Publication Data applied for

Library of Congress Cataloging-in-Publication Data applied for

ISBN 0 7190 6138 5 *hardback*
　　　0 7190 6139 3 *paperback*

First published 2003

11 10 09 08 07 06 05 04 03   10 9 8 7 6 5 4 3 2 1

Typeset in Adobe Garamond
by Servis Filmsetting Ltd, Manchester
Printed in Great Britain
by Biddles Ltd, Guildford and King's Lynn

Contents

Part III   Reflections

List of contributors

Gary Banham	Research Fellow in Philosophy, Manchester Metropolitan University
Andrew Benjamin	Research Professor of Critical Theory, Centre for Comparative Literature and Cultural Studies, Monash University
Jay Bernstein	University Distinguished Professor of Philosophy, New School University, New York
Andrew Bowie	Professor of German, Royal Holloway College, University of London
Howard Caygill	Professor of Cultural History, Goldsmiths College, University of London
Thomas Docherty	Professor of English, University of Kent, Canterbury
Jonathan Dollimore	Professor of English, University of York
Robert Eaglestone	Lecturer in English, Royal Holloway College, University of London
Joanna Hodge	Professor of Philosophy, Manchester Metropolitan University
John J. Joughin	Reader in English Literature, University of Central Lancashire, Preston
Simon Malpas	Lecturer in English, Manchester Metropolitan University
Mark Robson	Lecturer in English, University of Nottingham
Ewa Plonowska Ziarek	Professor of English, University of Notre Dame, Indiana

John J. Joughin and Simon Malpas

The new aestheticism: an introduction

The very notion of the 'aesthetic' could be said to have fallen victim to the success of recent developments within literary theory. Undergraduates now pause before rehearsing complacent aesthetic verities concerning truth, meaning and value, verities that used to pass at one time for literary criticism. The rise of critical theory in disciplines across the humanities during the 1980s and 1990s has all but swept aesthetics from the map – and, some would argue, rightly so. Critical theory, of whatever variety, presented a fundamental challenge to the image of the old-style academic aesthete sitting in his (and it was always his) ivory tower and handing down judgements about the good and the bad in art and culture with a blissful disregard for the politics of his pronouncements. Notions such as aesthetic independence, artistic genius, the cultural and historical universality of a text or work, and the humanist assumption of art's intrinsic spiritual value have been successfully challenged by successive investigations into the historical and political bases of art's material production and transmission. Theories of textuality, subjectivity, ideology, class, race and gender have shown such notions of universal human value to be without foundation, and even to act as repressive means of safeguarding the beliefs and values of an elitist culture from challenge or transformation. The upshot of this series of interventions has been the rapid expansion of the canon, as well as a profound questioning of the very idea of canonicity. Art's relations to dominant ideologies have been exposed from a number of perspectives, as well as its potential to challenge these ideologies. What has frequently been lost in this process, however, is the sense of art's specificity as an object of analysis – or, more accurately, its specificity as an aesthetic phenomenon. In the rush to diagnose art's contamination by politics and culture, theoretical analysis has tended always to posit a prior order that grounds or determines a work's aesthetic impact, whether this is history, ideology or theories of subjectivity. The aesthetic is thus explicated in other terms, with other criteria, and its singularity is effaced. Theoretical criticism is in continual danger here of throwing out the aesthetic baby with the humanist bathwater.

Yet, on theoretical grounds alone, the recent resistance to aesthetics remains puzzling, not least insofar as many of the theoretical advances of the last few years – the focus on the reader's role in the constitution of meaning, the possibility that texts are

open to a number of interpretations, the way in which literature troubles fixed definitions of class, race, gender and sexuality, etc. – might themselves be brought together
under the general rubric of 'the aesthetic function of literature'. Tied to actuality, in ways
that cannot be reduced to the empirical, aesthetic experience allows for the creation of
'possible worlds' as well as for critical experimentation. In a teaching situation (as
Thomas Docherty argues in his contribution to this volume) a reconceptualisation of
the aesthetic means making the most of an approach to 'education' which relies on an
openness to alterity, and developing a pedagogy that refuses to be prescribed by conventional or a priori categories. That these concerns are already rehearsed by the unravell-
ing of metaphysical 'givens' undertaken by contemporary theory could lead one to the
conclusion that, if theory has changed the conditions of teaching, then it will also enable
us to develop a more rigorous, non-foundationalist approach to aesthetics: one which
avoids the pitfalls and reductive unities of an old-style aestheticism. In the process,
though, theory will also need to look to its philosophical beginnings in aesthetics.

Two years ago, when the original proposal for the current collection was first sent
out for review, an early anonymous reader voiced some concerns about the project's
'philosophical' content. The specific cause for disquiet was that, while 'several of the
contributors happen to work in literature departments', the overall emphasis of the
volume was misdirected, and that, if the book was to get a green light at all, the editors
would at least 'have to decide whether it's about literature or philosophy'. This accusation concerning a migration across disciplinary lines is a curious one, not least
insofar as some of the best literary criticism of recent years has been penned by philosophers, while much of the work currently described as 'continental philosophy'
now emerges from departments of literature. But the reader's comments also serve to
remind us of the extent to which the dialogue which already exists between these two
subjects now needs to be made still more explicit. There are, after all, tensions to be
plotted here, as well as affinities.

In this respect of course there are other more tangible reasons why the anonymous
reader's distinction between literature and philosophy seems a less than helpful one.
Maybe the best response – at least it was the one that we gave at the time – is to say
that aesthetics is the theoretical discourse which attempts to comprehend the literary.
This of course is an unsatisfactory shorthand, and we will return to problematise the
position below, yet, loosely speaking, the relation between literature and philosophy
could be said to be symbiotic, in that each would be deficient without consideration
by the other. In this respect, as Andrew Bowie has recently reminded us:

> The rise of 'literature' and the rise of philosophical aesthetics – of a new philosophical
> concern with understanding the nature of art – are inseparable phenomena, which are
> vitally connected to changes in conceptions of truth in modern thought. . . . The need
> to integrate the disciplines of literary study and philosophy in new ways is, I propose,
> vital to the longer-term health of both disciplines. . . . Important work needs to be done
> . . . in showing how issues which emerge in relation to literature are, when connected to
> developments in contemporary philosophy, germane to issues concerning our self-
> understanding which do potentially play an important role in engaging with virtually
> any area of modern society.[1]

Bowie's case, that without 'an orientation towards understanding the truth-potential in art that is more than ideology, many of the most essential issues concerning the significance of art cannot even be discussed',[2] is, we would like to argue, compelling. Art is inextricably tied to the politics of contemporary culture, and has been throughout modernity. Aesthetic specificity is not, however, entirely explicable, or graspable, in terms of another conceptual scheme or genre of discourse. The singularity of the work's 'art-ness' escapes and all that often remains is the critical discourse itself, reassured of its methodological approach and able to reassert its foundational principles. In other words, perhaps the most basic tenet that we are trying to argue for is the equiprimordiality of the aesthetic – that, although it is without doubt tied up with the political, historical, ideological, etc., thinking it as other than determined by them, and therefore reducible to them, opens a space for an artistic or literary specificity that can radically transform its critical potential and position with regard to contemporary culture. In the light of this, we want to put the case that it might be time for a new aestheticism. This is not to argue that the critiques of aesthetics carried out under the various banners of theory are wrong or misguided. Of course the unmasking of art's relation to ideology, historical and political context, self-identification, gender and colonialism are immensely important for contemporary thought and politics. It is impossible now to argue that aesthetics is anything other than thoroughly imbricated with politics and culture. And this, without doubt, is an entirely good thing. None of those involved in this book set out to present any sort of rearguard defence of, or case for a return to, the notion of art as a universally and apolitically humanist activity presided over by a benign council of critical patriarchs. Rather it would be more accurate to say that the appearance of *The New Aestheticism* coincides with a conjuncture that is often termed 'post-theoretical' – both historically in the sense that in terms of historical sequence it comes after the initial impact of theory, but also conceptually in the sense that as 'theory' now enters a more reflective phase, there is an increased willingness among cultural theorists and philosophers alike to consider 'the philosophical origins of literary theory'.

Yet, in this respect, new aestheticism remains a troubled term and in current parlance it already comes loaded with the baggage of the 'philistine controversy' which first emerged in an exchange that originally that took place in the *New Left Review* during the mid-1990s. New aestheticism was identified there as a regressive tendency which in its 'pursuit of art and judgement' focused on 'ethical abstraction' to the exclusion of 'the pleasures of the body and the problems of contemporary art' – pleasures and brutalities that philistinism was better placed to explore as the 'definitional other' or the spectre of aesthetics.[3] Jay Bernstein and Andrew Bowie have by now made their own response as participants in the original debate,[4] but on reflection it is increasingly apparent that the two formations share a good deal of common ground: each is certainly opposed to the rootless aesthetic contingencies of cultural studies or lit. crit. postmodernism, and each registers an awareness of the constitutive antagonisms of modern culture (a theme to which we return ourselves below); so that, for example, one need only look at Jay Bernstein's contribution to the current collection to locate an aesthetic that is fully engaged with the contemporary brutalities of modern society.[5] Meanwhile, the label new aestheticist remains an opportunist one insofar as Bernstein himself only actually makes use of the term in passing during his introduction to *The Fate of Art* and only then to refer to the political project of German Idealism and Romanticism,[6] where the failure to reconcile art and politics remains a notorious trouble spot for those who would forge an aesthetic critique of modernity. In some ways the more rigorous term for this dilemma (and again it is one to which we will return below) is post-aestheticism. If the current volume allows room for a constructive difference of view on these and other issues, then it will partially have served its purpose.

The essays collected here, then, reflect a mixture of currencies. There are indeed new contributions from key players in the recent philistine controversy including Bernstein and Bowie, and while it remains the case that the majority of contributors happen to work in departments of literature or departments of philosophy rather than the history of art, film or media studies, we hope that further contributions from practitioners and theorists in other disciplines will follow. In an attempt to reassert the importance of aesthetics to contemporary theory and criticism, our aim throughout has been to offer a mix of established scholars from the first wave of theory whilst also securing contributions from younger second- or third-generation theorists. The new aestheticism does not claim to establish an orthodoxy; instead like any new constellation it circles restlessly around the very concept it attempts to grasp, and in doing so it lays open the field while remaining mindful of the need to attend to its own historical position. In what's left of the introduction we attempt a partial genealogy of the new formation.

The anti-aesthetic

The high-water mark of anti-aestheticism arguably coincided with the emergence of the so-called 'culture wars' of the late 1980s and early 1990s, wherein anxieties concerning the erosion of the high culture/popular cultural divide gained considerable publicity and became an industry in their own right, though mostly, it has to be said, the preoccupation of media pundits rather than academics. A good deal of unhelpful caricature of critical positions took place as a result, although actually, the attendant irony was that while those in the press bemoaned the decline of traditional values, for its part 'cultural criticism' had never been more self-consciously aware of its own complicity in upholding the literary canon. From the outset it had been the concern of materialist and political criticism to avoid the pitfalls of a transcendent critique – one which uncritically assumed the validity of its own position – and as a consequence critics working in the area of literary and cultural studies began to articulate a recurrent concern with positioning themselves simultaneously inside and outside the 'literary'. Here, for example, is Tony Bennett, speaking directly to the problem:

> There is no ready-made theoretical position outside aesthetic discourse which can simply be taken up and occupied. Such a space requires a degree of fashioning; it must be organised and, above all, won – won from the preponderant cultural weight of aesthetic conceptions of the literary. . . . As customary contrasts – between the 'literary' and

the non-literary, for example – lose their purchase, it is now possible to see not merely their edges but beyond their edges and, in realising the full implications of their historicality, to glimpse the possibility of a situation in which they may no longer order and organise the terms of literary production and reception. This is not merely to query the effect of a category ('literature') but concerns its functioning within and across an array of institutions and, accordingly, the challenge of organising positions – discursive and institutional – which will be not just outside 'literature' but beyond it in the sense of opening up new fields of knowledge and action.[7]

There can be no doubt that cultural critics are bound in certain ways to forms of academic hierarchy and as Bennett's comments suggest the hegemony of literature imposes constraints of its own, yet while his analysis usefully highlights some of the dilemmas facing an attempted politicisation of an established institution, a number of related issues still remain troublingly unresolved. Crucially, in calling for a refunctioning of the institution of 'literature' by which 'concepts and methods formed in aesthetic discourse' will be 're-assembled in new theoretical configurations'[8] his anti-aestheticist position is actually disingenuous insofar as it remains unwilling to think through the fuller implications of its dialectical dependency on what it would otherwise oppose. More seriously perhaps, in arguing that 'such positions [discursive and institutional] can be organised only by *prising* them away from aesthetic conceptions of literature'[9] Bennett also prevents any plausible account as to why one should be engaged in the study of literature in the first place, much less moving beyond it. How, one might ask, can such a transformation 'operate' if it fails to grasp the complexities of the discourse it claims to re-'fashion'?

One of the major limitations of the ideology critique of leftish criticism of the 1980s and 1990s is that in locating the aesthetic as a static or essentialist category or a dead 'cultural weight', it then fails to account for the enduring specificities of literature's cognitive significance. Such work falls short of a reconceptualisation of aesthetic discourse and often refuses to engage in any reflective fashion with the particularity of the work of art, much less the specificities of aesthetic experience.[10] In attempting to sever the aesthetic connection and in reducing literature to its determinants outside or beyond literature, Bennett's anti-aestheticism is committed to a 'sociology of social forms'[11] where the emphasis falls on exposing the regulatory character of 'cultural institutions' and on the need to bridge the gap between 'literature' and everyday life.[12] The slippage implied here between art, literature and 'lifeworld' is certainly one which some forms of affirmative postmodern cultural criticism have facilitated, and in recent years 'anti-aestheticism' has itself, at times, almost become a unifying device for articulating the shared concerns of what is actually an eclectic basket of theoretical positions. Compare Hal Foster in the mid-1980s concluding his introduction to what was to become a widely influential anthology of essays on postmodern culture:

'Anti-aesthetic' . . . signals that the very notion of the aesthetic, its network of ideas, is in question here: the idea that aesthetic experience exists apart, without 'purpose,' all but beyond history, or that art can now effect a world at once (inter)subjective, concrete and universal – a symbolic totality. Like 'postmodernism,' then, 'anti-aesthetic' marks a cultural position on the present: are categories afforded by the aesthetic still valid? (For example, is the model of subjective taste not threatened by mass mediation, or that of universal vision by the rise of other cultures?) More locally, 'anti-aesthetic' also signals a practice, cross-disciplinary in nature, that is sensitive to cultural forms engaged in a politic (e.g., feminist art) or rooted in a vernacular – that is, to forms that deny the idea of a privileged aesthetic realm.

The adventures of the aesthetic make up one of the great narratives of modernity: from the time of its autonomy through art-for-art's-sake to its status as a necessary negative category, a critique of the world as it is. It is this last moment (figured brilliantly in the writings of Theodor Adorno) that is hard to relinquish: the notion of the aesthetic as subversive, a critical interstice in an otherwise instrumental world. Now, however, we have to consider that this aesthetic space too is eclipsed . . .[13]

Foster's caricature of aesthetic autonomy aside, one needs to ask precisely what might be at stake in his questioning of 'the very notion of the aesthetic'. In common with other 'presentist' articulations of cultural criticism Foster is willing to discard the aesthetic as an outmoded category, insofar as the question of art's right to exist at a relative remove from social reality remains at odds with more immediately pressing and 'practical' concerns, yet clearly, a good deal hinges here on the terms by which this integration of 'art and empirical life' is achieved.[14] One of the chief characteristics of the 'avant gardism' of recent cultural criticism lies in its willingness to welcome the 'sublation of the difference between art and life' and thus secure the comforting illusion that art has been 'eclipsed' or come to an end;[15] yet this consolation only succeeds in betraying the extent to which art continues to attest to the divided condition of culture itself.

While Foster is willing to concede the 'brilliance' of Adorno's negative critique his emphasis on overcoming the constraints of aesthetic formalism prevents any consideration of the dynamic role that form plays in Adorno's conceptualisation of the aesthetic. Crucially, Foster's willingness to dispense with traditional aesthetic categories forecloses on the possibility of a more rigorous engagement with the historical processes by which such categories continue to be 'critiqued and renewed'. In contrast, and in his 'defence of autonomous art as socially critical', Adorno's aesthetic theory interrogates the extent to which cultural forms and the materials and techniques by which they are transfigured are already riven by 'the history sedimented within them'.[16] In this respect of course, as Adorno himself reminds us, the situation of the new in art is hardly new, so that, speaking of the 'hidden origins' of the new Viennese school he observes: 'Things that are modern do not just sally forth in advance of their time. They also recall things forgotten; they control anachronistic reserves which have been left behind and which have not been exhausted by the rationality of eternal sameness.'[17]

For Adorno, then, the participation of works of art in history and the 'determinate critique that they execute on history through their form'[18] necessarily needs to be construed in relation to the unresolved contradictions of society itself, and in this respect as Ewa Ziarek comments in her contribution to the current collection:

Adorno's argument [in *Aesthetic Theory*] does not repeat the modernist ideology of formalism, but, on the contrary, treats form as a dynamic social category linked to new technologies, economic structures of exchange, social relations of production as well as the intrinsic artistic forming of the always already historically shaped material.[19]

In his eagerness to assimilate art to its 'restorative' social function Foster's non-dialectical conceptualisation of aesthetic autonomy itself effectively fails to register art's own uncertainty concerning its 'right to exist'. In doing so he then also effectively surrenders the possibility of achieving a society free from domination.[20] As Jay Bernstein observes, whilst Adorno's 'aesthetic autonomy' might come at a 'high price' (in terms of its present remove from society) this position nevertheless remains integral to its critical potential: 'Only by sustaining its function of not now being socially formative can art enact a form of resistance to the rationality assumptions governing practice and be a place holder for what socially formative practice would be like.'[21]

For all their commitment to 'practice' and in their sensitivity to the local quotidian, recent democratising trends in cultural criticism tend to be secured on affect alone, so that, as Bernstein suggests: 'postmodern practice alters the empirical world without transforming it, its abstract affirmations belie the despair that sustains it'.[22] The failure of postmodern cultural theory to construe its emancipatory project in relation to aesthetics understood as 'social epistemology' means that, despite a tacit commitment to the ethico-political, new forms of cultural analysis often remain outflanked in political terms – unable to shape a response which engages in a properly reflective fashion with the validity claims on which their own emancipatory discourse of social transformation is implicitly based. While Adorno's scepticism concerning a socially formative function for art might have become unfashionable, many of the debates within cultural studies concerning the dissolution of a traditional concept of the humanities are still arguably unwittingly situated within the parameters of his diagnosis of the inability of art to achieve reconciliation with 'everyday life'. In fact, the yearning of cultural theory to secure a breach against the 'rationality assumptions' of its own institutional confinement is in every sense a traditional one. Yet, in its affirmation of a breach between disciplines, contemporary cultural theory is often too quick to forget the extent to which what Foster terms a 'cross-disciplinary' practice was always already a feature of an aesthetic criticism itself. Certainly, the early precursors of literary and cultural theory like Romantic philosophy, were, in any case, always hybrid assemblages rather than 'a unified discipline'.[23]

Somewhat paradoxically, then, as cultural theory has expanded its 'critical practice', its understanding of the philosophical and social determinants which govern its practice has contracted in almost equal measure. More seriously of course, the failure to construe a dialectical conception of aesthetic autonomy means that it is possible to track an inadvertent convergence between the anti-aestheticism of recent cultural theory and the complacency of the old-style aestheticism it would ostensibly seek to displace, insofar as each is reliant on a formulation of the aesthetic that is derivative of an 'over-simplified Kantianism',[24] so that, as Isobel Armstrong remarks of recent trends in cultural criticism:

> The traditional definition [of the aesthetic] has not shifted much, whether it is inflected as radical or conservative, undermined or confirmed. Neither radical critique

nor conservative confidence works with the possibility that social and cultural change over the last century might have changed or might change the category itself. Both in its deconstruction and consecration the model of the aesthetic remains virtually the same. And so the dialectics of left and right converge in an unspoken consensus that is unable to engage with democratic readings.[25]

In relying on an overly reductive caricature of art as a 'privileged realm' which exists at a non-cognitive remove beyond history, a 'politically committed' criticism is then unable to account for the persistence of art in anything other than reductively pre-scriptive and functionalist terms. Yet, if nothing else, the willingness of recent cultu-ral theory to historicise and relativise a fixed or unified notion of art, itself indirectly attests to the refusal of artworks to be exhausted by a continual process of appropria-tion and counter-appropriation in an endless variety of contexts. Indeed, one could say that the survival of literary texts over a period of time is less a product of their 'time-less' significance and more directly related to their ability to sustain interpretations which are often either contestable or politically opposed.[26] There can be no doubt that, in particular contexts at certain times, works of bourgeois culture have been util-ised as an instrument of oppression and social control, but then, as Andrew Bowie observes: 'why would one bother to concern oneself with the well-known products of Western culture, if it were not that they offer more than is apparent when their often quite evident failings with regard to contemporary social, ethical and other assump-tions are exposed?'[27] Moreover, what type of surplus 'knowledge' might be at stake here? As Bowie asks, 'are those insights [revealing the complicity of "great works" in securing "repressive discourses of race, gender, class, etc."] therefore themselves super-ior to what they unmask, offering a truth or revelation inaccessible to their object of investigation?'[28] For new aestheticists like Bowie, our understanding of the relation-ship between art, truth and interpretation is not merely dependent on an openness to the fact that literary texts transform meaning, but is also equally concerned with asking *how* this revelation is to be construed.[29] In this respect, an over-restrictively functionalist account of the reductions and inequities of canon formation falls short of a more reflective acknowledgement that the rise of literature is actually entwined with a more complex intellectual legacy: one which raises pressing philosophical as well as political questions to which we now need to turn.

Aesthetics and modernity

While the fraught relation between politics and art is as ancient as philosophy itself – so that art manifests a dissident potential that Plato saw fit to expunge from his ideal conception of the republic – the stakes are arguably raised still higher by art's ambivalent location within the philosophical project of modernity. It is no coinci-dence that the aesthetic has remained irreducible within modernity, and thus has appeared in a range of different guises always as a 'surplus' to the organising drive of instrumental reason. The analysis of the aesthetic is inseparable from a thinking of the complexities of philosophical and political modernity. Aesthetics emerged as an object of enquiry during the same period in which modernity was provided with the systematic underpinnings that gave rise to it as a sense of the world, and has remained inextricably tied up with many of modernity's self-reflections, ambitions and problems. It follows that an adequate thinking of modernity requires an investigation of the aesthetic and, reciprocally, the discussion of the impact of art and literature on contemporary culture needs a way of situating this culture in relation to the history of modern politics and philosophy.

Modernity develops from, and is closely linked with, the central progressive ambitions of the Enlightenment and Reformation, aspiring in its turn to generate knowledge and justice not from some metaphysical, historical or theological precondition but rather from the resources of reason itself. According to Jürgen Habermas, 'the secular concept of modernity expresses the conviction that the future has already begun: It is the epoch that lives for the future, that opens itself up to the novelty of the future.'[30] For modernity, then, reason becomes self-legislating and future-orientated: giving itself the rules for its own development and systematically discarding the beliefs and mystifications that had held it in check in the past. Modernity's central concepts thus derive from cognitive rationality, moral autonomy and the power of social-political self-determination. Although the historical origin of modernity is impossible to pin down as aspects of these defining philosophies occur in the work of figures writing from the late Middle Ages onwards, its emergence as a self-conscious discourse about the necessary interrelations of knowledge, morality, culture and history can be more reliably located at the end of the eighteenth century in the thought of German Idealism, and particularly the philosophies of Kant and Hegel who systematically delimit and map out the architectonic of modern reason.[31] In this respect, Bernstein argues that:

> With the coming of modernity – with the emergence of a disenchanted natural world as projected by modern science, a political language of rights and equality, a secular morality, a burgeoning sense of subjective consciousness, and autonomous art – the task of philosophy became that of proving a wholly critical and radically self-reflective conception of reason and rationality that would demonstrate the immanent ground for our allegiance to these new ways of being in the world.[32]

Perhaps the most important accounts of this notion of modernity are those that are developed from the work of Max Weber by contemporary writers such as Jürgen Habermas, Michel Foucault, Jean-François Lyotard and Cornelius Castoriadis who, despite their significant differences, share a sense of the internally differentiated nature of modern existence. Weber characterises modernity in terms of the destruction of metaphysical principles, first causes and religious worldviews in the work of eighteenth-century Enlightenment philosophers, which came to a head in the writings of Kant. He argues that modern experience has become separated into three spheres that are autonomous from one another and only formally connected, and whose interaction has become the site of intense theoretical, social and political debate. These spheres are, very briefly, scientific truth, normative rightness and beauty, which correspond to the philosophical disciplines of epistemology, ethics and aesthetics, and give rise to self-sufficient forms of social practice: the sciences and technology, the law and morality, and modern art, literature and more general culture. These practical disciplines in turn provide the ground for capitalist economy, bureaucratic administration and individual self-identification. Each of these spheres is internally lawful (it is able to legislate for its own constitution), and yet constantly impeaches upon, and is impeached upon by, the others. In other words, the relation between the spheres is one of semi-autonomy and troubled inter-implication, as forms of legislation coherent within a particular sphere impinge upon those legislations occurring in another. Developments in knowledge and technology require new forms of administration, for example, which may in turn inspire different modes of cultural representation.

This notion of conflictual coexistence between the spheres is opened up for analysis by the relationship between the faculties of pure reason, practical reason and judgement set out in Kant's three *Critiques*, which Habermas sums up with particular clarity:

> In Kant's concept of a formal and internally differentiated reason there is sketched a theory of modernity. This is characterised, on the one hand, by its renunciation of the substantial rationality of inherited religious and metaphysical worldviews and, on the other hand, by its reliance upon a procedural rationality, from which our justifiable interpretations, be they pertinent to the field of objective knowledge, moral-practical insight, or aesthetic judgement, borrow their claim to validity.[33]

In the absence of the 'substantial rationality' of a religious worldview, then, what remains is a formal rationalism, a 'procedural rationality', which, in Kant in particular and modernity more generally, is internally differentiated.

Kant's critical philosophy sets out to achieve two ends: to demonstrate the limitations of reason by describing how its attempts to grasp the totality of objective conditions dissolve into antinomy (particularly in the dogmatic thrust of pre-Enlightenment philosophy and theology); and at the same time to redeem thought and action by demonstrating the transcendental conditions of their possibility. In the first two critiques, of pure reason (epistemology) and practical reason (ethics), a chasm between truth and justice is opened. Between epistemology and ethics, Kant draws a division that cannot be crossed. By arguing that knowledge is bound by the 'limits of experience' which cannot be exceeded without falling prey to antinomy, he makes room for a separate ethical realm in which human freedom rests upon a 'categorical imperative' that is not reducible to knowledge because it is not generated by experience. The third critique, the *Critique of Judgement* in which Kant discusses aesthetics and natural teleology, sets out explicitly to form a bridge between epistemology and ethics. In the 'Introduction', Kant promises that reflective judgement will 'make possible the transition from pure theoretical to pure practical lawfulness, from lawfulness in terms of nature [knowledge] to the final purpose set out by the concept of freedom [justice]'.[34] In other words, the third critique aims to bring together the realms of epistemology and ethics, reconciling them in a system that will make possible a coherent account of the subject's place in the world. The almost universally acknowledged failure of the third critique in this endeavour provides the philosophical premises for the separation of the value spheres in modernity, and yet the thinking of aesthetics contained there provides a series of political and theoretical possibilities that have been taken up in the writings of both the Frankfurt school and the post-phenomenological arguments of thinkers such as Derrida, Lyotard, Lacoue-Labarthe and Nancy. In fact it is Kant's failure to reconcile epistemology, ethics and aesthetics in the third critique that opens a space for aesthetics within modernity which points towards the possibility of its having a transformative potential. As Bernstein argues:

> if art is alienated from truth and goodness by being isolated into a separate sphere, then that entails that 'truth' and 'goodness' are alienated, separated from themselves. Aesthetic alienation, then, betokens truth's and reason's internal diremption and deformation. . . . Art's exclusion from first-order cognition and moral judgement is, then, a condition of its ability to register (in a speaking silence) a second-order truth about first-order truth.[35]

Inadmissible to forms of criticism generated solely by pure or practical reason, art comes to occupy its own semi-autonomous realm presided over for Kant by aesthetic judgement. Although not telling the truth or being just in itself, art opens a space to question and challenge the 'first-order' formulations of epistemology and ethics that hold sway in the lifeworld. In other words, it is art's very 'alienation' and 'isolation' that provides the grounds for its political and philosophical potential in modernity.

Throughout the myriad political, cultural and philosophical discourses that have made up modernity, the term 'aesthetics' has retained the two key senses that emerge in the *Critique of Judgement*. The restricted sense is that aesthetics is the study of beauty in art and nature. More generally, though, it refers to the whole process of human perception and sensation – ideas about the body, imagination and feeling. As a particular discipline of enquiry it came into view during the eighteenth century with the work of the German philosopher Alexander Baumgarten, who posited the aesthetic as 'minor knowledge': sensation, affection and appetite (the lower powers) as opposed to scientific or theological rationality (the higher faculties). The implication of his arguments, however, is that these two powers are inextricably imbricated, and it is this implication that is taken up by Kant and modernity.

It is with Kant that aesthetics takes on its distinctly modern trappings. According to Hans-Georg Gadamer, aesthetics after the *Critique of Judgement* is

> no longer a mere critique of taste in the sense that taste is the object of critical judgement by an observer. It is a critique of critique; that is, it is concerned with the legitimacy of such a critique in matters of taste. The issue is no longer merely empirical principles which are supposed to justify a widespread and dominant taste – such as, for example, in the old chestnut concerning the origin of differences in taste – but it is concerned with a genuine a priori that, in itself, would totally justify the possibility of critique.[36]

In other words, because the 'transcendental function that Kant ascribes to the aesthetic judgement is sufficient to distinguish it from conceptual knowledge', aesthetics comes to require an investigation into the a priori foundation of its legitimacy that discusses it on its own terms rather than merely as an adjunct to empirical cognition.[37] And, as Gary Banham's chapter in this volume argues, the inter-implication of aesthetics in epistemology and ethics provides the means by which art can come to engage with issues in the cognitive and moral orders of the lifeworld.

The history of modernity is thus marked by a series of border conflicts between the value spheres and between the institutions that are governed by them. In this state of continual variance, the question of what the aesthetic is has invariably returned as a pressing issue. For Hegel, Marx and Freud, as well as thinkers such as Schopenhauer, Kierkegaard, Nietzsche, Arnold, Ruskin and Heidegger, the way in which the aesthetic is defined plays a key role in the development of a broader cultural-political analysis and has determined their respective notions of the importance and influence that are available to particular works of art or literature. Figures such as these, whose arguments provide the groundwork for much contemporary theory, open up the complexity and significance of the aesthetic for current cultural debates. Its anomalous position, continually in danger of being closed down by forms of truth-only cognition, is the subject of the essays collected in this volume, each of which attempts to work through a different aspect of our inheritance from modernity.

Post-aestheticism?

> Where philosophy ceases literature must begin . . .[38]

In some part of course the 'theory versus literature' debates of recent years have unwittingly shadowed the constitutive aporia of aesthetic theory itself, in that they indirectly register the truth potential which distinguishes art from other kinds of cultural production, but then fail to comprehend it, or at least comprehend it in under-reflective terms.

Art or literature eludes philosophy insofar as it is not susceptible to paraphrase, much less to systematic elaboration, yet the fact that art cannot be reduced to discursive analysis should not tempt us to settle for the consolation of art construed as a mere 'escape' from reality. If philosophy confines itself to propositional arguments which attempt to posit art's truth in relation to its empirical content or in terms of art's correspondence to an antecedent reality it then fails to confront the ways in which art exceeds its excluded status. 'Truth-only' accounts of art which attempt to legitimate art's status as an autonomous realm and which hinge on a fact/value distinction between the empirical and the transcendent cannot, by the same token, account for the process by which, in detaching themselves from the empirical world, 'artworks bring forth another world, one opposed to the empirical world'.[39] The transformative cognitive potential of the aesthetic and its world-disclosing capacity mark the emergence of art as an autonomous self-validating entity during modernity and make a new type of truth possible, producing new means of expression and unleashing the creative potential for new forms of social cognition. Yet even as aesthetic discourse provides new concepts and tools of analysis with which to challenge existing conceptual frameworks, the categorical separation of 'artistic truth' from other kinds of philosophical truth in modernity also presents a considerable dilemma for a modern aesthetic criticism and those who attempt to theorise art, so that as Bernstein observes:

> If art is taken as lying outside of truth and reason then if art speaks in its own voice it does not speak truthfully or rationally; while if one defends art from within the confines

of the language of truth-only cognition one belies the claim that art is more truthful than truth-only cognition.[40]

In a nutshell, then, the problem, as David Wood incisively puts it, is that 'poetic discourse may be able to say what philosophy can know it cannot'.[41] In this sense, of course, the very notion of 'aesthetic theory' is something of a contradiction in terms, so that as Schlegel puts it: 'What is called the philosophy of art usually lacks one of two things: either the philosophy or the art.'[42]

It is in confronting this dilemma that as Bernstein argues more recent 'post-aestheticist' philosophies of art like Adorno's actually take art's critical potential seriously by 'employ[ing] art to challenge truth-only cognition', while also facing the dilemma that 'philosophy cannot say what is true without abandoning itself to that which it seeks to criticise'.[43] While Bernstein's focus is on reading the post-aestheticist philosophies of art in Kant, Heidegger, Derrida and Adorno it would be possible to extend the implications of his thesis to recent currents of cultural criticism within the humanities. In this respect of course the lack of certainty concerning art exemplified by the culturalist theory of the 1980s and 1990s was already itself unwittingly 'post-aestheticist', not merely in the weaker sense of having broken with a reductive notion of aesthetic value or in consisting of postmodern anti-aestheticisms – but also in the potentially stronger sense that, in its indefatigable opposition to the formal constraints of the aesthetic, cultural criticism continued to deploy the cognitive import of the truth potential of the aesthetic against its own implication in disciplinary division, embroiled within what deconstructionists might term the problem of closure. Crucially, as Robert Burch notes:

> To the extent that such a [post-aestheticist] strategy challenges the fixed dichotomies and hierarchies upon which modern philosophy's claim to purity depends, it also threatens the firm distinction between the theory *per se* and its particular textual articulation. In the event, philosophical texts and aesthetic discourse come closer to artworks, since they will be bound to their determinate textuality or linguistic expression, as artworks are bound to the determinate materials of their production.[44]

This certainly catches something of the stylistic register of recent theoretical work in literary and cultural studies. Symptomatically, of course, cultural criticism at its best has become painfully aware of its own deficiency so that, in recording the collapse between 'theory *per se* and its particular textual articulation', much of the work bears the mark of its own ruination, insofar as ambiguous faultlines, ruptures, fissures, crises in representation and so on litter the corpus of cultural criticism during this period and frequently provide the foci for its activity. Again of course, there is a paradox to be remarked here, as, if in some respect the emergence of a 'new aestheticism' symptomatises the exhaustion of theory, then the tropes and conceptual motifs of 'theory' which articulated this shortfall were themselves resolutely aestheticist. As a result, the critical potential of the aesthetic has already proved crucially informative, not merely in productively accommodating the discontents of lit.crit.'s insular dislocation in recent years, but also in tacitly reshaping the direction cultural and literary studies have now taken.

The new aestheticism

The organisation of the current volume reflects something of this diversity and the collection opens with a cluster of papers that share an investment in staking out new positions for the aesthetic in contemporary culture and criticism. The polemical spirit and currency of these debates is immediately apparent in Thomas Docherty's opening chapter, where, in opposing philistinism, past and present, he argues that the role of aesthetic experience in education is to extend the possibility of thinking otherwise: a form of critical thinking which remains 'eventful' insofar as it refuses to be prescribed by predetermined categories. Docherty's objection is to philistinism in all its forms, and, as he demonstrates, this is as likely to include the 'radical' partisanship of theorists who oppose bourgeois art as the reductive anti-intellectualism of traditional criticism or the crude instrumentalism of contemporary education policy. In embracing the unlimited particularity of aesthetic experience as constitutive of culture, he argues that we need to g/host the unrealised possibility of the 'other reading' – as a potential 'guest' that should be accorded unconditional welcome or hospitality. Here, as with Jonathan Dollimore's contribution, the emphasis is on a form of unanticipated opening within an otherwise familiar discourse. Dollimore offers us a genealogy of aesthetic humanism that was always already internally riven: fascinated with the possibility of an aesthetic vision that contravenes its own imperative. In reconceiving the aesthetic as dangerous knowledge, insofar as it tells us 'there are things we should not know', the key issue becomes how we confront the *unheimlich* possibility of 'a non-human beauty whose power has something to do with its indifference to the human'.

The remaining three papers in this first section of the volume each offer us repositionings that are more directly engaged with contemporary literary-critical formations. Ewa Ziarek interrogates the recent history of feminist aesthetics and in a post-culturalist reading which draws upon advances within post-colonialism and feminism, including the theories of female masquerade and colonial mimicry of Joan Riviere, Frantz Fanon and Homi Bhabha, she offers a reformulation of Adorno's social history of mimesis in the context of a 'gendered and racial politics of modernity'. In a reading which resonates powerfully with Docherty's chapter Andrew Bowie reminds us that theory's suspicion of identificatory modes of thinking and its openness to otherness, are themselves variants of the singularity of aesthetic experience. And in asking 'What comes after art?' he reminds us that any sense of the demise of great art is premature. Instead he invites us to consider 'just how significant art may still be', directing us to a 'two-way relationship': an ongoing dislocation between the listening/viewing/reading subject, the forms of expression it encounters and the changed mode of understanding of the work which it often produces in the process. This sense of aesthetic 'encounter' is echoed in Simon Malpas's chapter, where he argues that the aesthetic can be located neither in the subject, as a form of psychological predilection or ideological mystification, nor in the work itself as a historical or formal identification, but rather as a 'touch' between subject and work, occurring in an instant that cannot be subsumed under a concept or final definition. Working through Jean-Luc Nancy's notions of the inoperative community and Being singular plural, Malpas questions the contemporary political and philosophical implications of art in a culture that is no longer capable of being thought according to modern conceptions of historical progress or political emancipation.

While several of these concerns also resurface in the second section of the volume, here the focus becomes more applied insofar as there is probably more by way of a direct engagement with particular aesthetic categories in relation to specific readings of given literary texts. Howard Caygill examines the movement between *aisthesis* as an open moment of excess and *ascesis* as a moment of discipline and closure, a movement that he characterises as 'Alexandrian' and also in some sense emblematic of the modern aesthetic. His reading traces the disruptive potential of this complex allegorical tension in the poetry of the Alexandrian modernists Ungaretti and Cavafy. In 'Defending poetry, or is there an early modern aesthetic?' Mark Robson invites us to consider the possibility that an aesthetic understanding of poetry can be identified in Sidney's *A Defence of Poetry*, which presents art as already alienated, and therefore capable of opening a space for critical reflection, before the Kantian delimitation of rationality in his critical philosophy. The chapter concludes with the case that 'prior to the Kantian critical philosophy is not a happily unified realm in which aesthetics might be observed in harmony with pure and practical reason', but that 'art as poetics, even before the rise of aesthetics, was always already alienated'. In contrast John Joughin reads the work of an early modern playwright in its subsequent historical contexts and offers us a theorisation of the phenomenon of Shakespearean adaptation as a way of rethinking our critical encounter with those texts that are in some sense 'exemplary'. In lending themselves to innovative forms of adaptation, Joughin argues that exemplary works maintain an originary power and thus serve to extend the ways in which we make sense of them. As the creation of the other, adaptation is without motive, a relinquishment of self that is also a response to a provocation of the works' own making. Joughin proceeds to theorise the open-endedness of exemplarity via Kant's discussion of genius as well as in relation to Shakespeare's critic-adaptor Hamlet.

The last two contributions in this section dwell on the forms of knowledge generated by an aesthetically aware critical practice. In 'Critical knowledge, scientific knowledge and the truth of literature', Robert Eaglestone argues that a criticism that pays attention to the aesthetic character of a work of art should conceive that work as providing an opening of a world in which the empirical truths of science can be produced. Tracking Heidegger's notion of truth as *alethia*, or unconcealment, Eaglestone investigates the key critical notions of form, genre and identification and in doing so develops a reading of Conrad's *Heart of Darkness*. In 'Melancholy as form: towards an archaeology of modernism', Jay Bernstein's focus is on what he terms the 'dialectic of spleen and ideal' as they are presented in Adorno's modernist philosophical aesthetics and as a constitutive feature of modernism itself. In exploring the 'collaborative antagonism' between 'forming-giving and decomposition' Bernstein offers us an Adornian inspired reading of Philip Roth's *American Pastoral*, a novel which interrogates the fate of American beauty, the history of that beauty and the 'intrinsic meaning of its normativity'. Bernstein argues that Roth's novel offers us nothing more nor less than an 'archaeology' of American modernism as the bearer of a secular ideal insofar as 'only in what fails the ideal is the authentic hope of the ideal to be found.'

The volume closes with a series of reflections on the crossings and intermediations of literature, philosophy and politics. In 'Kant and the ends of criticism' Gary Banham expands upon his work in *Kant and the Ends of Aesthetics* to consider the importance that Kant's aesthetics might have for contemporary criticism. He begins by remind-ing us that Kant discusses the aesthetic in all three critiques, and that its place in the *Critique of Judgement* is as a precursor to the analysis of teleological judgement which sets the scene for a thinking of culture as a self-legislating collective of subjects. From this perspective, Banham argues that a Kantian criticism opens a space not just for thinking art's relation to history and politics but also for a self-reflective questioning of that criticism's historical implication in the culture its own reading seeks to create. In 'Including transformation: notes on the art of the contemporary' Andrew Benjamin focuses on the complex relationship that obtains between contemporary art and politics. Arguing that an analysis of this relation requires a prior delimitation of the meaning and nature of the contemporary, the chapter proposes the categories of 'inclusion' and 'transformation' as a key means of thinking through the issues. According to Benjamin, the truth of the artwork lies in its capacity to bear conflicting interpretations, which means that any criticism must be based on a decision that pro-duces meanings for the work. Because the conflict between inclusion and transforma-tion can never be resolved or simply posited as an opposition, the chapter argues that art occupies a similar space to the refugee: the culture in which it arrives must trans-form itself if the work is to be included, and the task of criticism is to negotiate the politics of that movement. Finally, in a contribution that draws together two thinkers who have featured in close proximity in several of the previous chapters Joanna Hodge presents us with a provocative reconfiguration of the relationship between Adorno and Heidegger. Hodge argues that focusing on historicality rather than authenticity pro-vides the possibility of transforming the ways in which the relationships between aes-thetics, politics and history have been thought in contemporary philosophy. Mediated by Benjamin's critique of a-historical notions of rationality, Adorno's negative dialec-tic and Heidegger's Dasein are presented as ways of breaking with any notions of linear temporal development and presence. From this reading of the two philosophers, the chapter reworks the interrelations between aesthetics, politics and history in terms of a 'movement of ellipsis, a destabilised oscillation' between these categories, as well as between Adorno and Heidegger, as their reconfiguration opens a space in which one might 'contest the divided inheritance of Kant's thinking of imagination and art' with a recasting of aesthetics.

Positions, readings, reflections? The structure of the book might, to some, have an unfortunate resonance with those maps of teaching strategies so admired by educa-tionalists. But this collection is not the basis of a teaching strategy or a 'how to' manual. More than anything else it aims to be exploratory, opening the space for further discussion. The pieces included here do not add up to a coherent overall account of the aesthetic or provide a tool kit for a new style of criticism. Rather they form a constellation of approaches to art that, by taking seriously its imbrication with knowledge and ethics, indicate its potential for opening a range of ways of thinking culture. The collection is, thus, necessarily plural, as any work that takes the aesthetic seriously must be. Recognising the specificity of the aesthetic requires a significant shift in awareness of the possible modes and practices of critical enquiry, as well as a reconfiguration of the place of criticism in relation to philosophy, politics and culture. This collection is presented as a provocation to such a reconfiguration.

Notes

1 Andrew Bowie, *From Romanticism to Critical Theory: The Philosophy of German Literary Theory* (London: Routledge, 1997), pp. 1–2.
2 *Ibid.*, p. 8.
3 See D. Beech and J. Roberts, 'Spectres of the aesthetic', *New Left Review*, 218 (July–August 1996), 102–27 (pp. 102–3).
4 Cf. J. M. Bernstein, 'Against voluptuous bodies: of satiation without happiness', *New Left Review*, 225 (September–October 1997), 89–104 and A. Bowie, 'Confessions of a "new aesthete": a response to the "new philistines"', *New Left Review*, 225 (September–October 1997), 105–26.
5 For more on the philistine thesis, including all the material from the original *New Left Review* debate, as well as more recent responses, see D. Beech and J. Roberts (eds), *The Philistine Controversy* (London: Verso, 2002).
6 This sense of a Romantic new aestheticism also provides the spine for Walter Benjamin's 'The concept of criticism in German Romanticism' in W. Benjamin, *Selected Writings Volume 1*, ed. M. Bullock and M. W. Jennings (Cambridge, MA: Harvard University Press, 1996), pp. 116–200, and P. Lacoue-Labarthe and J.-L. Nancy's reading of the German Romantics in *The Literary Absolute: The Theory of Literature in German Romanticism*, trans. Philip Bernard and Cheryl Lester (Albany, NY: State University of New York Press, 1988).
7 T. Bennett, *Outside Literature* (London: Routledge, 1990), pp. 6–7. Also cf. A. Easthope, *Literary into Cultural Studies* (London: Routledge, 1991), esp. pp. 79–80.
8 *Ibid.*, p. 7.
9 *Ibid.*
10 Even those few literary critical works such as Terry Eagleton's monumental *The Ideology of the Aesthetic* (Oxford: Blackwell, 1990) that treat the specificity of different aesthetic theories are prone to fall prey to an urge to posit the aesthetic as a surface phenomenon that is generated and determined by ideology, psychology or history.
11 For more on the contemporary context of aesthetic/anti-aesthetic debates, including an insightful overview of Bennett's approach, cf. A. Singer and A. Dunn (eds), *Literary Aesthetics: A Reader* (Oxford: Blackwell, 2000), pp. 317–53 (cf. esp. pp. 332–3).
12 Though, in practice, the attempt to move 'beyond Eng. lit.' in cultural and literary studies has often only underlined the hermeneutic insularity of a brand of cultural criticism which, despite its fondness for an ironist take on cultural authority, is itself guilty of eliding the complexities of its own hierarchical remove from society. In fact, during the moment of 'high' theory in the late 1970s and early 1980s, the rising stock of non-traditional cultural critique in the academy effectively expanded at an inversely proportional rate to its ability to intervene in, let alone stem or prevent, the ravages of capital's advance on the public sphere. So much so, that by way of consolidating the material gains it had safely accrued

during Reaganism and Thatcherism, the ideological offensive of 1990s neo-conservatism, manifested during the so-called 'culture-wars', had very little difficulty in caricaturing and hijacking its radical 'opponent'. In this climate claims for the breach between institutional inside and outside, literary and non-literary look gestural at best.

13 H. Foster (ed.), *Postmodern Culture* (London: Pluto Press, 1985). Foster's collection was first published in America under the rubric *The Anti-Aesthetic* (Port Townsend, WA: Bay Press, 1983).

14 In its postmodern phase there can be no doubt that as Foster hints we are confronted with a complexification of 'cultural life', but how far can this then be said to constitute a transformation of 'the fundamental structures of everyday life' and the underlying problem of its social rationalisation? For a fuller critique of the 'naive optimism' of this form of postmodernist cultural theory see Jay Bernstein's 'Introduction' in J. M. Bernstein (ed.), *The Culture Industry: Selected Essays on Mass Culture* (London: Routledge, 1991), pp. 1–25 (cf. esp. pp. 20 and 21).

15 Again, we are directly indebted to Jay Bernstein here, cf. his 'Introduction', p. 21, but on the false comforts of the utopian impulse generally (to which Bernstein also alludes) cf. esp. T. W. Adorno in *Aesthetic Theory*, trans. and ed. Robert Hullot-Kentor (Minneapolis: University of Minnesota Press, 1997), p. 32: 'The new is the longing for the new, not the new itself: That is what everything new suffers from. What takes itself to be utopia remains the negation of what exists and is obedient to it. At the center of contemporary antinomies is that art must be and wants to be utopia, and the more utopia is blocked by the real functional order, the more this is true; yet at the same time art may not be utopia in order not to betray it by providing semblance and consolation. If the utopia of art were fulfilled, it would be art's temporal end.' The same tack is taken in Lyotard's postmodern aesthetics, influenced as it is by Adorno, in which the constant tension between innovation and the event is employed explicitly to contest the notion of art's development towards a utopian end. For a clear analysis of this, see 'The sublime and the avant-garde' in Lyotard, *The Inhuman: Reflections on Time*, trans. G. Bennington and R. Bowlby (Cambridge: Polity Press, 1993), pp. 89–107.

16 For a lucid elaboration of Adorno's attempt to understand art as 'essentially historical' and one to which we are indebted here and below, cf. Simon Jarvis, *Adorno: A Critical Introduction* (Oxford: Polity Press, 1998), pp. 90–123 (esp. pp. 90, 105, 123).

17 T. W. Adorno, *Quasi una Fantasia*, trans. R. Livingstone (London: Verso, 1992), p. 216, also noted by Jarvis, *Adorno*, p. 244, n. 65.

18 Adorno, *Aesthetic Theory*, p. 133.

19 See Ziarek, 'Mimesis in black and white: feminist aesthetics, negativity and semblance', p. 53, below.

20 Again compare Adorno, *Aesthetic Theory*, p. 1: 'All efforts to restore art by giving it a social function – of which art is itself uncertain and by which it expresses its own uncertainty – are doomed.'

21 Bernstein, 'Against voluptuous bodies', p. 96.

22 See Bernstein, 'Introduction', p. 22.

23 So that, in historical terms, as Andrew Bowie reminds us: 'Like Romantic philosophy, literary theory can be understood as part of a growing reaction against the separation of the everyday "life world" from the systematically determined spheres of science, technology and modern bureaucracy' (Bowie, *From Romanticism to Critical Theory*, p. 16). Meanwhile, of course, Adorno's own cultural criticism ranges across art, music, literature and a variety of other media, and evinces an engagement with a diversity of aesthetic forms of which any cultural theorist would be proud.

24 Or more accurately, perhaps, a quasi-Hegelian devaluation of the aesthetic that is achieved by bringing aesthetics under the ambit of another explanatory discourse – whether that be speculative philosophy, ideology, history or a generalised notion of the contemporary. On this problem, see Andrew Benjamin's piece in this collection: 'Including transformation: notes on the art of the contemporary', pp. 208–17, below.

25 I. Armstrong, *The Radical Aesthetic* (Oxford: Blackwell, 2000), p. 5.

26 For a thoroughgoing critique of the limitations of ideology critique see Bowie, *From Romanticism to Critical Theory*, esp. pp. 1–27.

27 See Bowie, 'What comes after art?' p. 70, below.

28 *Ibid.*

29 Cf. Bowie, *From Romanticsm*, p. 5.

30 J. Habermas, *The Philosophical Discourse of Modernity: Twelve Lectures*, trans. F. Lawrence (Cambridge: Polity Press, 1987), p. 5.

31 In fact one might, without being too outrageously reductive, argue that the conflict between Kantian and Hegelian conceptions of rationality provides the groundwork for some of the key debates in modernity as well as between the modern and the postmodern. For key examples of this formulation see, for example, Adorno, *Negative Dialectics*, trans. E. B. Ashton (London: Routledge, 1973); Jean-François Lyotard, *The Differend: Phrases in Dispute*, trans. Georges Van Den Abelee (Manchester: Manchester University Press, 1988); or Slavoj Zizek, *Tarrying with the Negative: Kant, Hegel, and the Critique of Ideology* (Durham, NC: Duke University Press, 1993).

32 J. M. Bernstein, *Adorno: Disenchantment and Ethics* (Cambridge: Cambridge University Press, 2001), p. 242.

33 J. Habermas, 'Philosophy as Stand-in and Interpreter', in K. Baynes, J. Bohman and T. McCarthy, (eds), *After Philosophy: End or Transformation?* (Cambridge, MA: MIT Press, 1987), pp. 296–315 (pp. 298–9).

34 I. Kant, *Critique of Judgement*, trans. W. S. Pluhar (Indianapolis and Cambridge: Hackett Publishing, 1987), p. 37.

35 J. M. Bernstein, *The Fate of Art: Aesthetic Alienation from Kant to Derrida and Adorno* (Cambridge: Polity Press, 1992), p. 5.

36 H.-G. Gadamer, *Truth and Method*, 2nd edn, trans. Joel Weinsheimer and D. G. Marshall (London: Sheed & Ward, 1989), p. 42.

37 Gadamer, *Truth and Method*, p. 41.

38 F. W. J. Schlegel, *Philosophical Fragments*, trans. P. Firchow (Minneapolis: University of Minnesota Press, 1991), p. 98 (translation adjusted).

39 Cf. Adorno, *Aesthetic Theory*, p. 1.

40 See Bernstein, *The Fate of Art*, p. 2.

41 D. Wood, 'Introduction' in D. Wood (ed.), *Philosophers' Poets* (London: Routledge, 1990), p. 2.

42 Schlegel, *Philosophical Fragments*, p. 2 (translation adjusted); also of course originally intended to serve as the ironical motto for Adorno's *Aesthetic Theory*.

43 Cf. Bernstein, *The Fate of Art*, pp. 4–9.

44 Robert Burch, 'The Fate of Art: Aesthetic Alienation from Kant to Derrida and Adorno', *Philosophical Quarterly*, 48 (1998), 132–4 (p. 133).

Part I

Positions

1 *Thomas Docherty*

Aesthetic education and the demise of experience

The philistine is intolerant.[1]

love naturally hates old age and keeps his distance from it [2]

In 1913, Walter Benjamin was a central figure alongside his teacher, Gustav Wyneken, in the 'German Youth Movement', agitating for substantial reforms in the German educational system and, beyond that, in German society. He placed one of his first serious publications, an essay entitled 'Experience', in *Der Anfang*, the magazine of the movement, as a contribution to the debates. In this essay, he points out that a society's elders have a bad habit of legitimising their views through recourse to their 'experience' (*Erfahrung*), their amassing of 'felt life', as we might call it, which is axiomatically greater than that amassed by youth. Youth – like a contemporary emergent 'modernism' – claims to offer something new, something requiring *synthetic* and not merely *analytic* judgement, in Kantian terms; but the old and established refuse to legitimise such novelty, and resist it, in a pragmatic world-weary analysis whose purpose is to assimilate the shocking to the normative and to contend that 'experience' will show youth the error of their ways and the validity of the elders' ways of thinking.[3]

Benjamin writes: 'In our struggle for responsibility' (by which he means something like youth's struggle for autonomy, for self-determination, or for the independence needed to determine a new and different future), 'we fight against someone who is masked. The mask of the adult is called "experience".' He goes on:

> But let us attempt to raise the mask. What has this adult experienced? What does he wish to prove to us? This above all: he, too, was once young; he, too, wanted what we wanted; he, too, refused to believe his parents, but life has taught him that they were right. Saying this, he smiles in a superior fashion: this will also happen to us – in advance he devalues the years we will live, making them into a time of sweet youthful pranks, of childish rapture, before the long sobriety of serious life. Thus the well-meaning, the enlightened.[4]

The present living of the youth – *Erlebnis* – is effectively evacuated of content. Youthful *Erlebnis* is denied substantive reality by this rhetorical manoeuvre practised by the elders; for reality, being the *amassing* of experiences (*Erfahrung*) is what, by definition, the youth has not yet attained.

Benjamin's point, arising from this, is that such thinking is precisely what substantiates and validates the philistinism of a culture whose terms are defined by the elders: 'herein lies his secret: because he has never raised his eyes to the great and the meaningful, the philistine has taken experience as his gospel'. Benjamin thus wants here to stake a claim for something 'other-than-experience', something characterised in terms of values or spirit, and, more precisely still, in terms of values or spirit that are in a profound sense 'modern', youthful, up-to-date: 'Why is life without meaning or solace for the philistine? Because he knows experience and nothing else. Because he himself is desolate and without spirit. And because he has no inner relationship to anything other than the common and the always-already-out-of-date.'[5] Benjamin's essay allows us to see that the effect of this, fundamentally, is to deny one kind of experience (*Erlebnis*: the *content* of the moment as it is lived in its intensity, the content of Baudelaire's 'transient, evanescent' moment; 'felt life') precisely as it validates another (*Erfahrung*: the accrued mass of such moments, no longer in their lived actuality, but rather in their general, abstract, total *form*: Baudelaire's 'eternal' or 'immutable'). As he puts it in 'The return of the *flâneur*', in terms indebted to Baudelaire, 'There is a kind of experience that craves the unique, the sensational, and another kind that seeks out eternal sameness'.[6] The elders legitimise the triumph of the latter, yielding a triumph of the sensible form of life over its sensual content; and the sense they give to such form is, paradoxically, senselessness itself, philistine 'meaninglessness'.[7]

Here is the kernel of Benjamin's 'modern' thinking. He notes the contest between, on one hand, the material content of a lived experience, transient if intense, and, on the other hand, the abstract and unreal ideality of the form that such an experience assumes when it is construed in terms of a 'monument of unaging intellect'. The absolute prioritisation of the latter is to be contested; and, in the present case, the aim is not simply to rehabilitate the lived actuality of material existence as such, but rather to claim that there is something valuable in the 'other-than-experience' constituted by the German Youth Movement's trajectory towards and into modernity, into a spirited occasionalism, or a being 'always-already-*up-to*-date'.

It is important to recall that for Benjamin, these elders were also 'teachers'. Benjamin saw education as being properly concerned with 'the nurturing of the natural development of humanity: culture'.[8] It would follow that if actual experience – the *Jetztzeit* – is denied, then culture is being denied; for culture is the activity of becoming, the educational development (*Bildung*) of the human into her or his being, and being requires that there be a content to the 'now-time', that there be substance and legitimacy in *Erlebnis*.

It did not trouble Benjamin that his movement was rather an elite and not at all a mass educational movement. In a letter to Wyneken, he writes: 'we are always very few, but we don't really care about that'.[9] My occasional references above to experience cast in terms of a 'felt life' have been intended to hint at an ostensibly unlikely collocation of Benjamin with the later Leavis. Leavis famously celebrated the elite (though not in the same terms as Benjamin), and resisted the idea of culture's availability to the mass. Both men share a conviction that a serious aesthetic education is necessary for resisting the advance of 'philistinism'. Leavis, however, explicitly excluded the mass from culture, arguing that the elite was itself under threat from a populist media (Northcliffe's newspapers) whose very vulgarity was damaging the existence of the 'public sphere' necessary for the maintenance of a literary civilisation. Against this, more recently, leftist theory has followed rather a later Benjamin, and has advanced the cause precisely of those 'excluded' from a supposedly 'normative' (if 'elderly') history of civilisation.[10] The question now concerns the place of aesthetic experience in education: the legitimacy of *Erlebnis* in the face of the authority of *Erfahrung*. Another way of putting this: how youthful is culture? My contention is that, in our time, aesthetic experience (like youth) is denied legitimacy by the elders (the dominant ideology of education) in a society (ours) that celebrates and legitimises a philistinism and vulgarity that deny human potential. This essay takes its stance against such a predicament.

Experience into event

For long, aesthetic experience – that feeling that provokes me to say 'I like this' in my encounter with art – has been disreputable. On one hand, it has been seen as the trivia of subjectivity, a local irrelevance in the face of the abstract general truths about art that can be derived from a *reasoned* response. In the eighteenth century, of course, aesthetics begins precisely from this contest between sense and sensibility; and reason is proposed as that which will effectively regulate the senses, enabling thereby a mode of criticism that is geared towards truth. On the other hand, however, experience is making a return, in the recent 'autobiographical turn' in criticism. Such a turn is, of course, the logical development of 'partisan' or committed criticism, in which the critic is seen not as a specific individual, but as an individual whose 'specificity' derives, paradoxically, from her 'representativeness' (as representative, exemplar, of a generalised class, gender, 'race', sexual orientation, and so on). My position here differs from both these tendencies, and derives from a fundamental question: 'Why are we so wary of the particularity of a specific aesthetic experience?' Such wariness is odd, if we see culture precisely as something experienced, lived, by specific individuals and their societies, rather than as something detached from human being and becoming as such.

Long predating Benjamin, there is another available instructive originary moment for this examination of our question. When he died on 10 February 1755, Montesquieu was blind, and had indeed suffered from near-total blindness during the last years of his life. Shortly after his death, when his fragmentary and still incomplete *Essay on Taste* was published, it became immediately apparent what such an affliction might have meant to him. In that essay (probably begun around 1726, and so contemporaneous with the 'birth' of aesthetics in the texts of Hutcheson[11]), Montesquieu had highlighted the primacy of vision in matters of aesthetic taste. In the section entitled 'Of Curiosity', he pointed out that: 'As we like to see a great number of objects, we'd also like to extend our vision, to be in several places at once, to cover more space . . . thus it's a great pleasure for the soul to extend its view into the distance.'[12] How to do this? What technology exists in 1726 to allow for such a prosthetic extension of vision? Montesquieu's answer is that it is art (and here, he means primarily visual art) that will enable such an advance. Art not only extends the possibilities we have for vision, for imaging, but, in doing so, offers us, as its primary content, the beautiful. The blind Montesquieu, then, is denied beauty, denied 'imaging otherwise' or, simply, imagination and 'youth'.

Montesquieu's thesis in his *Essay* starts from the proposition that we are always hungry for experience: growing and developing, we want to see as much as possible, to extend our view as far as possible (or even as far as *impossible*, into what we would now – post-Romanticism – term the imagination). We are never at rest, always seeking more experience, more engagements with objects whose difference and distance from us grant us our self-awareness or enable our autonomy. These objects, constituted through distance and difference, lead us always and inexorably further onwards and outwards in a restless desire for more and more experience.

As will be the case with Benjamin some two centuries later, experience (and particularly aesthetic experience) becomes constitutive of culture and of its acquisition. It is through the experience – intense moments of being or of becoming – offered by our engagement with art that we can imagine things undreamt of in our philosophies – or, to put this more simply, that we can *learn*. For Montesquieu, then, education depends on such aesthetic experience; as, for Benjamin, the lived experience of youth ought not to be discounted if we are to have an educational system that will contribute to culture rather than to the endorsement of philistinism.

However, our present elders are also suspicious of the validity of such 'mere' experience, preferring the instrumentalism of a reason that has been abstracted from our personal being or development. This, of course, is the poverty of that view of 'education' prevailing among European and American governments (however 'young' or 'modern' they may purport to be). Education is seen simply as the acquisition of a transferable skill, preparation of the individual for the taking of her or his place in an uncritical workforce; and, in such a state of affairs, the idea that an aesthetic education might have a value that is 'spiritual' or 'occasional' in Benjamin's terms, is simply anathema: aesthetics have value for our elders only to the extent that art contributes directly to the economy. This is the most extreme form of instrumentally rationalist abstraction: art and sensibility purely as commodity. Sadly, however, this conservative position is shared by that leftist theory or criticism that resolutely refuses to engage with the primacy of our aesthetic experience (spirited occasionalism) or with a non-quantifiable, non-computable (untheorised) 'sensibility'.

What might it mean for youth to engage with art in these circumstances? What might it mean to have an experience that is evacuated in advance of its content, to accept Jameson's 'texts come before us as the always-already-read'?[13] Agamben explicitly follows Benjamin in some recent work on *Infancy and History*, where he claims that:

> modern man's average day contains virtually nothing that can still be translated into experience . . . Modern man makes his way home in the evening wearied by a jumble of events, but however entertaining or tedious, unusual or commonplace, harrowing or pleasurable they are, none of them will have become experience.[14]

Things may 'happen', but they no longer acquire the *authority* of experience, as attested to by our elders, teachers, governors. This is akin to that situation in which we suspect that 'modern man' may spend the day reading books, hearing music, seeing pictures; but that it is all so vacuous, productive either of ignorance or of trite rehearsals of orthodox 'criticism'. This is one direct consequence of the age of 'information': the information/aesthetic overload allows no time to engage properly with any of it. We are thereby radically 'blinded', like Montesquieu; or, as Baudrillard has it, we prefer *simulacra* or *simulation*.

Vattimo addressed such a state of affairs in *The Transparent Society*. There, a key part of his argument is that the society of generalised communication and of mass media – and for him this is constitutive of the postmodern society – is one where we have, ostensibly, the promise of a pure transparency of experience. He comes at this through a consideration of the *Jetztzeit*, here called 'contemporaneity'. The contemporary world *is* contemporary, he writes, 'because it is a world in which a potential reduction of history to the level of simultaneity, via technology such as live television news bulletins, is becoming ever more real'.[15] The consequence of this is a 'radical revision of the very notion of history', such that 'the social ideals of modernity may in each case be described as guided by the utopia of absolute *self-transparency*'. The further result of this, however, is that, in the society of generalised communication, there is an eruption of myriad 'dialects' that question the assumed normative self-transparency of a previously central 'language'. This is a way of describing decolonisation, for instance, argues Vattimo; and it is also, of course, a way of explaining the tendency to assume that all dialects are *equally* sites of culture (thus: 'youth culture', 'football culture', 'business culture', 'rap culture', 'working-class culture'; and so on in various reifications of culture-as-commodity). Instead, then, of returning us to the fullness of the *Jetztzeit*, this state of affairs leads us back to Nietzsche's famous proposition that, perhaps, finally, the true world ends in a fable: that truth dissolves into a multiplicity of fablings. We might, thus, have experience; but there is no truth to such experience. Once more, *Erlebnis* becomes vacuous, despite our seeming validation of all kinds of experience; and, 'truthless', it has little relation to education.

Against this we might set Paul Zweig, who argues that our knowledge of adventure tends to be literary nowadays, rather than being drawn from our everyday life: 'adventures are precisely what few of us know from experience'. Yet, he suggests, our familiarity with adventure might be more common than we routinely think:

> Haven't all of us, now and then, experienced moments of abrupt intensity, when our lives seemed paralysed by risk: a ball clicking round a roulette wheel; a car sliding across an icy road; the excruciating uncertainty of a lover's response; perhaps merely a walk through the streets of a strange city? The cat's paw of chance hovers tantalizingly, and suddenly the simplest outcome seems unpredictable.[16]

Another way of putting this, of course, would be to say that with the unpredictability of the simplest outcome, we enter the realm of the 'event'.

This entry into the event is precisely the entry into youthful experience; more precisely still, it is the entry into play. Our critical task is to rehabilitate such experience, to refill it with content; and to regard such content as not only 'meaningful' but also 'eventful' and as serving education and culture materially, thereby. Zweig's case is that the entry into the event can be as banal as a walk in the streets of a strange city: that is, the event arises through the defamiliarising contact with the unknown. Another word for this, of course, is 'reading' or any such related aesthetic activity. The text 'always-already-read' by elders/teachers such as Jameson is the text paralysed; and it is also the reader/student blinded, the cultural event or history arrested.

Experience, life and death

Football isn't a matter of life and death; it's much more important than that.[17]

In his famous 'Theses on the philosophy of history', Benjamin proposed what has become a major insight for contemporary criticism, when he indicates the double-sided nature of 'cultural treasures' that embody what we call 'civilisation'. Famously, 'There is no document of civilization which is not at the same time a document of barbarism'.[18] This insight drives that major recent critical tendency – fundamentally semiotic-deconstructive, and operating as a 'corrective' to the norms of a bourgeois 'high culture' – indicating that values (especially aesthetic evaluations) are themselves shaped and conditioned by the political values of the 'victors' in the 'triumphal procession' that we call a history of civilisation. That is by now a commonplace.

Lurking within the observation is a yet more telling and a rather different question. If culture is genuinely double-sided, might it not also follow that 'there is no document of barbarism that is not also and at the same time a document of civilisation'? This would be the shocking possible corollary of Benjamin's famous thesis. The status of the document would thus become genuinely problematic: aesthetic documents – the artefacts of culture – are neither intrinsically civilised nor intrinsically barbaric; rather, the document manifests itself as the merest *potentiality* for *either* civilisation *or* barbarism. 'Culture' would now be the name that we give to the inhabiting of this potentiality; and intrinsic to such culture would be a fundamental aesthetic education. Those who decide the status of the document see culture, instead, as the *determination* of the potentiality, and thereby make the document (and culture itself) a commodity, an object, or a sum of objects (*Erfahrung*) rather than a process of eventful living (*Erlebnis*), living as itself the processing of contestations or of indeterminacy.

To put the question of experience in terms of a contest is also to understand experience in terms of Aristotelian *energeia*, energy. To explore this properly, we might relate Benjamin's concern for the (youthful) *Jetztzeit* to Agamben's understanding, derived from Aristotle, of potentiality. The simplest way to do this is to reconsider the metaphysics of presence. Augustine long pre-dates Derrida in being troubled over this. In both *Civitas Dei* and *Confessions*, Augustine famously pondered the issue of temporal being. Key to his thinking is that there is a distinction to be made between a present that is filled with substantial content, and a present that has a merely 'formal' existence, as a structural bridge enabling us to think the relation between past and future (or to think 'narrative', as it were). He begins from a consideration of the great transgressive moment of death. Meditating on a question whose theological basis is doubt about resurrection, Augustine asks whether it is possible to believe in ghosts: 'can one be living and dead at the same time?'. In response, he proposes a sophisticated argument in which he establishes an absolute opposition between being alive and being dead. That strict opposition then allows him to elide the very moment of dying itself, for at any given instance, he claims, one is either still alive or one is already dead; and therefore, one is 'never detected in the situation of dying, or "in death"'. Yet more importantly for our purposes here, 'the same thing happens in the passage of time; we try to find the present moment, but without success, because the future changes into the past without interval'.[19]

The consequence of this is not only that the moment of death is emptied of content, but so also is the moment of the present: the present is now marked always by the traces of past and future that crowd in on it and shape it, thereby stifling any self-presence therein. In other words, the present moment is merely a moment of potential. We might say that experience (in terms of the *Jetztzeit* or 'felt life') is thus only at best potential energy. By analogy, therefore, any 'present' engagement with an aesthetic object can be an engagement with either barbarism or civilisation; and it is the sustained inhabiting of that potential *energeia* that is 'culture'.

The realisation of the text is an act of realising potential, converting potential energy to kinetic (most usually, in the form of an avowed political energy). My contention here is that the premature politicisation – 'realisation' – of the text or of the aesthetic encounter is *always* barbaric and anathema to culture; for it actively denies the experience of the present moment, refuses the encounter with death that is at the centre of all art, an encounter that is actually a moment of transgression, a moment of engagement, an 'event' or an adventure whose outcome cannot be given in advance.

What I am resisting is the 'partisan' position whereby the preference for one reading 'kills' the other (14 May 1948 is *nakba*, say, thereby 'killing' the possibility of Israeli culture; *or* vice versa). Rather, I am stressing that the preference for one reading must always maintain the other reading, as unrealised potential or possibility; and that it must maintain it as 'ghostly', as a potential 'guest' in a spirit or occasion of hospitality. That hospitality is what I will now identify firmly with and as culture; or, as Derrida has it in a different context: 'Hospitality is culture itself and not simply one ethic amongst others.'[20]

This, then, is a counter to partisan reading or to a reading that is a priori determined by political choice, or by the premature decisionism that would lead a critic to place the commitment to a reading *before* the experience of reading. That partisanship – when it precludes the possibility of 'hospitality', as in cultural critique – is what I'll call, in our normal everyday sense of the term, *philistine*. While such determinism may be appropriate in the political sphere, it is out of place in the cultural; and while an analogy may be available between what happens in aesthetics and what happens in politics, it is a philistine error to elide the difference. Instead, the only commitment required is a commitment simply to the aesthetic encounter; but that commitment has itself some important consequences. The first is that 'culture' is not an abiding condition, but rather an episodic event: the spirited occasion in which it becomes possible to inhabit a potentiality.[21]

Criticism, play, dance

Montaigne opened his great essay on the force of imagination with a citation: *fortis imaginatio generat casum*, the strong imagination creates the event. We might compare here the great poet so beloved of aestheticists, Keats, in whose famous letter of 22 November 1817 to Benjamin Bailey we find that 'The Imagination may be compared to Adam's dream – he awoke and found it truth'.[22] Adam dreamt of *companionship*, and I shall return to the centrality of such companionship to our 'new aestheticism' in what follows. Montaigne's essay is about the strength of an imagination that can realise things in material actuality. For example, Montaigne writes, when he is in the presence of one who persistently coughs, he himself begins to experience pulmonary irritation: 'Someone insistently coughing irritates my own lungs and throat. I visit less willingly those ill people towards whom I have duties than I do those in whom I have less interest and who mean less to me. I seize upon the illness that I witness, and embed it in myself.'[23] Montaigne advances in the essay a materialist view of imagination, indicating that imagination realises itself through the body (as especially in sexual desire), and thus gives an actuality of experience to that which is ostensibly 'merely' imagination.

The usual way in which we have configured this question is, broadly, post-Romantic. It comes in the form of the question whether art makes any material difference to life. As a self-proclaimed 'last Romantic', Yeats, 'old and ill', put it thus, in what is possibly the most celebrated question of Irish literary history: 'Did that play of mine send out/Certain men the English shot?'; to which Auden would, equally famously, reply that 'poetry makes nothing happen . . . it survives, / A way of happening, a mouth'.[24] At issue between Yeats and Auden, however, is rather the centrality of play and more especially of the play of imagination; for it is this kind of play that is, really, another word for the potentiality of which I write here.

The idea of play as central to aesthetics is not new, of course. Schiller had been at pains to stress the importance of play, *Spielen*, and of the 'play-drive', *der Spieltrieb*, in his *Letters on Aesthetic Education* (specifically in Letter 24). For Schiller, this (deliberately ambiguous) term, hovering between notions of theatricality and of childhood self-entertainment, effectively regulates the opposition in our consciousness between the two competing drives of 'sense' and of 'form' (or between sensibility and reason; between particulars and universals; or, more pertinently here, between event and the dead-weight of elderly authority, between *Jetztzeit* and philistine 'maturity'):

> The sense-drive demands that there shall be change and that time shall have a content; the form-drive demands that time shall be annulled and that there shall be no change. That drive, therefore, in which both the others work in concert . . . the play-drive, therefore, would be directed towards annulling time within time, reconciling becoming with absolute being and change with identity.[25]

Such 'play' gives a content to time *while also* giving it a formal sense; it reconciles the particular experience with the more general socio-cultural general authority. Recently, using entirely different sources, Isobel Armstrong argued something similar: 'Play, that fundamental activity, is cognate with aesthetic production . . . I understand play . . . as a form of knowledge itself. Interactive, sensuous, epistemologically charged, play has to do with both the cognitive and the cultural.'[26] Here, *inter alia*, Armstrong is writing against the crude philistinism of a British educational system that has become increasingly Gradgrindian in its concentration on education as pure instrumentality. Play is now seen as a waste of time by politicians who regard children simply as fodder for political statistics or the achievement of 'targets'. Just like:

> Thomas Gradgrind, sir. A man of realities. A man of facts and calculations. A man who proceeds upon the principle that two and two are four, and nothing over, and who is not to be talked into allowing for anything over . . . With a rule and a pair of scales, and the multiplication table always in his pocket, sir, ready to weigh and measure any parcel of human nature, and tell you exactly what it comes to.[27]

Or, as the much later Adorno and Horkheimer have it in their devastating critique of a crude 'Enlightenment', 'whatever does not conform to the rule of computation and utility is suspect'.[28] Oh, that we had some of Dickens's anger now.

Thankfully, Armstrong does. Armstrong rightly wants to rehabilitate youthful play as a central pedagogical activity. She considers childhood play, in which 'things lose their determining force', or, in my preferred terms here, where things become pure potentiality. Play, she argues, transforms perception, as when a stick becomes a horse, say, where the stick 'becomes a "pivot" for severing the idea of a horse from the concrete existence of the horse, and the rule-bound game is determined by ideas, not by objects. Play liberates the child into ideas'.[29] 'Quadruped. Graminivorous. Forty teeth . . .' and so on, if taken as definitive of a horse, does not. The former is culture; the latter constitutes Gradgrindian-like barbaric government 'not to be talked into allowing for anything over', a barbarous criticism as practised by the 'man of realities'.[30]

The poem is such a pivotal object, releasing its reader into the experiencing of ideas, into thinking as such. That 'eventful' thinking, eventful precisely to the extent that its outcome cannot be predetermined, is what we might properly call culture, but culture-as-activity, culture-as-potentiality, or, more simply, *education*: the forming and informing of a self in the spirit of growth, development, and imagining the possibility that the world and its objects might be otherwise than they are. Another word for this, of course, is metaphor; but metaphor as a practice of thought, or, in the words of Ricoeur, as a process of 'cognition, imagination, and feeling'[31]: in my own terms, a thinking that is always hospitable to otherness, and is thus 'companionable'.

A useful way of characterising the play at issue here is to see it as dance. Valéry, in particular, made great play with dance as a key figure in philosophy; but it is more recently Badiou who has argued for dance 'as a metaphor of thought'. For Badiou, following Nietzsche, dance is 'all that the child designates', an always new beginning prompted by the 'altering' event. Dance is a 'wheel that moves itself', a 'circle that draws itself and is not drawn from outside', a pure and simple act of affirmation.[32]

This, however, is not the dance that is imposed from without, regulated by external forces (be it that of choreography, rock music, or the rhythms of mechanical/industrial production); it is dance that does not submit to an external regulation. By analogy, we need a criticism that is self-determining, autonomous: playful, between sense and form. For Nietzsche, the opposite of dance is 'the German', marching to the military beat with her or his strong legs. Dance, by contrast, resists what Nietzsche called such 'vulgarity', the vulgarity marked by the spontaneous reaction of the body to external forces.

Badiou appropriates Nietzsche in these terms: 'Dance would be the metaphor of all real thinking linked to an event. For an event is precisely that which remains undecided between taking place and no-place, an emergence that is indistinguishable from its disappearing.'[33] Dance, in these terms, is what allows experience to occur as event:

> Thus we see that dance has to play time into space. For an event founds a singular time from its nominal location. Traced, named, inscribed, the event designs, in the 'it happens that' (*le 'il y a'*), a before and an after. A time brings itself into existing . . . Dance is that which suspends time in space.[34]

We should here recall Montesquieu, for whom play is pleasurable because it satisfies our avarice for experience, and, within such play, dance in particular pleases us by its lightness, grace, beauty and

> by its link to music, the person who dances being like an accompanying instrument; but above all it pleases thanks to a disposition of our brain, which is such that dance secretly encompasses the idea of all movements under certain movements, of most attitudes under certain attitudes.[35]

Lurking more explicitly behind Badiou, however, is Valéry. In *L'ame et la danse*, Valéry offers a Socratic dialogue, in which Phèdre tells Socrates to look at a young dancer: 'Look at her fluttering! You'd say that the dance comes out of her like a flame', to which Socrates replies:

> What is a flame, my friends, if it is not the *moment itself*?. . . Flame is the act of that moment between earth and sky. My friends, all that passes from a heavy to a subtle state passes through the moment of fire and light . . . Certainly the unique and perpetual object of the soul is that which does not exist; that which was, and which is no more; – that which will be and which is not yet; – that which is possible, that which is impossible, – there indeed is the business of the soul, but not ever, *never*, that which is![36]

Valéry argues that the body of the dancer, in refusing to be localised in one place as a simple object, thus becomes multiple: playful. Such play, in its multiple release of possibility, is itself also thought – but thought in the form of event, or thought realised as potentiality. This is the materiality of imagination; and by extension, it is the materiality also of reading.

Reading thus becomes a matter of companionship. By this, I do not mean to suggest that (as in Booth, say) there is an implied relation between reader and writer,[37] nor (as in Leavis) that an elite 'common pursuit' is established between teacher and student.[38] Rather, I mean that reading-as-culture produces an attitude of readiness for companionship; and in this, it is like dance, where movement is autonomous yet also ready for relation with – hospitable to – the movement of other partners. Cultural reading such as this is that which happens *between* determinacy and indeterminacy: culture, we might say, is the *potentiality* for culture.

In this regard, Socrates learns a deal from Diotima, in Plato's *Symposium*. Discussing the nature of love, Diotima first of all rejects the simple oppositions between good and bad, wisdom and ignorance, beauty and ugliness, reinstating the middle terms whose occlusion proves so useful to Augustinian sophistry. Love, she then argues, is itself such indeterminacy: 'Love is between mortal and immortal . . . He is a great spirit, Socrates. Everything classed as a spirit falls between god and human.'[39] If culture is also such indeterminacy, then we might say, modifying Derrida, 'love is culture itself and not simply one ethic among others'. The aesthetic attitude I propose, then, is one that aligns love, companionship, hospitality; and it is the *inhabiting* of these, not as stable conditions but as episodic events, *potentiality*, that is culture.

The dancer may then be like the *flâneur*:

> As he walks, his steps create an astounding resonance on the asphalt. The gaslight shining down on the pavement casts an ambiguous light on this double floor. The city as a mnemonic for the lonely walker: it conjures up more than his childhood and youth, more than its own history.[40]

And it is this *flâneur* that the aesthetic must accompany, rehabilitating memory, youthful *Erlebnis*, ambiguity and the exponential potential for *more*: more dance, more love, more hospitality, more experience.

Coda

All art is good; if it is not good, it is not art. The critic needs an attitude of potentiality, an attitude that releases thought like a dance, like an event; and such an attitude is one of a deep hospitality. What, then, is 'bad art'? The notion that there is such a thing as 'bad art' is one that can be seen in the tabloid newspaper outrage at some contemporary works; but it is also visible in the outrage of the partisan critic at various forms of 'bourgeois' art, or in the crude anti-intellectualism of Carey, say.[41]

Both attitudes are equally philistine. The philistinism of contemporary governments and of their education departments hardly requires assistance from those within the institutions of education who should, by definition, know better; and who should, in practice, be more hospitable to the possibilities for culture and to culture as potentiality.

Notes

1 W. Benjamin, 'Experience' in M. Bullock and M. W. Jennings (eds), *Selected Writings Volume 1: 1913–1926* (Cambridge, MA: Harvard University Press, 1996), pp. 3–5 (p. 5).
2 Agathon, in Plato, *Symposium*, trans. C. Gill (Harmondsworth: Penguin, 1999), p. 29.

3 Benjamin, 'Experience', pp. 3–5. See also I. Kant, *Critique of Pure Reason*, 2nd edn (1787), trans. J. M. D. Meiklejohn (London: Dent, 1946), p. 30.

4 Benjamin, 'Experience', p. 3. I suggest the alignment with modernism so that we can see the emergence of these new forms for what they might have been: the revolt of youth against its immediate forebears, or 'modernism as adolescence'.

5 *Ibid.*, p. 4.

6 W. Benjamin, 'The return of the *flâneur*' in W. Jennings, H. Eiland and G. Smith (eds), *Selected Writings 2: 1927–1934* (Cambridge, MA: Harvard University Press, 1999), pp. 262–7 (p. 266); cf. C. Baudelaire, in C. Pichois (ed.), *Critique d'art* (Paris: Gallimard, 1992), p. 355.

7 For Benjamin, 'philistine' is an ambivalent term. On one hand, it is the slang term (*Philister*) for the townfolk in a university town, to distinguish them from educated students; on the other, Benjamin knew the Philistines as a tribe from the Old Testament, those occupying the land we can now identify as Palestine.

8 See M. Brodersen, *Walter Benjamin: A Biography*, trans. M. R. Green and I. Ligers (London: Verso, 1997), p. 49.

9 Cited in Brodersen, *Benjamin*, p. 48.

10 See F. R. Leavis, *Mass Civilisation and Minority Culture* (Cambridge: Minority Press, 1930), pp. 3–4, 8 and *passim*. The views here expressed are variously reiterated throughout Leavis's career, especially in those essays dealing with the sociology of culture, as in *For Continuity* (Cambridge: Minority Press, 1933); *Education and the University* (London: Chatto & Windus, 1943); *The Living Principle* (London: Chatto & Windus, 1975), and in the post-humously collected papers in *The Critic as Anti-Philosopher*, ed. G. Singh (London: Chatto & Windus, 1982). The leftist criticism of the past thirty years, suspicious of Leavis and of his emphasis on experience, now finds itself, paradoxically, validating experience – specifically the experience of the oppressed.

11 For more on this, see my *Criticism and Modernity: Aesthetics, Literature and Nations in Europe and its Academies* (Oxford: Oxford University Press, 1999).

12 Montesquieu, *Essai sur le goût* (Paris: Payot & Rivages, 1994), p. 17 (my trans.).

13 F. Jameson, *The Political Unconscious* (London: Methuen, 1981), p. 9.

14 G. Agamben, *Infancy and History*, trans. Liz Heron (London: Verso, 1993), pp. 13–14.

15 G. Vattimo, *The Transparent Society*, trans. David Webb (Cambridge: Polity, 1992), p. 17.

16 P. Zweig, *The Adventurer* (London: Dent, 1974), pp. 3–4.

17 Bill Shankley, one-time manager of Liverpool FC.

18 W. Benjamin, 'Theses on the philosophy of history', *Illuminations*, trans. H. Zohn (London: Fontana, 1973), pp. 245–55 (p. 248).

19 Augustine, *City of God*, trans. Henry Bettenson (Harmondsworth: Penguin, 1972), p. 512. Samuel Johnson uses a similar tactic, attacking Optimism, in his review of Soame Jenyns's *Free Inquiry*. For my commentary on how this relates to deconstruction as a 'modern, Optimistic' thinking, see my *On Modern Authority* (Brighton: Harvester, 1987), p. 235 *et seq.*

20 J. Derrida, *On Cosmopolitanism and Forgiveness*, trans. M. Dooley (London: Routledge, 2001), p. 16.

21 A useful analogy here is in Sheldon Wolin's 'Fugitive democracy' in S. Benhabib (ed.), *Democracy and Difference* (Princeton: Princeton University Press, 1996), pp. 31–45. There, Wolin distinguishes 'politics' ('continuous, ceaseless, endless') from 'the political' ('episodic, rare'); culture, I contend, is not politics, but rather political, in this sense. See my *Criticism and Modernity*, p. 113, on this.

22 J. Keats, *Selected Poetry and Letters*, ed. R. H. Fogle (San Francisco: Rinehart, 1951), p. 305.
23 Michel de Montaigne, *Essais* (Paris: Garnier-Flammarion, 1969), 1, p. 143, (my trans.).
24 W. B. Yeats, *Collected Poems* (London: Macmillan, 1950), p. 393; W. H. Auden, *Collected Poems*, ed. E. Mendelson (London: Faber & Faber, 1976), p. 197.
25 F. Schiller, *On the Aesthetic Education of Man*, ed. E. M. Wilkinson and L. A. Willoughby (Oxford: Clarendon, 1967), p. 97.
26 I. Armstrong, *The Radical Aesthetic* (Oxford: Blackwell, 2000), p. 37; cf. Leavis's insistence that a literary-critical education is one that trains 'intelligence and sensibility together' in *Education and the University*, pp. 34, 38, 67–8 and 70.
27 C. Dickens, *Hard Times*, ed. T. Eagleton (London: Methuen, 1987), p. 16.
28 T. W. Adorno and M. Horkheimer, *Dialectic of Enlightenment*, trans. J. Cumming (London: Verso, 1979), p. 6.
29 Armstrong, *Radical Aesthetic*, p. 38.
30 Note that this does not imply a 'two cultures' mentality. I stress that the latter mode here is *not* to be identified with the mode of the hard sciences, for these too require the inhabiting of potentiality that is culture: these too are aesthetic. If an opposition is required, let it be 'Business Studies' that has no place in a university.
31 P. Ricoeur, 'The metaphorical process as cognition, imagination, and feeling' in S. Sacks (ed.), *On Metaphor* (Chicago: Chicago University Press, 1979), pp. 141–57.
32 A. Badiou, *Petit manuel d'inesthétique* (Paris: Seuil, 1998), p. 92 (my trans.).
33 *Ibid.*, p. 97 (my trans.).
34 *Ibid.*, p. 98.
35 Montesquieu, *Essai*, p. 31.
36 P. Valéry, *Morceaux choisis* (Paris: Gallimard, 1930), pp. 250–1.
37 See W. C. Booth, *The Company We Keep* (Berkeley and Los Angeles: California University Press, 1988).
38 See Leavis, *The Living Principle*, pp. 33–5.
39 Plato, *Symposium*, p. 38.
40 Benjamin, *Selected Writings*, 2, p. 262.
41 See J. Carey, *The Intellectuals and the Masses* (London: Faber, 1992).

Art in time of war:
towards a contemporary aesthetic

In times of war

In September 1914 an agonised Hermann Hesse writes of how war is destroying the foundations of Europe's precious cultural heritage, and thereby the future of civilisation itself. Hesse stands proudly for what he calls a 'supranational' tradition of human culture, intrinsic to which are ideals essentially humanitarian: an 'international world of thought, of inner freedom, of intellectual conscience' and a belief in 'an artistic beauty cutting across national boundaries'.[1] Even in the depths of war, insists Hesse, a German should be able to prefer a good English book to a bad German one. Three years later he writes along similar lines to a government minister telling him that he would be a more humane leader in this time of conflict were he to read 'the great authors' and listen to great composers like Beethoven.[2]

Much later (1946) Hesse comments as follows on these and other similar writings:

> When I call [them] 'political' it is always in quotes, for there is nothing political about them but the atmosphere in which they came into being. In all other respects they are the opposite of political, because in each one of these essays I strive to guide the reader not into the world theatre with its political problems but into his innermost being, before the judgement seat of his very personal conscience. In this I am at odds with the political thinkers of all trends, and I shall always, incorrigibly, recognize in man, in the individual and his soul, the existence of realms to which political impulses and forms do not extend.[3]

Here is an uncompromising expression of that spiritual, essentialist individualism which underpinned Hesse's equally uncompromising universal humanism. Here too is the corollary of both the humanism and the individualism – a profound distrust of the political.

Though not beyond criticism – he was little known outside Germany and so wanted to avoid his own books being banned there – Hesse was implacably opposed to the barbaric nationalism of his own country from around 1914 onwards. He went into self-imposed exile in 1919, and never returned to Germany. He was awarded the Nobel Prize for literature in 1946, but for most of his life remained a struggling, exiled, writer. His books were eventually banned in Germany in 1943, and that was a severe blow. He begins his Nobel Prize letter of thanks with the reasons he cannot be present in person: 'the hardships of the National Socialist period, during which my life work was destroyed in Germany and I was burdened day after day with arduous duties, undermined [my health] for good. Still, my spirit is unbroken. . .'.[4]

Art in time of war: my title refers not just to the literary encounter with war, but the way wars in the last century compelled artists and intellectuals into rethinking the aesthetic – its scope, its power and its dangers. One question is paramount: is literature most compelling when in the service of humane values, or when it departs from them? And why begin with Hesse, this once celebrated, sometime cult figure, now much neglected? I begin with Hesse because the full significance of an aesthetic humanism becomes apparent in relation to artists like him in a way it doesn't in, say, the squabbles within the English literary critical tradition in the last quarter of the twentieth century. More specifically, the critique of humanism which helped provoke those squabbles never properly engaged the example of people like Hesse, preferring instead much easier targets in academic literary criticism. In other words, within both the humanist tradition and the theoretical critique of it, the historical conditions of thought matter, and it especially matters that many recent critics of humanism have been formed entirely within an education system – from school to university – which is itself the product of relative security and prosperity in the post-war period.

Right now it's especially revealing to reconsider the life and writing of advocates of a high European humanism like Hesse. The reasons are several, including the obvious fact that debates about the relevance (or not) of artistic culture to numerous contemporary malaises are more urgent and conflicted than ever. I was about to remark the crucial proviso that our lives are not, as was Hesse's and millions of others at that time, devastated by world war. Indeed they are not, and yet we might recall that Britain has been involved in several major wars in the last two decades, and wonder about what part, if any, Hesse's ideal of a supranational, European cultural tradition played in those conflicts. And although the historical conditions are indeed quite different, we too live in a time of acute distrust of, and perhaps despair about, the political realm which Hesse would have understood. Additionally, in Britain there is an increasingly bitter debate about just how integrated with Europe – how 'supranational' – we should become, and nationalism, cultural and economic, remains a potent force, literally breaking up major political parties and stirring potent if as yet localised racism. Some predict that it will only take another economic depression for the reappearance in Britain of the barbarism witnessed in Eastern Europe in the 1990s. Finally, as Hesse well knew, the realm of the aesthetic, even or especially when it tries to stand above the political, never escapes it.

Days after my writing the above in 2001 there occurred the September 11th terrorist attacks on New York and Washington, subsequent to which Britain signed up to another war, one whose scope and extent was, and remains, unknowable. If the rhetoric is similar – the need to defend Western civilisation against barbarism – the conditions of this war are so different as to be unimaginable for those like Hesse. A hastily formed international coalition against terrorism claims to proceed in the name of civilisation but it does not need – indeed is embarrassed by – the old humanist universals. We know how arrogant and unheeding Western humanism could be in relation to cultural and racial difference, not least within its own colonial and imperialist domains. That's one reason why, in Western democracies, a confident humanism has given way to an ethic of multiculturalism; for sure, an assumption of underlying similarities is not entirely absent, but it is subordinate to a cautious embrace of cultural difference. Which is why Britain's prime minister, as he commuted the world in October 2001 shoring up support for the coalition against terrorism, allowed it to be known that, as he travelled, he read translations of the Koran.

What has become truly supranational is, of course, the very capitalism which Hesse and others saw as humanism's enemy. At one level global capitalism needs and nurtures the multiculturalism which has superseded humanism; at another it promotes a cultural imperialism more arrogant than humanism and underpinned by popular rather than high culture – Hollywood and McDonalds' rather than Shakespeare and Harrods. This is an economic and military imperialism which exacerbates cultural antagonisms. And that means that multiculturalism (or hybridity) can shift very quickly from being an ameliorating influence on those antagonisms to being an opportunity for them to intensify. Terrorism may thrive on the multicultural; a certain kind of terrorism presupposes it. The United Kingdom and the United States are desperate to show that this new war is not being waged against Islam precisely because there are many Muslims, including some residing in Britain, who regard it as precisely that, or at least as a conflict between irreconcilable cultures and religions. Just as it seemed as if the 'global' antagonisms of the kind focused in the Rushdie affair had been fudged into history, they erupted again on September 11th, and with a terrible ferocity. One irony of the Rushdie affair was that a work of literature provoked rather than ameliorated those antagonisms. In recent months I listened in vain for significant voices promoting art as a human activity transcending cultural and religious antagonism.

More war and the decline of humanist faith

What precipitated the decline in humanist faith? Well, all three aspects of Hesse's cultural philosophy – its universal humanism, spiritual individualism, and distrust of the political – were the object of fierce criticism by almost all the strands of so-called theory (literary, cultural and critical) during the 1980s and 1990s, and with a degree of success which helped generated the so-called culture wars. Culture became 'politicised' as never before, and almost always around the issue of who was excluded from the humanist universe. Some academics and politicians trying to cling to the humanist tradition blamed 'theory' for its demise. This is too easy and often plain diversionary: the problem goes much deeper, and back much further. Quite apart from the growing antipathy to Western humanism among other cultures and world religions, there were deep misgivings within the tradition itself.

Let us go back to the outbreak of another war. W. H. Auden's poem '1st September 1939' – widely invoked in relation to September 11th – offers a response to the impending Second World War reminiscent of Hesse's to the First:

> Defenceless under the night
> Our world in stupor lies;
> Yet, dotted everywhere,
> Ironic points of light
> Flash out wherever the Just
> Exchange their messages:
> May I, composed like them
> Of Eros and of dust,
> Beleaguered by the same
> Negation and despair,
> Show an affirming flame.[5]

Reminiscent, yes, but so different. There is the speaker's poignant hesitancy, his unsureness, composed as he is of Eros and dust, and beleaguered by negation and despair, as to whether he is strong enough to sustain the affirming flame. And now the contact between the civilised is furtive; Hesse's image of a supranational humanism operating as an overground unity across and above the strife is replaced here by one suggesting an underground hiding from it; erratic, clandestine communications occur at night between the fragmented and the dispersed. And then there's the description of these communications as 'ironic': perhaps, in retrospect, nothing was more indicative of the diminishing faith in the humanist salvation of Europe than the turn to irony. In art no less than in life itself, and never more so than in the writing of Hesse's compatriot, contemporary, and fellow exile, Thomas Mann, irony becomes part confession of, part defence against, the failures of that vision. Irony becomes the crutch of 'late' humanism, at once guarantee of its sophistication and confession of its uncertainty. No surprise then Auden's subsequent and infamous downplaying of the importance of art and the artist; 'we live in a new age', he wrote a decade later, 'in which the artist neither can have . . . a unique heroic importance nor believes in the Art-God enough to desire it'.[6]

Though Hesse's own faith never faltered, by the end of the Second World War it was tempered. In that acceptance message for the Nobel Prize, as well as that for the Goethe Prize, both awarded in 1946, he affirms again the belief that 'culture is supranational and international', but speaks too of a 'deathly sick Europe' and his own temptation to abandon European culture altogether and turn to the wisdom of the Orient. It's a temptation resisted, but the influence of the Orient is indeed central to his new realisation that the fundamental message of mankind's greatest teachers is stoicism, a spiritual renunciation of worldly things as the precondition for discerning the mystical unity in all being. In these final years there is an even greater insistence on the individual soul as the touchstone of integrity, perhaps now at the expense of humanism.[7]

In short the Second World War confirmed, for many, the bankruptcy of Enlightenment humanism. And now we are talking not just of its inability to prevent barbarism, but its complicity with it. Theodor Adorno and others in the Frankfurt school detected in Enlightenment humanism the origins of the very problems which Hesse imagined it to be an answer to.[8] Adorno declared the worthlessness of 'traditional culture', coming as it now does 'neutralized and ready made', adding, famously, that 'to write poetry after Auschwitz is barbaric'.[9] Later those like Baudrillard would take this critique to its limit: 'the "Human" is from the outset the institution of its structural double, the "Inhuman". This is all it is: the progress of Humanity and Culture are simply the chain of discriminations with which to brand "Others" with inhumanity and therefore with nullity.'[10] Even as a thumbnail sketch of western humanism this is grossly reductive; indeed, that assertion – 'This is all it is . . . simply the chain of discriminations etc.' – is so reductive as to be itself a kind of terrorism, the intellectual counterpart of the reductive fundamentalism of actual terrorists.

Today's anti-intellectual guardians of traditional culture love to tell us that Marxism is obsolete, and heavy-duty continental theory just nonsense. That's an argument for another day. I don't rely on dubious theorists like Baudrillard, or even great ones like Adorno; I bypass this culture-wars stand-off by invoking George Steiner's passionate and seminal essays of the 1960s collected as *Literature and Silence*. Steiner gives a blunt, untheoretical elaboration of Adorno's argument: not only did the Nazis destroy 'central European humanism', but the barbarism of the twentieth century 'prevailed on the very ground of Christian humanism, of Renaissance culture and classic rationalism'. Recall Hesse's confident advice to that war leader in 1917, and compare it with this from Steiner in 1966: 'We know now that a man can read Goethe or Rilke in the evening, that he can play Bach and Schubert, and go to his day's work at Auschwitz in the morning. To say that he has read them without understanding, or that his ear is gross, is cant.' 'What', speculates Steiner, 'are the links, as yet scarcely understood, between the mental, psychological habits of high literacy, and the temptations of the inhuman?'[11] What indeed.

In today's international context it is not just Hesse's idea that salvation might lie in a reaffirmation of a universal, spiritual and ethical humanism that rings hollow, but also its underlying premise, namely that art is a humanising force. The extraordinary thing is, our culture industry and our humanities education system still depend upon that premise. The centrality of the arts within the humanities, most especially of English literature, has always rested on the claim that they have a civilising influence promoting national if not transnational humanitarian values.[12] Sir Claus Moser, speaking in October 2000, puts it well: 'I speak with a passionate belief in the enriching force of the arts in the life of each one of us and of society as a whole.' Complaining of those philistines in today's society, some in high places, 'who fail to appreciate . . . what the arts bring to a civilised society, to our quality of life . . . [and] that a civilised society demands fine culture at its core', Moser endorses President Kennedy's belief that 'the life of the arts . . . is a test of a nation's civilisation'.[13] For Hesse and numerous others in earlier generations, the humanist aesthetic was a liberating expression of profoundly civilising sympathies. For Moser in 2000 humanism remains just that. I respect Hesse writing in 1917; I can't but see Moser, writing in 2000, as deeply complacent. Far from being liberating, the humanist aesthetic has become a way of standing still amidst the obsolete, complacent and self-serving clichés of the heritage culture industry and the arts establishment. It's like an edifice which stands still, but on rotten foundations, propped up by vested interests.

But my argument is not just that Hesse's humanism is untenable and unpersuasive now, 'after Auschwitz', but that it was already so at the time in which he proposed it. In fact, I believe it hardly survived the insight of autobiographical works of his own like *Steppenwolf.* Without doubting Hesse's sincerity, I've often wondered whether other artists haven't always paid lip service to the humanist defence of art by way of licensing an aesthetic vision which they knew contravened it. One is reminded in this connection of literary didacticism in earlier periods, especially when state censorship prevailed: such didacticism, far from foreclosing on subversive thought, was often its precondition. Consider a simple example. The ending of an Elizabethan or Jacobean play is often didactic – the villains get their just deserts and some kind of conventional and/or providential moral order is vindicated. In the mid-twentieth century a gener-ation of critics tried to convince themselves that this didactic dénouement effectively discredits or at least neutralises the subversive questioning and thought which pre-ceded it. Unfortunately for them, from a creative, a theatrical and an intellectual per-spective, the didactic dénouement does not so much close off that questioning as enable it: it subscribes to the law's letter precisely in order to violate its spirit; far from foreclosing on it, a conforming framework actually licensed a subversive content.

I make this point about the tendentious objective of didacticism because it's one of several respects in which the 'modern' conception of the aesthetic I want to propose is already old; I'm advocating a departure which is also a return. Steiner struggles to redeem something of the humanist aesthetic from its ruins in the twentieth century; in contrast I abandon that aesthetic in favour of another, one which becomes visible in those ruins, and in relation to those challenges, because it was always there.

My case for saying literature all the time violates the humanist imperative could proceed by invoking the views of those who have wanted to censor art, from Plato, through the anti-theatrical prejudices to advocates of modern state censorship. But again I justify this aesthetic not with reference to the enemies of art (though I do argue that they are not as philistine as some would claim) but from within its practice and its defence.

Similarly, I could make my case for the daemonic tendencies of the creative mind with reference to disreputable kinds of writing like pornography, or the semi-respectable, like gothic fiction or Jacobean tragedy. Instead, in recent books like *Sex, Literature and Censorship* I've argued the case with texts taken from the heart of canon-ical respectability.[14]

I'll return to this but first, as a way of further following the fate of humanism, I consider further the core premise of the humanist aesthetic, namely that art is a pro-foundly humanising force. I mentioned just now that it remains as a rationale for humanities education and the culture industries. More surprisingly perhaps is that critics of humanism also adhere to it, albeit in an appropriated and radicalised form. The stand-off here is not so much one between the humanists and the anti-humanists, as between a conservative and a progressive humanism. Consider one of the most con-frontational examples of all, namely the cultural materialist critique of humanism. At first sight it opposes the humanist project in every respect. Certainly beleaguered aca-demic humanists see it that way. For example, John M. Ellis laments the threat to a humanist education posed by this critique's obsession with gender, race and class. Ellis

pines for a humanities education which enabled students to become 'enlightened citizens'; which produced a society of people educated 'for full and intelligent participation in a modern democracy'; which helped us 'develop a richer understanding of
human life and to train the mind', which taught us to enjoy and to love literature;
which taught the still viable classical precept that poetry 'delighted and instructed',
and so on.[15] Those like Ellis are right to this extent: the materialist critique resolutely
rejects all three of the tenets I've attributed to Hesse (universal humanism, essentialist individualism, an aesthetic realm standing above the political); instead it sees art
as either appropriable for the oppressed and exploited, be they defined in terms of
class, and/or sex and/or race, or as an instrument of their oppression, or a merging of
both positions.[16] In so doing it clearly retains humanitarian ideals albeit under
another name, with changed terms and constituencies, and a scepticism about how
art, *as currently conceived*, contributes to those ideals. The argument now is whether
or not, or to what extent, aesthetic discourse has a 'democratic and radical potential'.[17]

But there's a sense in which these arch-enemies, the humanist and the materialist,
are competing for the same ethical high ground. To invoke Ellis again, both humanists
and materialists would endorse the idea of a society of people educated 'for full and
intelligent participation in a modern democracy', while disagreeing about (i) what such
a society looks like; (ii) the proximity of actual existing societies to that ideal; (iii) the
part canonical artworks, and an education based on ideas of the aesthetic as conventionally understood, actually play in promoting democracy and participation. Additionally,
from the example of a latter-day humanist like Richard A. Etlin, we can see how the
humanist has already conceded ground to the political/ethical agenda of the materialist. Etlin defends nineteenth-century novelists against Edward Said's claim that they
were complicit with imperialism. But far from saying, as his predecessors might have
done, that such political considerations are irrelevant to aesthetic ones, Etlin not only
marshals those novelists' own anti-imperialist and antislavery sentiments, but reads
their novels for evidence of the same.[18] He thereby implicitly extends the humanist
agenda to partially accord with that of his opponents, even while trying to discredit their
arguments.[19] It's difficult not to conclude that the materialists have already won the high
ground, although they've also extended its terrain. At the very least, the old argument
that such political considerations are irrelevant to the aesthetic vision has gone for good.
While Etlin refuses to accept Said's assertion that politics and culture, far from being
different spheres are 'ultimately the same', he can only counter it with an evasive generalisation: the humanist refuses to conflate the two spheres 'in all times and in respects'.[20]
The irony of all this is that the survival of humanism may well depend on its critics. In
its conservative form as defended by Ellis and Etlin it's a tired convention; in its appropriated form, on the extended terrain of the materialists, it's at least still alive.

Returns

From within the same materialist critique something else was emerging much more
germane to my purpose than this struggle for the ethical high ground. As the constituencies of the oppressed were refined and enlarged, and the operations of power

understood in all their (often counter-intuitive) complexity, so attention turned from the 'conscious', manifest and apparently unified project of the artwork, to a consideration of its 'unconscious' or latent tendencies, its internal *dis*unity. More often than not the work was read not for its explicit content but for its tensions, conflicts and contradictions; for what it did not say, yet half-revealed. In a sense – a sophisticated sense – it was read against itself. This was part of a significant change in ways of reading culture more generally: the centre came to be understood in relation to its margins, the 'other' in relation to the 'same', the dominant in relation to the subordinate, the sane in relation to the insane, the heterosexual in relation to the homosexual, and so on. A paradoxical dialectic became visible in which the 'in relation to' became strangely 'implicated with' and even 'dependent upon': via a violent dialectic the excluded, the inferior and the irrelevant return to haunt and terrorise the identity and well-being of their dominant others, perhaps striking at the literal and symbolic centre of their being.

The violent dialectic between the dominant and the subordinate was something which humanism could not comprehend – hence, in part, the so-called 'anti-humanism' of the critique which explored it. It also became apparent from this critique that certain types of literature had always contained their own imaginative understanding of this dialectic, and, if only implicitly – perhaps even unintentionally – a challenge to the very humanism which sought to appropriate them. Many of the canonical works of literature claimed by and for the humanist vision so obviously threaten rather than confirm it: put very simply, they reveal too much. And so a new challenge emerges, one importantly different from the materialist challenge to the limitations of aesthetic humanism, it's blindness to the fact of exclusion, the way its supposed 'universality' was not universal at all. The challenge now is to understand the tension between the aesthetic and the humane as commonly understood; to understand that the aesthetic vision has been most captivating precisely when it exceeds and maybe violates the humanitarian one. Captivating yes, but also potentially dangerous: there can be no guarantee that (for instance) the imaginative exploration of the return of the repressed will be conducive to the health of either the individual or the society; only the utterly naive can believe that all repression/suppression is bad.

Those who love art and live by it refuse to recognise this potential challenge, believing instead that art is the most exalted expression of civilised life. They promulgate well-intentioned lies, telling us that great art and the high culture it serves can only enhance the lives of those who truly appreciate them; that such art – unlike, say, propaganda, popular culture or pornography – is incapable of damaging or 'corrupting' us. Such an attitude not only fails to take art seriously enough, but rests on a prior process of pro-art censorship more effective than anti-art state censorship. Their defence *of* art is more often than not a defence *against* art, and an exaggerated respect for it becomes a way of not engaging with it. Those who love art the most also censor it the most. To approach literature insisting on an alignment of the ethical conscience and the creative imagination is to be blind to the fact that some of the most compelling writing is about the tension between, if not the incompatibility of, these two things. If I allude to *Sex, Literature and Censorship* again here it's simply because I only now have time to sketch and develop the argument outlined there.

We know that the aesthetic vision can challenge reactionary social agendas. Indeed, for most defenders of art today, though by no means all, that's welcome enough because theirs is a moderately liberal agenda. But art can also challenge progressive and humanely responsible social agendas. For that reason, to take art seriously is to recognise that there are some reasonable (i.e. rational) grounds for wanting to control it. I'm not claiming that art is inhumane in the sense that it insidiously legitimates the interests of the powerful at the expense of the dispossessed, exploited, etc., although there are indeed some canonical works which have been plausibly read in such terms. Nor is my argument a transhistorical one about all art, or even all literature. It is obviously more applicable to some genres, periods and movements wherein a knowledge of what profoundly disturbs psychic and social equilibrium, of what threatens prevailing notions of civilised life, is central – e.g. Greek tragedy, the drama and epics English Renaissance (especially Spenser and Milton), countless modernist texts, including some which have been interpreted quite otherwise.

Again, a disquieting half-realisation of this has often occurred even within conservative aesthetic perspectives. We can detect it in the most basic category of the humanist aesthetic, that of 'character'. Time and again, and literally across centuries if not millennia, the most compelling individual creations are the daemonic ones: the vice figures in medieval moralities had vitality and wit on their side; the malcontents in Elizabethan and Jacobean tragedy are charismatic, insightful anti-heroes whose deep insight into corruption is enabled by their complicity with it; Milton's Satan in *Paradise Lost* has a perverse integrity which at the very least problematises, and for some readers discredits, the didactic project of the entire epic. In *Paradise Lost* the devil is in the structure as much as the detail. Critics have always tried to avoid this by arguing that such imaginative identifications with the immoral and the inhumane are ultimately contained, placed or neutralised by some over-arching ethical vision or structural closure of the literary work.

There is a strange affinity between an aesthetic identification with the daemonic and the theological and ethical impulse to exact a full look at the worst. For instance, what we encounter in *Paradise Lost* is the courage – or arrogance, and perhaps paranoia – of the most formidable kind of theology, that which believes it can most effectively overcome what threatens it only by knowing it to the full. In Milton's case the need for such a confrontation would be intensified by the experience of revolutionary defeat. In *Paradise Lost*, the damage to didactic intent derives from performing this impulse not only as theology but as tragic literature, arguably the definitive expressive medium of defeat. And even if it could be shown that Milton never made, or never intended, such identification (which it can't), it would still be the case that he made it possible for others to so identify, including two of his most influential readers, Blake and Shelley.[21] Two points about their readings: first they indicate how cultural pressures at the time of reception will, if powerful enough, always over-ride formal strategies of closure, reactivating and privileging dissident currents in a work; second, their somewhat risky identifications with Satan are made not against but on behalf of the humanitarian project; in fact they are significant moments in the development of aesthetic humanism.

Even so, such readings of Satan were dangerous enough for God and his followers, if no longer for the rest of us. And that's my point: we allow such readings when they no longer challenge us. And yet literature is full of knowledge which is dangerous for us: it discloses understandings of the world which our own modes of civilised life cannot or do not want to recognise, perhaps *should not* recognise. I argue, for example, that modernists like W. B. Yeats and D. H. Lawrence, under the influence of Nietzsche, offer an exhilarating celebration of an amoral aesthetics of energy. As readers have admired and identified with, say, Yeats's poetic voice they've found themselves uncomfortably close to an aesthetic which allowed artists and intellectuals to identify with fascism. My claim though is not that Yeats should be censored as a fascist but that his verse offers us a different and disturbing insight into recent history and ourselves. To understand the poetry is not to transcend its violence but to enter its seductive sublimations. When the poet is free from politics in the narrow sense he can be most effective in articulating some of the deeper fantasies which contributed to millions making certain political identifications and affiliations which in turn led to the death and torture of millions of others. These fantasies remain very alive today. To put it bluntly, a certain reading of Yeats and Lawrence reveals fascist fantasies as a more or less repressed constituent of modern cultures. So: to insist that literature never escapes the political (which I do) is quite different from demanding that it be responsibly political (which I don't); for me, the value of Yeats and Lawrence lies centrally in their not being politically responsible because all such responsibility rightly entails repression.

Of course this is an argument which commits me to a view of aesthetic appreciation as in certain respects cognitive, that is, possessing a truth or knowledge content. Such an account is associated most immediately with Adorno[22] but again, has a longer, quite conventional history both as working assumption and as theory. Even conservative aesthetic theories embrace it, for example those, including neoclassicism, which regard art as offering generalised, universal truths about the world, though once again the question as to what kind of truth is being offered is one too few stop to answer or even ask. Arguably art has more often than not been assumed to possess cognitive content of some kind, and it is only in relation to theories of art as non-referential that it becomes an issue. The dissociation of art and knowledge is relatively recent. As J. M. Bernstein puts it in *The Fate of Art*, 'the experience of art *as aesthetical* is the experience of art as having lost or been deprived of its power to speak the truth . . . This loss . . . I shall call "aesthetic alienation"; it denominates art's alienation from truth which is caused by art's *becoming* aesthetical, a becoming that has been fully consummated only in modern societies'.[23] To see art as cognitive does not preclude it having specific and even unique types of formal properties (language, style, genre and so on), nor does it diminish their importance. But it does challenge claims that such aesthetic specificity renders the cognitive element of a work as secondary or even irrelevant. And since such claims are relatively recent the onus of proof is on those who make them.

Yet another respect in which a 'conservative' or established dimension of the aesthetic harbours a challenge to the humanitarian agenda it was supposed to endorse is latent within the theory of aesthetic appreciation as 'disinterested'. Such appreciation involves a profound uniqueness of perception which is both detached from and sees beyond the mundane world of politics and interest – the idea in other words of aesthetic perception as, in Kant's words, 'disinterested and free'. This idea has its own unique route to the non-humane or the inhumane, in for example Schopenhauer's reworking of Kant; now aesthetic disinterestedness releases us from the will to live and requires the death of the self – an eradication of one's individuality and even of one's humanity.[24] This aesthetic draws us to the sublime and that fascination with a non-human beauty whose power has something to do with its indifference to the human. Subsequently the aesthetic of disinterestedness mutated into a specifically human distaste for, or indifference towards, the human – again most notoriously when beauty is the object of its gaze. There are so many examples from the twentieth century: Lawrence/Birkin's fantasies of a universe aesthetically cleansed of the 'foul . . . defilement' which is humanity;[25] the symbolist poet who declared of an anarchist bomb attack, 'What do the victims matter if the gesture is beautiful?' Or Wilde's remark about Thomas Wainewright: 'When a friend reproached him with the murder of Helen Abercrombie he shrugged his shoulders and said, "Yes; it was a dreadful thing to do, but she had very thick ankles".'[26] Finally, and returning to my war theme there is Mussolini's indebtedness to the Futurists when he compared bombs exploding among fleeing civilians to flowers bursting into bloom.[27] Karlheinz Stockhausen allegedly said that the events of September 11th were the greatest work of art imaginable.[28] Might it not be that, inside the outrage which greeted these remarks, and the prompt decisions to cancel performances of his work, was a disavowal? At the very least we know that millions the world over watched the events compulsively, over and over again, experiencing a range of emotions: anger, shock, compassion and a horrified fascination at a spectacle which seemed to exceed the cinema's most sublime special effects, thereby giving a new, awful sense to the idea that life might imitate art.

To recap – it is in such respects that the aesthetic I'm outlining is already apparent within the Western tradition: the tendentious function of didacticism, the fascination and identification with the daemonic, the cognitive dimension of the work of art, and the way aesthetic detachment enables amoral perception.

Know to know no more: dangerous knowledge

This aesthetic is surely most apparent in the artistic preoccupation with dangerous knowledge – the kind of knowledge which disturbs rather than consolidates social and psychic order. Here we're concerned not just with the dissident perspective of some writers, but the organisation of human culture. An individual identity is composite, a partial organisation more or less complex, and always entailing a greater or lesser degree of repression, suppression and exclusion: identity is constituted by what something is not, as well as by what it essentially is. So too are cultures and civilisations, albeit inconceivably more elaborate both in their organisation and their exclusions.

The more complex the organised unity, the more vulnerable it is to being destabilised, especially by, or in relation to, its exclusions. Further, what is excluded remains inseparable from what is included, which means it is never fully outside. This is one reason why the most potent threat to something operates internally, in terms of its structure and organisation; ruin is an internal not an external process, disintegration from within rather than destruction from without. The alien beast may be slouching towards Bethlehem, but the greater danger lies in the fact that things fall apart and the centre can't hold. Intellectually speaking this has become a modern commonplace, largely thanks to the likes of Darwin, Marx, Nietzsche and Freud. There are other terms for the same or related processes of internal ruin, most of them loaded with disapprobation: to degenerate, decompose, dissolve (dissolution, dissolute), unravel, unbind, regress. And of course revolution, in both its old and its newer senses.

In every case of perceived unbinding urgent political questions arise: is this really a threat to our modes of cultural organisation, or might it be incorporated with minimal change? And if the change required is more extensive, does it promise adoption and survival, or disintegration and loss of identity? That such questions will be answered differently depending on position, vested interest and existing relations of power and conflict indicates the complexity of both the process and its perception. That some literature enacts disintegration is obvious: why else censorship? But we know too that even literature overtly on the side of binding also necessarily explores the forces which unbind, and time and again it is these forces which prove the most fascinating: the depiction of utopias never matches that of dystopias, and writers come most alive when exploring that convergence of forbidden desire and dangerous knowledge.

As Roger Shattuck and others have shown, forbidden knowledge has always been a feature of human cultures, most obviously in the concepts of taboo and heresy.[29] Ignorance is bliss, we say. In *Paradise Lost* Milton gives us this picture of Adam and Eve, sleeping innocently:

> These lulled by nightingales, embracing slept,
> And on their naked limbs the flow'ry roof
> Show'red roses, which the morn repaired. Sleep on
> Blest pair; and O yet happiest if ye seek
> No happier state, and know to know no more.[30]

In a phrase, 'Be lowly wise'. Adam and Eve disobey, and their transgressive desire for forbidden knowledge brings death and disintegration into the world, into desire. In other words, it kick-starts history.

To observe the injunction not to know (or, more accurately, for *some* people, often the majority, not to know) has been regarded as a precondition of social and psychological well-being, and the survival of civilisation itself – again implicit in the very idea of censorship. Against that, the breaking of the injunction has been regarded as profoundly liberatory, albeit with tragic consequences, though sometimes also with revolutionary ones. Straddling that opposition are some of the great trangressive figures of myth and literature including Eve, Prometheus, Faust/us, Mary Shelley's Frankenstein, Flaubert's Madame Bovary, Thomas Mann's Aschenbach and Joseph

Conrad's Kurtz. Others, like Robert Louis Stevensons's Jekyll/Hyde, embody the real-isation that knowledge of evil is more intimate with genius than with barbarism, while those like Shakespeare's Macbeth, Dostoyevsky's Raskolnikov and Nietzsche's creator as supreme amoral artist, confirm Pascal's observation that there is a kind of evil which often passes for good because 'it takes as much extraordinary greatness of soul to attain such evil, as to attain good'.[31] Indeed, if most of these figures carry a sense of the dangerous, as well as the liberatory, potential of the forbidden, this is because the knowledge that is forbidden so often reveals the underlying proximities of evil to good. Freud suggests why:

> the objects to which men give most preference, their ideals, proceed from the same perceptions and experiences as the objects which they most abhor, and . . . they were originally only distinguished from one another through slight modifications . . . Indeed . . . it is possible for the original instinctual representative to be split in two, one part undergoing repression, while the remainder, *precisely on account of this intimate connection* undergoes idealization.[32]

Dangerous knowledge indeed

In proverb and myth, in theology and philosophy, one human language after another tells us there are things we should not know, things we should not do, and things we should not see,[33] places we should not go, and of course desires we should not gratify. Thus the importance of Nietzsche contrasting the Dionysiac conception of art with the humanitarian, and in terms of two distinct kinds of sufferer – those who suffer from a superabundance of life and those who suffer from an impoverishment of life. The former 'want a Dionysian art as well as a tragic outlook and insight into life', and willingly confront 'the terrible and questionable . . . every luxury of destruction, decomposition, negation'; while the latter need 'mildness, peacefulness, goodness in thought and in deed . . . a certain warm, fear-averting confinement and enclosure within optimistic horizons'.[34] In Nietzsche we see so clearly that transgressive desire, even when explicitly erotic, aims not just for forbidden pleasure, but forbidden knowledge too.

The humanist wants literature to confirm who and what we essentially are or should be. The aesthetic I'm exploring confronts us with what we are not; or rather, it confronts us with the psychological cost of being who we are, or perhaps the social cost of becoming what we would like to be, had we but courage equal to desire. It means we can never be complacent about the benign influence of art, any more than we can about knowledge per se. To take art seriously is to know it comes without the humanitarian guarantees which currently smother it. We may agree that the suppression of 'truth' is harmful socially and ethically, while remembering that it happens in all cultures, including 'democracies'. 'Why do they hate us so much?' was the bewildered, anguished response of some Americans on September 11th, seemingly unaware of so much: unaware that their country was indeed hated with a vengeance of the kind wreaked on that day; unaware that they were vulnerable to such an attack; unaware even of who their enemies actually were. In that case we grieve for the ignorance as well as the loss of life because if more people had been better informed history might, just might, have been different. But it does not follow that a full access to knowledge is always socially and ethically beneficial. To believe it is must be one of the few remaining naiveties of Enlightenment humanism. As that humanism declines many of the older voices it displaced are to be heard once again, distant but compelling. One especially haunts me: in much wisdom is much grief, and he who increaseth wisdom increaseth sorrow. Artists have increased both.

Notes

1 H. Hesse, *If the War Goes On: Reflections on War and Politics* [1946], trans. R. Manheim (London: Pan Books, 1974), pp. 15–17.

2 *Ibid.*, p. 20.

3 *Ibid.*, p. 11.

4 *Ibid.*, p. 141.

5 W. H. Auden, '1st September 1939' lines 78–88, in *Collected Shorter Poems 1930–1944* (London: Faber, 1950).

6 W. H. Auden, *The Enchafed Flood or the Romantic Iconography of the Sea* (London: Faber, 1951), p. 150.

7 Hesse, *If the War Goes On*, pp. 123–4, 145, 149.

8 I'm thinking here of not only T. W. Adorno's and M. Horkheimer's seminal *Dialectic of Enlightenment*, trans. J. Cumming (New York: Seabury Press, 1972) but also Herbert Marcuse's important collection *Negations: Essays in Critical Theory*, trans. J. J. Shapiro (Harmondsworth: Penguin, 1968).

9 T. W. Adorno, *Prisms*, trans. Samuel and Shierry Weber (London: Neville Spearman, 1967), p. 34.

10 J. Baudrillard, *Symbolic Exchange and Death* [1976], trans I. Hamilton Grant, introd. Mike Gain (London: Sage Publications, 1993), p. 125.

11 G. Steiner, *Language and Silence: Essays on Language, Literature and the Inhuman* (New York: Athenium, 1977), p. ix.

12 Witness the title of a recent book by one of humanism's most strident contemporary advocates: Harold Bloom's *Shakespeare: The Invention of the Human* (London: Fourth Estate, 1999).

13 Lecture delivered to the Royal Society of the Arts, 23 October 2000; printed in an abridged form in the *Independent* (25 October 2000), see 'Wednesday Review', p. 4.

14 J. Dollimore, *Sex, Literature and Censorship* (Cambridge: Polity, 2001).

15 J. M. Ellis, *Literature Lost: Social Agendas and the Corruption of the Humanities* (New Haven: Yale University Press, 1997), pp. 3–4, 33, 49, 51.

16 The appropriation of the humanist aesthetic by and for those traditionally excluded from it is an important aspect of its history – see esp. J. Rose, *The Intellectual Life of the British Working Class* (New Haven: Yale University Press, 2001). As I argue here, though, this appropriation is also a transformation which threatens some of humanism's founding principles.

17 Cf. I. Armstrong, *The Radical Aesthetic* (Oxford: Blackwell, 2000), p. 2.

18 R. A. Etlin, *In Defence of Humanism: Value in Arts and Letters* (Cambridge: Cambridge University Press, 1996), pp. 114–22.

19 As an aside one notes here a typical strategy of the conservative humanist: s/he resists change for as long as possible, but when such resistance is no longer possible gives some ground

reluctantly, either pretending s/he hasn't or, if shown to have done so, claiming this was what was meant all along. As a strategy of course nothing could be more 'political' in the narrowest sense of the word. Generally, I find Etlin's beautifully produced book devoid of understanding of the arts in proportion to its tasteful appreciation of them.

20 Etlin, *In Defence of Humanism*, p. 114.

21 See J. A. Wittreich Jr. (ed.), *The Romantics on Milton* (Cleveland, OH: Western Reserve University, 1970), esp. pp. 35, 98, 528–41.

22 For an instructive account of Adorno's theory see S. Jarvis, *Adorno: A Critical Introduction* (Cambridge: Polity, 1998).

23 J. M. Bernstein, *The Fate of Art: Aesthetic Alienation from Kant to Derrida and Adorno* (Cambridge: Polity, 1992), p. 4, emphasis original; see also James O. Young, *Art and Knowledge* (London: Routledge, 2001).

24 A. Schopenhauer, *The World as Will and Representation*, trans E. F. J. Payne (New York: Dover Publications, 1958), I, pp. 179, 196–8; II, p. 371.

25 D. H. Lawrence, *Women in Love* [1921] (Harmondsworth: Penguin, 1977), p. 142.

26 O. Wilde, 'Pen, pencil and poison' in *Intentions* [1891] (London: Methuen, 1925), p. 86.

27 Cited from M. Jay, ' "The aesthetic ideology" as ideology: or what does it mean to aestheticize politics?' in *Force Fields: Between Intellectual History and Cultural Critique* (London: Routledge, 1993), pp. 71–83 (p. 73).

28 Stockhausen later claimed that he had said 'the greatest work of art by Lucifer'. What exactly he did or didn't say isn't the point; rather it's people's response to what he was reported as saying – see the *Guardian* (20 September 2001). More recently Damien Hirst has apologised for describing the attack as 'a visually stunning work of art'. Other writers have been more cautious; in a recent article Peter Conrad speaks of the 'inadvertent, possibly shameful wonderment' at the event shown by Ian McEwan, 'who thought that the towers collapsed with a "malign majesty" ', and Martin Amis, 'who thrilled to the "opulently evil" flames' ('The presumption of art', *Observer Review* (8 September 2002), p. 6.

29 See R. Shattuck, *Forbidden Knowledge: From Prometheus to Pornography* (New York: St Martin's Press, 1996); T. Ziolkowski, *The Sin of Knowledge: Ancient Themes and Modern Variations* (Princeton: Princeton University Press, 2000).

30 J. Milton, *Paradise Lost*, Book IV, lines 771–5, in *Milton: Poetical Works*, ed. D. Bush (Oxford: Oxford University Press, 1969).

31 B. Pascal, *Pensées*, trans. and introd. A. J. Krailsheimer (Harmondsworth: Penguin, 1966), p. 215.

32 S. Freud, 'On repression' in The Pelican Freud Library, vol. 11, *On Metapsychology: The Theory of Psychoanalysis*, ed. A. Richards, trans. J. Strachey (Harmondsworth: Penguin, 1984), p. 150 (my emphasis).

33 On 'ocular prohibition' in myth see especially Shattuck, *Forbidden Knowledge*, pp. 18–21.

34 F. Nietzsche, *The Gay Science*, ed. B. Williams, trans. J. Nauckhoff (Cambridge: Cambridge University Press, 2001), p. 234.

Mimesis in black and white: feminist aesthetics, negativity and semblance

As Sarah Worth suggests, despite well-established feminist work in literary criticism, film theory and art history, feminist aesthetics 'is a relatively young discipline, dating from the early 1990s', and thus still open to contestation and new formulations.[1] In this context it might seem paradoxical that one of the founding texts of feminist aesthetics, Rita Felski's *Beyond Feminist Aesthetics: Feminist Literature and Social Change*, proclaims its impossibility. Felski concludes that 'no convincing case has yet been made for a gendered aesthetics' because there are 'no legitimate grounds for classifying any particular style of writing as uniquely or specifically feminine'.[2] Felski associates the project of feminist aesthetics with a desire to ascribe immanent gendered meanings to literary forms and styles, and thus with a problematic conflation of literary and political values:

> The notion of a feminist aesthetics presupposes that these two dimensions (the political and the aesthetic) . . . can be unproblematically harmonised, assuming either that an aesthetically self-conscious literature which subverts conventions of representation forms a sufficient basis for a feminist politics of culture . . . or that texts which have been politically important to the women's movement are automatically of aesthetic significance.[3]

As an alternative, she proposes dialectical mediation between aesthetics and feminist politics (even though she admits she stresses the feminist side of this dialectics) – a mediation that would repoliticise art on the levels of both production and reception, without however reducing it to an instrumental political use value. And what would provide the means of such mediation is the notion of a feminist counter-public sphere which, instead of direct attribution of political meaning to particular styles, contextualises women's art vis-à-vis social and ideological conditions of production/reception.

Felski's work, including her most recent *Doing Time*, raises many provocative questions – for instance, why the project of feminist aesthetics should be defined in such reductive terms (which are then indeed disclosed as reductive), and more importantly, why her own approach to women's art is 'beyond' aesthetics. Although it seems new in the context of feminism, this claim about the impossibility of feminist aesthetics is after all strangely familiar – it inadvertently repeats the Hegelian thesis of the death of art without any awareness of the long history of the critical engagements with this thesis.[4] Hegel's claim, let us recall, does not announce the end of artistic production but rather points to the eclipse of the inherent and irreducible social function of art, which for that reason 'no longer satisfies our supreme need'.[5] And if art is not thereby simply reducible to enjoyment, if it still carries social meanings, they are no longer in harmony with the sensuality of its form and thus their complexity can be more adequately analysed by the conceptual language of philosophy, science or, in our terms, cultural studies. We hear an uncanny residue of this sentiment of dissatisfaction in the opening sentence of Felski's essay, 'Why feminism doesn't need an aesthetic (and why it can't ignore aesthetics)', except that now it extends from the field of art production to aesthetics as such: 'My dissatisfaction with feminist aesthetics does not stem from a belief that there are no connections between art and gender politics. Rather, I do not think that feminist aesthetics helps us understand these connections adequately.'[6] In this context it is not surprising that Felski's critique of the French and American feminist approaches to aesthetics – the lack of sufficient historicisation of the female subjectivity and gender ideology on the American side, the abstract fetishisation of the formal innovation on the French side – repeats Hegel's critique of the opposition between historicism and formalism together with his call for the overcoming of art for the sake of the more appropriate means of social mediation. And if the Hegelian solution consists in the subsumption of art by philosophy – that is, in the sublation of art's sensuous dependence on the particular image, form and affect by conceptual articulation – Felski's more Habermasian option, despite her call for a mediation between aesthetic and political domains, privileges in fact the subordination of art to the feminist politics of counter-public sphere based on the problematic notion of a common gender identity.

I begin with Felski because her influential work provides a symptomatic expression of three difficulties in the revisions of modern aesthetics from the perspective of gender, race and cultural studies. We are confronted first of all with the inability to redefine the specificity of aesthetics in the context of the cultural politics of race and gender without, despite all the claims to the contrary, falling into the trap of either apolitical formalism or the political 'death of art'. Thus, when the justifiable critiques of the modernist ideologies of formalism are accompanied by the uncritical desire 'to allow art to return to its social context',[7] they all too often collapse into the opposite reductive tendency, namely, the re-enactment of the political 'death of art'. Second, there is the persisting difficulty of studying the interconnection between gender, race and sexuality in the cultural politics of modernity, despite all claims to the contrary. The juxtaposition of Paul Gilroy's *The Black Atlantic: Modernity and Double Consciousness*, devoted to a brilliant analysis of the black, but mostly male, counterculture of modernity, and the protracted feminist discussions of 'the gender of modernism' is a paradigmatic example of this problem. And finally, there is the dependence on the category of mimesis, which is never interrogated historically. Used in a double sense as representation and identification, mimesis figures prominently not only in Felski's preference for realist art but also in her project of a feminist politics based on identifications with a common gendered identity. Reproducing the deadlock of the debate between Lukács and Adorno, this demand for mimesis produces, as Henry

Louis Gates Jr. remarks, 'an overly mimetic conception of oppositional literature'.[8]
Yet, this often unexamined interconnection between the 'mimetic' and the 'oppositional' produces what Paul Gilroy diagnoses as the politics of fulfilment, that is, politics 'content to play occidental rationality at its own game'.[9] By legitimating the
contextual integration of aesthetics into cultural logic, even if it is a logic of opposition, this ahistorical appeal to mimesis, I would claim, neglects not only the aesthetic
process of production but also the changing historical forms of mimesis. Context-
ualising aesthetics all too frequently occurs, therefore, at the price of a disavowal of
the historicity of aesthetic categories.

In order to elaborate an alternative approach to a feminist aesthetic theory, it is
necessary to address the political implications of modern aesthetics without either
sublating art by politics or making abstract claims about the 'subversiveness' of experimental form. By thinking through the contradiction between aesthetic autonomy and
the critical social function of art, such an approach would contest the historical separation not only between political and aesthetic spheres but also between gender and
'the colour line' fracturing these spheres from within, while remaining suspicious of
their false reconciliation. Put in a different way, feminist aesthetics has to find new
ways of mediation between the aesthetic autonomy of art and the sexual, racial politics of modernity without overcoming the productive tension between them. Rather
than subsuming art by politics, this mediation should assume the form of a careful
redefinition of all the crucial modern aesthetic categories – such as autonomy, form,
mimesis, sensibility, negativity and utopia – by taking into account discontinuous histories of aesthetics, social antagonisms and diverse artistic practices.[10] In particular,
we will have to begin with the critical interrogation of the historical status of mimesis
in the context of a gendered and racial politics of modernity – the problem on which
I want to focus in this essay.

Needless to say, my approach to feminist aesthetics is influenced by Adorno's aesthetic theory. Although Adorno hardly ever considers black, non-European, or
women writers, there are nonetheless several aspects of his work relevant to my
project: first, there is the relation between form, history and social antagonism;
second, there is the ambivalent function of modern art, suspended between subversion and complicity with the structures of domination; and finally, there is the historical diagnosis of the ideological status of mimesis in modernity. By rethinking both
form and mimesis in the context of the new forms of power in modernity, Adorno
allows us to formulate the relation between form and content beyond the impasses of
the contextualism/formalism debate. One of his most original claims is that the
unsolved and unacknowledged contradictions in society are reflected primarily not at
the level of content, where they are easily assimilated into the predominant forms of
rationality, but at the level of form: 'The unsolved antagonisms of reality return in artworks as immanent problems of form.'[11] Obviously, Adorno's argument does not
repeat the modernist ideology of formalism, but, on the contrary, treats form as a
dynamic social category linked to new technologies, economic structures of exchange,
social relations of production as well as the intrinsic artistic forming of the always
already historically shaped material.

This emphasis on form as a modality of social making rather than a means of representation does not mean that the feminist theory of aesthetics should abandon the crucial category of mimesis. On the contrary, it means that mimesis should be redefined in the context of the historical investigation of its ideological status in modernity. Toward this end, I will reformulate Theodor Adorno's social history of mimesis, understood both as an aesthetic means of representation and as a psycho-political term of identification, in light of the influential theories of female masquerade and colonial mimicry proposed by Joan Riviere, Frantz Fanon and Homi Bhabha. This diverse configuration of theorists not only shows the structural intersections between race, gender and sexuality in the formation of modern subjectivities but also reveals a new modality of mimesis as semblance and its ambiguous ideological status. By juxtaposing Riviere's notion of masquerade as 'a compromise formation' with the social regulation of mimetic behaviour stressed in different ways by Bhabha and Adorno, I argue that this new modality of mimesis in modernity not only provides an imaginary resolution of racial and gender antagonisms but also performs a perverse reconciliation of sensibility and rationality, jouissance and the law, in the service of domination. On the psychic level, the colonial and gender masquerade functions as a compromise formation between the id, ego and superego; on the cultural and political levels, it contains the contradictions between the imperial metropolis and the colonised peripheries, between the modern ideal of freedom and economic, colonial and gender domination, between identity and difference, between social prohibitions and libidinal gratifications, and finally between the autonomy and the commodification of art. Consequently, on the colonial and gendered peripheries of modernity, mimesis reveals a new form of domination that is based on fusion of sensibility and intelligibility, carnality and rationality rather than on their diremption as is the case in the imperial metropolis. I would argue therefore that the enormous ideological appeal of mimesis lies not just in the reduplication of reality, or in the reproduction of the status quo, but in the semblance of the perverse reconciliation between rationality and sensibility, prohibition and enjoyment that is missing in reality. Consequently, through the fetishistic substitution of the utopian consolation for the degraded present, mimetic semblance provides an indispensable compensatory supplement to what Claude Lefort describes as the disembodied, abstract regime of power in modernity. In this context, the critical function of modern art is perhaps more complex than Adorno initially postulated: it lies primarily not in the recuperation of sensible particularity but in the negation of this compensatory supplement sustaining modern power and the subsequent re-enactment of the alterative relation to carnality and otherness beyond the opposition between diremption/reconciliation of sensibility and rationality.

Influenced by anthropology, psychoanalysis, sociology, art and philosophy, Adorno's history of mimesis unfolds in the double – socio-psychological and aesthetic – register. It is intertwined as much with the changing modalities of subject formation, social relations and the organisation of labour as with the history of aesthetics. This critical genealogy reveals a profoundly ambiguous role of mimesis in modernity – it is both an index of the forgotten, unconscious history of libidinal investments and fantasies and a controlled, regulated practice in the service of domination. As such, this historical investigation not only diagnoses an entwinement of rationality, sensibility and power, but also hopes to disclose the possibility of an alternative, non-appropriative relation to objects. Mimesis is a notoriously difficult and obscure concept in Adorno's work partly because he wants to stress its socio-political ambiguity, and partly because he wants to uncover its forgotten pre-philosophical, libidinal history. From its earliest manifestations in the cry of terror and the uncontrolled somatic reactions of the body frozen in fear where the organism in order to survive approximates the inanimate nature, to the impersonations of the threatening nature in ritualistic or magical practices, this pre-philosophical notion of mimesis has very little to do with representation but, on the contrary, is intertwined with the sensible, carnal receptivity to the outside, or what Adorno calls the non-identical. In contrast to abstract, general philosophical concepts, these mimetic acts of response and adaptation to the other reflect, according to Karla Schultz and Michael Taussig,[12] particular, sensuous modalities of the expressivity of the body. By bearing a trace of the dependence of thinking on its other (carnality, sensibility, the non-identical), mimesis enables a contestation of the hegemony of abstract rationality and its destructive tendency toward immanence. As Jay M. Bernstein points out, the dependence of mimesis on its other reveals the non-identical, which eludes all forms of identification, as a paradoxical condition of identification: the non-identical 'grounds and makes identifying thought possible while making its claim to totality impossible'.[13]

Adorno argues, however, that even these early mimetic impulses at work in the uncontrolled responses of the body, magical impersonations of nature, or ritual performances of dance and song, are dominated by fear and the instinct of self-preservation. Thus, the mimetic affinity and dependence on the other are from the outset intertwined with the desire for the mastery of the internal and external antagonistic forces. Born out of terror in the encounter with the unknown, this phobic mimesis – which Frantz Fanon will make a privileged object of his investigation – is in complicity with the rational domination of nature through the division of labour, technology and science. Reduplicating the mythic fear of the other in a sublimated form,[14] the rational subject/object dialectic of pure immanence obliterates alterity, 'because the idea of outsidedness is the very source of fear'.[15] Although modern reification is itself a mimesis of death,[16] instrumental rationality nonetheless 'outlaws' and confines to oblivion uncontrolled, libidinally invested mimesis because it still bears witness to the threatening proximity of the outside and to the receptivity of the body: 'Civilization has replaced the organic adaptation to others and mimetic behavior proper, by organized control of mimesis, in magical phase; and, finally, by rational practice, by work, in the historical phase. Uncontrolled mimesis is outlawed.'[17] In modernity, the social control of mimesis assumes three main forms: instrumental rationality, modern consumerism and the phobic projections of fascism. In knowledge, the absorption of the other into the same – the conceptual constitution of the object and its abstraction from sensuous particularity – takes the place of the mimetic adaptation to the other. In consumption, the compulsive identification and the phantasmatic introjection of what Karla Schultz calls the prefabricated 'image of self-realization' appeases a modern anxiety of non-identity.[18] As the history of racism and

anti-Semitism shows, the obverse side of the imaginary identifications with the narcissistic fulfilment promoted by commodity culture is the morbid projection of prohibited mimetic impulses on racialised others:

> Those blinded by civilization experience their own tabooed mimetic feature only in
> certain gestures . . . which they encounter in others and which strike them as isolated
> remnants, as embarrassing rudimentary elements that survive in the rationalized envi-
> ronment. What seems repellently alien is in fact all too familiar: the infectious gestures
> of direct contact suppressed by civilization . . .[19]

Projected onto dominated groups, these remnants of the prohibited mimetic impulses
– 'the urge to lose oneself in the other', 'the lure of base instincts, reversion of ani-
mality' – evoke anger and aggression because they are reminders of the fear of the
outside and the yearning for jouissance, which nonetheless 'must be forgotten' in
order to survive 'the new conditions of production'.[20] And yet, what is forbidden is
nonetheless enjoyed 'craftily' on the condition that it is externalised and despised in
the other, just as the 'bad smell' can be enjoyed under the rationalising pretext of 'dis-
infection'. Consequently, political anti-Semitism 'rehabilitates' the weakening of prohibition and the regression to the archaic in the name of 'rational interests': 'the
anti-Semites gather together to celebrate the moment when authority permits what is
usually forbidden'.[21] Mobilised by fascism in a paranoid fashion, this libidinal
economy of phobic projections, devoid of any critical reflection, becomes an organised mimesis to a second degree: an administered imitation of the mythical mimesis,
a perverted compromise between enjoyment, aggression and social regulation.

If we take seriously Adorno's and Horkheimer's claim that the social regulation of
mimesis in modernity is in complicity with racism and commodification then it
becomes clear that mimesis (in its function of identification and realist representation)
cannot be evoked uncritically as a basis of either feminist politics or progressive aesthetics. Nor can it be simply rejected for the sake of abstract formalism, which, when
divorced from 'mimetic impulse' and carnal sensibility, remains in complicity with
instrumental rationality and reifications of modern life. Consequently, to exit this
double bind and to recover a critical potential for mimetic impulse in modern art, a
feminist theory of aesthetics has to diagnose the new modalities of mimesis, which,
under the guise of semblance, provide not only an imaginary resolution for racial and
gender antagonisms but also a perverse compensation for the diremption of sensibility and intelligibility, jouissance and the law, in modernity. Yet it is precisely at this
point that Adorno's and Horkheimer's historical critique is insufficient because, in its
failure to account for the new forms of mimetic semblance characteristic of gendered
and racialised identifications, it misses the new modality of power. Despite its 'empty'
and disembodied character, this power operates, as Foucault has taught us, on and
through the body. Consequently, in order to account for the ideological compensa-
tions of mimetic semblance, we need to supplement Adorno's work with the feminist
and postcolonial theories of mimicry proposed by Riviere, Fanon and Bhabha.[22]

Published in 1929 in the *International Journal of Psychoanalysis*, only a year after
the publication of a phenomenal number of major modernist texts by women writers,

such as Woolf's *Orlando*, Barnes's *Ryder* and *Ladies Almanac*, or Rhys's *Quarter* (originally titled *Masquerades*),[23] Riviere's 'Womanliness as a masquerade' is a major modernist theoretical exploration of the ambiguous role of mimesis at the historical moment of women's entry into and negotiation with the gendered, racial structures of the public and literary spheres of modernity. Extremely influential in feminist theory, especially in the 1980s, Riviere's essay, and in particular, its claim that a masquerade and genuine femininity are the 'same thing', has been read frequently as an early, anti-essentialist, performative formulation of gender.[24] Yet, despite the critical potential of this recovery of mimetic semblance in place of authentic identity, female masquerade remains in complicity with modern power, social anxieties about homosexuality,[25] phallic rivalry, racism and the fear of retribution. When read as a new modality of mimesis, the masquerade of imperial womanliness becomes a symptomatic expression of the compensation and social regulation of the colonial, sexual and racial antagonisms of modernity.

What makes masquerade a particularly useful trope for diagnosing the contradictions of mimesis in the formations of white metropolitan femininity is the repeated oscillation of the master/slave dialectic, which, as we shall see in a moment, is reminiscent of the colonised/coloniser dialectic. In fact, a masquerading woman alternates between the positions of mastery and subjection, without, however, transcending their impasses. Ostensibly, Riviere focuses on the case of the white, intellectual, ambiguously homosexual woman, who suffers from a masculinity complex supported by the unconscious fantasy of the possession of the paternal phallus – a fantasy acted out in her intellectual performances, through which she unconsciously displays and seeks a public recognition for her phallic mastery. Nonetheless, the phallic mastery purchased by masculine identification is paid for with the intense fear of retribution from authority figures and the ferocious threat of the superego, reflecting social regulation. As a defence against the castration threat the woman adopts the mask of a slave: to hide her phallic possession, she compulsively re-enacts a masquerade of a castrated, degraded femininity. To evoke Adorno's critique of mimesis, we could say that in the case of female masquerade the critical potential of the mimetic impulse is arrested by the structures of domination, fear and an instinct of self-preservation.

The ambiguity of mimetic semblance is further compounded by its subtext of racist fantasies.[26] In her dreams, Riviere's patient, a white American from the South, sees herself attacked by a black man, whom she plans to seduce and then deliver 'over to justice', which, as Jean Walton suggests, can only be a euphemism for castration and lynching.[27] In this fantasy, the incompatible psychic formations of aggression, phallic enjoyment and the defence against paternal authority are negotiated through a projective identification with the 'Negro' – a contradictory fantasmatic figure of phallic jouissance, the punishing superego, and the punished victim delegated to take the blame for woman's theft of the phallus. Paradoxically, in order to function as a defence mechanism, the masquerade of womanliness has to be reinforced by another masculine identification – but this time not with the insignia of white power but with the racist stereotype of black masculinity. In this contradictory identification with the punished victim/punishing superego, we see here a feminised figure of Negrophobia, which Riviere and her numerous feminist critics fail to analyse and which Fanon puts at the centre of colonial domination. Consequently, it is the black mask of the white womanliness that consolidates the fragile compromise between sensibility and power, between the defences of the narcissistic ego, the punishing cruelty of the superego, and the sadistic aggression of the id, and, in so doing, provides an ideological support for the racist imaginary.

What has also been ignored in most interpretations of Riviere's essay, and what is nonetheless crucial to understanding the new gendered modalities of mimesis, is not only the paranoid projections of Negrophobia but also the perverse fixation on the pre-Oedipal relations with the mother. Following Melanie Klein, Riviere argues that woman's appropriation of the paternal phallus is an unconscious act of reparation for her earlier sadistic wishes of the dismemberment of the maternal body: thus the woman 'steals' the paternal phallus not for herself but in order to restore it to the mother. As Catherine Millot remarks, 'in this case . . . the father is no more than an appurtenance of the mother, one of the attributes of maternal power, the equivalent of fetish'.[28] By maintaining a contradictory attitude to the imaginary maternal phallus – its absence is at once acknowledged and negated through the act of sacrificial restoration – the fetishistic turn of the female masquerade is at once a cipher of longing for excised sensuality and the maternal genealogy as well as a mark of the daughter's servitude to the mirage of the phallic mother: 'her efforts to . . . make reparation by restoring the penis' to the mother 'were never enough; this device was worked to death; and sometimes it almost worked her to death'.[29] In light of Kristeva's 'Women's Time', we can read this deadly dedication to the myth of archaic mother as an 'archetype' of the utopian belief in 'a good and pure substance' without antagonism, frustration or division.[30]

If the unacknowledged Negrophobia puts female masquerade squarely in the context of colonial domination, its other features – in particular, the mimetic identification with masculine power, the aggressive rivalry for the possession of the phallus and the prohibition of the superego against such possession – can be compared to the assumption of a white mask by a colonised subject analysed in different ways by Homi Bhabha and Frantz Fanon. In the context of this comparison we could say that the impasses of the master/slave dialectic in the position of metropolitan femininity repeat the oscillations of colonised/coloniser dialectics. Yet, such a comparison reveals not only the intertwining of racial and gender antagonisms in mimetic semblance but also the first striking difference in the mode of its social and psychic regulation: If in the case of metropolitan female masquerade we are dealing with a prohibition of masculine identification and the transgression of this prohibition, in the case of colonial mimicry we are dealing with the imperial demand for the identification with whiteness and an instituted failure in the structure of this demand.

It is of course Homi Bhabha who brilliantly diagnoses this new modality of the psycho-social regulation of mimetic semblance in the maintenance of Western imperialism. Like Adorno, he links the ambiguity of the mimetic impulse both to the structures of domination and to the possibility of subversion. Bhabha argues that colonial mimicry is one of the most elusive strategies of colonial power, the effectiveness of which comes from yet another compromise formation – this time, a compromise between the contradictory demands for identity supporting the panoptical vision of domination and a diachronical sense of difference. It is thus a compromise, to use Kalpana Seshadri-Crooks' apt formulation, between the 'visibility and historicity' of the signifier of race.[31] To justify the civilising mission of colonialism and the disciplinary surveillance of the colonised, the colonial power demands the imitation of whiteness and at the same time erects a prohibition against such an identification, evident for instance in the difference between being anglicised and being English. The colonial power has to produce, therefore, not only an enforced imitation of European ideals but also a slippage, a failure of identification. This faulty 'colonial mimesis' constitutes the colonised subject as a partial presence, as a defective semblance – 'almost the same *but not quite*'[32] – of whiteness, just as the masquerading woman is ultimately a defective semblance of the male intellectual. And yet, these two figures of semblance, like mirror reflections of each other, are in fact symmetrical opposites: note in particular that the oppressive demand of colonial mimesis (the demand for the partial identification with the colonising power) mimics the transgressive aspects of female masquerade (its refusal of the prohibited identification with phallic power). This means indeed that the colonial mimesis puts the colonised masculinity in a peculiar feminised position; however, not in a position of traditional femininity, as it has been often argued, but in the place of an ambiguous homosexual woman passing for a man passing for a woman. Just as feminist critics fail to notice Negrophobia in the unconscious structures of female masquerade, Bhabha fails to notice this profound ambiguity of sexuality – almost male but not quite – in his analysis of the ambivalence of colonial power.

Like Adorno, Bhabha argues that the contradictory political regulation of mimetic semblance is motivated by the fear and subjugation of alterity. Yet if Adorno interprets this obliteration of alterity as a consequence of the abstraction of power /knowledge from sensuous particularity and almost complete repression of the prohibited mimetic impulses, Bhabha points out that this repression is lifted on the colonial margins. Consequently, the perverse colonial mimesis provides a compensatory supplement to the disembodied forms of political power in modernity. Similarly, the subjugation of alterity assumes a different form in colonial mimesis: it is not just a conceptual subjugation of the non-identical in the dialectic of pure immanence but a libidinally charged, fetishistic disavowal of difference. Simultaneously acknowledged and negated, the otherness of the colonised is replaced by an imaginary substitute, 'a product of desire that repeats, rearticulates reality as mimicry'.[33]

It is precisely this fetishistic character of the colonial regulation of mimetic semblance that challenges the authority of the colonial power and the Manichean dualism on which it depends just as the fetish splits the ego into two contradictory attitudes: 'The *menace* of mimicry is its *double* vision which in disclosing the ambivalence of colonial discourse disrupts' its epistemological, political and, we have to add, masculine authority. The very partiality and default of imitation alienates the model from itself and discloses its wholeness as a metonymy of presence. As Bhabha puts it, 'on the margins of metropolitan desire, the *founding objects* of the Western world become the erratic, eccentric, accidental *objets trouvés* of the colonial discourse'.[34] Thus the enforced slippage of colonial mimesis threatens to turn into a mockery of colonial regulation, into a site of the emergence of the otherness of the colonised and the 'interdicted' desires, which resist and threaten the colonialising process. By revealing ambivalence, incompleteness and doubling of both the white authority and the black subjectivity,[35] the instituted flaw of colonial mimesis not only intensifies disciplinary surveillance but constitutes a possibility of resistance. As Antonio Negri and Michael Hardt sum up:

> the colonized's mimicry of the colonizer's discourse rearticulates the whole notion of identity and alienates it from essence; cultures are always already partial and hybrid formations. This social fact is the basis on which a subversive political project can be conducted to destroy the binary structures of power and identity. . . . The postcolonial political project, then, is to affirm the multiplicity of differences so as to subvert the power of the ruling binary structures.[36]

Yet, Negri and Hardt fail to note that what is at stake in colonial mimicry is not only the emergence of 'the partial and hybrid formations' but also a perverse compromise between prohibition and enjoyment, sensibility and power – a compromise that compensates for the disembodied character of power and abstract culture in metropolitan modernity. By turning to Frantz Fanon's analysis of colonial mimesis, we can diagnose the nature of this compromise more precisely: we not only note a shift to a different libidinal economy of colonial power (from fetish to phobia) but also confront what has been hitherto evoked only obliquely – namely the black masculine body as the site of both contradictory libidinal investments and the political regulation of mimesis. By focusing on the 'epidermalization' of mimesis, Fanon locates the political regulation of colonial mimicry in the process of the deflection of the specular I into the social reality of colonial domination – in psychoanalytic terms, in the shift from primary to secondary narcissism, in Fanon's terms, from bodily schema to racialhistorical schema. The central figures of this regulation are paranoid projection, Negrophobia and the abjection of the black body.

As is well known, Fanon interprets the coloniser's phobic reaction to the black body in terms of a paranoid projection of aggressivity and incestuous jouissance: 'projecting his own desires onto the Negro, the white man behaves "as if" the Negro really had them'.[37] In so doing, Fanon returns us to the problematic of phobic mimesis and the resurgence of the mythical fear of the other in the colonial situation. Similar to Adorno's discussion of the projection of the prohibited mimetic impulses at work in anti-Semitism, Fanon's diagnosis of the paranoia of colonial power emphasises not so much the emergence of the threatening otherness of the colonised but a certain compromise between enjoyment and prohibition of the libidinal aspects of archaic mimetic impulses – jouissance and death drive: 'the civilized white man retains an irrational longing for the unusual eras of sexual licence, of orgiastic scenes, of unpunished rapes, of unrepressed incest'.[38] Let us notice, therefore, that Fanon's diagnosis of the libidinal economy of colonial power stresses not only the contradiction between the demanded and prohibited imitation of whiteness but also the perversion, or the turning aside, of the prohibition against incestuous jouissance. Neither giving up nor accepting prohibition, the perversion of colonial power regulates enjoyment by externalising the punishing cruelty of the superego and the prohibited incestuous longing for lost jouissance in the black body. As a result of this projective identification, the sexualised black body – the body of noxious enjoyment – is experienced in the racist imaginary as a 'biological' threat to the imaginary integrity of the white body. As Fanon points out, 'the Negro, because of his body, impedes the closing of the postural schema of the white man'.[39] Because of this projective 'epidermalisation' of the prohibited mimetic impulses, the specular black image is overlaid with racial-historical schema constituting the colonised body as the repository of the repugnant jouissance and the unassimilable aggressivity of the death drive. On the margins of metropolis, the libidinally invested black body is turned therefore into an at once fascinating and repulsive memorial of mythical fear and incestuous jouissance, which must be forgotten in the capitalist mode of production.

For Fanon as for Bhabha, the effects of this phobic mimesis are ambiguous. On the one hand, as the repository of what is 'the unassimilable'[40] within the imaginary and the symbolic registers, the black body sustains the <u>méconnaissance</u> of the ideological coherence of whiteness. The paranoid projection allows the white ego to enjoy what is prohibited by displacing the internal ambivalence, jouissance, and the archaic fear onto the imaginary other who retrospectively seems to threaten the integrity of the white body from without. Yet, on the other hand, despite the epidermal barrier protecting whiteness against the encroaching proximity of the real, the phobic narcissism reveals both the compromise between prohibition and jouissance and the fortified identity of whiteness to be perpetually threatened. As Homi Bhabha argues, 'the colonizer is himself caught in the ambivalence' of projective identification, 'alternating between fantasies of megalomania and persecution'.[41] In other words, the black body as a phobic object is a correlative of the white body in the grips of mythical fear, loathing, and yearning.

For the black subjectivity, however, the devastating effects of colonial mimesis are radically different. That is what Fanon suggests when he argues that 'the Negro suffers in his body quite differently from the white man'.[42] For Fanon the enforced and prohibited identification with whiteness manifests itself not only as the defective semblance of white presence but as a traumatising fragmentation and expulsion of the body: 'What else could it be for me but an amputation, an excision, a hemorrhage that spattered my whole body with black blood?'[43] Paradoxically, the impossible dilemma of white identification – '*turn white or disappear*',[44] which sounds like a colonial perversion of Lacan's forced choice between symbolic 'life' or being – does not merely constitute the black subjectivity as a partial semblance but expels the black body from the symbolic universe: 'my shoulders slipped out of the framework of the world, my feet could no longer feel the touch of the ground'.[45] The traumatic effect of the crumbling of the bodily schema under the weight of the projected racial-historical schema is the loss of the symbolic support of the body. Because of this invasion of the body by the real, 'a Negro', Fanon writes, 'is forever in combat with his own image'.[46]

When juxtaposed with Bhabha and Riviere, Fanon allows us not only to analyse the default of the colonial identifications – being almost white, almost male, but not quite – but also to diagnose different responses to the threat of the imperial superego along gender and racial lines: in particular, we see here a striking divergence between the protective mask of white womanliness and the 'amputation' of the black body. Thus, if the defensive assumption of the mask of a castrated femininity 'saves' the white skin, the partiality of colonial mimicry produces a tragic disjunction between the 'white masks, black skin' which, as Stuart Hall and Homi Bhabha rightly point out, does not characterise the duality of the coloniser and the colonised but describes the immobilising shattering of black masculinity from within. Ultimately, what these three figures of mimesis – the defensive mask of imperial femininity, the phobic narcissism of white authority, and the 'corporeal malediction' of the black skin – foreground, is the compromise between enjoyment, prohibition and social regulation and its simultaneously compensatory and destructive function. In contrast to the theft and sacrifice of phallic enjoyment enacted in female masquerade, colonial mimicry is intertwined with the traumatic encroachment of the repulsive enjoyment, which shatters the bodily image of the colonised subject. Thus, if the coloniser enjoys by projecting the threatening jouissance onto the other, if the woman turns herself into a perverse instrument of the enjoyment of the phallic mother, the black man objectifies and amputates his body in order to get rid of the repulsive jouissance attributed to him by the white other.

By reading Adorno, Riviere, Bhabha and Fanon together, I have tried to show that the new psychic economies and social regulations of mimetic semblance in modernity provide a dubious and ideologically suspect alternative to instrumental rationality and the disjunction between abstract universality and sensible particularity on which it is based. Operating on the margins of metropolitan power/knowledge, these gendered and racialised modalities of mimesis perform a compensatory semblance of reconciliation between rebellion and complicity, between enjoyment and prohibition, between the fetishisation of white femininity and the abjection of racialised bodies, between a utopian resolution of antagonisms and the damaged reality of exploitation. The belief in this compromise can be maintained only by disqualifying those who bear the burden of its proof as defective yet fascinating semblances of Western subjectivity. The mimetic semblance of reconciliation is thus preserved at the price of the externalisation of antagonisms, contradictions and enjoyment in the dominated others. To refer to psychoanalytic terminology for a moment, we can say that this perverse compromise formation, achieved through the disavowal of symbolic inconsistencies and negativity, is intertwined with the imaginary construction of the phallus as 'the ultimate white mask'.[47] By throwing a veil over the phallus as the signifier of lack, female masquerade provides support for its imaginary status as a token of masculine mastery and colonial domination. The imaginary equation of the phallus with white masculinity reinterprets the lack in the symbolic in ideological terms as a default of the colonial imitation of whiteness while displacing the frightening proximity of the enjoyment onto the abjected black skin. Consequently, the other side of the disavowal characteristic of mimetic semblance is the abjection of the racialised body associated with enjoyment or perverse servitude to the jouissance of the other. Instead of being a signifier of lack, of the symbolic castration of every subjectivity, the phallus becomes in these fantasmatic transactions an imaginary object – a 'desired bit of whiteness', as Fanon puts it – the appropriation of which could either legitimate colonial power or compensate for the ravages of exploitation. However, rather than supporting resistance, this imaginary compromise reproduces a rapacious dialectic of 'having', which, by renouncing lack, instrumentalises the question of 'being'.

In the end I would like to pose briefly a question about the critical function of modern art in relation to these new modalities of the social regulation of mimesis in modernity. In what sense can the precarious status of art, which itself is merely a semblance, negate the compromises and the disavowals of antagonisms, contradictions and negativity produced by mimetic semblance? Modern art can perform this critical function only insofar as aesthetic semblance is intertwined, as Lambert Zuidervaart reminds us,[48] with a double negation: first, the artwork has to negate the semblance of external reality it produces (negation of representation) and second, it has to negate the artistic autonomy emerging from the first negation (negation of art as in-itself separated from the social). Consequently, unlike the imaginary reconciliation and the disavowal of negativity produced through mimetic semblance, artistic semblance turns against itself and its own complicity with domination in order to foreground the inconsistencies and internal contradictions 'between what the artwork appears to be and what it is'.[49]

Let us look at this double gesture of negation more closely. In a more obvious way, abstract and experimental art negates the mimetic function of the traditional novel because the illusion of external reality denies the materiality of form and the process of artistic production. In a less obvious way, however, this emphasis on the materiality of form also negates the subjective projections and disavowals by externalising/objectifying the subject in the artistic material. The work of art both re-enacts the rational/subjective control over the material and 'extinguishes' the subject in the materials: the subject 'takes part in objectivity when his energy, even that of his misguided subjective "projection," extinguishes itself in the artwork'.[50] Thus, the critical distance from masquerade does not reclaim a more 'authentic' identity but, on the contrary, 'unmasks' its imaginary status by breaking down the default identifications sustaining colonial power and by 'sacrificing the sacrifices'[51] they entail – the sacrifice of one's being, the abjection of black skin or the perverse renunciation of enjoyment to the Other.

It is by turning against its own aesthetic illusions of external reality and subjective control that modern art can expose the contradictions and negate the compensatory function of mimetic semblance operating already on psychic, cultural and aesthetic levels. On the psychic level, let us recall, mimetic semblance functions as a compromise formation between the id, the ego and the superego, producing a perverse reconciliation between enjoyment and prohibition, sensibility and the socio-symbolic order. On the cultural level, this compromise, implicated in the politics of self-preservation and the reproduction of colonial domination, contains the contradictions of modernity between imperial power and colonial mimicry, between the abstract commodity form and the sensuality of female and racialised bodies, and finally, between high and low art. On the aesthetic level, it produces a fetishistic substitution of the utopian promise of reconciliation for the damaged present. Because the compensatory nature of these multiple compromises obfuscates antagonisms and diremption in reality, and thus remains in complicity with domination, the negation of mimesis in modernism becomes a historical necessity. Consequently, by contesting the aesthetic reproduction of mimetic semblance operating already in reality, modern art, as Adorno aptly observes, does not just reject representation but 'rebel[s] against the semblance of a semblance that denies it as such'.[52] Let me just remark that in the case of the modernist texts of the prominent women writers (such as Woolf's *Orlando*, Rhys's novels or Larsen's *Passing*) this rebellion against 'the semblance of a semblance' occurs by turning the racial and gender masquerades into the principle of formal construction.

As many critics of modernism have pointed out, the negation of mimesis could deteriorate into aestheticisms or the fetish of formal subversiveness. This is for instance the basis of Felski's scepticism about modern experimental art. Yet, what these criticisms disregard is the second negation that the progressive art must perform – this time, the negation of its artistic autonomy. As Adorno puts it, the illusion of autonomy 'became an embarrassment because the gapless being-in-itself, after which the pure artwork strives, is incompatible with its determination as something humanly made and therefore as a thing in which the world of things is imbedded a priori'.[53] Although indispensable for the critique of the social regulation of mimesis, the semblance of art as in-itself, as an autonomous object, disavows the social character of artistic materials, the link between form and social division of labour, and finally the irreducibly social and subjective mediation of artistic making: 'For everything that artworks contain with regard to form and materials, spirit and subject matter, has emigrated from reality into the artworks and in them has divested itself of its reality.'[54] Since this disavowal is in complicity with reification, art has to negate its autonomy, on which its critical function also depends.

It is only in the aftermath of this double negation of the compensatory compromises of mimetic semblance and the reifications of aesthetic autonomy that art can redeem its own status as semblance and preserve the critical function of the mimetic impulse. For Adorno this secular redemption of semblance through the labour of the negative achieves a 'tour de force', which points to the future reconciliation of social antagonisms even though such a reconciliation is as yet impossible in reality: 'Those [works] that are a tour de force, a balancing act, demonstrate something about art as a whole: They achieve the impossible.'[55] Consequently, the mimetic impulse of artistic semblance is counterfactual: it negatively presents the utopian promise as non-existent and thus as an impetus for a change rather than a compensatory semblance of the present fulfilment. By turning against itself and its complicity with domination, art thus can redeem a critical mimetic impulse at the price of foregrounding its own internal contradiction: in contrast to the disavowals, projections, consolations and compromises of mimetic semblance, progressive art has to envision future reconciliation and at the same time to negate it as non-existent. In Adorno's words, modernist artwork has to 'testify to the unreconciled and at the same time envisions its reconciliation'.[56] Thus, the critical mimetic impulse can be redeemed only when its utopian aspirations refuse to substitute aesthetic reconciliation for the conflicts and diremptions of an unreconciled reality.

Notes

1 S. Worth, 'Feminist aesthetics' in B. Gaunt and D. McIver (eds), *The Routledge Companion to Aesthetics* (London: Routledge, 2001), pp. 437–46 (p. 437).

2 R. Felski, *Beyond Feminist Aesthetics: Feminist Literature and Social Change* (Cambridge, MA: Harvard University Press, 1989), pp. 156, 19. This view is modified but not fundamentally challenged in her subsequent works, *The Gender of Modernity* (Cambridge, MA: Harvard University Press, 1995) and *Doing Time: Feminist Theory and Postmodern Culture* (New York: New York University Press, 2000).

3 Felski, *Beyond Feminist Aesthetics*, p. 180.

4 For very different responses to 'the death of art', see for instance T. W. Adorno, *Aesthetic Theory*, trans. and ed. R. Hullot-Kentor (Minneapolis: University of Minnesota Press, 1997), pp. 3–4. Hereafter abbreviated AT. See also, F. Jameson, '"End of art" or "end of history"' in *The Cultural Turn* (London: Verso, 1998), pp. 73–93; G. Vattimo, 'The death or decline of art' in *The End of Modernity*, trans. J. R. Snyder (Cambridge: Polity Press, 1988), pp. 51–64 and J. D'Hondt, 'Hegel et la mort de l'art', *Esthétique de Hegel*, ed. Véronique Fabbri and Jean-Louis Veillard-Baron (Paris: Harmattan, 1997), pp. 89–105.

5 G. W. F. Hegel, *Introductory Lectures on Aesthetics*, trans. Bernard Bonsaquet (Harmondsworth: Penguin, 1993), p. 12.

6 Felski, *Doing Time*, p. 175.

7 Worth, 'Feminist aesthetics', p. 443.

8 H. Louis Gates Jr., 'Critical Fanonism' in Nigel C. Gibson (ed.), *Rethinking Fanon: The Continuing Dialogue* (Amherst: Humanity Books, 1999), pp. 251–68 (p. 259).

9 P. Gilroy, *The Black Atlantic: Modernity and Double Consciousness* (Cambridge, MA: Harvard University Press, 1993), p. 38.

10 I thus agree with Felski's call for mediation; where I disagree is in the particular model of mediation she proposes – that is, the sublation of art by the feminist politics of counter-public. This model fails to interrogate the historicity of aesthetic categories, and, despite all the precautions, risks the reduction of art to the political use value.

11 AT, p. 6.

12 K. L. Schultz, *Mimesis on the Move: Theodor W. Adorno's Concept of Imitation* (New York: Peter Lang, 1990). Schultz writes, 'mimesis . . . is responsive and concrete. It works through images rather than concepts and approaches the other . . . as something different yet related. . . . It responds emotionally, intuitively' (p. 3). This point is also elaborated in the most comprehensive history of mimesis offered by M. Taussig, *Mimesis and Alterity: A Particular History of the Senses* (London: Routledge, 1993). For other illuminating discussions of Adorno's concept of mimesis, see B. Engh, 'Of music and mimesis' in M. O'Neill (ed.), *Adorno, Culture and Feminism* (London: Sage, 1999), pp. 161–73; L. Zuidervaart, *Adorno's Aesthetic Theory* (Cambridge, MA: MIT Press, 1994), pp. 180–5; and M. Jay, 'Mimesis and mimetology: Adorno and Lacoue-Labarthe' in T. Huhn and L. Zuidervaart (eds), *The Semblance of Subjectivity: Essays in Adorno's Aesthetic Theory* (Cambridge, MA: MIT Press, 1997), pp. 29–54.

13 J. M. Bernstein, 'Why rescue semblance?' in *The Semblance of Subjectivity*, pp. 177–212 (p. 188).

14 M. Horkheimer and T. W. Adorno, *Dialectic of Enlightenment*, trans. John Cumming (New York: Continuum, 1993), p. 181. Hereafter abbreviated DE.

15 DE, p. 15.

16 For a discussion of mimesis of death, see J. M. Bernstein, 'The horror of nonidentity: Cindy Sherman's tragic modernism' in P. Osborne (ed.), *From an Aesthetic Point of View: Philosophy, Art and the Senses* (London: Serpents Tail, 2000), pp. 107–44 (pp. 126–7).

17 DE, p. 180.

18 Schultz, *Mimesis on the Move*, pp. 42–7.

19 DE, p. 182.

20 *Ibid.*

21 *Ibid.*, p. 184.

22 Joan Riviere, 'Womanliness as a masquerade' in V. Burgin, J. Donald and C. Kaplan (eds), *Formations of Fantasy* (London: Methuen, 1986), pp. 35–44, originally published in *International Journal of Psychoanalysis*, 10 (1929). Hereafter abbreviated WM. For the most influential theories of colonial mimicry see F. Fanon, *Black Skin, White Masks*, trans. C. Lam Markmann (New York: Grove, 1967) and H. Bhabha, 'Of mimicry and man: the ambivalence of colonial discourse' in *The Location of Culture* (London: Routledge, 1994), pp. 85–93. Hereafter abbreviated BS and LC.

23 For a discussion of 'the women of 1928' see B. Kime Scott, *Refiguring Modernism: The Women of 1928* (Bloomington: Indiana University Press, 1995), pp. 183–257.

24 For the influential interpretations of Riviere's theory of masquerade, see, among others, J. Butler, *Gender Trouble: Feminism and the Subversion of Identity* (London: Routledge, 1990), pp. 43–57; D. Cornell, *Beyond Accommodation: Ethical Feminism, Deconstruction, and the Law* (London: Routledge, 1991), pp. 105–6; Mary Ann Doane, 'Film and the masquerade: theorizing the female spectator', pp. 17–32 and 'Masquerade reconsidered: further thoughts on the female spectator', pp. 33–43 both in *Femmes Fatales: Feminism, Film Theory, Psychoanalysis* (London: Routledge, 1991); S. Heath, 'Joan Riviere and the masquerade' in *Formations of Fantasy*, pp. 45–61; C. Johnston, 'Femininity and the masquerade: Ann of the Indies' in E. Ann Kaplan (ed.), *Psychoanalysis and the Cinema*, (London: Routledge, 1990), pp. 64–72.

25 For this critique, see for instance J. Butler, *Gender Trouble*, pp. 43–57; Sue-Ellen Case, 'Toward a butch-femme aesthetics' in H. Abelove *et al.* (eds), *The Lesbian and Gay Studies Reader* (London: Routledge, 1990), pp. 294–306; and T. de Lauretis, *The Practice of Love: Lesbian Sexuality and Perverse Desire* (Bloomington: Indiana University Press, 1994), pp. 108–9.

26 As Walton writes: 'By fantasizing a black man, Riviere's patient is calling upon a figure whose relation to the phallus is as tenuous as her own.' 'Re-placing race in (white) psycho-analytical discourse', *Critical Inquiry*, 21 (1995), 775–804 (p. 784).

27 *Ibid.*, 785.

28 C. Millot, 'The feminine superego' in P. Adams and E. Cowie (eds), *The Woman in Question* (Cambridge, MA: MIT Press, 1990), pp. 294–314 (p. 300).

29 WM, p. 42.

30 J. Kristeva, 'Women's time', trans. A. Jardine and H. Blake, in T. Moi (ed.) *The Kristeva Reader* (New York: Columbia University Press, 1986), pp. 187–213 (p. 205).

31 K. Seshadri-Crooks, *Desiring Whiteness: A Lacanian Analysis of Race* (London: Routledge, 2000), pp. 20–1.

32 LC, pp. 86–9.

33 *Ibid.*, p. 91.

34 *Ibid.*, p. 92.

35 *Ibid.*, p. 62.

36 M. Hardt and A. Negri, *Empire* (Cambridge, MA: Harvard University Press, 2000), pp. 144–5.

37 BS, p. 165.

38 *Ibid.*

39 *Ibid.*, p. 160.

40 *Ibid.*, p. 161.

41 LC, p. 61. Bhabha makes a similar argument in 'Remembering Fanon: self, psyche, and the colonial condition': 'paranoia never preserves its position of power for the compulsive identification with a persecutory "they" is always an evacuation . . . of the "I" ', in *Rethinking Fanon*, pp. 179–94 (p. 190).

42 BS, p. 138.

43 *Ibid.*, p. 112.

44 *Ibid.*, p. 100.

45 *Ibid.*, p. 138.

46 *Ibid.*, p. 194.

47 For the discussion of the phallus as the white mask, see D. Boyarin, 'What does a Jew want?; or the political meaning of the phallus' in C, Lane (ed.), *The Psychoanalysis of Race* (New York: Columbia University Press, 1998), pp. 211–40.

48 Zuidervaart, *Adorno's Aesthetic Theory*, pp. 178–212.

49 AT, p. 101.

50 *Ibid.*, p. 175.

51 For the definition of the Lacanian separation as 'the sacrifice of the sacrifice', see S. Zizek, *Enjoy Your Symptom: Jacques Lacan in Hollywood and Out* (London: Routledge, 1992), pp. 167–8.

52 AT, p. 102.

53 *Ibid.*

54 *Ibid.*, p. 103.

55 *Ibid.*, p. 106.

56 *Ibid.*, p. 168.

What comes after art?

Kafka's last completed story has become something of an allegory of contemporary theoretical approaches in the humanities. In 'Josefine, the singer, or the mouse people', the narrator, a mouse, ponders the phenomenon of Josefine, a mouse who sings. The problem with Josefine is that she actually seems to make the same kind of noise as all the other mice, but she makes a performance of it, claiming that what she does is very special. She is able, moreover, to make a career out of being a 'singer', despite the doubts voiced by some of her audience. Kafka's story plays with various versions of aesthetic theory, linking Josefine's apparent highlighting of the ordinary to make it extraordinary, for example, to what sounds like Russian formalism's concept of *ostranenie*. The narrator is never convinced by what Josefine does, but is also never finally prepared to write it off. Given that the story was written by someone who had painfully devoted his life to 'literature', and who knew he was dying, the question as to whether he might just have been writing texts like everybody else, and thus doing nothing special really, becomes especially poignant. However, it seems clear that the ironic amusement produced by the fact that this deep text on aesthetics takes place in a world of highly articulate mice takes the story into realms which a discursive account of the issues could not. In this sense, Kafka's story is a great 'literary text' with aesthetic value, and this seems to me important.[1] *Why* it is important takes us to the heart of some much-discussed issues in the humanities.

In recent years some theoretically informed work in the humanities has increasingly focused on revealing the extent to which traditional assumptions informing the investigation of cultural phenomena are likely to obscure dimensions of those phenomena which should lead us to be suspicious both of their aesthetic appeal and of their 'canonical' status. One obvious consequence of these approaches has been that invocations of the aesthetic status of a text or other cultural artefact as the decisive factor in its reception can lead to some version of the accusation of failing to see that, as Walter Benjamin put it, documents of culture are always also documents of barbarism.[2] The problem with many of the contemporary versions of this stance is that the critic ends up placing herself in something like the position of the narrator-mouse of Kafka's story, aware that she is deeply ambivalent about what she is confronted with, yet still obsessively concerned to get to the bottom of its nature. Added to this, though, is the lurking suspicion that, in the last analysis, there may not be very much to get to the bottom of. Kafka's narrator asks whether Josefine's song might not be just a fraud, and claims that it will disappear anyway when she dies.

We can project the sort of thing that developed out of the issues Kafka's story highlights onto some recent theory as follows. Isn't art in the strong aesthetic sense essentially a product of the bourgeois era, and isn't part of the contemporary crisis in art's status a result of the revelation of the ideological nature of how art was used by the dominant classes to cover up social contradictions in the name of an illusory harmony said to be present in the work of art? Furthermore, did not Marcel Duchamp's 'ready-mades' reveal the extent to which art is in fact a result of the functioning of certain institutions in which objects can be located? In future 'art', in a more attenuated sense, might instead be seen mainly as one resource for enriching the contexts of everyday life, as, of course, it had been in some respects prior to the rise of the great bourgeois traditions. In consequence, so the argument goes, we will be able to do without the crypto-theology which lies at the heart of aesthetically oriented accounts of art, and which allowed the ethnocentric, gender- and class-biased, Western tradition to exert such a problematic influence. The same kind of story has been told about 'literature' and the fact that, as Kafka's story itself reflects, there may be nothing to distinguish literature in any fundamental way from other kinds of text. Interestingly, it is harder to do the same with music, though that has not stopped people trying.

These are obviously large and difficult issues, and the caricature just offered does not do justice to the more reflective suspicions of the aesthetic in recent theory.[3] However, there does seem to be a crucial division in the debates around the issue of aesthetics, which has been suggested by a thinker as concerned to deflate metaphysical pretension and diminish human cruelty as Richard Rorty. Contrasting the implications of Fredric Jameson's and Harold Bloom's positions for cultural and other politics, Rorty argues that the difference between their adherents is not 'between those who take politics seriously and those who do not'. Rather it is 'between people taking refuge in self-protecting knowingness about the present and romantic utopians trying to imagine a better future'.[4] The former think that their theoretical insights are the key to unmasking the elevated status of the high culture which they link to the roots of the predicaments of the present; the latter think that significant art cannot be adequately responded to in this manner and that we should be looking to what it can offer us for the future. Behind Rorty's version of this issue lies what seems to me to be a decisive question. The question can be posed quite simply, as we will see in a moment, but the exploration of its implications for the future of the humanities is anything but simple.

The main point of serious investigation of the significant products of Western culture – and this can include everything from Bach, to jazz, Shakespeare, to new forms of independent film – has become, for some recent theory, to explore the extent to which these products contribute to or escape from repressive discourses of race, gender, class, etc. Many approaches put in question by such theory aim, in contrast, to understand how great culture opens up worlds of the imagination which provide new resources of meaning in all kinds of different social and historical contexts. The

simple question is this: are the semantic resources offered by the former positions confined to their insights into the delusions and repressions of Western culture (delusions
and repressions which, I should stress, I have no concern to deny)? More provocatively: are those insights therefore themselves superior to what they unmask, offering
a truth or revelation inaccessible to their object of investigation? In short: having done
the negative critical work, what is on offer as a positive alternative from theories whose
primary aim is to unmask, or is this asking too much of them? Was what an aesthetic
approach saw in the best of Western and other culture *merely* an illusion from which
we should now be liberated? Now this is obviously a very schematic way of putting
the issue, and the crude opposition of theoretical attitudes just suggested does not do
justice to the fact that many approaches to cultural issues combine something of both
sides. However, even allowing for this proviso, the doubts created by these sorts of
questions seem to me to be part of what has opened up the space for the contemporary renewed interest in aesthetics.

To put it another way: why would one bother to concern oneself with the well-
known products of Western culture, if it were not that they offer more than is apparent when their often quite evident failings with regard to contemporary social, ethical
and other assumptions are exposed? An uncomfortable alternative presents itself here
for those to whom Rorty imputes 'self-protective knowingness'. The first possibility is
that these works are so powerful that the prime task of the theorist is to defuse their
ideological power, which means, of course, both that the nature of this power requires
a lot more explanation and that the explainer must possess special insight to be able to
see through it. The second possibility is that the works are in fact merely what happened to be the focus of the existing forms of study in the institutionalised humanities, and are therefore used to exemplify what the theorist already believed anyway. In
both cases aesthetic questions cannot be ignored. In the first case the task is to establish how it is that what had, from the perspective of aesthetics, been understood to
offer new resources for hope and meaning that transcend existing ways of thinking and
feeling, is in fact more important for its exemplification of repressive ways of thinking.
In the second case the question has to be answered as to why one concerns oneself with
works which might be seen as more apt for aesthetic than for ideological investigation,
rather than doing research into changing social and cultural attitudes in contemporary
society or in the historical period in question.[5] The justification for taking 'high'
culture – which is anyway increasingly marginalised in large parts of Western societies
– as one's object seems quite hard to find, unless, of course, one accepts the first position. By accepting this position one is, though, likely to end up by trying to acknowledge the power of something which one is at the same time effectively trying to reduce
to being a mere contingent product of a history marked by barbarism.

Clearly we should all want to disabuse those whom we teach, and those around us,
of racist, sexist and other regressive attitudes. Whether this is best achieved by, for
example, looking at colonialism via *The Tempest*, or sexism via Schumann's song-cycle
Frauenliebe und -leben, seems questionable, unless there are other compelling reasons
for reading Shakespeare and listening to Schumann. These reasons would seem to
depend on the fact that these are major artists who did something nobody else suc-

ceeded in doing. That this fact matters little in large parts of the contemporary cultural world seems to me to suggest that either one sees one's task as revealing to people that they are missing something important, or that one should do something else. The emergence of the orientation in cultural studies towards 'popular culture' of all kinds is in this respect a logical response to the suspicion that works from the great traditions may now no longer (if, of course, they ever did) have a decisive influence on political and social life. This does not, however, obviate aesthetic questions, even in relation to popular culture. The danger here is that an apparent openness to what supposedly (and sometimes actually) elitist positions have unjustifiably ignored can in fact be based on another kind of failure of openness. Both concentrating on popular culture, and using major works from the tradition predominantly to reveal ideological and other distortions can lead precisely to the situation where one ends up just confirming what one thought and felt anyway. The point of real aesthetic experience, though, is surely that it should take one somewhere else, not just to where one has already been or already is.

Does this mean, then, that the revelation of the history of patriarchy manifest, for example, in Western drama from the *Oresteia*, to Strindberg's *The Father* and beyond, a history which was almost wholly invisible until the emergence of feminist criticism, is missing the aesthetic point of these monuments of Western culture, and so should give way to more traditional approaches? I don't think so. Such readings have opened up a new world which would have remained unarticulated without the perspectives they revealed in these texts. Crucially, though, such perspectives did not need to be forcibly imposed on the texts: they emerge from a new interpretation of the structural tensions in the texts that form part of their aesthetic power. Does the revelation of the patriarchal assumptions of the *Oresteia*, where the myth of Athene being born without a mother is blatantly invoked to reveal the primacy of the male, take away from the fact that the trilogy has a unique power to convey the trauma involved in the transition from one social order to another, however unjust we may find *both* the orders in question? The patriarchal assumptions may be repellent, but many attitudes apparent in works of art, like the questionable aspects of the work of Richard Wagner, repel us, without our assuming we therefore already know more than what such art can convey. If art is, then, in Heidegger's terms, a form of 'world-disclosure', critical readings that show new and problematic dimensions of a work can form an essential part of what that art is.

What I am saying might, though, seem now to leave the door open for a lazy pluralism, in which the *Oresteia* is just as good for explaining patriarchy to a class as anything else, so that the same might be achieved in cultural studies by examples from a TV soap. If we wanted to read the *Oresteia* in the perspective of the history of Athenian justice, then that would be fine as well. It all depends on what one is trying to do: the circularity of interpretation will always mean that one gets results relating to what one started out looking for. In certain respects this pluralism, like the circular structure of interpretation, is inescapable. As a result of the growth of theoretical reflection the humanities have developed new perspectives which make it more and more clear that the idea of finding a definitive method for approaching any aspect of culture is simply mistaken. The tools we need for one kind of task may be of little use for another, and each may be of great value in their own realm of application. However, this leaves two issues wide open, and they are hardly negligible ones. Indeed, they go to the heart of questions about value and communication that are at the core of the humanities.

First, there are unavoidable and fundamental clashes between the tools for differing tasks, such as those for literary biography based on authorial intention, and those for analysis of discourse based on the primacy of linguistic and literary resources before those writing within them. Where do we go to negotiate such clashes? Cultural judgement has not least to come to terms with the fact that the modern world has shown there are an indefinite number of different ways of approaching cultural products. The crucial issue is, then, how we are to arrive at the ability to choose approaches which are most revelatory and most productive. This, as we shall see, is one of the decisive questions in the history of aesthetics, and is the core of the justification for making the humanities central to education. Second, the critical revelation of the failure of cultural artefacts to live up to the normative demands of the present presumably reaches a limit when that revelation has been achieved. This limit, though, forces one to ask what such an approach is to undertake next, and to ask what the value of this could be. It can, of course, also be that this revelation itself has a hidden repressive aspect. Might criticism based on the critique of ideology actually obscure the potential *political* import of a work by blocking off responses to that work which might enable the reader/listener/viewer to develop new horizons not countenanced by a view which seeks to make art the location of ideological unmasking? Although we should always attempt to police our awareness of the possible repressive consequences of how we speak and of what we value, there must also be a place for creative exploration of the things that positively make our lives more meaningful, without which we would be immeasurably impoverished. It is this possibility which seems to be missing from so much 'knowing' theory that wishes to unmask its object. The great pianist Artur Schnabel talked of music that is better than it can ever be played, and the same can apply to texts which transcend the ways in which they come to be read.[6]

A tension emerges at this point, though, which is paradigmatically manifest in the work of T. W. Adorno. Is it not a form of self-deception to concentrate on the value of aesthetic 'appearance',[7] if the task should be to make the real world itself more tolerable and humane? The basic problem in Adorno emerges from the conflict between the need for a negative critical perspective which suspects an 'affirmative' culture of complicity in the ills of the modern world, and the need for affirmative resources if motivation for change of all kinds, from the political to the personal, is to be generated. This leads him into paradigmatic difficulties, which reveal much about why aesthetics has been such a contentious area of recent debate. When Adorno claims, for example, that 'The aesthetic totality is the antithesis of the untrue totality', his assertion depends upon there being a wholesale opposition between the state of a world seen in the light of the Holocaust and of the continuing dominance of capitalist exploitation, and the genuine work of art.[8] It is not, though, that the beauty of the work is per se a criticism of the essentially ugly nature of the commodified world. This is because, for Adorno, the kind of beauty which manages to be both expressive and formally integrated, in the manner of the great tonal works of music, from Bach to Mahler, is now almost certain to have been appropriated by the culture industry. Adorno is therefore led to an implausible elevation of certain works of aesthetic modernism – such as those of Kafka or Schoenberg – to being virtually the only source of non-deluded insight into a 'reified' reality. This, of course, makes the status of his own theoretical claims problematic: do the artworks need his philosophy, or is it vice versa?

Now the difficulties in Adorno are of a quite specific nature, stemming from his totalising verdict on the effects of commodification on modern culture. This verdict leads to the idea of a world where repressive identification, the reduction of things to the ways they can be manipulated for human purposes that is most obviously present in the commodity form, is the key to the most significant problems of modernity. He consequently adverts to what cannot be construed in these terms, which he thinks is manifest in the work of artists who, by refusing to be seduced by instrumental and commercial aims, engage most fully with the immanent problems and demands of their materials. Adorno's present growing popularity seems, though, to depend in part on the fact that some of his assumptions coincide with certain aspects of other theorists of the kind touched on above, who, unlike Adorno, are suspicious of the aesthetic dimension in any positive sense, and who at the same time, like Adorno, are distrustful of the ways in which thinking functions in terms of reductive identification. The question which arises here is the following. Given both that a major aspect of thinking in the aesthetic tradition from Kant onwards is a concern with irreducible particularity, and that an idea often adduced by many recent theorists is the danger of repressing 'alterity', why is a concern with aesthetic experience so questionable in certain influential areas of the contemporary humanities?

A great deal depends here on the kind of story about the history of aesthetics one tells, and on how that story informs the development of contemporary theoretical assumptions. It seems clear to me that the stories which have dominated some theoretical debate rely upon a too limited conception of the history of aesthetics, as well as on questionable assumptions about the nature and role of art. This is not least because some of the notions most frequently employed in theories concerned to unmask the aesthetic in fact rely on ideas that emerged as part of the history of aesthetic theory. Let us go back to the question of judgement, which involves a series of revealing problems in this respect.

One of the assumptions of traditional literary or other artistic education is that its job is to promote the development of people's ability to judge well, a skill which is part of being able to live well. The reasons why the development of skill in judging is both so important and so tricky were shown by Kant. In any judgement about something in the world one is confronted with a dilemma which has no solution that can be formulated algorithmically. Even in cognitive judgements one has to be able to make a move from the particular empirical manifestation one is examining to subsuming that manifestation under a rule which identifies it. There can be no rule for doing this, though, because one would get into a regress of the rule for the rule for the rule, etc., and thus could never judge at all. Finding the general rule for a particular always entails the ability to eliminate an indefinite number of possible applicable rules, most of which will be actually irrelevant, but none of which can just be excluded a priori. We are often able successfully to apply rules because our unthematised background knowledge somehow already excludes most of what is irrelevant.[9] This is why robots can have such trouble in performing many tasks we find simple: if one tries to codify background knowledge algorithmically one just adds even more rules, thus making the task more and more difficult. For Kant judgement involves the active capacity of the subject to make choices which are not necessitated and thus cannot be reduced to a method.[10] Kant's account of aesthetic experience develops from his general account of the nature of judgement, and the implications of his account of the relationship between the two are too often ignored in contemporary theory in the humanities.

Arriving at new knowledge depends precisely on the ability to bring a series of different particular phenomena under a new rule which specifies what makes them identical. It is a commonplace of theory of the kind developed by Adorno that this ability can function repressively. In an essay of the early 1930s, 'Theses on the language of the philosopher', for example, Adorno ponders the issue which Kant is trying to solve in his epistemology, namely how an empirically infinitely diverse world can be brought under unifying rules. The danger, as Adorno sees it, is that the forms of identity employed for this unification will be inherently reductive, because they will depend, as Kant claims, on the functioning of the thinking subject: 'If multiplicity's unity is subjectively impressed on it as form, such form is necessarily thought of as separable from the content.'[11] The 'content' is therefore what these days is seen in terms of 'alterity', and Adorno is concerned precisely with the 'non-identical' aspects of that content, which are threatened in a world where rule-bound judgements are increasingly the basis for the functioning of all levels of society. The danger of reductive identification is therefore inherent in the nature of the subject, which seeks to control the world by imposing forms of identity on a world of irreducible difference.[12] The problem is that the search for identity can easily become irrational, invading areas where it has no place. The sort of thing Adorno means is apparent in gender, racial and other kinds of stereotyping (though he sometimes, for example in the really hyperbolic passages of *Dialectic of Enlightenment*, extends it to theorising in the natural sciences, which is more problematic).

Like Lacan, Derrida and others, Adorno insists that the subject depends on a language which is not wholly in its power. For Adorno this language is itself in part the product of the repressive history of the subject's attempt to dominate the other. The crucial point here is that the subject's self-transparency, upon which its aim of control is based, is always a delusion. In the 1933 book on Kierkegaard Adorno claims that, 'If language is the form of communication of pure subjectivity and at the same time paradoxically presents itself as historically objective, then, in language, objectless inwardness [which is supposed by Kierkegaard to constitute the subject's resistance to transient external historical developments] is reached by the external dialectic'.[13] Language therefore subverts the sense in which the subject can sustain itself as a pure origin against the objective pressure of the world. How, then, does this relate to the Kantian questions about judgement?[14]

The most important thing in the present context is that Kant thought aesthetic experience was made possible by the fact that even cognitive judgement is, for the reasons we saw above, not necessitated. We can therefore engage in a 'free play' of judgement when we do not attempt to determine the object conceptually, but instead allow our ability to judge in differing ways to work of its own accord. He regards the capacity for aesthetic appreciation which this makes possible as a self-justifying aspect of our existence, and he sees it as contributing to the development of our ability to judge well in cognitive and other contexts. Such appreciation is, it is important to remember, not based on the mere pleasure of a stimulus. Kant already insists in 1769–70 that 'Contemplation of beauty is a judgement, and not a pleasure', and the aim of such judgement is to reach universal agreement, despite the inherently particular nature of aesthetic experience.[15] The essential issue here lies, then, in the relationship between aesthetic experience's reliance on the idea of the activity of the subject, and Adorno's concern with the extent to which the subject functions within linguistic and other constraints. These constraints are more powerful than the subject and may not be transparent to it, even though they have been generated in the history of the self-preservation of the species which makes the individual's existence possible.

Kant's aim of universality in aesthetic judgement depends, then, on the freedom of the subject which seeks a community of agreement with others in relation to its affective and other responses to art and natural beauty. For Adorno universality, in contrast, is precisely likely to be the result of objective pressures for conformity of the kind which recent theory analyses in terms of the repression of the other. The source of such repression is at least in part linguistic, in the form of the prejudices built into particular discourses by the circumstances of their development. Adorno's subject may think it is free, but it is in fact always already formed by such objective pressures. The question is, though, whether a wholesale rejection of what Kant intended does not obviate the *point* of the critical perspective that gives rise to the rejection. If there is no access to what could be understood in some way as taking us *beyond* our being determined by objective social pressures, the sense that these pressures are a problem at all becomes hard to understand.

In its extreme versions Adorno's position therefore seems to lead to a kind of negative aesthetic theology. Only art which is so uncompromising that it could not possibly be thought of as commanding any kind of consensus in contemporary society can be true to the historical situation after Auschwitz. In analogous manner, the sort of 'knowing' theory cited by Rorty leads to a farewell to art as a source of insight or pleasure of a kind that theory cannot provide. This leaves one wondering, though, what the culture that would emerge if the critique were successful could possibly look like, once the cleansing of illusions is complete. How can one aspire to something which seems to have so little positive content? In both cases the model of the subject involved in the theory seems to be predicated to such an extent on what Adorno terms the 'primacy of the objective', the determining power of the world over the subject, that the aim of opposing this primacy itself appears illusory.

One significant part of the tradition of aesthetic thinking that concerns me here seeks to understand what possibilities there can be for the modern subject in a world where objective pressures of all kinds do indeed continually increase. Adorno is characteristically ambiguous on this issue. He himself offers a more illuminating way of addressing the problem of the modern subject than is available in the parts of his work which repeat the ideas of *Dialectic of Enlightenment*, in the tension he identifies between 'expression' and 'convention' in modern art. The difficulty for modern artists lies, Adorno argues, in the fact that, as the means of expression are expanded, the space for individual innovation diminishes, because in time live resources for articulation will necessarily become mere conventions.[16] The Western traditions of modern literature, music or visual art offer exemplary models of the playing out of this dialectic, and the best aesthetic theory shows how vital it is to the understanding of modern culture.

My worry is that we seem to be in danger of losing sight of the exemplary nature of those traditions, and of the theoretical reflections that accompanied them. Culture thrives on critical judgement, and criticism needs models which, without becoming fetishised, can reveal the deficiencies of inferior cultural production. If such models are neglected, in favour of other critical and ideological aims, or of the attempt, in the name of avoiding elitism, to elevate the merely local to the measure of what is culturally valid, the endeavours of those who sought to expand our means of articulation by both assimilating and transcending the weight of objective cultural pressure are devalued.[17] The likely result of this neglect is a self-deceiving, narcissistic relationship to culture, in which what Novalis termed the 'aesthetic imperative' of seeking to transcend one's limits by doing justice to major works of art is forgotten. It is important to remember here that the undoubted elitism that may, for example, have affected the reception of 'high' culture in the nineteenth century cannot, in a Western world where the best cultural products are widely available in affordable form via mass reproduction, just be transferred to the present. The way in which such elitism continues is now more likely to be through the failure to provide the right kind of access to great culture in education. The danger here, of course, is that 'knowing' theory may lead to such access no longer being regarded as a pedagogical priority.

How the development of the kinds of attitude which are merely suspicious of the Western tradition of art affects contemporary Western society cannot be adequately understood in the short term. However, the spread of theories in recent times which seem to depend on cultural amnesia and on the narcissism of seeking confirmation of prejudices rather than openness to the way great works can take one beyond one's prejudices may be a sign of deeper cultural problems. The reason why can be suggested by another aspect of the aesthetic tradition which begins with Kant. This is the demand that one legitimate to others one's judgement about cultural products which can reflect the most intimate dimensions of oneself. It is not, as is too often claimed, that the attempt to arrive at a *sensus communis* is something actually achievable (even if Kant himself seemed to think it might be a way of at least symbolically revealing our shared 'intelligible' nature). The real point is that there can be no definitive way of concretely achieving such a consensus, even though it can remain a unifying point of orientation. The idea of consensus must instead, then, remain a 'regulative idea', not an achievable state of affairs.[18]

We acknowledge the legitimacy of this idea if we are prepared to engage in dialogue about cultural experience in which our own particular judgements must be regarded as both inherently fallible and yet not merely arbitrary. The key to this aspect of the aesthetic has best been described by Stanley Cavell, when he claims: 'It is essential in making an aesthetic judgement that at some point we be prepared to say in its support: don't you see, don't you hear, don't you dig? . . . Because if you do not see something, *without* explanation, then there is nothing further to discuss'.[19] Without the possibility of a shared level of appreciation which cannot be theorised, the point of aesthetic judgement dissolves. We may not empirically get to this shared level, but the important thing is the possibility of appealing to it. This combination of the need for legitimation with the realisation that such legitimation relies on an appeal to something which cannot be definitively established also means that what is most essential about aesthetics is immune to arguments which associate it with the repression or denial of difference. At the same time, it should be remembered that the 'non-identical' aspect of aesthetic experience, its resistance to explanation, would be mere mystification without the attempt to render it more generally accessible through critical dialogue and the development of cultural communication.

Now it is important to be clear at this point that I am *not* in any way claiming that the developments in the recent theory and practice of literary and cultural studies, which have, for example, led to attention to what was excluded by the dominant Western critical canon – women's writing, writing by cultural and ethnic minorities, etc. – have been mistaken. These have led to a whole series of new and exciting perspectives which have had important social and political effects. To the extent to which aesthetic thinking contributed to the exclusion of works and aesthetic practices from cultures or from groups of people not previously endorsed by Western academic culture, a critique of 'aesthetics' is clearly justified in the name of what it has excluded. It is vital, however, that the standards of achievement set by the greatest works – standards which are testified to by their offering semantic potential in ever new contexts – can still come into the evaluation of what had been excluded. This should, though, not preclude a rejection of those standards if they are inadequate to the new object's capacity for changing perceptions of what is aesthetically valid.[20] It does seem odd, then, in the context of reflections on the ethnocentric nature of some of what resulted from aesthetic thinking, that aesthetics as a whole has often got such a bad name. The idea that someone like Friedrich Schlegel, for example, who effectively invented serious literary history and who had a immense cosmopolitan awareness of world literature, as well as being a groundbreaking aesthetic thinker, could be seen as part of a problematic tradition, is indefensible. The real question, of course, as I suggested above, is *which* tradition of aesthetics is at issue.[21]

One answer to the question of how the traditions of aesthetics are often conceived is the (questionable) philosophical story common to Heidegger, Gadamer, Derrida, Lyotard, in some respects Adorno, and others. In this story modernity is seen as dependent on the idea that the 'certainty of all being and all truth is founded on the self-consciousness of the single ego: *ego cogito ergo sum*' (Heidegger), and this has too often been used to characterise 'aesthetics' as well. The link to aesthetics from the philosophical story of the domination of being by the subject in science and technology is often made via the idea that art becomes reduced to something dependent upon the contingent individual feeling of the subject. One way of subverting this view of the subject as the source of judgement is, as we have seen, to show how the language in which it makes its judgements is prior to it. Another way, proposed by Gadamer in particular, is to claim that the real significance of art results from its transcendence of its reception and its revealing a truth beyond the subject: 'The "subject" of the experience of art, that which remains and persists, is not the subjectivity of the person who experiences it, but the work of art itself.'[22] Clearly the arbitrary and contingent nature of individual aesthetic production and reception – where one sleeps through some vital part of the play or the symphony, or is not 'feeling right' for the work in question – is not the basis of serious understanding of art's significance. Whether this means one should therefore exclude consideration of the subject in the manner Gadamer does is, however, questionable. It is only if one thinks that the history of thinking about the subject is a history in which the subject is universally regarded as the philosophical *foundation* for grasping the nature of the truth of modernity that such an extreme option has to be adopted.

It is surprising how many contemporary theoretical positions tacitly or unconsciously adopt some of this kind of account. The power of the account is obvious: the theory wave in the humanities has made many people aware of the potential for self-deception inherent in the ways we think about culture. This potential derives particularly from the failure to see the extent to which subjects are what they are both because of objective pressures and because they are not the masters of their language. However, 'theory' has also tended to overplay the *extent* to which we can gain higher insight into those deceptions by locating them as part of linguistic and other practices that connect, for example, to the exercise of power in society or to commercial pressures. What is missing in such approaches can be illustrated by consideration of two related topics which have played a very subordinate role in recent theory. A major factor in the rise of aesthetic theory is the change in the status of music during the second half of the eighteenth century. Related to this is the re-evaluation of the nature of 'feeling' that takes place in the same period, which is also linked to the emergence of the discipline of aesthetics. If, as some people begin to do at this time, one makes music into the art which is the key to understanding all art, one has, of course, already precluded a wholesale subordination of the aesthetic to ideology. Music's non-representational status does not allow one to make direct inferences to ideological matters. This does not mean that music, and, above all, talk about music, cannot be ideological. They evidently can: all art is situated in social contexts that involve links between cultural production and mechanisms of power. What matters, though, is the realisation that there are dimensions of cultural articulation which transcend what we can say about them, which are not necessarily usable for ideological purposes, and which are crucially connected to the ways we try to understand ourselves as subjects. Although music's transcendence of the sayable has too often been used as a means of fetishising art, it is a mistake therefore to assume that the *only* possibility for the critic is to unmask mystifications, rather than reveal the ways in which music and, by extension, other art can bring us up against the limits of more discursive forms of articulation.

Suspicion of discussion about feeling is these days usually directed towards the fact that feeling is linguistically and symbolically mediated. However, this does not mean that feeling is wholly articulated by the symbolic forms we habitually employ. The motor of new articulation in modernity is often the sense that, in Adorno's terms, convention has taken over from expression, and that new expression is demanded by what cannot adequately be conveyed by existing means. Anthony Cascardi suggests in relation to Kant's *Critique of Judgement* that 'Feeling . . . remains cognitive in a deeper sense; affect possesses what Heidegger would describe . . . as "world-disclosive" power'.[23] There is, as Cascardi indicates, an important sense in which insistence on the 'mediated' nature of feelings – on the idea that they rely on what can be stated propositionally – gets things the wrong way round. Kant says that 'The general validity of pleasure [in beauty] and yet not via concepts but in intuition is what is difficult' in giving an account of aesthetics.[24] Kant's concentration on pleasure here and elsewhere is admittedly too limiting: the point can better be made in terms of the validity of world-disclosure through feeling. The important point is, though, that if aesthetic validity were of the kind that is arrived at via conceptual agreement, feelings would be reducible to the kind of consensus that is possible in conceptual judgements, and this would obviate the point of the aesthetic. Part of the motivation behind Adorno's work is that he thinks that the point of the aesthetic *is* being obviated in many aspects of modern culture. Much of the culture industry, as he claims, does rely upon the schematisation of feelings into standardised forms which are then provided for by that industry. To the extent that views based on the primacy of ideological aims try to reduce art to what is already known or felt in some other respect, they can actually conspire with this situation.

Modernity need not, then, be understood merely in terms of the reduction of feelings to standardised forms. The explosion of expressive resources in the music composed from the period during which aesthetics emerged at the end of the eighteenth century onwards is a striking illustration of the importance to modernity of forms of articulation which transcend what can be conceptually grasped. The decisive aspect of this explosion is that it involves a two-way relationship between the subject and the forms of expression. The new music both gives rise to new forms of feeling and is a result of the changed self-understanding of those who produce and listen to it. These two aspects cannot be methodologically separated. The subject is on the one hand subjected to existent forms of articulation, and at the same time can refashion these forms to signify something which they previously did not signify. Establishing where one aspect stops and the other begins demands the kind of separation between scheme and content which more and more recent philosophy rejects as a misapprehension of the nature of our being in the world. The account of the subject as the self-deceiving locus of attempted domination of the other is, when looked at in relation to the best aspects of the traditions of aesthetics and modern art, only part of a much more complex story. One of the reasons why so much recent theory, in which music plays a minimal role, is prone to misjudge aesthetic issues lies, then, precisely in its failure to appreciate the significance of the non-conceptual form of music for any account of the subject. The best Romantic aesthetic theory, from Hölderlin to Schlegel and Schleiermacher, regards the essential issue for us as subjects as our *failure* to be transparent to ourselves, and sees aesthetic production and reception as means of coming to terms with the divided nature of the self, not as another way in which the world is reduced to the measure of the human. In this view the aesthetic is a resource for critical self-transcendence, rather than always being the location of self-deception.[25]

To conclude: I think there is actually a significant political point to this opposition between theoretical attitudes to the aesthetic. One of the oft-repeated recent worries about theory in the humanities has concerned the growing distance of theorising about art from what non-academic performers, readers, listeners and spectators value when they engage with art. This worry can be use to hide a merely reactionary attempt to re-establish the status quo, which does not bother to ponder why that status quo came under such attack, and this is not what interests me. How, though, might we arrive at a more effective division of intellectual labour, one which does not lose sight of the reasons for which we might have engaged in the first place with the works about which we theorise? These reasons are, of course, the kind of reasons which move anyone to engage with art. The real challenge is, then, to steer a course between mere theoretical 'knowingness' and mere unreflective aesthetic enjoyment. There is no way of mapping out such a course in advance: my claim is simply that the balance has in recent times moved too far in the direction of knowingness, and this has been reflected in some of the theories that have become decisive for many humanities subjects. Although we should keep in mind the worry which permeates the Kafka story with which we began, the worry that there is nothing ultimately significant about art, we still need to take into account the fact that through that very worry Kafka wrote texts which far transcend the texts of writers who were convinced that what they were writing was art. A combination of critical self-doubt with the intuitive sense that there can always be another, perhaps better, way of articulating what concerns us seems to me characteristic of the best we can learn from the traditions of aesthetic theory and from the art to which they were the accompaniment. The contemporary tendency to argue as though we were already in a situation where we know what comes after art precludes such a combination. Contemporary aesthetic production may be more decentred, and the era of the great works may for that reason even belong to the past, but that is not a reason to underestimate what great works do that nothing else can. Perhaps, then, we are not reaching the end of the significance of great art from the Western traditions, but are instead only at a point where some of the academic world seems to have lost sight of just how significant that art may still be.

Notes

1 In an entertaining essay Karl Markus Michel plays this story off against Adorno's *Aesthetic Theory*, granting it greater insight than Adorno (in B. Lindner and M. W. Lüdke (eds), *Materialien zur ästhetischen Theorie Th. W. Adornos. Konstruktion der Moderne* (Frankfurt: Suhrkamp, 1980)).

2　It is worth remembering that, whatever one thinks of the statement, the opposite does not apply.

3　I have, for reasons of space, generally not attached my critical remarks to specific thinkers in this essay, and am relying on something like 'ideal types'. This admittedly runs the risk of failing to engage with the detail of the positions in question, but has the advantage of suggesting broader links between contemporary tendencies.

4　R. Rorty, *Achieving Our Country* (Cambridge, MA: Harvard University Press, 1998), p. 140.

5　'New historicism' arguably does the latter, albeit often beginning the investigation with an aesthetically significant text.

6　It should perhaps be added that works which seemed canonical in one era can die in another. Whether they may be revived in a later period is then the crucial question.

7　The meaning of the German word 'Schein', which is so central to aesthetic theory, is notably ambiguous between 'appearance', which need have no negative connotations, and 'illusion', which clearly does have negative connotations.

8　T. W. Adorno, *Ästhetische Theorie* (Frankfurt: Suhrkamp, 1973), p. 429.

9　I shall not deal with the detail of Kant's answer to this dilemma, which would take us too far beyond the scope of this essay. The view suggested here has been best outlined by Hilary Putnam. See also, A. Bowie, *From Romanticism to Critical Theory: The Philosophy of German Literary Theory* (London: Routledge, 1997).

10　Kant thinks the categories, the a priori forms of judgement, are the exception to this situation. Without the categories we could, he argues, not even begin to have cognitive dilemmas, because we would have no forms of objectivity of the kind present in maths that organise the material of cognition in ways about which we can disagree.

11　T. W. Adorno, *Philosophische Frühschriften* (*Gesammelte Schriften* Vol. 1), (Frankfurt: Suhrkamp, 1973), p. 366.

12　The most obvious source of this idea is Nietzsche's 1873 essay 'On truth and lie in the extra-moral sense'.

13　T. W. Adorno, *Kierkegaard. Konstruktion des Ästhetischen* (Frankfurt: Suhrkamp, 1979), p. 53. There are close parallels between Adorno's critiques of Kierkegaard and Husserl, and Derrida's deconstruction of self-presence in Husserl.

14　At an epistemological level, a view like Adorno's suggests that even the notion of pure a priori categories is undermined by their dependence on a language which is historically formed. A significant part of the post-Kantian aesthetic tradition, incidentally, already made this point, which was first raised in the work of Hamann and Herder, who rejected 'pure' concepts because of their dependence on natural languages to be understood at all.

15　I. Kant, *Schriften zur Ästhetik und Naturphilosophie*, eds M. Frank and V. Zanetti (Frankfurt am Main: Deutscher Klassiker Verlag, 2001), p. 109.

16　It could, incidentally, even be argued that the 'theory wave' is in part a result of the perception of the dominance of convention in art. So much has now been done in the major forms of art that we are increasingly inclined to see what is the same, rather than experiencing what is different.

17　The contemporary attempts to re-evaluate the notion of the 'Philistine' fall into this trap. See D. Beech and J. Roberts, 'Spectres of the aesthetic', *New Left Review*, 218 (July–August 1996), 102–27; and cf. A. Bowie, 'Confessions of a "new aesthete": a response to the "new philistines" ', *New Left Review*, 225 (September–October 1997), 105–26.

18　Wholesale consensus would, as Albrecht Wellmer points out, obviate meaningful communication anyway: what would the point of it be?

19 S. Cavell, *Must We Mean What We Say?* (Cambridge: Cambridge University Press, 1976), p. 93.

20 It may well be that many cultural expressions have their value within local communities, and thus should not be measured with inappropriate means relating to universalising claims. Even then, however, if these expressions are not to stagnate, it is likely that a confrontation with more demanding forms of expression will result. Think of the move of jazz from the brothels of New Orleans to Carnegie Hall.

21 I have explored this issue at some length in the revised version of *Aesthetics and Subjectivity: From Kant to Nietzsche* (Manchester: Manchester University Press, 2002). Some of the points made here in brief are dealt with in detail in that book.

22 Hans-Georg Gadamer, *Wahrheit und Methode* (Tübingen: J. C. B. Mohr, 1975), p. 98.

23 A. J. Cascardi, *Consequences of Enlightenment* (Cambridge: Cambridge University Press, 1999), pp. 50–1.

24 Kant, *Schriften zur Ästhetik*, p. 137.

25 See Bowie, *Aesthetics and Subjectivity*.

Touching art: aesthetics, fragmentation and community

Art has hitherto been considered, in all possible ways, in terms of both 'creation' (*poiesis*, genius, and so on) and 'reception' (judgement, critique, and so on). But what is left in the shadows is its befalling or devolving, that is to say, also its chance, event, birth, or encounter – which, in other terminologies, has been called the 'shock', 'touch', 'emotion', or 'pleasure', and which participates indissociably in both 'creation' and 'reception'.[1]

Throughout the history of literary and art criticism the focus has fallen, as Jean-Luc Nancy argues, on the creation or reception of works and texts. Theories of genius, authorial psychology and the material or historical conditions of production have revalued the creative processes that give rise to art in a range of different ways. Equally, important questions about reception that deal with notions of canonicity, ideology and the construction of subjectivities in texts have been generated by critical movements that seek to investigate the politics of literature, art and culture. Stripped down to a minimal point, however, the question of art's immediate impact (what Nancy refers to as its 'shock' or 'touch') remains a space for thinking a politics of the aesthetic that might helpfully be explored. Art has always been political: emerging from a given community, it comments on the identities, needs and desires of sections of its members, and criticism seeks in a variety of ways to uncover the modes in which those issues are generated by the work or text. The danger with some approaches to the work, however, is that they sideline its particularity as art, treating it as just one more commodity in cultural circulation and thereby eliding its specific transformative potential. The focus here will be to think the specificity of the aesthetic processes by which works and texts come to raise questions about the nature of community, and hence of the political problems of our being in common. The key question, then, is what is it that is particular to the work of art that raises the question of community?

The aim of this chapter is to begin to open a space for the investigation of the place of the aesthetic in the contemporary world. It will take as its object the notion of the artistic fragment that emerges within modernity, and consider the ways in which modern art functions as a fragmentary form.

The relationship between art, fragmentation and modernity is summed up succinctly by Theodor Adorno:

Ever since Beethoven's last works those artists who pushed integration to an extreme have mobilised disintegration. The truth content of art, whose organon was integration, turns against art and in this turn art has its emphatic moments. Artists discover the compulsion toward disintegration. . . . The category of the fragmentary – which has its locus here – is not to be confused with the category of contingent particularity: The fragment is that part of the totality of the work that opposes totality.[2]

The art of modernity mobilises disintegration: in the drive to completion and closure, it opens itself to its own fragmentation not as a contingent factor pointing to its lack of completion, but essentially – as a constituent moment in its drive toward self-integration. Throughout modernity there have been numerous movements of aesthetic thought that have approached art and literature in terms of this fragmentary status. Since the Romantic period, art has been conceived over and again in terms of the challenges it poses for attempts to construct the world as a systematically ordered totality. This disruptive potential tends to be derived from the ways in which artistic fragmentation is posited as a disturbance of or challenge to the closure and completion of systems of thought or politics. On this reading, the work of art or literature is irreducible to critical, political or cultural explanation or assimilation – it always has the potential to signify more than can be summed up in a single reading or analysis – and yet it remains indissociable from, and opens questions about, the social space within which it appears. In this respect, Adorno's formulation of art's problematic autonomy helpfully captures the disruptive relations obtaining between art, the empirical world and historical specificity: art, he argues, 'harbours what is empirically existing in its own substance. . . . Even the most sublime artwork takes up a determinate attitude to empirical reality by stepping outside of the constraining spell it casts, not once and for all, but rather ever and again, concretely, unconsciously polemical to this spell at each historical moment'.[3] Art is not constrained by the structures of the actual, but figures and refigures actuality by taking it as a point of departure for aesthetic production. It is not, however, a separate realm cut off from the world, but rather acts as a potential site for a continually changing disturbance of the conceptualisation of the actual in particular historical circumstances. Aesthetic representation generates a moment in which reflection can begin because of the way its presentation estranges, disrupts and fragments the actual. But in what might this fragmentary aesthetic excess consist? And how might it be able to mobilise a critique of contemporary systems of thought, culture or politics? By tracing a genealogy of this fragmentation in the writings of Friedrich Schlegel and the critique launched against it by G. W. F. Hegel, this chapter will identify a fragmentary Romantic residue in contemporary aesthetics. It will argue that the issues that are at stake in the disagreement between these two key thinkers have not passed away into history but continue to provoke the most profound questions about the value and role that art holds for us now.

Modernity and fragmentation

The notion of the fragmentary artwork first comes to gain a modern formulation in the literature and thought of the Romantic period. According to Philippe Lacoue-

Labarthe and Jean-Luc Nancy, the fragment opens up a space at the limits of modern politico-philosophical systematisation:

> in the very same moment and gesture of fragmentation, the fragment both is and is not System. . . . This same gesture, which is simply the writing of the fragment, conse-quently serves to subtract this fragment from the Work, within the continually renewed ambiguity of the *small* work of art, thus serving, in sum, to fragment the fragment . . . and in this respect it is legitimate to recognize in romanticism's specificity a kind of per-sistence or resistance, within idealism, of at least an element of the Kantian notion of *finitude*.[4]

For the Jena Romantics who set out the first definitions of the Romantic fragment, the totality to be challenged was that presented by idealist philosophy, which found its most comprehensive articulation in the work of Hegel. In the journal *Athenaeum*, published between 1798 and 1800, the concept of the fragment and its problemat-isation of systematic philosophy are worked out. In *Athenaeum* fragment 116, Friedrich Schlegel posits Romantic poetry as a 'progressive universal poetry': an art that aims to 'mix and fuse poetry and prose, inspiration and criticism, the poetry of art and the poetry of nature'.[5] This idea of poetry, in which it both strives to become a 'mirror of the whole circumstances of the world, an image of the age' and yet also 'hover[s] at the midpoint between the portrayed and the portrayer, free of all real and ideal self-interest, on the wings of poetic reflection', figures the notion of the aesthetic as unbounded fragment.[6] Beneath what may appear to modern ears as somewhat overblown rhetoric is a sense of the poetic that transcends generic identification and closure, and opens up a space for aesthetic self-reflection, analysis and critique. This aesthetic (and for Schlegel poetry is the supreme moment of aesthetics) is impossible to pin down and define, to grasp in a particular passage or figure from a poem, text or work but rather in Schlegel's formulation is caught up in a continual process of contextual transformation:

> The romantic kind of poetry is still in the state of becoming; that, in fact, is its real essence: that it should forever be becoming and never perfected. It can be exhausted by no theory and only a divinatory criticism would dare try to characterise its ideal. It alone is infinite, just as it alone is free. . . . The romantic kind of poetry is the only one that is more than a kind, that is, as it were, poetry itself.[7]

The explicit notion presented here is that because of its resistance to subsumption under a system of critique, poetry assumes a state of constant becoming: 'free' and 'infinite', it is open to continual rereading and reconfiguration by the discourses that approach it. Never completed or perfected, the poetic fragment is orientated towards future readings and new openings: as Schlegel states in 'Ideas' 48, 'Where philosophy stops, poetry has to begin'.[8] Because it is inexhaustible by critique, and impossible to fix with a single meaning, poetry transcends any present critical reading or philosoph-ical definition and gestures towards a future different from what is currently the case.

   In contrast to Schlegel's valorisation of a poetry and aesthetic of the future, Hegel's *Aesthetics* is premised on the 'pastness' of art. Coincident with the arrival of specula-tive modernity, he argues that philosophical reason has become the key means by which the issues and challenges facing the world can be approached, and that this marks the 'end of art':

> just as art has its 'before' in nature and the finite spheres of life, so too it has an 'after', i.e. a region which in turn transcends art's way of apprehending and representing the Absolute. For art has still a limit in itself and therefore passes over into higher forms of consciousness. This limitation determines, after all, the position which we are accustomed to assign to art in our contemporary life. For us art counts no longer as the highest mode in which truth fashions an existence for itself . . . With the advance of civilization a time generally comes in the case of every people when art points beyond itself.[9]

Because, according to Hegel, art's vocation is to 'unveil the *truth* in the form of sensuous artistic configuration', the emergence of a modern consciousness from the increasingly technological, scientific and philosophical understanding of the world developed during the Enlightenment produces a modern culture in which art's sensuous presentations can no longer fully grasp and present the complexities of the life-world, and it therefore ceases to be able to provide a guide for thought and action.[10] Modernity, in this respect, appears 'after art'; it represents itself as the 'after' of art, the point at which art's self-transcendence into philosophy has become necessary. It is the age in which art can no longer play the role it had hitherto undertaken for society: because art can only present the 'outward' or 'sensuous' form of the Absolute, and with the advance in Spirit that is marked by modernity, 'there dwells in the spirit the need to satisfy itself solely in its own inner self as the true form for truth to take'.[11] Yet, the 'end of art' does not mean that no more works are created. Instead of disappearing or becoming nothing more than the heritage of a bygone age, art, in Hegel's slightly strange formulation, 'points beyond itself'.

Hegel's description of the meaning of art's 'pointing beyond itself' that follows the occurrence of the phrase in the 'Introduction' to the *Aesthetics* repeats his argument in the *Phenomenology* which states that Spirit simply moves beyond art to dialectical reason and philosophy. Thus, Hegel states quite simply that, although one 'may well hope that art will always rise higher and come to perfection . . . the form of art has ceased to be the supreme need of the spirit'.[12] Art is surpassed as a means of generating truth: sublated in the movement of dialectical speculation it becomes just another one of the 'Particular interests' that are 'destroyed in the process' of 'conflict and destruction' from which reason and the Absolute emerge.[13]

Modernity's art is thus effectively excluded from the speculative system: it is surpassed as a 'way of apprehending and representing the Absolute' and thereby, in Jay Bernstein's words, 'loses its capacity to speak the truth concerning our most fundamental categorical engagements and commitments'.[14] In short, art 'falls out' of philosophy as it ceases to be the 'supreme need' of the new spirit of the age. Yet, this 'falling out' seems to contradict a cardinal rule of Hegel's system because in the movement of the dialectic nothing is beyond speculation, and therefore philosophy must have no remainder, must leave no 'fall out'. Lacoue-Labarthe identifies this apparently contradictory state of affairs in the following terms in an essay on Hegel and German Romanticism:

Philosophical discourse excludes nothing, especially not what it represents to itself as being of an 'order' not its own. And even when it attempts to exclude (if it ever wants to), its 'sublating' power is such that what is excluded never fails to return, so that not only must philosophy negotiate with it, but it can also claim it, (re)adopt it, or even, at the limit, pride itself on it. Philosophy divides, decides, and *criticizes*: but what it severs, it also constitutes on both sides, and the whole as such (be it rearranged) *returns* – in all senses – to philosophy.[15]

Thus, despite Hegel's gesture of setting art free from the search for truth, it 'returns' to haunt philosophical modernity, sucked back into the vortex of speculation by the force of the movement of dialectical negation. What Lacoue-Labarthe calls Hegel's 'gigantic "war machine" directed against aesthetics in general' fails both to eliminate art and to exclude it from systematic thought.[16]

When Hegel returns to the problem of the 'end of art' later in the *Aesthetics*, he seems to recognise as much, and the meaning given to art's 'pointing beyond itself' changes significantly:

in this self-transcendence art is nevertheless a withdrawal of man into himself, a descent into his own breast, whereby art strips away from itself all fixed restriction to a specific range of content and treatment, and makes *Humanus* its new holy of holies: i.e. the depths and heights of the human heart as such, mankind in its joys and sorrows, its strivings, deeds, and fates. . . . This is a subject-matter which does not remain determined artistically in itself and on its own account; on the contrary, the specific character of the topic and its outward formation is left to capricious invention, yet no interest is excluded.[17]

In this formulation of the 'beyond', art, in ceasing to be the 'sensuous revelation of *truth*' comes to figure a 'withdrawal of man into himself': the human subject replaces 'the Divine [as] the absolute subject-matter of art', and, as such, ceases to be truly Absolute.[18] The implication of Hegel's argument here points to another sense of artistic fragmentation: for pre-modern societies, art figured the divine essence of a community (the Egyptian temple, Greek statuary, and so on), but that divine essence is no longer available for sensuous presentation and so art's figuring is refocused on the particularity of individual actors and ideas. Ceasing to present community as a whole, its focus on the individual fragments the sense of its presentation of a being in common.

Brought together, what Schlegel and Hegel formulate in their very different ways is the end of the 'total' work of art: the art that encompasses the most fundamental shared beliefs of a society, and depicts and disseminates its goals. What remains is, on the one hand, the infinitely becoming plurality of fragments and, on the other, the 'capricious invention' broken off from the path of society's progress. More than this, though, the differences between the two thinkers point to a tension in modern aesthetics that opens a space for a contemporary politics of art.

Hegel's critique of Schlegel and the Jena Romantics turns on the notion of art's withdrawal into subjectivity, and his most pressing condemnation of Romanticism pinpoints its apparent grounding of the aesthetic in the subjectivity of the artist as an individual genius. Aside from some barbed comments about Schlegel not being a proper philosopher but a dilettante literary critic, the key concern raised by Hegel is that Romanticism substantialises Fichte's formalist arguments about the dialectical movement between the transcendental structures of the I and not-I which give rise to knowledge. This move from a formal to a substantial I transforms Fichte's transcendental analysis into an empirical-psychological positing of the personal I of the genius poet or artist who invents the world according to her or his own interest and caprice. He argues that for the positing ego of the Romantic artist, 'everything appears to it as null and vain, except its own subjectivity, which therefore becomes hollow and empty and itself mere vanity'.[19] In other words, Hegel detects in Romanticism a focus on the creative genius who acts as a guarantor for the work, which in turn becomes cut off from the objective world as it explores remorselessly the joys and sorrows of the (artist's) human heart.

If Hegel's critique of Romantic subjectivity and genius is accurate then it is clearly devastating.[20] The notion of a self-creating subjectivity has little currency today outside of the realms of ultra-free-market individualism, and there is little need even to resort to theoretical concepts such as the 'death of the Author' to grasp the problems that emerge here. What it does not challenge, however, is art's futural structure: although art no longer figures the aims and goals of social progress and has ceased to be the key means of deploying truth and knowledge, it remains a site of disruption, challenge and critique.

Thus the art of modernity, which, although redundant at the moment of its inception, cannot be suppressed (repressed?) by speculation but rather 'returns – in all senses – to philosophy' is what Schlegelian Romanticism announces in the fragment. Stripped by Hegel's critique of any substantive or subjective authenticity (or genius), the work itself retains an openness to the future. In other words, the fragment is the art that exists on the threshold of speculative modernity: no longer able to tell the 'truth' in its 'true form' or ground itself in a governing creative genius, but not yet excluded from thought as a medium of mere relaxation and escapism, it holds out the possibility of difference and disturbance within systematic organisation. Appearing at the moment of the 'end of art', the fragment's attempts to 'reveal the truth in the form of sensuous artistic configuration' are already outmoded from modernity's perspective and result only in failure. It thus exists, in Thomas McFarland's phrase, only as 'the forms of ruin', as scraps, contingencies and 'capricious inventions' that 'remain broken or indifferent to the objective world' of philosophical modernity.[21] And yet, even as ruin, art is continually drawn back into the speculative system by the 'sublating power' of the dialectic. Neither inside nor outside, the aesthetic fragment exists at the limit of the 'Work' of philosophical modernity, 'completing and incompleting' the universalising movement of the speculative system which it fragments through a 'continually renewed ambiguity of the small work of art': the art that has come undone from speculation's striving after the Absolute and thus has no claim to the totalising perspective of a grand narrative. For this reason, Lacoue-Labarthe and Nancy claim that 'what interests us in romanticism is that we still belong to the era it opened up', and in fact that, a 'veritable romantic *unconscious* is discernible today, in most of the central motifs of our "modernity" '.[22] At the opposite end of modernity from Romanticism, Adorno's materialist thinking of the imbrication of art in the modern echoes the sense of its fragmentary nature:

> Art is modern when, by its mode of experience and as the expression of the crisis of experience, it absorbs what industrialisation has developed under the given relations of production. This involves a negative canon, a set of prohibitions against what the modern has disavowed in experience and technique; and such determination is virtually the canon of what is to be done.[23]

Art stands out against the rationalising and industrialising drives of the modern, fragmenting them by recapturing the techniques and experiences disavowed in the continual striving for progress and development. This, for the critics of modernity, is art's fundamental critical potential.

Fragmenting the fragment: contemporary aesthetics and the possibility of community

The fragmentary space of the aesthetic opens up a vantage point from which a critique of the modern can emerge. Art thus holds the capacity to disrupt the closure of systematic rationality, fragmenting its categories and structures. The question I want to pose, though, is how might we think art in relation to the often-posited destruction of these modern systems? Or, in other words, what happens to the artistic fragment when the world itself becomes fragmentary? In order to begin to propose an answer to this question I want to turn now to an investigation of the work of Jean-Luc Nancy, and particularly to his notion of the singular plural.

Recent developments such as the globalisation of capitalism, gradual loss of power of the nation state, transformation of communications systems and fracturing of consensus about social structures and values that were founded on discredited gender and racial hierarchies have called into question the idea of a rational, progressive development of modernity. Contemporary thought seldom strives for the systematic rationality of Hegelian speculation.[24] Rather, the notion of difference – whether it is thought in terms of gender, the postcolonial, historicism or deconstruction, to name but a few approaches – provides the structure for enquiry in the contemporary humanities. In this sense, as thinkers such as Lyotard, Deleuze and Nancy argue, there is no longer a 'sense of the world' available for thought. At the beginning of a book that takes this phrase as its title, Nancy posits the 'end of the world':

> There is no longer any world: no longer a *mundus*, a *cosmos*, a composed and complete order (from) within which one might find a place, a dwelling, and the elements of an orientation. . . . There is no longer a Spirit of the world, nor is there any history before whose tribunal one could stand.[25]

For many contemporary theorists, the 'grand narratives' of modernity (to borrow Lyotard's phrase) no longer have any legitimacy when it comes to thinking and organising the world, experience and history. In this vein, Zygmunt Bauman argues that the 'deepest meaning conveyed by the idea of globalisation is that of the indeterminate, unruly and self-propelled character of world affairs; the absence of a centre, of a controlling desk, of a board of directors, of a managerial office'.[26]

In the face of the fragmentation of contemporary cultures, there is little possibility of recourse to a universal governing notion of truth or emancipation. According to Nancy, 'Our time is the time . . . when this [grand narrative] history has been suspended: total war, genocide, the challenge of nuclear powers, implacable technology, hunger, and absolute misery, all these are, at the least, evident signs of self-destroying humanity, of self-annihilating history, without any possibility of the dialectic work of the negative'.[27] It is not that these histories are no longer being written, or that speculative thought no longer attempts to grasp the world; rather, this thinking no longer appears adequate to the plurality that appears in contemporary worldhood and the fragmentation of experience in today's cosmopolis. For Nancy, the plurality of the contemporary presents the contemporary as the space of a radical absence of sense, or rather a space in which the absence has itself become our sense.

Nancy expands upon and fleshes out his thinking of the plurality of worlds in *Being Singular Plural*. Here he links the thought to the post-Marxist (and, again following Lyotard, postmodern) sense of the development of the 'spectacular-market society' in which 'commodity fetishism' and the global domination of capital are accomplished in 'the production and consumption of material and symbolic "goods" that all have the character of being an image, illusion, or appearance'.[28] Subjectivity becomes a function of wealth: the capacity to purchase new images, identities and even bodies becomes the basis of who we are. The political and philosophical stakes of this are that 'universal commerce [becomes] constituted by a representation wherein existence is both an invention and a self-appropriating event. A subject of representation, that is, a subject reduced to the sum or flux of representations which it purchases, is the placeholder that functions as the subject of Being and history'.[29] This is the basis for the postmodern idea of culture as it appears in writers such as Baudrillard and Jameson, and even to a certain extent Lyotard.[30] However, Nancy takes a different tack from these thinkers in refusing either to attempt to delve below the surface of spectacle in the hope of recovering a Marxian base (à la Jameson), or to celebrate the hyperreality of a surface-spectacle without depth in the manner of Baudrillard. Arguing that both of these approaches work through untenable notions of an opposition between good and bad representation, his move is rather to rethink the ontological structure of the social bond in terms of being-in-common, or as the title of his book suggests, being singular plural.

The notion of being singular plural sets out from the Heideggerian concept of Dasein, which Nancy argues is necessarily and inextricably tied up with Mitsein. By working through section 26 of *Being and Time*, Nancy argues that Being-with is an irreducible moment in the formation of Dasein that remains underdeveloped in Heidegger's analysis. For Heidegger, any question of the meaning of Being, any question of meaning, is necessarily communal: 'Dasein is essentially Being-with. . . . Not only is Being towards Others an autonomous, irreducible relationship of Being: this relationship, as Being-with, is one which, with Dasein's Being, already is. . . . So far as Dasein *is* at all, it has being-with-one-another as its kind of Being.'[31] Being, for

Heidegger, is always therefore a Being-with in which the 'with' is primordial and not just a modification of a pre-established Being. Rather than being based on a pre-given self-consciousness, one's identity and existence in the world necessarily emerges from relations with others.

For Nancy, the problem with Heidegger's thinking of Being through Dasein occurs in the relegation of Being-with to 'average everydayness'. He argues: 'One cannot affirm that the meaning of Being must express itself starting from everydayness and then begin by neglecting the differentiation of the everyday, its constantly renewed rupture, its intimate discord, its polymorphy and its polyphony.'[32] In Heidegger, the question of the other, or the differences between others, is not explicitly worked through. According to Nancy, on the other hand, the others who come to stand up against the self in Being-with are not only different from that self, but also different from one another in and of themselves rather than modifications of some model or archetypal other. Each other is singular, unique and irreducible to the mass (even when part of a mass). This means that what we receive with these singularities is:

> the discreet passage of *other origins of the world*. What occurs there . . . is an origin; it is an affirmation of the world, and we know that the world has no other origin than this singular multiplicity of origins. The world always appears each time according to a decidedly local turn [of events]. Its unity, its uniqueness, and its totality consists in a combination of this reticulated multiplicity, which produces no result.[33]

Rather than employing modern categories to think experience through a subject–object distinction or politics through the relation between an individual and society (oppositions that always privilege one side or the other of the binary), the analysis of existence is opened to the workings of a singularity that is always already in relation to a plurality of other singulars. What emerges from this is an analysis of community conceived in terms of the singular plural in which subjectivity does not occur on the basis of some form of modified Cartesian identity, but rather happens in the moments of encounter with each unique and irreducible other. Subjectivity is irreducible and unique, and yet indissociable from relations with the plurality of others (each of whom will also be singular). Community thus obtains in this plurality of singularities each existing on the basis of its relations with others, which makes it irreducible to systematic universal analysis or, as Nancy puts it, inoperative.[34]

The question this raises for my account of artistic fragmentation is what space does this notion of the singular plural leave for a thinking of art? In debates about the post-modern, two versions of the place of art dominate, which (for want of a more detailed analysis) might be identified as the Jamesonian and the Lyotardian. In the former, the critical edge of modern art has fallen into the self-ironising sentimentality of pastiche that is cut off from the political and social developments of late capitalism.[35] Those following Lyotard, on the other hand, argue that art continues to play the role that it did within modernity – to 'wage a war on totality' by opening up the system to disruption.[36] The alternative that I want to explore here, however, returns to the Schlegelian/Hegelian conflict that was outlined in the last section in order to think art's relation to community.

Nancy returns to artistic fragmentation in *The Sense of the World*, where he begins to open the question of what is at stake for contemporary thought in the notion of 'romantic incompletion' developed in *The Literary Absolute*. In the light of the collapse of speculative or systematic totalities, the status of the artistic fragment is transformed, which means that:

> One must know first of all what remains in the fragments. . . . In other words . . . if one supposes that fragmentation has properly dislocated the essence on which it supervened, one must ask oneself if this 'essence' has not itself been delivered, thrown, projected, and offered like what one would have to call, twisting Benoit Mandelbrot's word, a 'fractal essence'. . . . In still other words, in what direction are we to take the step from a fragmented cosmetics to an aesthetics of a sensible tracing [*frayage*], and beyond this to the fragile permanence of 'art' in the drift of the 'worldly'?[37]

As the quotation with which this chapter began suggests, the response to this question lies in the reading of art as event. This draws on the Heideggerian notion of art's ability to disclose the world, to open the setting into work of truth in the appearance, birth and encounter of the event of disclosure. However, in distinction from Heidegger, Nancy's notion of what is disclosed by art draws on the sense of the fragmentation of our already fragmented Being-with. For Nancy, art 'neither operates nor ensures the continuity and homogeneity of being', but is rather 'the presentation of presentation' insofar as this presentation is 'without presentness . . . does not possess a truth as does (the subject of) being. Rather, presentation itself *is* truth'.[38]

What does this notion of artistic presentation as 'truth' consist in? Thrown back on the fragmentary nature of our being singular plural, we are called upon by art to respond to its interruption of the circle of signification and its exposure of the fragility of signified sense. The argument that presentation itself is truth does not ascribe to it some transcendental status, but rather posits art as a disclosure of truth as 'the secret of that which comprises nothing other than the multiple, discreet, discontinuous, heterogeneous, and singular touch of being itself'.[39] This is not therefore the presentation of or that there is an unpresentable, but rather the presentation that presentation is itself singular plural, that there are multiple origins of the world, that the world is constituted in and by our Being-in-common, which itself is finite and fragmented. For Nancy, what remains of the Romantic fragment is the sense of incompletion and the lack of a Work. Now, however, the fragment discloses 'the fragmentation of sense that existence *is*'.[40] Without guide or rule we as viewers, listeners or readers who are ourselves exposed to our singular plurality are called upon to respond.

On the basis of this thinking of the aesthetic, art responds to the fragmentation of the contemporary with a presentation of the difference at the heart of being-in-common. It intervenes in the present, opening up identifications (be they ideological or psychological) to difference: works present the discontinuities implied in the process of communal existence and question our everyday sense-making procedures. This presentation is intrinsically political as it provides a ground for questioning the rules, conventions and customs that strive to govern this existence, sort groups and factions from each other under the banners of homogeneity, and direct the behaviour of each towards a unified end (whether that end is national, racial, gender, religious or political identity). Art, whether it is classified as high or popular, activates the sense that difference is. If it doesn't do this, it isn't art. It doesn't matter whether the work exists as part of a canon or recognised collection; art is what touches upon the differences between us that form the basis of community, and reminds us of the necessity of being in common. In the surprise fragmentation of sense elicited by the work there is the possibility of touching on the sense of a plural community.

Notes

1 J.-L. Nancy, *The Sense of the World*, trans. J. S. Librett (Minneapolis: University of Minnesota Press, 1997), p. 133.

2 T. W. Adorno, *Aesthetic Theory*, trans. R. Hullot-Kentor (London: Athlone, 1997), p. 45.

3 Adorno, *Aesthetic Theory*, p. 5.

4 P. Lacoue-Labarthe and J.-L. Nancy, *The Literary Absolute: The Theory of Literature in German Romanticism*, trans. Philip Bernard and Cheryl Lester (Albany: State University of New York Press, 1988), pp. 50–1.

5 F. W. J. Schlegel, *Philosophical Fragments*, trans. P. Firchow (Minneapolis: University of Minnesota Press, 1991), p. 31.

6 Schlegel, *Fragments*, pp. 31–2.

7 *Ibid.*, p. 32.

8 *Ibid.*, p. 98.

9 G. W. F. Hegel, *Aesthetics: Lectures on Fine Art*, 2 vols, trans. T. M. Knox (Oxford: Oxford University Press, 1975), vol. 1, pp. 102–3.

10 Hegel, *Aesthetics*, vol. 1, p. 55.

11 *Ibid.*, p. 103.

12 *Ibid.*

13 These quotations are taken from the passage on the 'cunning of reason' in G. W. F. Hegel, *Lectures on the Philosophy of World History. Introduction: Reason in History*, trans. H. B. Nisbet (Cambridge: Cambridge University Press, 1975), p. 89. Jay Bernstein provides an excellent gloss of this sense of the end of art in *The Fate of Art: Aesthetic Alienation from Kant to Derrida and Adorno* (Cambridge: Polity, 1992): 'To speak of the end of art is to claim that art is no longer for us the place in which the truth (of who and how we are, and of how 'things' are for us) occurs; art is no longer unavoidably formative for our experience of ourselves or the world; it no longer constitutively presents or even represents what is absolute for us. The death or end of art denotes not the halting of historical movement, nor, then, the cessation of an activity and the concerns surrounding it; but a dislodgement, as it were, of those activities and concerns from the (metaphysical-historical) centre to the periphery.' (p. 73).

14 *Ibid.*, p. 5.

15 P. Lacoue-Labarthe, 'The unpresentable', trans. C. Sartiliot, in *The Subject of Philosophy*, ed. T. Trezise, trans. Trezise *et al.* (Minneapolis: University of Minnesota Press, 1993), pp. 150–1.

16 Lacoue-Labarthe, 'The unpresentable', p. 151. A similar discussion of the deconstructive potential of art for Hegelian philosophy is generated in J.-L. Nancy, *The Muses*, trans. P. Kamuf (Stanford, CA: Stanford University Press, 1996). See especially the essay entitled

'The girl who succeeds the Muses' (pp. 41–55), which makes a similar case to the one I am attempting to develop here about the inextricability of poetry and philosophy: 'poetry finds itself confronted with the *prose* of thinking. This prose would therefore be, by rights, the element in which it would finally come to be dissolved, and all art and arts with it. . . . But this non-art shows a singular ambiguity: it is at once the index of pure interiority withdrawn into itself, of the 'pure element of thinking' that receives into itself a thoroughly sublated exteriority. . . . [Thus, it turns out that, confronted with this prose,] art is again 'given body', reincarnated as it were at the very limit of its dissolution, and that in 'reincarnating' itself, it again grants a place to the set of 'particularizations' that are essential to it.' (p. 43).

17 Hegel, *Aesthetics*, vol. 1, p. 607.

18 *Ibid.*

19 *Ibid.*, p. 65.

20 The conditional in this sentence is deliberate. A number of writers have made convincing cases that Hegel misrepresents Romantic subjectivity. Perhaps the most accessible argument against his reading of Schlegel comes from Judith Norman's 'Squaring the Romantic circle: Hegel's critique of Schlegel's theories of art' in W. Maker (ed.), *Hegel and Aesthetics* (New York: State University of New York Press, 2000), pp. 131–44.

21 T. McFarland, *Romanticism and the Forms of Ruin: Wordsworth, Coleridge, and the Modalities of Fragmentation* (Princeton: Princeton University Press, 1981), see especially the chapter entitled 'Fragmented modalities and the criteria of Romanticism', pp. 3–55.

22 Lacoue-Labarthe and Nancy, *The Literary Absolute*, p. 15.

23 Adorno, *Aesthetic Theory*, p. 34.

24 Clearly there is a sense in which the system has never been more total than it is in the present climate of a capitalist 'new world order' where IMF and World Bank projects bring those on the margins under the sway of free-market economics – frequently with devastating consequences. Modern notions of totality still hold sway in the world, often in the noxious forms of fundamentalism, whether of the Muslim or Christian variety, and the conflicts between them affect peoples throughout the world. An emancipatory politics cannot, however, be based on such fundamentalist assumptions. What I am trying to think here is an alternative critical/aesthetic stance to what seems to be the increasing tribalisation of contemporary politics.

25 Nancy, *The Sense of the World*, p. 4.

26 Z. Bauman, *Globalization: The Human Consequences* (Cambridge: Polity, 1998), p. 59.

27 J.-L. Nancy, 'Finite history' in *The Birth to Presence*, trans. B. Holmes *et al.* (Stanford, CA: Stanford University Press, 1993), pp. 144–5.

28 J.-L. Nancy, *Being Singular Plural*, trans. R. D. Richardson and A. O'Byrne (Stanford, CA: Stanford University Press, 2000), p. 49.

29 Nancy, *Being Singular Plural*, pp. 49–50.

30 Lyotard's version of this position defines contemporary capitalism as 'a vanguard machine dragging humanity after it, dehumanising it'; see J.-F. Lyotard, *The Postmodern Condition: A Report on Knowledge*, trans. G. Bennington and B. Massumi (Manchester: Manchester University Press, 1984), p. 63.

31 Martin Heidegger, *Being and Time*, trans. J. Macquarrie and E. Robinson (Oxford: Blackwell, 1962), pp. 156, 162–3.

32 Nancy, *Being Singular Plural*, p. 9.

33 *Ibid.*

34 See J.-L. Nancy, *The Inoperative Community*, ed. P. Connor (Minneapolis: University of Minnesota Press, 1991), especially pp. 1–42.

35 The basis of this position is set out in F. Jameson, *Postmodernism, or the Cultural Logic of Late Capitalism* (London: Verso, 1991).

36 Lyotard, *The Postmodern Condition*, p. 82. Lyotard develops a more nuanced account of the critical capacity of art in *The Inhuman: Reflections on Time*, trans. G. Bennington and R. Bowlby (Cambridge: Polity, 1991) and, in a way that is most interesting for this chapter, *Soundproof Room: Malraux's Anti-Aesthetics*, trans. R. Harvey (Stanford, CA.: Stanford University Press, 2001).

37 Nancy, *The Sense of the World*, p. 124.

38 *Ibid.*, p. 138.

39 *Ibid.*, p. 137.

40 *Ibid.*, p. 139.

Part II

Readings

The Alexandrian aesthetic

> For the most central pathway in this city is more vast and more impassable than even that extensive and untrodden desert that it took Israel two generations to cross.[1]

Still the most unreal of the unreal cities, Alexandria remains emblematic of the modern aesthetic, with its most significant monument dispersed between the Embankment in London and Central Park, New York.[2] The exile of the monumental fabric of the city to the capitals of modernity testifies to Alexandria's condition as a figure for diaspora as well as emphasising the fascination that the city continues to hold for modernity and modernism. As the home of diaspora, Alexandria has been celebrated since antiquity for its equivocal hospitality for cultural differences whether linguistic, religious, scholarly or sexual.[3] The city famed for both its orgies and its libraries stands both for the prodigal scattering of seed, with all its pleasures and disasters, and its gathering together, cataloguing and storage, with all *its* pleasures and disasters. This movement of dispersal and collection also informs what might be described as the Alexandrian aesthetic – a movement between *aisthesis* as a moment of pleasurable openness and *ascesis* as the moment of discipline and closure – a movement that underlies the experience of the 'allegorical'.

For it is not only the monuments of Alexandria that have been carried over into the heart of metropolitan modernity, but also the entire aesthetic temper of allegory. In tracing the origins of the modern allegorical aesthetic in *The Origins of German Tragic Drama*, Walter Benjamin described its unstable movement between excess and discipline as essentially Alexandrian. The peculiar complicity between aisthesis and ascesis that Benjamin finds in allegory has its origins in the figure of the Alexandrian, a figure that through various routes and vectors has been carried over into modernity and modernism. Yet in the course of dissemination, what is crucial to the Alexandrian – namely a certain poetics of diaspora or of scattering and re-collection, the traffic between aisthesis as sensible pleasure and ascesis as rational discipline – has itself been disciplined. The equivocal tension between aisthesis and ascesis – the diasporic – has largely been sacrificed to the desire to resolve the multiple movements into a disciplined progression from the confusion of the senses to the discipline of reason. The self-destructive movements of Christian allegory that Benjamin identified in the baroque prefigure the attempt to dissolve aisthesis into ascesis that informs modern aesthetics. Yet in spite of attempts to reduce the disorientation of allegory to the unilinear governance of the symbol, the allegory of the Alexandrian aesthetic remains in movement – or, to use the figure ubiquitous throughout Alexandrian culture – it continues in a 'procession' moving backwards and forwards between aisthesis and ascesis.

The processional movement of aisthesis and ascesis adopts many guises and can be described in many ways. It is present in the processions between the many to the one, between dispersal and unification, between the senses and the intellect, between pleasure and abstinence, pollution and purity, between even perdition and redemption. Yet these polar oppositions are not strictly sustainable – the procession does not move from one pole to another, but, rather like Ptolemy of Alexandria's epicyclical explanation for the movements of the planets in the *Almagest* (AD127–141), it inextricably entwines progressive and retrograde movements. Yet this is not simply the antinomian confirmation of opposites by means of their inversion – the discovery of intellect at the extremes of sense, literality at the extreme of metaphor or even redemption at the extreme of perdition – that characterises gnosticism and a certain extreme of allegorical thought and practice also analysed by Benjamin, but the mutual implication of each in the other. There is a procession but not a progression from one term to the other, there is no orderly and unilinear movement but an inextricable intertwining of tendencies. The Alexandrian aesthetic is to be found in this procession between aesthesis and ascesis, but the time in which this procession unfolds is itself complex. The movement in question does not assume an unequivocal orientation of time but weaves together past, present and future. For just as the city is geographically suspended between desert and the sea, so too its allegorical figure recurs as at once the Egyptian exile, the desert of Exodus and the promised land.

The origins of Alexandrian allegory in the mutual procession and recession of aisthesis and ascesis are closely related to the emergence of aesthetic in the narrower sense of the 'philosophy of art'. The latter represents the peculiar ascesis visited upon works of art that constitutes the philosophical 'aesthetic'. The vast library and museum of Hellenistic Alexandria enabled a vast labour of scholarly commentary, reflection and translation that might be described as the first 'aesthetic', if by this is understood the disciplined philosophical reflection on the interpretation of texts and works of art. The gathering of the texts and their interpretation was not motivated solely by philological preoccupations, but also by an undefined commitment to the distinction between aisthesis and ascesis. This commitment is most evident in the neo-platonism characteristic of the city – in its Pagan, Jewish and Christian variants – that saw in aisthesis a doctrine of sensible experience considered as a vehicle, more or less apt, for an approach to the ideas. The ideas were cloaked in sensible experience and could thus be revealed through a work of reflection and interpretation that departed from the data of sensibility. The reflection on texts and works of art thus formed part of the disciplined movement, procession and in some accounts even the Exodus from the realm of sense to the realm of ideas. Sensible experience and its works were, in short, allegorical, pointing beyond themselves and calling for interpretation. The movement from the sensible to the ideal thus not only involved the elaboration of interpretative protocols, but also implied a process of ascesis, the mortification of the body or text for the sake of salvation in the revelation of meaning and truth.

Walter Benjamin's alignment of the allegorical aesthetic with the ascetic mortification of the body in the *Origin of German Tragic Drama* rehearses the Alexandrian origins of allegory. Apart from its prodigious library and the erudition of its scholars, Hellenistic Alexandria was also celebrated for its anatomy, sometimes, reputedly, involving live human subjects. It subsequently pioneered Christian ascetic theology with its accompanying monastic ascetic practice and was the source of the vicious controversies concerning the nature of the body of Christ that violently divided – and still divide – Christianity. This mortification of the flesh whether for the sake of knowledge or salvation contrasted violently with the neo-platonic procession from the sensible to the ideal – a link between ascesis and knowledge sanctioned above all by Plato's *Phaedo* and figured as a cosmic procession in the *Phaedrus*.

The passage between aisthesis and ascesis would be restated by Baumgarten in his reinvention of aesthetic – the *Reflections on Poetry* (1735) – commentary on Horace's *Ars Poetica* structured around what it identifies as a patristic, but is more accurately a neo-platonic distinction between aisthesis and *noesis*. It is also central to his incomplete *Aesthetica* which attempted to reorient aisthesis and noesis largely but by no means exclusively through the hierarchical subordination of the former to the latter. Yet even he, while stressing the importance of the rational education of the senses, insisted that they not be suppressed but developed through the experience of sensible perfection of the beautiful. Nevertheless, Baumgarten introduced rational ascesis into modern aesthetics through the notion of the education of sensibility, a tendency advanced by Schiller in his *Aesthetic Education*.

The modern subordination of the aesthetic to the ascetic in terms of a stage in the progression from sensibility to reason contrasts with the Alexandrian view of it as the site of a complex processional movement combining progressive and recessive tendencies. For the latter, the movement between the sensible and the ideal is not an ascent but a complex and equivocal alignment – the descent of the soul, for example, requires the ascent of the body and both may indeed imply other more complex, underlying movements. The significance of the complex rising and falling procession is evident in the peculiar location of Alexandria in the economy of salvation – it simultaneously figures the fleshpots of Egypt, the desert of Exodus or the site of repentance, and the promised land. The complexity of the movements that make up the aesthetic – underestimated by Baumgarten and the aesthetic tradition after him, with the exception of Kant – may be revealed through reading of the classic Alexandrian allegorists and neo-platonists (Philo and later Plotinus) who plotted a figure of the aesthetic that still has the capacity to disrupt the more ascetic version advocated by Baumgarten and his modernist successors. The complexity of this movement between ascesis and aisthesis can be appreciated from a different perspective in the work of the Alexandrian modernists such as Giuseppe Ungaretti (1888–1970) and C. P. Cavafy (1863–1933) with their poetry of exile and nostalgia exploring the complex movements of loss, errancy and salvation through the diasporic languages of Italian and Greek.

Allegory – the ascetic aesthetic

The outrage that followed the Alexandrian church father Origen's act of self-castration was provoked not so much by the deed itself – with its proximity to extreme ascetic pagan practices associated with the worship of Cybele – as by its motivation by a *literal* reading of Matthew 19:12. The literality of Origen's interpretation betrayed an unexpected lapse of allegorical sensitivity in one who was heir to a sophisticated tradition of allegorical interpretation of biblical and other texts. The self-mutilation testifies not only to a painful over-investment in literality, but also to a victory of ascesis over aesthesis. The ambiguous and ambivalent relationship between the two was here, like the Gordian knot, resolved by a single cut. Origen's gesture may be said to have consolidated an alliance between the investment in the literal (the unnegotiable fixing of meaning, its promised land where meaning is brought home for good) and the antiaesthetic extreme of asceticism that finds meaning in the mortification of the flesh.

It points also to the characteristically Alexandrian elision of textual interpretation, sexuality and the body. For Origen's self-mutilation, on closer inspection, anticipates the unilinear and progressive movement of sensibility to reason characteristic of the modern aesthetic. The ascent from the senses to the ideal is cast as a violent ascetic movement of liberation from the body and its pleasures towards a higher, sublimated state. In this ubiquitous interpretative strategy, stress is laid upon the achievement of literality; the meaning of a journey is found in the destination rather than the journey itself, in the arrival at the promised land rather than the formative forty years of errancy in the desert. This concatenation of themes was already highly developed in the work of the first-century neo-platonic Jewish philosopher, Philo of Alexandria. Philo pioneered the allegorical interpretation of the Torah, producing a large number of extended and sophisticated allegorical readings. Yet Philo's allegories exemplify, sometimes in spite of themselves, the complex syncopation of ascent and descent that characterises the equivocal procession between sense and ideal characteristic of the Alexandrian aesthetic.

Philo's three 'Allegorical Interpretations' ('Legum allegoriae') offer not only a programmatic statement of the allegorical method of interpretation applied to the account of the creation of the world offered in the book of Genesis, but also an uneasy reflection on the meaning of pleasure and the role of pleasure in meaning. In these allegories, the pleasures of the senses are given the allegorical figure of 'Egypt', collapsing together the 'fleshpots' of biblical Egypt with the temptations of Philo's contemporary Alexandria. Yet even here there are the beginnings of a characteristic ambivalence with respect to the city – does it represent only the Egyptian 'house of bondage', or is it, as for Dionysos of Alexandria, the Sinai desert or even the promised land?

To complicate matters further, Philo carries over the biblical metaphor or 'Exodus pattern' into the aesthetic through the parallels between the biblical and the philosophical Exodus, from the pleasures of the senses to reason, and the philological exodus, from the letter to the meaning of a text. The same ascetic method is assumed to be at work in the biblical, philosophical and the philological orders. Yet the complex issue of this method is nicely revealed in the third of the 'Allegorical

Interpretations' where Philo describes his own attendance at the Alexandian orgies already famed in antiquity:

> for when I have gone to entertainments where no respect was paid to discipline, and to sumptuous banquets, whenever I went without taking reason with me as a guide, I became a slave to the luxuries that lay before me, being under the guidance of masters who could not be tamed, with sights and sounds of temptation, and all other such things as work pleasure in a man by the agency of his senses of smell and taste. But when I approach such scenes in the company of reason, I then become a master instead of a slave . . .'[4]

Here the appeal to ascesis seems familiarly unilateral: pleasure and the temptations of the senses tend to slavery, reason to mastery. But it is crucial to note that Philo 'approaches' scenes of pleasure in the company of reason. He is not urged by reason to shun them; reason even serves as his '*guide*' to excessive pleasures. In short, reason is far from committed to an ascetic anti-aesthesis. The complexity of Philo's view of pleasure and reason is evident in his allegorical interpretation of the subtlety of the serpent in Genesis 3:1. The serpent has a powerful role in Philo's sexualised biblical cosmogony: 'God, who created all the animals on the earth, arranged this order very admirably, for he placed the mind first, that is to say, man, for the mind is the most important part in man; then outward sense, that is woman; and then proceeding in regular order he came to the third, pleasure.'[5] The figuration of the mind as man (Adam) and sense as woman (Eve) is commonplace, but the figuration of pleasure as a serpent has more interesting implications. Philo's analogical justification of the figure holds that:

> as the motion of the serpent is full of many windings and varied, so also is the motion of pleasure. At first it folds itself around a man in five ways, for the pleasures consist both in seeing and in hearing, and in taste, and in smell, and in touch, but the most vehement and intense are those which arise from connection with woman, through which the generation of similar beings is appointed by nature to be effected.[6]

Unlike some later Platonists, Philo is not a gnostic; he does not decry sexual reproduction as contributing to the continuance of a fallen world created by an evil demiurge. Quite the contrary, he implies that pleasure, and its figure the serpent, are an essential part of creation. Such approbation of pleasure seems far from the conventional ascetic tendency to negate the body and its pleasures in the name of reason. For Philo there is a pleasure of the senses that may be approached and enjoyed in the company of reason.

Philo quickly retraces his steps, distinguishing between different kinds of pleasure in a way that anticipates Kant's later distinction in the *Critique of Judgement* between disinterested and interested pleasure. Philo introduces a distinction between 'the pleasure which arises from the contemplation of pictures or statues; and all other works which are made by art' and the 'pleasures of the belly' or of sense.[7] The division of pleasures between those of the soul and those of the senses brings with it a doubling of the figure of the serpent, who is now called to figure the ambivalence of pleasure. The pleasures of sense, also described as those of 'the multitude' or of the 'houses

in Egypt', 'bring on death', but not death as the separation of soul and body, celebrated in Plato's *Phaedo* as the liberation of the soul from its prison in the body, 'but
that [soul death] which is the destruction of the soul by vice'.[8] The serpent that brings
on soul death will prevail until both body and soul 'turn to repentance'. Philo suggests that this turn or movement is achieved not by the simple destruction of the
serpent – as in Origen's self-mutilation – but through the creation of a second serpent,
the serpent of the pleasures of the soul. Moses' creation of the brazen serpent – a work
of art – is read allegorically as a figure of those pleasures of the soul that would after
Kant be known as disinterested 'aesthetic' pleasures. These are the peculiar pleasures
of the third critique in which reason and sensibility 'accompany' each other to the
scene of pleasure. The second serpent is a remedy to the threat of soul death posed by
the first. Philo interprets Genesis 21:6 in terms of Moses' remedy for the children of
Israel in their Exodus who suffer from the memory of the pleasures of Egypt: 'for if
the mind that has been bitten by pleasure, that is by the serpent which was sent to
Eve, shall have the strength to behold the beauty of temperance, that is to say, the
serpent made by Moses in a manner affecting the soul, and to behold God himself
through the medium of the serpent, it shall live.'[9] Interestingly, the soul *can only* see
God through the eyes of the second serpent, through art or the pleasures of the soul.

The antagonistic serpents were destined to have a long life, with Moses' serpent
being called by the Alexandrian Christian heirs of Philo allegorically to figure Christ,
or for Pagans, the God of healing Asclepius. It was also carried over into the Genesis
narrative, with the escape from Egypt, the land of serpents, assisted by the brazen
second serpent. The allegory of the serpents points to a complex relationship between
ascesis and aesthesis. There would be no need for the figure of the second serpent if it
served only to extirpate the first – the pleasures of the senses – through an act of
ascesis. For ascesis here does not simply suppress the pleasures of the senses but enjoys
them in the company of reason; the second serpent stands for a pleasure in which both
the ascesis of reason and the aesthesis of sensibility are implicated.

The mutual implication of ascesis and aesthesis is central to the work of Plotinus,
the leading representative of the Alexandrian school of neo-platonism during the third
century. It is unfolded in the complex reflection upon the relationship between the
movement of ascesis and the pleasure of the senses in the sixth tractate of the first
Ennead, 'On beauty'. This meditation is characterised by the mutual animation of
ascesis and aisthesis, choreographed as an opposition resolved into complementarity.
The ascetic moments of Plotinus's text stress the separation of the soul from the body:
the soul has descended into the body and has now to reverse the movement through
an act of dieresis or separation. That the act of separation is not simply a suppression
is evident in its various figures – as a separation of pure gold from ore, as a lustration,
and as the liturgical procession of a mystery religion – but all involve the abstraction
of a pure substance from a mixture. The gold is 'worked out' of the ore, the soul is
'washed clean of all that embodiment has daubed it with' and the initiates who would
'mount to the temple sanctuaries must purify themselves and leave aside their old
clothing, and enter in nakedness'.[10] Yet this ascesis is a means to the liberation *of*, not
a liberation *from*, aisthesis. Aesthetic beauty always testifies to the idea in its purity; it

embodies a memory of the idea that needs to be drawn out or abstracted from its material distortions but not necessarily liberated from them.

The joint works of ascesis and aisthesis are combined in the celebrated metaphor, drawn from Plato's *Phaedrus*, of the sculptor 'working at the statue'. The sculptor's work consists in drawing out the beautiful form implied in the matter, not in imposing form upon recalcitrant matter: 'he cuts away here, he smoothes it there, he makes this line lighter, this other one purer, until he disengages beautiful lineaments in the marble'.[11] The work of clarifying matter is also figured in terms of a procession or exodus. For Plotinus, 'The fatherland for us is there whence we have come' and indeed where we always are. But to arrive where we were, are, and will always be requires 'a new manner of seeing' through which 'remaining here you have ascended aloft'.[12] Remaining in the senses while having ascended above them in the company of reason marks for Plotinus the negotiation between aisthesis and ascesis or 'new way of seeing', the view from Philo's brazen serpent. It may be figured as the home of diaspora – the Egypt of the body that is to be abandoned, the desert the site of the body's errancy and the promised land where the body has always been.

These fragmentary analyses of the Alexandrian aesthetic have brought out two salient characteristics. The first is a concern with troping – with movements and turns, ascents and descents, departures and arrivals – that make dynamic the relationship between sense and reason and complicate the temporality of the aesthetic. The second is a preoccupation with pleasure, and in particular with its distribution between the pleasures of the senses and those of the senses accompanied by reason. The figure of the two serpents or the account of the discovery of the idea in matter and the senses respects the mutual implication of ascesis and aisthesis. Neither dominates the other. What holds for the classical statement of the Alexandrian aesthetic holds also for its modern expressions. Both characteristics define the work of the two main Alexandrian modernists – Giuseppe Ungaretti and C. P. Cavafy – Alexandrian authors of diasporic oeuvres subsequently claimed by the Italian and Greek national traditions that respect the mutual implication of ascesis and aisthesis, the one departing from the standpoint of the trope, the exodus pattern or procession, the other from the standpoint of the doubling of pleasure achieved through unrepentant retrospection, a turn that converts the pleasures of the senses not into a pillar of salt but into the pleasures of the soul. Both are Alexandrian, with Ungaretti writing from the strange time of simultaneously being at home, in exile and returning, and Cavafy from the time of recollection that returns to scenes of earlier passion, but always in the company of reason, never to condemn but through art to relive and in some way perpetuate them.

Ungaretti's poetics of diaspora

Giuseppe Ungaretti was born in Alexandria in 1888 to Italian parents who ran a bakery in a suburb of the city. In 1912 he left Egypt for Paris, where he studied with Bergson and frequented the circles of avant-garde painters and poets. With the outbreak of the First World War he moved to Milan and was mobilised in 1915. His first collection of poems, *Il porto sepolto*, was published in 1916, republished with amendments in 1919 as *Allegria di Naufragi*, then with more amendments as *Allegria* in 1931 and 1936, and in a final version for the collected works *Vita d'un uomo: poesie i L'Allegria 1914–19*. This first collection comprises poems 1914–19 that confront the poet's Alexandrian childhood with his experience of metropolitan modernity and modernism, above all with the experience of mechanised trench warfare.

Ungaretti begins the 'Nota introduttiva' that accompanies his collected works, *Vita d'un uomo: Tutte le poesie*, with a commentary on his poem 'Eternity' that, like a manifesto, opens *L'Allegria*: 'From a flower picked to the other given inexpressible nothing'.[13] Ungaretti's own commentary identifies this poem as an allegory of Alexandria. The commentary identifies in 'nothing' and 'eternity' the 'constant destruction produced by time', an experience that is not abstract, but linked inseparably to Alexandria:

> Alexandria is in the desert, in a desert in which life is more intense than the time of its foundation, but where life does not leave any trace of permanence in time. Alexandria is a city without a monument, or better with hardly a monument to recall its ancient past. It changes incessantly. Time carries it away, at all times. It is a city where the sense of time, of destructive time is present to the imagination before everything and above all.[14]

Yet this intense and specific childhood experience of transience – the city disintegrating into the desert of time or submerged in its sea (*Il porto sepolto* was Ungaretti's first title for the collection[15]) – is extended to the condition of modernity. Speaking specifically of *L'Allegria,* Ungaretti carefully claimed that this experience of temporal and spatial transience 'Does not just concern philosophy, it concerns a concrete experience from a childhood passed in Alexandria and necessarily intensified, embittered, deepened and crowned by the 1914–1918 war'.[16] Yet this experience was complex: it involved not just the melancholy 'constant recall of death' provoked by the 'annihilating landscape' of the desert[17] (although this is nevertheless a vital moment) but also that of exhilaration before the open horizon of the sea and the promise of adventure that it seemed to offer. Alexandria is for him the port between past and future, death and life, hovering like a mirage between them both.

The poems of *L'Allegria* speak of the city from the standpoint of both the desert and the sea, from the standpoint of death and fear of loss and of desire and love for the future, not that these are strictly separable in Alexandria. In his prose commentary on 'Eternity' Ungaretti describes this ambiguity in terms of the nothing that is death and the desire of love that is life, but remaining alert to the possibility of mirages – whether of life or death – a suspicion that he shares with fellow Alexandrian Cavafy: 'I am from Egyptian Alexandria: other oriental places may have the "Thousand and One Nights," Alexandria has the desert, has the night, has the nothing, has mirages, the bare imaginary that falls hopelessly in love and causes to sing in a way without voice.'[18] This song without voice – Ungaretti repeatedly evokes the call of the city watchman at night *uahed* – which turns its back upon both desert and sea is also the voice of a war poet for whom the exterminating landscapes of childhood have become the entirely modern landscape of trench warfare. The child's experience of Alexandria is completely compatible with the adult's destructive experience of metropolitan modernity. The voiceless songs of *L'Allegria 1914–1919* thus weave together the memories of an Alexandrian childhood with the violent experience of trench warfare. Yet in this major work of North African/European modernism, the aesthetics of childhood memory and the violent discipline of warfare are not kept apart, but drift into proximity through the simultaneously destructive and redemptive figure of Alexandria. The pivot of the movement between memory and hope is located in the omnipresence of death – allegorical insofar as the death that is omnipresent itself dies in Alexandria – confirming Benjamin's description of the saving irony of allegory – its total destructive movement turning back upon itself – total negation negating itself. (Cavafy makes a similar turn with love and the repetition of desire.) Out of the extreme experience of transience and the proximity of death figured in desert and the trench, emerges hope for the future – the sea or peace. Alexandrian troping forever insinuates hope into despair and despair into hope – Egypt is the exile is the desert is the promised land.

The parallels that Ungaretti draws between Alexandria and the landscape of modern warfare are most evident in the earlier versions of *L'Allegria*. The changes between the early and the later editions indicate an attempt to make less explicit the local, Alexandrian specificity of the collection, most notably in the suppression of one section, 'The Panorama of Alexandria of Egypt', and the reassignment of its poems under the more generic title 'L'Ultime'.[19] The transition from Alexandria to Europe and modernity – which was also the departure from the home that was already itself part of the Italian diaspora – is the subject of the pivotal poem 'Levant'. The liminal character of this poem is evident in its internal windings and unfinishable state, testified by radical changes it underwent between 1915 and 1942. In all its complex and often baffling windings the poem presents an epitome of Ungaretti's Alexandrian aesthetic and its translation into modernity and modernism:

> *Levant*
>
> The line
> dies vaporously
> on the distant circle of the sky
>
> Clicking of heels, clapping of hands
> and the clarinet's arabesque squawk
> and the sea is ashen grey
> trembles softly troubled
> like a pigeon
>
> In the poop Syrian emigrants are dancing
>
> In the prow a youth is alone
>
> On Saturday night at this time
> Jews
> down there
> carry away
> their dead

in the spiralling funnel
swaying
of alleys
of lights

turbulent water
like the noise of the poop that I hear
in the shadow
of
sleep[20]

The poem has a complicated genesis, the definitive version under the title 'Levant'
appearing in the 1942 edition. Before this it appeared under the title 'Mist', which
was itself a revision, in 1919, of a rather different poem 'The Supplicants' published
in the Florentine journal *Lacerba* in 1915 and absent from *Il porto sepolto*. The final
version is the outcome of a sustained process of distillation that, beginning with an
inelegant autobiographical account of a voyage shared with emigrants, was transformed into a magnificent meditation upon migration, death and commemoration.

'Levant' is structured in terms of a procession, with the voice located on a ship
moving slowly away, leaving Alexandria. It seems to speak from the point or at the
moment – the poem is literally at sea in the gloaming – when the last trace of the city
dips below the horizon and finally disappears, from vision if not from memory.[21] The
ambiguous mood of the poem – retrospective and prospective – is already set with
respect to the line that 'dies vaporously' on the distant circle of the sky. It is left open
whether this is a horizontal line – the mist surrounding the distant city which with
distance resolves into a misty blur on the line of the horizon, about to merge with it
and disappear – or the vertical plume of steam from the ship's funnel which is dispersed in the distant circle of the heavens.[22] Whichever it is, or even, most likely, if it
is both, there is no doubt that the vaporised lines die on the distant circle (horizontal
and/or vertical) of the sky. (Indeed, *morire* ('to die') is the first verb of the poem).[23]
The vapour itself does not escape ambiguity, serving as a figure of life – breath – as
well as a figure for the dissolution of liquid into its constituent drops that is inversely
analogous with the sand of the desert, whose pulverised and pulverising grains are
associated by Ungaretti with disintegration and death.

The liquid states evoked in the poem shift drastically in the course of the action,
moving from the opening vapour to the ashen expanse of the swelling sea and ending
with the turbulence left by the ship's propellers. Associated with these different liquid
states is a movement in the place of the narrated gaze, from the stern to the poop to
the bows of the ship and then again back to the stern. The shifts in viewpoint are
accompanied by shifts in affect that can be indicated in a preliminary way by cataloguing the very few verbs that follow 'to die': 'squawk', 'tremble', 'dance', 'carry away'
and 'hear'. These verbs swirl around to form a figure of movement and death and help
identify the poem as itself a funeral procession, with all the complex affects associated
with carrying away the dead.[24] The ambiguity surrounding what it is that dies by
being reduced to vapour is thus compounded by the spectral movement of the voice

and point of view around the ship. If the opening line is oriented vertically, the ship's smoke rising into the sky, then the voice of the first half of the poem can be located in the bows – looking up, then looking back at the dancing emigrants, and then, via the memory of the Jewish funeral processions, moving to the stern. If the opening line is oriented horizontally as the vaporous dissolution of a now distant Alexandria, then the voice begins to speak in the stern, is interrupted by the dancing emigrants, then speaks from the prow and then again from the stern. In both cases the movements are complex, even more so if they are combined, for then the viewpoint is simultaneously oriented forward and up and backwards and down – establishing a spiral form whose presence is enforced by the many explicit references in the poem to spirals – the clarinet's arabesque howl, the spiralling alleys of Alexandria and the spiral of turbulence left in the ship's wake. The viewpoint and place of utterance is unstable, even in terms of its movements around the ship itself let alone when oriented with respect to the ship's movements between points of departure and destination. There is also a suggestion, amplified by the reference to the Jewish funeral procession and the intimated parallel between the ship and a coffin, that the entire poem may be a view of the funeral procession from the standpoint of the ghost of the corpse.

The meditative gaze, whether back to the city or up to the dying plume of steam and smoke, is suddenly interrupted by the sound of music and dancing. The reverie is rudely interrupted by revelry, by the clicking of heels and the clapping of hands and the squawk of the clarinet coming from what are subsequently identified as emigrants dancing in the poop to celebrate their passage, which is, of course, from their past to their future.[25] But the elation of the dance is immediately modulated by a literal undertow; the dancing on the ship is countered by the soft tremor of the ashen sea. The implausible likeness of the sea to a pigeon is ostensibly motivated by their shared characteristic of colour – greyness – and the likeness between the tremor of the pigeon's breast and the gentle waves of the Mediterranean. Yet there are less obvious aspects of the metaphor that become apparent in the variants. The earlier versions have the sea 'gently trembling' ('trema dolce') like restless pigeons whose breasts are swollen by a 'loving wave' ('d'onda amorosa'), thus likening pigeons to the sea and the sea to pigeons. Both, it seems to be suggested, bear witness to an almost cosmic pulse of desire and love that runs through them. But there is also another aspect to this wave that is evident in an earlier poem from 1915 published in *Lacerba*: 'Il paessagio d'Alessandria d'Egitto' ('The landscape of Alexandria of Egypt'), in which the swelling chest of the pigeon is likened to the song of the 'fella' – the ululation or song without voice of the desert. This invests the seascape with desire, establishing a link between the gentle swelling of the waves, the swelling of the breast of the pigeon and the song without voice of the desert and, finally, of the poem itself. This song 'without voice' underlies the swell of the waves and establishes an immediate contrast with the raucous music of the emigrants, a discord which is resolved in the poem through the suggestion that both musics give voice to nostalgia for what has been lost and longing for what is to come.

The encounter of the two songs – the sombre music of the sea and the raucous music of the emigrants (the inseparable songs of death and life) – coincides with the translation of the poetic voice from the stern to the prow of the ship – 'At the prow a young man is alone'. (Ungaretti later commented ironically, 'It is of course me'.) In the 1931 version he is to be found leaning on the railings and 'looking like a shadow', emphasising a little too bluntly the questionable presence/absence of this figure who managed to survive the otherwise radical editing of the poem. But although in the forward position, at the cutting edge of the ship, which it may be recalled is also the position Mallarmé ironically yields to his younger contemporaries in his toast to the avant-garde *Salut*, the young man is sunk in retrospection, remembering the Jewish funeral processions (in which, Ungaretti noted, 'I assisted in Alexandria'[26]).

The memory of the Jewish funeral processions drives the poetic spiral that begins with death and moves through song to end in turbulence. It is also the matrix of the poem, the original experience that fuelled the intense process of condensation that issued in the final poem. Indeed, the final and definitive 1942 title of the poem – 'Levant' – refers back to the description of the Jewish funeral processions in the 1915 and 1919 'versions'.[27] The 1915 poem 'Supplicants' that would mutate into 'Mist' and finally 'Levant' is greatly indebted to Apollinaire's 'Zone' for its structure, and at one point in its autobiographical narrative evokes an intense shipboard experience of light and colour in the fog:

> Those covers of rough material
> that the Jews of the Levant use
> carrying away their dead on a Saturday night[28]

The memory of the Jewish funeral processions is thus borne into the poem by the colour of the fabric; the lemon yellow evokes the memory of the 'coperto di crespo' used by the Jews of the Levant in their funeral processions. This almost incidental evocation of the memory serves as an illustration of chromatic intensity and provokes powerful consequences even for the 1915 poem, let alone its subsequent incarnations. In 1915 the autobiographical improvisation slips into a sombre key. The entry of death and the funeral procession causes the sky almost to touch the earth and underlines the finality of the departure from Alexandria.

In the 1919 version, the memory of the Jewish funeral procession has been divested of its role as chromatic simile, appearing now as a verse in its own right. The residual reference to colour, 'nothing can be seen / except the swaying / of light / covered in *crespo*', is evident only in the reference to crespo. This will persist into the 1931 version but by 1942 has completely disappeared. In all the versions from 1919 onwards, the only colour to survive the chromaticism of the first version is grey. At the same time as the colour fades into the fog and out of the poem, the reference to the Jews changes its geographical character. The reference to 'Jews of the Levant' is carried over into the 1919 version but is thereafter replaced by 'Jews down there' ('ebrei laggiu'), referring specifically to the Jews of Alexandria and situating their processions in the winding alleys of that city.

The memory of the funeral procession becomes increasingly insistent, forming the gyre of the poetic spiral. Its original motivation as a chromatic simile is already succeeded in the second version of 1919 and in all subsequent versions by an explicit tem-poral parallel – 'On Saturday night at this time'. The time of the poem and the time of the funeral procession are thus linked, not accidentally but structurally. At the same time as the Jews carry away their dead in Alexandria, the poet is carried away in a ship from Alexandria. The elation of a voyage to a new life expressed in the songs and dancing of the emigrants is not shared by the poet. In a typical Alexandrian trope, the voyage to the future is likened to the last journey of the dead to their graves. The sea is ash and bears on its back a ship/coffin.

The poem ends with a parallel between the labyrinthine streets of Alexandria through which the dead are carried on the shoulders of the living and the labyrinthine turbulence – the *confusa acqua* – of the sea. The poem exemplifies the complex trop-ings of the Alexandrian aesthetic, combining a number of progressive and regressive movements, locating Egypt, the desert and the promised land with the Alexandria that has been left behind. The movements traced by this poem are almost dizzying in their complexity. The linear movement of the ship away from the port of Alexandria across the Mediterranean to Genova – from past to future – is qualified by the undulating movement of the waves and the allegorical correspondence between the ship on the sea and the coffin bobbing on the shoulders of the mourners in Alexandria. The journey in a straight line across the sea is also a journey between an African past and a European future, but one in which the voyager is already dead. Then there is the movement of the dancers, the emigrants who, borne by the movements of the boat ahead and up and down, dance patterns within it. This is opposed to the shadow in the bows who seems passive, but of course is himself in motion. For in the course of the poem he moves between stern and prow, between retrospect and prospect, from looking back to looking forward, from waking to sleep. All in a tumble of movements figured in the final turbulence that is the response to the vaporisation of death that opens the poem.

Ungaretti's 'Levant' may be read as an allegorical evocation of Alexandria as the allegorical city. The attempt to move away from the city that figures destruction and death for this poet brings this experience with it. The attempt to leave the movement of destruction only translates it into the diaspora. The complex tropings of this and other poems in *L'Allegria* make this collection a work of scattering and recollection. It is the complex movements that make this work diasporic. In it there is no home, no point of rest – even the ship provides a site for restlessness. The ship leaving the city becomes a fixed point around which everything else moves – as does the coffin on the shoulders of the mourners, the dead body replete with significance for being empty of it.

'apo ten polu anome edone' – Cavafy's dates

If Ungaretti's Alexandrian poems consummately explore the complex movements of exile, homelessness and return that are central to the Alexandrian aesthetic, those of his fellow Alexandrian C. P. Cavafy focus on the aspect of pleasure and its embalm-ment in art. Although born in Alexandria, Cavafy spent much of his childhood in

England and wrote his first poetic work in English. However, there is no nostalgia for England comparable to Ungaretti's nostalgia for Alexandria, and Cavafy's work in Greek focuses largely on the pleasures and regrets of the city of Alexandria where he spent all of his adult life.

Cavafy's work presents an intense exploration of the intrication of ascesis and aestheis but one which, unlike in Ungaretti, is not projected upon the city as the coffin/ship bearing within it the destruction of past and future, but rather on the city as a desired body and especially on the desired bodies of some of the city's inhabitants. His preoccupation with incarnation – in all its guises – takes the form of a series of allegories of pleasure, usually framed in terms of recollection of sexual pleasure, or rather more frequently, regret at missed opportunities for it. Pleasure in Cavafy has always already happened or not-happened, or is about to happen or not-happen. The poem 'In the Street' has the artistic-looking youth drifting aimlessly 'as though still hypnotised by the illicit pleasure, / the very illicit pleasure that he's just experienced'.[29] The poetic is not the anomalous pleasure, but the hypnotic even anaesthetised state that succeeds it, its recollection and repeated transformation into something new. Cavafy's work exemplifies the movement between Philo's two serpents – the Egyptian serpent of sensible pleasure and the brazen serpent that recollects it, from the sexual desert of the present to the promised land of pleasure that has already happened and had seemed to have been lost for ever.

Yet Cavafy's work should not be mistaken as the lyrical cameo to Ungaretti's Alexandrian epic of exile and impossible return. His lyrical introspection is deliberately untrustworthy, cast within a strategy of adopting personae that marks one of the more astonishing developments of the legacy of Robert Browning. This is evident above all in his constant resort to seemingly precise but not entirely reliable dates. While Ungaretti fixes a moment and a place – twilight at sea – Cavafy cites a date. The date fuses the persona and the lyrical, and becomes one of Cavafy's preferred means to transform occasions of real or imagined sexual pleasure into the brazen serpent of disinterested art.

Cavafy's work is consistently Alexandrian in its preoccupation with processions, but his are not the funeral processions remembered by Ungaretti, but the processions of lovers – all combining the sensual and the ideal, but not by any means adding up to a progression. In retrospect he too sees no line but a turbulent procession through the winding byways of desire. In this unruly procession of rough trade mingled with sensitive aesthetes it is the precise memory of dates that offers a common denominator and allows the procession to adopt a tangible shape. The dates are a turning to the past that transforms it, a pagan repentance that turns past pleasures and missed pleasures of the senses into pleasures of the soul.

Such a transformation is evident in an undeclared series of poems scattered through Cavafy's oeuvre – the five 'days of' poems: 'The Days of 1903' written in March 1909 and published in 1917[30]; 'The Days of 1908' written in July 1921 and published in 1932; 'The Days of 1896' written in 1925 and published in 1927; 'The Days of 1901' published in 1927 and finally 'The Days of 1909, '10 and '11' published in 1928. The ironically nostalgic formula 'The Days of . . .' conceals a complex

relationship between the past and the present, one that is governed first of all by a
queer aesthetic of the concealment and revelation of homosexual pleasure and then
by an Alexandrian aesthetic similar to Ungaretti's of a complex trope that brings past
experience – in this case homosexual pleasure – into the present and transforms it
from a pleasure of the senses to a pleasure of the soul. It marks the return or even the
redemption of an exiled sexuality to the promised land that it passed by because dis-
tracted by convention – 'society / totally narrow minded, had all its values wrong'.[31]

The trope of turning to the past that informs the series is inaugurated in a pair of
early dated poems from 1903 that remained unpublished during Cavafy's lifetime.
Although they do not use the formula 'Days of . . .' their complex temporal structure
and shifts in mood anticipate the act of recollection that informs the other poems of
the series. As inaugural poems of the series they present more visibly the complexity
of the poetic act that is performed in the later poems.

'September 1903' is made up of three verses, one of two lines, one of five and
one of four. Within these Cavafy employs a complex metrical pattern of 13-11,
12-12-11-12-12 and 11-12-13-11[32] that serves to reinforce the use of repetition in
the poem, but also qualitatively to distinguish between the repetitions. This distinction between repetitions reveals the transformation of the experience by the act of recollection.

> *September 1903*
>
> At least let me now deceive myself with illusions
> so as not to feel my empty life.
>
> And yet I came so close so many times.
> And yet how paralyzed I was, how cowardly;
> why did I keep my lips sealed
> while my empty life wept inside me,
> my desires wore robes of mourning?
>
> To have been so close so many times
> to those sensual eyes, those lips,
> to that body I dreamed of, loved-
> so close so many times.[33]

The poem begins by locating itself in a present 'empty life' the feelings of which may
be anaesthetised by self-deception through illusions. However, the second verse does
not present an illusion, but a state of disillusion. It is in the form of a question, beginning with a statement of regret that announces the first of the poem's many repetitions, here of the formula 'And yet' – 'And yet I came so close so many times' 'And yet
how paralyzed I was, how cowardly'. The incantation of 'And yet' prefaces two lines
of twelve syllables which, far from evoking a consoling illusion, present the very
feeling of regret that would seem to make up 'my empty life'.

The experience of the 'empty life' of regret is intensified by the question 'why did
I keep my lips sealed / while my empty life wept inside me, / my desires wore robes of
mourning?' Here a level of ambiguity sets in that begins to transform the anaesthesia

of the empty life into something more vital. In what sense are these lips sealed – are they silent or did they deny a kiss to the lover, or both? The empty life of regret in the present is subtly located in the past as the cause of the experience of regret. The emptiness in the present of then not having spoken or opened the lips to the lover is the cause of present not speaking. The weeping empty life of then – the past – becomes the empty life of the present. And yet, at this point another ambiguity emerges around the way in which the question is framed: is it 'why did I keep my lips sealed' followed by the suggestion of two answers 'while my empty life wept inside me, my desires wore robes of mourning'; or is it a rhetorical question, 'why did I keep my lips sealed / while my empty life wept inside me' with the answer '[because] my desires wore robes of mourning'? The metrical pattern of 11-12-12 is neutral, but the implications of the ambiguity are considerable. In the first, the tears of the empty life and the mourning desire are the same, while in the second, the silence and refused kiss as well as the weeping empty life arise from nursing 'desires in robes of mourning'.

The second position seems marginally endorsed by the final stanza where the mourned, but also 'dreamed of' body was indeed loved – but 'loved-' with a typographically striking dash on love- (to be repeated and made the subject of the companion poem 'December, 1903'). The dash leaves open the question of whether the dreamed of body was enjoyed or loved in being mourned and dreamed of. The question of mourning and the dream is here put in terms of the desired body. What loss are these desires mourning? How is it that a desire, oriented towards future enjoyment and fulfilment, should already be mourning the loss of the desired object? Is the object of desire then impossible – unattainable within human time – or is it that the fulfilment of the desire discharges it? The latter case makes sense of the movement of this poem, in which the pleasure of the desired, enjoyed and rejected body, a pleasure unambiguously of the senses, is transformed into another kind of pleasure enjoyed in a different kind of time.

This is confirmed by the main structural feature of 'September 1903', namely repetition, a trope associated by Walter Benjamin with allegory. This concerns not only the repetitions of 'empty life' and 'And yet' – the first temporally ambiguous (the link between the empty lives of the present and the past), the second a formal repetition – but most significantly the repetition of the phrase 'so close so many times'. The phrase, which is itself about repetition, changes meaning through its repetitions and emerges as the site for the transformation of the pleasure. The first statement of it is preceded by 'And yet I came' which gives 'so close, so many times' the sense of an opportunity repeatedly missed, a repeated approach that never arrived. The first repetition of the phrase, however, finds it changed: at the beginning of the third verse 'To have been so close so many times' suggests regret, but then this is changed by what follows – for 'To have been so close so many times / to those sensual eyes, those lips, / to that body I dreamed of, loved-' is a memory of fulfilment, a repeated act of love with the beloved whose absence now is the cause of the empty life. The second verse in retrospect (we have turned and are looking back in almost the same way as Ungaretti in the boat leaving Alexandria) is regret not for unfulfilled desire but for a desire that was fulfilled, was repeated, but not repeatable to eternity. The latter is accomplished in the final line and final repetition of the poem. The past perfect tense of 'To have been so close so many times' becomes, after 'loved-' the continuous present -'so close, so many times'. Repeated to eternity. In this the moment of pleasure is perpetuated, and ceases to be a finite encounter or pleasure of the senses and becomes an infinite pleasure of the soul. The repetition of repetition, rather like the Hegelian negation of the negation, thus becomes something different, something new.

But then, maybe it is this continuous present of repeated, recollected pleasure that is the deceptive illusion. The repetition is the illusion, and was always. And perhaps it is the desire to repeat that is the mourning desire – repetition can never be accomplished and so is lost. What is crucial in any decision about the redemptive potential of repetition now emerges as the meaning of 'love-', the theme which is explored in the companion poem 'December 1903':

December 1903

And if I can't speak about my love-
And if I don't talk about your hair, your lips, your eyes,
still your face that I keep within my heart,
the sound of your voice that I keep within my mind,
the days of September rising in my dreams,
give shape and colour to my words, my sentences,
whatever theme I touch, whatever thought I utter.[34]

Set two months after the despair of September and its consoling illusion of repeated repetition, 'December 1903' proposes another solution, although perhaps it will turn out to be another deceptive illusion. The sealed lips lamented in September are now granted an allegorical reversal, a movement whose authority is reinforced by setting the argument within one verse, thus reducing the uncertainty provoked by the breaks in thought between the verses in 'September 1903', but even more so by beginning with a metrical falter of 12-17 and then proceeding with a remorseless catena of lines of 15-15-15-15-15 syllables. The attempt continually to repeat the feeling of the proximity of the lover's body – that feeling of repetition in the continuous present that would overcome the feeling of the empty life – is abandoned in the first two lines. Employing an ascetic trope from negative theology, the inability to open his lips and to speak the lover's attributes is no longer a cause of suffering and emptiness. By ascetically denying speech, in not speaking 'about my love-', not speaking about his hair, lips and eyes (according to the December catalogue – September evoked his eyes, lips and body), the silence is no longer born of despair, but of excess. The 'love-' which cannot be spoken, both the beloved and the feeling of love itself, far from being absent and an object of mourning, now becomes omnipresent – it is everywhere and in every time. The ascetic denial of the lover, the refusal of the alleviations offered by continuous repetition in September, provoke the allegorical reversal or turn that allows the lover to fill the 'empty life' of the present.

In December, the pleasure of the soul is achieved not by the repetition of love in an eternal present, but by acknowledging its omnipresence. If the lover's attributes cannot be spoken, nevertheless, and here begins the chain of fifteen-syllable allegorical lines, his face is kept in the heart, his voice in the mind, and the days of September in dreams. The lover is totally present – in passion (in the heart), in reason (in the mind) and in desire (dreams). As such his attributes cannot be analysed or felt, because they are the condition of all acts of feeling, reason and desire. The ubiquity of the lover is evident not in the object of words and sentences but in their 'shape and colour' – it informs 'whatever theme I touch, whatever thought I utter'. The latter is both a description and a promise, a declaration of fidelity that goes beyond a particular beloved and becomes a condition for life. It is an experience that in another, religious context might be described as the turn of 'repentance' – a looking back that does not provoke the despair of being chained to repetition.

Postscript

To a certain degree the work of Ungaretti and Cavafy continues to be troubled and shaped by a series of preoccupations that were already evident in classical Alexandrian aesthetics. These preoccupations inhabit the margins of the modern aesthetic – they mark a diversion of the attempt to reduce the pleasures of sensibility to the ascesis of reason that has characterised aesthetics since Baumgarten. However, they also mark a moment that is latent in varying degrees to the modern aesthetic – Baumgarten and Kant both admit the complexity and the errancy of beauty, its movement that does not necessarily pass from the senses directly to reason, but may take other routes in other company. Similarly with the theme of pleasure and the body; especially for Kant, the question of the relationship between interested and disinterested pleasure is central and by no means given a single or definitive answer. Finally, the religious undertow of modern aesthetics is rendered explicit and central in the Alexandrian, for which the questions of exile, diaspora and redemption are ineluctable features of the aesthetic. This dimension is evident in work as diverse as that of Ungaretti and Cavafy, both of whom struggle with the questions of exile, loss and redemption. If a conclusion is possible perhaps it should be framed in terms of the wish that these fragments of an Alexandrian aesthetic will, if nothing else, contribute to complicating and hopefully even intensifying the character of the modern aesthetic.

Notes

1 Dionysius of Alexandria in *A Dictionary of Early Christian Beliefs*, ed. David W. Bercot (Peabody, MA: Hendrickson Publishers, 1998), p. 8.
2 Cleopatra's needle was itself looted in the first century AD from upper Egypt and remains a strange prefiguration of concept art occupying an extra-territorial, extra-temporal site on the Embankment – lapped by the Thames on three sides it is neither on land nor in water. It is also uncannily without time, dating back millennia to 1475 BC it was brought violently into the Victorian present of 1878 and beached on the Embankment with bronze texts celebrating the achievement of its theft. Buried beneath it are everyday items of nineteenth-century daily life. Overall it gives the disturbing sense of not yet having arrived at its final destination.
3 Most elegantly stated on the opening page of Lawrence Durrell's *Alexandria Quartet*

(London: Faber, 1962): 'Capitally, what is this city of ours? What is resumed in the word "Alexandria"? In a flash my mind's eye draws me a thousand dust-tormented streets. Flies and beggars own it today – and those who enjoy an intermediate existence between either. / Five races, five languages, a dozen creeds: five fleets turning through their greasy reflections behind the harbour bar. But there are more than five sexes and only demotic Greek seems to distinguish between them' (p. 17).

4 Philo, *The Works of Philo*, trans. C. D. Yonge (Hendrickson Publishers, 1997), p. 68.

5 *Ibid.*, p. 45.

6 *Ibid.*

7 *Ibid.*, p. 46.

8 *Ibid.*

9 *Ibid.*

10 Plotinus, *The Six Enneads*, trans. S. MacKenna and B. S. Page (Chicago: Encyclopaedia Britannica Inc., 1952), I, vi, 6.

11 *Ibid.*, I, vi, 9.

12 *Ibid.*

13 G. Ungaretti, *Vita d'un uomo: tutte le poesie*, ed. L. Piccioni (Milano: Oscar Mondadori, 1992), p. 5.

14 *Ibid.*, p. 497.

15 Speaking of the matrix of *Il porto sepolto*, Ungaretti cited Jean and Henri Thuile and their library inherited from their father, out in the desert: 'They spoke to me of a port, of a submerged port, that preceded the Ptolemaic era, proving that Alexandria was a port already before Alexander, that already before Alexandria there was a city. Of which is known nothing. That city of mine consumes and annihilates itself moment by moment. How could we know of its origins if nothing remains even of what happened a moment ago?' (p. 498).

16 *Ibid.*, p. 517.

17 'A sense of death, from the beginning, and surrounded by an annihilating landscape: everything reduced to fragments . . . everything with but a minute duration, everything precarious. I was prey in that landscape, that presence to the reminder, the constant recall of death' (p. 499).

18 *Ibid.*, p. 505.

19 While not wishing to anticipate a later discussion, this seems an apt point at which to mention the poem published in Lacerba in February 1915, 'Il Paesaggio d'Alessandria d'Egitto', not published in *Il porto sepolto*. Contemporary with the other Alexandrian poems and with the first version of 'Levant', it is like them dedicated to producing a 'landscape' or 'panorama' of the city as spatial and temporal mirage.

20 Ungaretti, *Vita d'un uomo*, p. 7.

21 Although the first version, the 1915 'Supplicants', is five nights into the voyage, the later version brings the action back to the night of departure. In the 1919 version the proximity to Alexandria is spelt out ('And we finally lose track of the city / and proceed with the sky above'), as is the nostalgia ('O my hot country I have nostalgia tonight'), an emotion that is even more overwhelming in the final version for not being declaimed.

22 The 1931 variant – published in *popolo* 14 June 1931 – is *vaporosamente muore* 'dies vaporously' (Ungaretti, *Vita d'un uomo*, p. 596) the adverb emphasises, perhaps too bluntly (as in the translation), that death occurs through vaporisation, an observation that is indirectly, mistily, sustained by the adjectival *vaporosa*.

23 Ungaretti also suggests an archaic sense of *morire*, namely to extinguish.

24 The importance of the figure of the funeral procession for Ungaretti will become apparent below – it is a figure that recurs in his work, most poignantly in his elegy for Moammed Sceab, who committed suicide in Paris ('In Memoria', Ungaretti, *Vita d'un uomo*, pp. 21–2). There are few comparable poems in the European tradition, even in the European modernist tradition, devoted to the sufferings of the immigrants to the European metropolises – 'He was called / Moammed Sceab / Descended / from nomadic emirs, committed suicide, because he no longer had a country . . .'.

25 In 'Supplicants' the noisy everyday presence of the emigrant families is emphasised over their dancing and their music, as is a reference to the cold mist – 'faceva fredo' – that survived into the 1919 version, where the ambient noise of children and their mothers has been silenced, but where the music is that of a 'piffero' rather than the raucous clarinets of the final version.

26 Ungaretti, *Vita d'un uomo*, p. 519.

27 I can only speculate on Ungaretti's motives in choosing this title in 1942, especially given that a version of the poem under the title 'Mist' was published in the fascist *popolo* in 1931.

28 Ungaretti, *Vita d'un uomo*, p. 354.

29 C. P. Cavafy, *Collected Poems*, trans. E. Keeley and P. Sherrard (London: Chatto & Windus, 1998), p. 48, lines 7–8.

30 It is perhaps indicative of the complexity of the memorial strategy employed in the series that the 'Days of 1903' was originally entitled 'Days of 1907' – what is important is not the actual date but the fact that the experiences are datable.

31 'Days of 1896', Cavafy, *Vita d'un uomo*, p. 105, lines 21–2.

32 For descriptions of the Greek metrical patterns adopted by Cavafy, see Keeley and Sherrard, p. 190.

33 Cavafy, p. 138.

34 *Ibid.*, p. 139.

Defending poetry, or, is there an early modern aesthetic?

Is there an early modern aesthetic?

Or, better:

What does one call the space currently occupied by aesthetics before aesthetics emerges?

This question appears within the space occupied by what has become known in certain literary-critical circles as the *early modern* period, broadly defined as 1500–1700.[1] Formulation of the idea of the early modern can be taken as an exemplary moment in the permeation of a 'new' historicism through literary studies since the early 1980s, most obviously through the twin historicisms of cultural materialism and cultural poetics (or 'new historicism').[2] The periodising title *early modern* is part of a movement away from notions such as 'the English Renaissance' or from 'the Tudor period', although such names are retained by some of historicism's adherents.[3] That the emergence of the phrase 'early modern' seems to mark a strategic attempt to delineate what otherwise appears to be a depressingly familiar ramification of what I suppose we must now term 'old' historicism doesn't diminish its institutional effectivity.[4]

One area that has created concerns about the new historicist project is its treatment of aesthetics. 'Cultural poetics', previously Stephen Greenblatt's preferred term for his form of criticism, makes clear the expansion of 'poetics' into a domain that is no longer strictly associated with 'poetry' (widely conceived).[5] Aesthetics has been expanded as a term within new historicist discourse to encompass any form of symbolic interaction that is susceptible to (literary-) critical analysis. As Catherine Gallagher and Greenblatt have argued:

> In the analysis of the larger cultural field, canonical works of art are brought into relation not only with works judged as minor, but also with texts that are not by anyone's standard literary. The conjunction can produce almost surrealist wonder at the revelation of an unanticipated aesthetic dimension in objects without pretensions to the aesthetic.[6]

This sense of wonder is crucial to Greenblatt's (and Gallagher's) project.[7] Eschewing theoretical formulations, new historicism favours an attention to 'particularity' over what is considered to be the universalising impulse of more rigorously delineated critical projects.[8] Thus the readings of 'social energies' produced, encompassing objects and practices that are not bounded by an aesthetics that takes art as its focus, deliberately offer no systematic place for the aesthetic.[9] Part of the reasoning behind this is a desire to avoid falling back into a conservative notion of the 'special' quality of art in which, as Gallagher and Greenblatt put it, 'The rest of human life can only gaze longingly at the condition of the art object, which is the manifestation of unalienated labour, the perfect articulation and realization of human energy'.[10] Certainly such an aesthetic idealism does not seem to offer a fruitful avenue for enquiry. But does a more narrow conception of the aesthetic than that offered by new historicism necessarily entail such a vision of unity, lack of alienation and perfection? Part of the purpose of this essay is to suggest that this form of idealism was always an illusion, but that this does not mean that it can so easily be dismissed.

Tellingly, in the narrative given in *Practicing New Historicism,* one of the main impulses behind the authors' approach comes not from within early modern culture, but instead from Herder.[11] Thus new historicism locates itself within the ambit of German Romanticism/Idealism and its inheritances, seeking to read the early modern in terms of an aesthetic that is post-Kantian (although not Kantian) rather than being itself early modern. This should not be surprising. Indeed, new historicist discourse frequently foregrounds its imbrication with present concerns, but tends to be selective about what those concerns are.[12] So while it would not be possible simply to avoid the impact of a modern notion of aesthetics on contemporary critical practices, it is worth giving further consideration both to the relationship between modernity and *early* modernity, and to the role of the aesthetic within modernity itself. It will then be possible to look to an early modern text on the role and functions of art, Sidney's *A Defence of Poetry*, in order to begin to address more fully my opening question.

Hugh Grady has been one of the most consistently interested critics of recent years in the modernity of the early modern, and in a series of books he has focused his work on Shakespeare.[13] As Grady has pointed out, however, the term *early modern* has itself been employed with a certain degree of ambivalence:

> Widespread use of the term *early modern* expresses much of the ambiguity [around the question of Shakespeare's modernity] by positing both continuity and difference: the era is part of modernity but it's 'early' modernity. While Stephen Greenblatt has called for something like a revival of Burckhardt's idea of Renaissance modernity, critics such as Catherine Belsey and Jonathan Dollimore have followed T. S. Eliot, making of the Renaissance a premodern transitional age in which discourses from an earlier medieval mentality overlap newer ones from the Age of Absolutism and an embryonic modernity.[14]

Leaning more towards what he identifies as Greenblatt's view, Grady suggests that rather than seeing Shakespeare (who here almost seems to stand in for the early modern *tout court*) as caught between a residual medieval position and a modern humanistic one (a view which he sees particularly in Belsey's work), it is possible 'that Shakespeare was working from a mentality that was specific to his own phase of early modernity'.[15] One aspect of the problem is that the term *early modern* is a slippery and ill-defined one for the most part, especially in its relation to the modern, and consequently in different contexts '*modern* and *early modern* overlap and compete with each other'.[16] When Grady comes to discuss his sense of Shakespeare's modernity in this essay, he provides a familiar set of characteristics which he wishes to call modern: instrumental reason, power and autonomous subjectivity. Any philosophical notion of aesthetics becomes submerged in talk of the effects of a 'postmodern' aesthetic of discontinuity, and Shakespeare emerges as 'distant enough from modernity to be its critic, implicated in its logic and dynamics enough to speak to us of its unfulfilled possibilities'.[17] The aesthetic here, then, is almost entirely negative. It is seen to be part of a modernity that it is not significant in shaping in conceptual terms, and its role for Grady is as a marker of critical distance and a reminder of *unfulfilled* possibilities. What of the possibilities that were fulfilled? They are seemingly not Grady's concern. For Grady, then, the early modern (as Shakespeare) is not modern, but it remains modern enough to be recognisable in its differences from modernity. This is plausible enough, since anything that was *absolutely* different would be unrecognisable. It seems clear, though, that Grady's ambivalence to the term *early modern* hinges on a concept of the early modern that is itself ambivalent. Further, what lies behind this is a more deep-seated ambivalence towards modernity itself. Grady's attempt to find a 'mentality' specific to the early modern period, rather than one defined as between the modern and the medieval, should suggest that we look more closely at what lies within both modern and early modern aesthetic discourses.

Aesthetics and modernity

To repeat: *What does one call the space currently occupied by aesthetics before aesthetics emerges?* Let me recall what prompted me to consider such a question in the first place. In part, I was motivated by a series of concerns about definitions of modernity that necessarily impact upon the emergence of the idea of the early modern. Reading *The Fate of Art*, Jay Bernstein offered what seemed in many respects to be a compelling delineation of modernity, which Bernstein sees as beginning with the Kantian critical project, remarking that 'it is Kant's third *Critique* that attempts to generate, to carve out and constitute, the domain of the aesthetic in its wholly modern signification'.[18] We have to begin with this wholly modern signification. Outlining Kant's attempt to separate the categories in the process of delimiting pure and practical reason, and thus to establish a division of art from truth and goodness that persists in the notion of autonomous art, Bernstein notes the crucial role that aesthetics plays in the articulation of Kant's critical philosophy as a whole. Indeed, the question of philosophical aesthetics is the question of philosophy as system. For Kant, as for Hegel, the role of the aesthetic is crucial to the elaboration of a systematic critical project, that is, for the possibility of the closure of this thought as system. The aesthetic, then, is not something to be added to philosophy, nor is it simply one branch of philosophy among others. It is, rather, that which allows for a crucial step in philosophy's project of completing itself. We might say that a philosophy without aesthetics is not a philosophy, and certainly not a critical philosophy. Equally, we must not think of aesthetics in terms of a category that is separated or separable from this philosophical context, from a context which always conceptualises the aesthetic in relation to (in Kantian terms) theoretical and practical reason.[19]

Reason, then, always provides the framework for the discussion of aesthetics. The context for this post-Romantic 'story' of aesthetics is usefully reconstructed by Andrew Bowie, following Gadamer. In a trajectory which stretches from Kant and Baumgarten through German Idealism to Nietzsche and Schopenhauer, Bowie suggests that the crucial aspect of the story of aesthetics is 'the relationship between competing claims to truth' but that, as Gadamer indicates, 'one cannot presuppose that the nature of the division between philosophy and art can be truly defined by philosophy'.[20] In freeing art from instrumental social functions, German Idealism stresses the role of the imagination in going beyond particular rules of and for art: 'Instead of being conceived of principally in terms of mimesis, representation, or entertainment, art begins to be conceived of in terms of its ability to reveal the world in ways that may not be possible without art.'[21] This is a shift, then, not just in how art is conceived as an object, but also in terms of its functions. The terms which are here being abandoned, such as mimesis and representation, are central to early modern debates about art, and to the classical tradition from which these debates are derived, and I will return to these ideas later. The central thing to note at this point is the connection between art and truth.

The truth offered or revealed by art is the point from which Bernstein begins. The categorial separation of domains in Kant's critical philosophy does not in itself, suggests Bernstein, offer any real problems to those who believe in a notion of enlightened modernity, but it must be related to the parallel move to use aesthetic judgement to prove the underlying unity of reason. This far less successful Kantian move, argues Bernstein, opens the space in which it is possible to read the emergence of the critique of enlightened modernity, since the fragmentation of reason that the categorial separation reveals may be seen to mirror the fragmentation of modernity itself. This establishes a line of critical thought that we might for convenience's sake call Hegelian. From this recognition of the failure of Kant's move in the *Critique of Judgement*, and its consequences for the idea of the autonomous artwork in modernity, Bernstein puts forward his notion of 'aesthetic alienation'.[22] In this alienated form, aesthetics suffers mourning for its separation from reason and morality, and the 'fate' of art of Bernstein's title refers to this alienation from truth. Having stressed the importance of a sense of mourning to modernity, Bernstein reads in the third critique what he calls a 'memorial aesthetics', in which pain is brought together with the experience or production of pleasure. Bernstein cites Kant's own example in the third critique of the possibility of feeling some pleasure in a painful experience, which is that of the mourning widow who simultaneously remembers both her loss and the worth of her dead husband. It is tempting to read the widow as an allegorical figure for the position of the philosopher who wishes to preserve both the critical and systemic ambitions of the critical philosophy.

For Bernstein, the loss of the systematic unity of Kant's critical project is not to be read as a purely negative fall from a rational grace, since the critical element of the project need not be abandoned. To those who would wish to save Kant from his troublingly aporetic reading of the third critique, Bernstein proposes that 'Resistance to the memorialization of aesthetics on the grounds that it destroys the universality of Kant's critical system through the introduction of an essentially aporetic moment, a non-recuperable indeterminacy at the core of determinate reason, is nonetheless misplaced since it ignores the fact that his metaphysics was aporetic from the beginning', adding that 'to ignore the moments of limit and opacity in the critical system is to render it uncritical'.[23] Resistance is, then, misplaced if it is motivated by a desire to preserve an illusory integrity, since the unity for which it offers to stand guard can only be sustained by ignoring the *critical* integrity of the critical system. In other words, to be critical is more important, ultimately, than to be systematic, and clearly any system could only be produced through and as a result of the critical integrity of any rational approach. One way to think through this might be to say that the critical aspect of Kant's project is doubled or enfolded, in that it acts as a form of resistance to its systemic ambitions. It remains necessary to be systematically critical, even if that critical element disrupts the system that it is supposed to guarantee.

It seems pertinent to consider further what relationship Grady's ambivalent periodisation bears to Bernstein's Habermasian characterisation of modernity, and thus to turn again to the question embedded in my title: is there an early modern 'aesthetic'? One of the problems for a historicist attempt to answer this question is that the spectre of anachronism is involved here, not least because it is well accepted that the term 'aesthetics' itself is first used by Baumgarten in 1735, and that the system of the arts to which it refers emerges in the eighteenth century.[24] The emergence of aesthetics in this period marks an attempt to make a decisive shift away from discourses of art that focus upon rules and prescriptions; in other words, aesthetics emerges as that which is not poetics or rhetoric. As Cynthia Chase has argued: 'The rise of aesthetics happens concurrently with the fall of rhetoric: it is the institutionalised discipline of "Rhetoric" that is displaced by aesthetics, and it is the power of "rhetoric" that is castigated in the literature and the politics which in this respect it may be right to call "romantic".'[25] Rhetoric is not then just replaced; it is explicitly abjected in romanticism. It is this negative valuation of rhetoric within the post-romantic tradition that we must think beyond if we are to encounter that which occupies the space of aesthetics in the pre-romantic period, and yet it must not simply be assumed that this is possible. In part this is because any notion of a sudden division of pre- and post-romantic thought is dubious as well as hard to define, but it is also because any rational enquiry must proceed according to categories, concepts and procedures fully imbricated with this romantic inheritance.

From cultural poetics to poetics

Certainly, 'aesthetics' in the post-Kantian terms with which we are familiar did not exist in the sixteenth and seventeenth centuries in England, and the matter of aesthetics must be traced in a submerged form in discussions of poetics and rhetorics in this period, as well as reconstituted from what is frequently a very self-reflexive literary culture.[26] The treatment of rhetoric identified by Chase inevitably raises the question of what precisely is being abjected. Alongside reading the often prescriptive 'how to' manuals of poetics and rhetoric, it is important in attempting to assess early modern discourses on art to look to the various prefaces, epistles, dedications and other para-texts that frame both literary and non-literary texts, as well as to read those moments in the texts themselves in which their own textuality becomes an explicit matter of concern.[27] Metatheatricality has long been a topic of critical interest in the study of Renaissance drama, and there are similarly metapoetic and metarhetorical elements to be found in verse and prose.[28]

Of course, in constituting this reflexivity, much of this material reflects a classical inheritance, which often follows and disrupts the 'Aristotelian' division between poetics and rhetoric. The question of poetics is opened up in Aristotle's work through an emphasis on mimesis, and all of the poetic forms that he discusses are treated as 'modes of imitation', including not just poetry (in the linguistic sense) but also music (flute-playing and lyre-playing).[29] In this, Aristotle is picking up on the discussion in Book X of Plato's *Republic*, in which the poet also appears as an imitator.[30] Here it is part of an argument about the relationship between appearance, reality and truth, and art is thought of in terms of other forms of making (that is, as *poiesis*). Again, it is the relationship of art to truth that is central to the debate. The notably negative concep-tion of poetry in this section of the *Republic* condemns poets, like all imitators, to a position at 'the third remove from truth', arguing that 'the imitator knows nothing worth mentioning of the things he imitates, but that imitation is a form of play, not to be taken seriously, and that those who attempt tragic poetry, whether in iambics or heroic verse, are all altogether imitators'.[31] Such a view of art as fundamentally non-serious and parasitic upon reality continues even into the work of modern ('analytic') philosophers such as J. L. Austin.[32]

Poetry in this Platonic and/or Aristotelian sense includes everything that we have come to call literature. Against this emphasis on mimesis in the definition of poetics, in rhetoric, for Aristotle, 'The modes of persuasion are the only true constituents of the art: everything else is mere accessory'.[33] Rather than being a second-order repre-sentation of a first-order reality (or in Plato's terms a third-order imitation of a second-order reality that is itself a weak model of the Form), the rhetorical dimensions of linguistic works have a direct impact on the world in working upon the listener or reader. Since both poetics and rhetoric are primarily arts of language, however, there are points at which Aristotle's categories intersect, and as Clark Hulse argues, '"poetics" never exists in isolation, and is always overlapping, contesting, combining, and separating from the other arts, especially the arts of rhetoric, music, philosophy, theology and even geometry. It is precisely in those zones of interaction that theorists are best able to work out the important issues of poetics, concerning the nature, func-tion, and forms of literature'.[34] It is for this reason that Hulse employs the term 'aes-thetics', in order to mark the co-implication of poetics with other domains of artistic production and enquiry, in particular those which are non-linguistic. Yet this does seem to leave aesthetics as a largely strategic category in which all discourse on art (broadly conceived) might be contained. As such, it fails to occupy a systemic posi-tion similar to that envisaged in the Kantian critical project.

This mimetic inheritance can be read a little differently. Translation of *mimesis* as 'representation' rather than 'imitation' offers a way out of the problem posed by the apparent secondariness of literature, but we need to remember that in the early modern period imitation does not itself have negative connotations.[35] Equally, linguistic arts are frequently related to the other arts, even in attempts to define poetry itself. As Sir Philip Sidney proposes in *A Defence of Poetry*, perhaps the most famous of English Renaissance treatises on art: 'Poesy is . . . an art of imitation, for so Aristotle termeth it in the word μίμησις [*mimesis*] – that is to say, a representing, counterfeiting, or figuring forth – to speak metaphorically, a speaking picture – with this end, to teach and delight.'[36] Here we see a positive valuation of imitation (*mimesis*), but one that is valued in particular because it has a specific purpose, to teach and to delight. The figure of the 'speaking picture' recognises that the figures and images of poetry are already metaphorically crossing from language into another realm (and this is, of course, what metaphor means, 'to carry across'). For Sidney, both pleasure and moral content must be present. The teaching invoked here is what Brian Vickers has called the ethical-rhetorical function of early modern literature, and Sidney recognises that this lesson is unlikely to be successful if the mode of instruction is unpalatable.[37] This is in part why, for Sidney, poetry is to be preferred to historical writing, or indeed philosophy. Literature, according to this definition, fails to recognise a clear distinction between poetics and rhetoric, partaking of both in its attempts to delight as it persuades. There is seemingly no purity or autonomy to poetics, in that it always attempts to act within the world, but what is the nature of this action? What is it that literature as poetry teaches?

The eminence of poetry, for Sidney, comes from the idea that the poet is a maker. Picking up on the Greek word ποιεῖν as the root of poetics, Sidney uses this to suggest that poetry cannot be relegated to the status of mere copying.[38] Noting the reliance of the astronomer, the geometrician and arithmetician, philosophers both natural and moral, the lawyer and historian, and others, on objects and rules (including in this the world and nature), Sidney argues that:

> Only the poet, disdaining to be tied to any such subjection, lifted up with the vigour of his own invention, doth grow in effect another nature, in making things either better than nature bringeth forth, or, quite anew, forms such as never were in nature, as the Heroes, Demigods, Cyclops, Chimeras, Furies, and such like: so as he goeth hand in hand with nature, not enclosed within the narrow warrant of her gifts, but freely ranging only within the zodiac of his own wit. Nature never set forth the earth in so rich tapestry as divers poets have done; neither with so pleasant rivers, fruitful trees, sweet-smelling flowers, nor whatsoever else may make the too much loved earth more lovely. Her world is brazen, the poets only deliver a golden.[39]

Here, then, is a treatise on poetics that emphasises the possibility of going beyond rules and prescriptions. Instead of a comparison between nature and art in which the representation is able to go in only one direction, from nature to art, nature is held up to the richness of art and is found wanting. There is a line of argument in the Platonic inheritance that would accept this reversal of the relationship of art to nature while retaining a sense of art as a secondary manifestation. Here it could be argued that art offers access to the Forms that is equivalent to that offered by objects in nature (that is, to sense-experience), and is thus not tertiary compared to a secondary reality, but is still no better than secondary. Despite this secondarity, Sidney asserts the possibility of moving beyond sense-perception, beyond the world, beyond 'subjection', beyond history (conceived of as the constraint of saying 'what really happened'). What might be read as irresponsibility in the face of history is revealed to be in the service of a higher notion of truth. Such a truthful element, which might be seen as a moment of utopian invention, carries with it (like all utopias) the negative recognition that the world of the senses from which it is freeing itself is imperfect, or fallen. Such a recognition would certainly accord with Sidney's Protestantism. But from the perspective of our discussion, this movement beyond history may be read as an attempt to offer a truly historical cognition of the world.

In this allusion to a truth beyond a mimetic relation to the world, Sidney is also able to combat charges that poets are liars. Sidney argues that 'though he [the poet] recount things not true, yet because he telleth them not for true, he lieth not' (53). The truth lies in the moral example, not in the fiction through which it is conveyed, and the emphasis is again on persuasion, since as he notes earlier in the *Defence*, 'a feigned example hath as much force to teach as a true example' (36). The truth of the true example has no moral validity beyond that of the truth which may appear through a fiction, but this does not entail upon the writer any necessity to claim that the fiction is itself true. This insight is not the subject of unalloyed joy, however. Only poetry can deliver a vision of the golden world, but the pleasure that this produces cannot free itself entirely of the painful tarnish of its brazen counterpart. Brass is, of course, an alloy, a combination of elements that could only mistakenly be associated with purity. The poet may be able to offer a glimpse of this purity, but his status as maker firmly places his work within the world of objects. Poetry, as defined here by Sidney, is co-extensive with the world but opens the space for critical engagement with that world. Its speaking pictures, as mirrors up to nature, open a space for *reflection*.

Back to modernity

In this context of debates around the term *early modern*, everything hinges on the word 'modern' (although it would also be worth, in another place, pausing over the word 'early').[40] If we simply abandon the modern sense of aesthetics on the grounds of some notion of fidelity to periodised chronology, can the concept of the early modern be retained, or must it similarly be jettisoned? The Habermasian view of modernity that Bernstein elaborates makes clear the centrality of the aesthetic to its definition, however alienated that aesthetic may be, and indeed aesthetics is crucial to post-Kantian accounts of philosophical modernity *as* modernity. The consequences for those attached to the term *early modern* would seem to be that, without the elaboration of an effective role for what we would now call aesthetics, the *early* modern will cease to bear any relation to modernity that might afford any genuinely critical purchase. The force of the term *early modern* threatens to dissipate along with the aesthetic, revealing itself as an indefinable concept, without any referent in the 'world' (and there are several possible ways in which world might be conceived here).[41] In other words, the narrativisation of modernity that the term *early* modern implies would reveal that the sense of the word modern would have to remain open, perhaps even empty. Furthermore, the concept of the early modern would also appear to have no necessary relation to the concept and narrative of history upon which historicism depends. What seems on the verge of appearing, then, is a historicism with no securely knowable connection to history. If historicism does not seem to provide a reliable conceptual scheme, then, how *are* we to think about the relationship between literature, aesthetics and history?

One answer would seem to be offered by a return to rhetoric and poetics, here conceived precisely in terms of their combination of persuasion and force with pleasure. Rhetoric opens the relation of text to world, recognising that language as art (the arts of language) can only be gifted autonomy through a violent separation. This is fundamental to early modern notions of poetics that stress an ethical-rhetorical dimension to art. It is this dimension that promises art's connections to truth and cognition. Early modern discourse on the aesthetic domain itself exhibits an awareness of the interrelation of pleasure and pain, and this is activated through the dual recognition that (as part of the world) it always occupies a fallen, secondary position with respect to a transcendental realm, and simultaneously that any glimpse of that realm is only possible through an act of invention, imagination or desire. As an act, art does not fall outside that which is available to sense-perception, but it is not simply bounded by it. Indeed, it is this doubled or enfolded act of (re)cognition that art makes possible, both in spite of and because of its secondarity (as mimesis or representation). Kantian modernity, precisely located in this violent separation and in the mourning that ensues, is a doubling of the recognition that the interaction of poetics and rhetoric ensures. Prior to the Kantian critical philosophy is not a happily unified realm in which aesthetics might be observed in harmony with pure and practical reason, and this is what spurs Kant on, but the mourning that Bernstein posits is itself an enfolded version of the pleasure and pain that art produces through and as (rhetorical) force. Such a force offers the pleasurable pain of reflective thought (of thought as reflection). Rhetoric and poetics, at the points at which they intersect, always seem to be aware of their loss (the golden world of unity). Modernity's sense of loss is thus a doubling, a double mourning; we have lost the unity of reason, but have also lost the rhetorical/poetical discourse that allowed us to recognise that such unity was always already lost. The recognition of this loss can only come about through a questioning of aesthetics itself; it cannot simply be thought from a position securely 'outside' it. Art as poetics, even before the rise of aesthetics, was always already alienated. This is what an early modern 'aesthetic', in the form of rhetoric and poetics, can tell us.

Notes

A version of this piece was presented in a session organised by John Joughin and Simon Malpas at *Post-Theory: Politics, Economics and Culture*, De Montfort University, 6–8 September 2001. I am grateful to them, to the conference organisers (Gary Day and Andy Mousley), and to the participants for comments.

1 Both ends of this period have been the topic of some debate, and it is stretched at times from 1450 to around 1800. This is not the place to reopen such discussions.

2 For definitions of new historicism see, among many possible sources, H. Aram Veeser (ed.), *The New Historicism* (London: Routledge, 1989); R. Wilson and R. Dutton (eds), *New Historicism and Renaissance Drama* (Harlow: Longman, 1992); and L. A. Montrose, 'Renaissance literary studies and the subject of history', *English Literary Renaissance*, 16 (1986), 5–12.

3 On the term itself, see, among many other texts which might be cited here, D. Aers, 'A whisper in the ear of the early modernists; or, reflections on literary critics writing the "history of the subject"' in Aers (ed.), *Culture and History 1350–1600* (Detroit: Wayne State University Press, 1992), pp. 177–202; L. Charnes, 'We were never early modern' in J. Joughin (ed.), *Philosophical Shakespeares* (London: Routledge, 2000), pp. 51–67; H. Dubrow, 'The term *early modern*', *PMLA* 109 (1994), 1025–6.

4 New historicism is not confined to Renaissance studies, but this has been the area upon which it has had the strongest impact. Like 'theory' in general, the new historicism has, of course, been pronounced dead. I take up this notion elsewhere in a piece entitled 'theory.after.life' (forthcoming).

5 See Greenblatt's essay, 'Towards a poetics of culture' in *Learning to Curse: Essays in Early Modern Culture* (London: Routledge, 1990), pp. 146–60.

6 C. Gallagher and S. Greenblatt, *Practicing New Historicism* (Chicago: University of Chicago Press, 2000), p. 10.

7 See, for example, Greenblatt's essay, 'Resonance and wonder' in *Learning to Curse*, pp. 161–83 and his *Marvelous Possessions: The Wonder of the New World* (Oxford: Clarendon Press, 1991). For a rigorous analysis of 'wonder' in Greenblatt's work, see C. Colebrook, *New Literary Histories: New Historicism and Contemporary Criticism* (Manchester: Manchester University Press, 1997), ch. 9, esp. pp. 214–19.

8 Sadly, such attention to particularity is rarely extended to other critical modes.

9 'Social energy' becomes a key term in Greenblatt's work in his *Shakespearean Negotiations: The Circulation of Social Energy in Renaissance England* (Oxford: Clarendon Press, 1988).

10 Gallagher and Greenblatt, *Practicing New Historicism*, p. 11.

11 *Ibid.*, pp. 5–8, 13. For a sense of Herder's place within the German Romantic/Idealist context, see D. O. Dahlstrom, 'The aesthetic holism of Hamann, Herder, and Schiller' in K. Ameriks (ed.), *The Cambridge Companion to German Idealism* (Cambridge: Cambridge University Press, 2000), pp. 76–94.

12 A general, if far from generous, sense of this rubric might be discerned in Harold Bloom's aligning of new historicists (in several places in his work) with what he calls the 'School of Resentment'. For a typically polemical passage, see the prologue to his *How to Read and Why* (London: Fourth Estate, 2000). Also typically, when Gallagher and Greenblatt respond to Bloom he is not even named (never mind cited) in the text, his name appearing only in the index.

13 See H. Grady, *The Modernist Shakespeare* (Oxford: Oxford University Press, 1991); *Shakespeare's Universal Wolf* (Oxford: Oxford University Press, 1996); and, as editor, *Shakespeare and Modernity: Early Modern to Millennium* (London: Routledge, 2000).

14 H. Grady, 'Renewing modernity: changing contexts and contents of a nearly invisible concept', *Shakespeare Quarterly*, 50: 3 (1999), 268–84, p. 272. The cited passage ends with a note to Greenblatt, *Renaissance Self-Fashioning: From More to Shakespeare* (Chicago: University of Chicago Press, 1980); C. Belsey, *The Subject of Tragedy: Identity and Difference in Renaissance Drama* (London: Methuen, 1985); and J. Dollimore, *Radical Tragedy:*

Religion, Ideology, and Power in the Drama of Shakespeare and his Contemporaries, 2nd edn (Hemel Hempstead: Harvester Wheatsheaf, 1989).

15 Grady, 'Renewing modernity', p. 276.

16 *Ibid.*, p. 278.

17 *Ibid.*, p. 284.

18 J. M. Bernstein, *The Fate of Art: Aesthetic Alienation from Kant to Derrida and Adorno* (Cambridge: Polity, 1992), p. 5.

19 For an elaboration of this sketch, which suggests that this concern for aesthetics character-ises what is called continental philosophy, see P. Osborne (ed.), *From an Aesthetic Point of View* (London: Serpent's Tail, 2000).

20 A. Bowie, 'German Idealism and the arts' in Ameriks (ed.), *The Cambridge Companion to German Idealism*, p. 242.

21 *Ibid.*, p. 243.

22 Bernstein, *The Fate of Art*, pp. 4–5.

23 *Ibid.*, p. 64. Kant's example is to be found in the opening paragraph of §54 of the *Critique of Judgement*.

24 On the relation between spectrality and anachronism, see Derrida, *Spectres de Marx: L'État de la dette, le travail du deuil et la nouvelle Internationale* (Paris: Galilée, 1993)/*Specters of Marx: The State of the Debt, the Work of Mourning, and the New International*, trans. P. Kamuf (New York: Routledge, 1994).

25 C. Chase, 'Literary theory as the criticism of aesthetics: De Man, Blanchot, and Romantic "allegories of cognition"' in C. Caruth and D. Esch (eds), *Critical Encounters: Reference and Responsibility in Deconstructive Writing* (New York: Rutgers University Press, 1995), pp. 42–91, p. 44.

26 See C. Hulse, 'Tudor aesthetics' in A. F. Kinney (ed.), *The Cambridge Companion to English Literature, 1500–1600* (Cambridge: Cambridge University Press, 2000), pp. 29–63; T. J. Reiss, 'Cartesian aesthetics' in G. P. Norton (ed.), *The Cambridge History of Literary Criticism: Volume 3 The Renaissance* (Cambridge: Cambridge University Press, 1999), pp. 511–21. For a discussion which touches on these concerns, see J.-F. Lyotard, 'Defining the postmodern', and P. Lacoue-Labarthe, 'On the sublime', trans. G. Bennington, in L. Appignanesi (ed.), *Postmodernism: ICA Documents* (London: Free Association, 1993 [1989]), pp. 7–18. Both take up this question of the relation of aesthetics to its prehistory. There is perhaps an analogy to be drawn between the line of enquiry that I am following here and the problem posed by psychoanalysis. Greenblatt, for example, suggests that 'psychoanalysis is the historical outcome of certain characteristic Renaissance strategies'. He further suggests that: 'psychoanalytic interpretation seems to follow upon rather than to explain Renaissance texts . . . psychoanalytic interpretation is causally belated, even as it is causally linked: hence the curious effect of a discourse that functions *as if* the psychologi-cal categories it invokes were not only simultaneous with but even prior to and themselves causes of the very phenomena of which in actual fact they were the results.' It should be noted, however, that historicism can differentiate itself from psychoanalysis only by refer-ence to psychoanalysis. In this sense it always comes after psychoanalysis, and cannot (itself belatedly) be rigorously separated from it. See Greenblatt, 'Psychoanalysis and Renaissance culture', in *Learning to Curse*, pp. 131–45, pp. 144 and 142.

27 For a fascinating discussion, see G. Genette, *Paratexts: Thresholds of Interpretation*, trans. J. E. Lewin (Cambridge: Cambridge University Press, 1997). Originally published as *Seuils* (Paris: Éditions de Seuil, 1987).

28 My use of terms beginning with 'meta-' is purely strategic. It is by no means certain that it

would be possible to distinguish clearly between a language that was poetic/rhetorical and a language that would be able to comment upon poetics/rhetoric from a 'safe' distance. This parallels the comments by Derrida and others about metalanguage, to the effect that 'there is no metalanguage, which is another way of saying that there is only metalanguage'. For a clear summary, see J. Culler, *On Deconstruction: Theory and Criticism after Structuralism* (London: Routledge, 1983), p. 199.

29 Aristotle, *Poetics*, in *The Complete Works of Aristotle*, ed. J. Barnes, 2 vols (Princeton: Princeton University Press, 1984), 2, p. 2316 (1447a).

30 Plato, *The Collected Dialogues, including the Letters*, eds E. Hamilton and H. Cairns (Princeton: Princeton University Press, 1961 [1989]), p. 821 (596e).

31 Plato, *Republic*, X, p. 827 (602b).

32 In a much-discussed passage, Austin writes: 'Language', spoken on stage, used in a poem or soliloquy, 'is in special ways – intelligibly – used not seriously, but in ways *parasitic* upon its normal use – ways which fall under the doctrine of the *etiolations* of language. All this we are *excluding* from consideration.' See *How To Do Things With Words*, 2nd edn (Oxford: Oxford University Press, 1976), p. 22.

33 Aristotle, *Rhetoric*, in *The Complete Works of Aristotle*, 2, p. 2152 (1354a).

34 Hulse, 'Tudor aesthetics', p. 35.

35 See, for example, the comments of T. M. Greene: 'The imitation of models was a precept and an activity which during that era embraced not only literature but pedagogy, grammar, rhetoric, esthetics, the visual arts, music, historiography, politics, and philosophy. It was central and pervasive', *The Light in Troy: Imitation and Discovery in Renaissance Poetry* (New Haven: Yale University Press, 1982), p. 1.

36 Sidney, *A Defence of Poetry*, ed. J. A. Van Dorsten (Oxford: Oxford University Press, 1966 [1991]), p. 25.

37 B. Vickers, 'Introduction', in Vickers (ed.), *English Renaissance Literary Criticism* (Oxford: Oxford University Press, 1999), pp. 1–55, p. 10.

38 For a recent text which begins from a similar recognition, see J.-L. Nancy, *Résistance de la poésie* (Bordeaux: William Blake & Co., 1997).

39 Sidney, *A Defence of Poetry*, pp. 23–4.

40 I am grateful to Nicholas Royle for a gentle reminder of the necessity of paying attention to 'early', and I hope that he will accept this promise to do so, even if I cannot fulfil that promise here.

41 See, notably, J.-L. Nancy, *The Sense of the World*, trans. J. S. Librett (Minneapolis: Minnesota University Press, 1997). First published as *Le sens du monde* (Paris: Galilée, 1993).

Shakespeare's genius: *Hamlet*, adaptation and the work of following

Adaptation: the following work and the work of following

> The issue of Shakespeare's uniqueness keeps coming up . . . as cause both for acclaim and for dismay, together with a repeatedly documented cause for alarm concerning the indiscriminate appropriation of Shakespeare to underwrite, or to neutralize, cultural and political oppression. I suppose I am to be counted among those who take Shakespeare's 'position' here as indeed a matter of his appropriability, as when Brecht shows us how to consider the opening scene of *Coriolanus* from the side of the rebellious populace. Such inspirations to appropriation, or counter-appropriation, point a way to articulate our persistent, or recurrent, intuition of Shakespeare's all-too-superhuman 'humanity'. I imagine this emphasis is prompted by, and finds ratification in, the perception of our age, in the theatre of the West, as one less of innovation in the composing of plays (and operas) than originality in their productions or readings, our unpredicted reconsiderations of works from any period.[1]

The survival of Shakespeare's plays continues to demonstrate that literature means different things to different people in different contexts. To say that this facility for reinvention and restaging seems to be valued is not to reduce the evaluative to a prescriptive form of interpretation – indeed, the range of ways in which those texts we now term canonical continue to be valued and reinterpreted, often from diametrically opposed points of view, suggests rather the contrary.

In considering the question of Shakespeare's 'uniqueness', Stanley Cavell points us to the simple truth that the continued proliferation of Shakespearean adaptations and productions, in an ever-burgeoning variety of media, itself confirms that a particular play's afterlife is nothing more or less than a constant process of origination. In doing so, he remains willing to allow that our relation to literature is open-ended and creative rather than predetermined or rule following, commenting elsewhere that 'a work such as a play of Shakespeare's cannot contribute the help I want from it for the philosophical issues I mention unless the play is granted the autonomy it is in one's power to grant, which means, seen in its own terms'.[2] Clearly, Cavell is not seeking a return to an autotelic or self-contained notion of 'the-text-in-itself', much less some spurious sense of original authenticity or immutable literary value. Rather, his interest is linked directly to the originary governance of the work of art and the hermeneutic yield of what he terms 'our unpredicted reconsiderations of works from any period'. This surplus potential, manifested by the plays' 'appropriability', is perhaps especially evident in the case of theatrical appropriation where, as Mark Fortier reminds us:

> Interpretation in the form of theatrical conceptualising or performance . . . can and sometimes must take license in ways that literary criticism narrowly defined does not. . . . Theatrical adaptation, especially radical rewriting and restaging of an existing work, goes one step further: although adaptations of Shakespeare's work may be driven by a belief in fidelity to something about Shakespeare, and although in large measure they are forms of critical and interpretative practice, questions about the accuracy of adaptation have little practical meaning.[3]

Theatrical adaptation is arguably 'less constrained' than other modes of interpretation. As such it offers us a way of rethinking the fuller implications of our hermeneutical encounter with those works which are in some sense 'exemplary' – not only insofar as these texts enable continued rewriting and restaging, but also in the sense that they then often remain paradigmatic, as radical or 'ground-breaking' adaptations. By speaking of these works as exemplary, then, I mean to suggest not only those texts which survive over a long period of time, but those works which in doing so maintain their originary power and thereby serve to extend the ways in which we make sense of them.[4] In this respect, as Fortier's distinction suggests, it makes little sense to speak of the 'accuracy' of adaptation. Yet this of course raises a series of related issues: why is it that, even in the case of contemporary evaluations of the playwright's work, some Shakespearean adaptations remain more memorable or significant than others? More problematically still, even if we acknowledge the originary power or qualitative distinction of some adaptations over others, how can we then do so without merely reinstalling traditionalist clichés concerning Shakespeare's eternal value?[5]

It is evident that the apparent opposition between originality and adaptation actually needs to be construed more rigorously, and in this chapter I will argue that we need to theorise adaptation not only in relation to the singularity of our encounter with exemplary or originary works, but also in terms of our capacity to receive the 'new sense' of those works which must by definition remain unprecedented and non-thematisable. In the first half of my argument this opens the way to a reconceptualisation of Kant's notion of original works in his discussion of genius via the intermediary concept of the exemplary, and in specific relation to the elaboration of this term as a central concern of modern aesthetic discourse.[6]

Rather than regarding Shakespeare as a poor unwitting adjunct of reason or as a means of underwriting 'cultural and political oppression', I want to argue that the *resistance* of the playwright's work to definitive interpretation or conceptual control might finally turn out to be a far more crucial resource for critical thought, as, only in understanding the resistance or refusal of the text are we are 'exposed' to its otherness. In this respect, as Gerald Bruns remarks of Cavell's account of the hermeneutical encounter, 'The idea is not to accommodate the text to our way of thinking but to recognize its alienness, its otherness, as a question put to us, such that understanding the text will mean understanding the question, what it asks of us'.[7] In reminding us that the succession of any literary text customarily manifests itself in the form of exposure to the other which cannot be readily construed or subsumed within the framework which attempts to confine it, and in emphasising the limits of the hermeneutical situation, Cavell's sense of the ethical significance of aesthetic response could be directly aligned with the work of Levinas and Derrida. In the case of all three thinkers this means remaining responsive to the irreducible otherness of the other in an encounter with alterity which is 'refractory to categories' and which foregoes philosophical 'knowing', if that 'knowing' is construed in the narrower sense of mere objectification.[8] In Cavell's account, the desire for certainty within the modern philosophical tradition is itself exposed as a form of scepticism which barely conceals a rage at the non-identity of the other. So that, within the hermeneutical encounter, it is precisely because scepticism is forced to concede the limits of an experience beyond its grasp that it exposes us to the possibility that we might 'acknowledge' the 'otherness of the human'.[9]

For Cavell, then, if Shakespeare's texts are philosophical dramas, it is because they retain an ethical dimension within the limits of those social, historical and linguistic conventions which simultaneously remain in need of redress and actually conjure an ethical situation into being. Evidently, these distinctions concerning the locatedness of our hermeneutic experience and its ethical implications go to the heart of literary tradition itself insofar as it constitutes a hegemonic process that is dynamic and contingent and which allows for the possibility of intervention as well as future change and transformation. By Cavell's 'measure of resistance', however, the question of how we relate to literary texts and the profession of literary criticism (insofar as it purports to 'profess' anything) occurs at a type of limit, and as such it is a matter of unsettling con-sequence and self-estrangement. The critical act is curiously non-appropriative – a form of possession that all too often dispossesses – in a process that challenges 'our prepossessions, our preoccupations with what we think we know about what our intellectual or cultural fathers or mothers have instilled in us'.[10] Yet insofar as those texts we recognise as literary continue to offer us 'new resources for hope' in creative forms that promise to transcend 'existing ways of thinking and feeling', literary criticism also necessarily embraces the possibility of transformation.[11] In either case the key question remains how can one succeed, or adapt to that which continues to remind us of the limitedness of our present condition and thereby in some sense refuses to be followed? This is a fate exemplified to some extent by Shakespeare's Hamlet, the proto-intellectual and critic-adaptor to whom I'll want to turn in the second half of this chapter.

In summary, then, one might say that each critical act is a form of adjustment, yet paradoxically adaptation – the work of following as well as the following work – encapsulates a hermeneutic process that stages the impossibility of following in the very process of attempting to follow or locate the measure of the work. Yet importantly *how* we negotiate, adapt or ad-just to the alterity of adaptation also necessarily constitutes its own measure of creativity; furthermore the work of adaptation reminds us that aesthetic experience is itself dynamic and historically variable. It follows that in its dependence on an endless adaptation to the other and the non-identical, the work of following is conjoint with a certain responsibility, or more accurately perhaps, demands a certain responsibility of us, and in this respect the question of a text's successivity, of how we attempt to measure up to it, or vice versa, might also disclose more than radical criticism has previously allowed for.

From genius to exemplary work?

To speak of 'Shakespeare's genius' is of course already an act of provocation, evoking as it does a notion of the 'transcendent bard' that the recent historicist turn in literary and cultural studies has helped to dislodge and demythologise. Yet the refusal to think of Shakespeare's work in terms of this most traditional category is curiously unhistorical, and not only constitutes a failure to engage with the critical history of what is a key concept in aesthetics, but also arguably comprises a missed opportunity for the critique and renewal of the category itself. As it appears in Kant's third critique, genius is a fairly new concept, yet its critical prehistory includes some clear association with the playwright's work, most notably perhaps in Edward Young's influential *Conjectures on Original Composition* (London, 1759) where, notwithstanding his 'faults', Shakespeare is adjudged 'an Original' in contrast to Ben Jonson the classically correct imitator:

> *Shakespeare* mingled no water with his wine, lower'd his Genius by no vapid Imitation. *Shakespeare* gave us a *Shakespeare*, nor could the first in antient fame have given us more. *Shakespeare* is not their Son, but Brother; their Equal, and that, in spite of all his faults. . . . Jonson, in the serious drama, is as much an Imitator, as Shakespeare is an Original.[12]

In fact, as Jonathan Bate reminds us, this contest between 'originality' and imitation is as old as the First Folio itself, as, in attempting to account for the source of Shakespeare's distinctiveness, the various early dedications to the plays oscillate restlessly between intimations of Shakespeare as a 'natural genius' on the one hand, and Shakespeare as the consummate craftsman on the other – precisely, that is to say, between the accusation and counter-accusation of originality and adaptation, creating and making.[13]

In Young's treatise, as elsewhere, the focus is as much on ancient exemplars of 'original genius' as it is on the 'modern' and the accent is not exclusively Shakespearean,[14] yet by the eighteenth century, as Bate reminds us, a sense of the exemplary status of Shakespeare's genius already clearly plays an important literary-critical function within a more public domain. To follow debates in the pages of *The Spectator* or the *Tatler* during this period, or within the growing archive of commentary and editorial glosses that quickly surround the recuperation of the playwright's work, is to witness something of the potential hermeneutic yield that accrues from the singularity of the Shakespearean text. Even in its Renaissance context this transformative potential of literature, as well as its generative power, is clearly bound up with the sense in which the 'principal books' of a particular age survive as a form of exemplary presiding spirit or '*genius* literarius'.[15] Yet as these discussions become increasingly codified within an emergent public sphere, Shakespeare's 'genius' rapidly emerges as a category which reveals compliance with and deviation from the formal aesthetics of which it is part. Here, the playwright's refusal to submit to existing rules or to correspond to any antecedent begins to insinuate an important leglislative function, and disputes concerning the nature of Shakespeare's artistic creativity are crucially implicated in producing new forms of social interaction and in helping modify the criteria for taste and judgement. In the process of helping to situate and contest existing contemporary cultural norms concerning truth, value and meaning it follows that, just as Shakespeare becomes aesthetical, he becomes political and contentious too. So that as Margreta de Grazia observes, the playwright's work is central to:

> the neo-classical critical tradition of determining Beauties and Faults, an exercise that required and refined the generally interchangeable faculties of Taste, Judgement and Reason. Analysis of an author's Beauties and Faults (Excellencies and Blemishes) involved major critical issues, the rivalry between art and nature, for example, or between rules and genius. Dryden was apparently the first to apply the categories to Shakespeare, but the major eighteenth-century editors from Rowe (1709) to Samuel Johnson in 1765 regarded the judging of Beauties and Faults as one of the editor's major duties.[16]

Here again of course Shakespeare's heuristic function is a direct product of his resistance to interpretation. Indeed as de Grazia reminds us:

> Shakespeare is quoted in all these publications – anthologies, editions, periodicals, and critical essays – because, in all of his irregularity, he offers 'the fairest and fullest subject for Criticism', providing the critic with both positive and negative examples of moral probity and literary decorum. . . . It was precisely because Shakespeare afforded, in Pope's words, 'the most numerous as well as the most conspicuous instances, both of Beauties and Faults of all sorts' that he provided the best material for developing and refining Taste.[17]

Viewed in an eighteenth-century context, then, notions of the playwright's genius clearly retain a subversive quality that remains beyond regularisation and in so doing provides the very exception that proved the rule. In the process of making Shakespeare 'fit' for consumption Restoration editors, adaptors and critics alike are forced to concede that in its untheorisable excess the playwright's work sustains its relative exclusivity by 'authenticating' a claim to validity which is somehow unique, yet simultaneously also exceeds the restrictive demands of empirical truth which governs the neo-classical criticism of the period. In its 'British' context, the pressure of situating these variant truth claims in relation to Shakespeare's work in some part serves to locate the inherently contradictory formation of an emergent 'national literary criticism' itself. As Christopher Norris reminds us, such is the 'paradoxical consequence' of Dr Johnson's editorial project that:

> On the one hand Shakespeare has to be accommodated to the eighteenth-century idea of a proper, self-regulating discourse which would finally create a rational correspondence between words and things, language and reality. . . . On the other hand,

allowances have to be made for the luxuriant wildness of Shakespeare's genius, its refusal to brook the 'rules' laid down by more decorous traditions like that of French neo-classicism.[18]

As Norris's comments suggest, these divergences concerning the indeterminacy and opacity of Shakespeare's work go to the heart of key questions concerning the hetero-geneous affiliation of a native culture and its values, and in time they become the proving ground for emergent senses of national and cultural identity in other contexts too. Indeed, discussions concerning the nature of Shakespeare's genius arguably site one of the earliest conjunctures through which to view an emergent relationship between literary criticism and aesthetic theory in something approximating to a modern European context.[19] Yet it is, as Bate reminds us, in Germany that early English literary criticism marks perhaps its most complex antecedent relationship in providing a crucial developmental spur to 'the growth of what we now think of as Romantic aesthetics'.[20] Such is the impact of the playwright's work that by 1812 Friedrich Schlegel observes: 'German Shakespeare translations [have] transformed the native tongue and the range of national consciousness.'[21] By the beginning of the twentieth century Friedrich Gundolf goes still further, claiming that the German tongue had literally 'embodied Shakespeare's *Seelenstoff,* his *anima* or "soul sub-stance". . . . Shakespeare has not been translated into the German language it *has become that language*'.[22] As George Steiner observes, 'The notion is, at one level, absurd, at another of the greatest philosophic-linguistic interest'.[23] Crucially, of course, in its hermeneutic context the pivot of this 'philosophic-linguistic interest' concerns a shift in understanding about the nature of language itself. For German Romanticism, the semantic indeterminacy of Shakespeare is directly linked to the emergence of a new native 'literary language' which cannot be subsumed under exist-ing rules, as, beyond the systematic endeavours of modern philology to establish a science of language, 'literature becomes the realm of language which arises for its own sake and is not bound to representation' or to descriptive analysis.[24]

In the same tradition, a more explicitly philosophical justification for reading genius as an acategorical category is provided by Kant's *Critique of Judgement,* which also of course in some part itself sets the agenda of modern aesthetics. Kant locates some helpful distinctions which serve to clarify several of the points we have touched on so far. Firstly, in the course of his conceptualisation of genius, Kant confirms that the 'product of genius' could be said to evade definitional procedure insofar as it is without antecedent.

> [G]enius (1) is a *talent* for producing that for which no definite rule can be given: and not an aptitude in the way of cleverness for what can be learned according to some rule . . . consequently *originality* must be its primary property. (2) Since there may also be original nonsense, its products must at the same time be models, i.e. be *exemplary,* and, consequently, though not themselves derived from imitation, they must serve the purpose for others, i.e. as a standard or rule of estimating.[25]

Genius then cannot be subsumed within book learning or 'academic instruction' insofar as it exhibits a talent 'for producing that for which no definite rule can be given and not an aptitude in the way of cleverness for what can be learned according to some rule'.[26] Again this non-subsumability of genius ensures its leglislative (canonical) function. Moreover, as Kant goes on to remind us, the products of genius are distinguished by being exemplary. Paradoxically, this means that whilst genius is beyond comprehension by standard definitions it simultaneously provides its own measure in serving as a standard or model for others. In short, as we have already inferred, genius is rule breaking but also rule making.

As Jay Bernstein suggests, in the course of Kant's analysis originality 'becomes manifest in two modes: destructively and constructively'.[27] In respect of the former the provocation of exemplary items is transgressively to overturn a conventional understanding of what has previously passed as art. Yet, as Bernstein points out, for Kant 'originality must involve more than breaking rules; its deformations must allow for the possibility of reformation'.[28] In this sense the open-endedness of exemplarity is secured in terms of its successivity and can be construed as 'serving the purpose for others' in providing 'new ways of making sense'.[29] So that as Kant puts it:

> Following [succession] which has reference to a precedent, and not imitation is the proper expression for all influence which the products of an exemplary *author* may exert upon others – and this means no more than going to the same sources for a creative work as those to which he went for his creations, and learning from one's predecessor no more than the mode of availing oneself of such sources.[30]

Again, importantly, Kant distinguishes between imitating and following works of genius: the former is 'slavish' and 'would mean the loss of the element of genius, and just the very soul of the work'; while the following work of genius runs the risk 'of putting talent to the test', in 'one whom it arouses to a sense of his own originality in putting freedom from the constraint of rules so into force in his art, that for art itself a new rule is won'.[31] This is a crucial distinction and evidently comes close to the idea of adaptation I have already outlined above, i.e. the work of following as a form of creative con-sequence.

In one respect Kant's sense of the succession of an exemplary work could be said to 'provide possibilities in the plural, that were not previously available; and . . . may alter what we conceive those possibilities to be' only by reference to a precedent.[32] Yet by extension we might say that modern adaptations often themselves only disclose the provocation of an original work precisely by 'virtue of succeeding it'.[33] Thus such an affinity through distance might only materialise unevenly over a period of time. Moreover an adaptor might 'acknowledge' the relation between exemplarity and succession by 'producing the successive works themselves'.[34] This helps us view say Baz Luhrman's *William Shakespeare's Romeo + Juliet* as disclosing something newly 'Shakespearean' in the course of simultaneously constituting its own form of unprecedented innovation. Bernstein offers a clarification of the connection between exemplarity and succession and the production of succeeding works by referring us to the example of modernist art:

> Here . . . exemplarity means the opening up of new possibilities without the item or items that do the opening up being able to be accounted for in terms of its or their

antecedents. Exemplary items provide the measure, with only their provocation, on the one hand, and succession on the other, 'measuring' (without measuring) them.[35]

In some sense I would want to argue that the production of successive works and their exemplification of a measureless measure could be construed as analogous to the indeterminate process of (Shakespearean) adaptation itself. However, as Bernstein rightly points out, in conceiving of succession in terms of one genius 'followed by another genius', Kant 'does not quite see this possibility' for exemplary works.[36] As such, Kant's analysis still arguably runs the risk of imposing a uniformity on the potentially measureless possibilities of the exemplary. Yet as Bernstein argues, this would be to reduce 'the indeterminacy of the exemplary instance to unity' and 'to reduce the new rule won through exemplarity to a single case'.[37] Meanwhile, insofar as Kant understands the *act* of genius as constituting 'free action [and] as creative and legislative rather than rule following',[38] this also serves to suggest that artistic practice might itself be open to reconceptualisation in terms of its proto-political and ethical potential within the public domain. These are possibilities I shall want to return to below.

A thrust enters history . . .

The origin of the artwork is art. But what is art? Art is actual in the artwork. Hence we first seek the actuality of the work. In what does it consist? Artworks universally display a thingly character, albeit in a wholly distinct way. The attempt to interpret this thing-character of the work with the aid of the usual thing-concepts failed – not only because these concepts do not lay hold of the thingly feature, but because, in raising the question of its thingly substructure, we force the work into a preconceived framework by which we obstruct our own access to the work being of the work. Nothing can be discovered about the thingly aspect of the work so long as the pure self-subsistence of the work has not distinctly displayed itself.[39]

We need to push the concept of exemplarity still further. How does one apprehend the measureless possibilities of the exemplary? And in what sense can we argue that there is a qualitative distinction in the succession or survival of great works, and their open disclosure of transformative possibilities over a period of time? Bound up with how we interpret, remember or testify to the enduring semantic power and signifying possibilities of literary works, Heiddeger's remarks on 'The origin of the work of art' offer us a more 'generalised thinking of the Kantian notion of genius', and in doing so help tease out the historical implications of exemplary artworks.[40]

In some sense, as Heidegger's comments suggest, we need to confront the actuality of the artwork. But then if the artwork or the play is the thing, what type of thing is it? Heidegger's key point here of course is that an artwork's distinct thingly character remains beyond the grasp of the usual thing-concepts, which fail because they force the work into a preconceived framework and thereby obstruct our own access to what he terms 'the work being of the work'. As Heidegger implies, conventional approaches to the question of the authenticity of artworks operate according to a correspondent model of truth in which art's relationship to the world is conceived in terms of a naive mimeticism which posits the truth of an anterior or pre-existent reality, of which art is then a 'true' re-presentation. So far so good of course, insofar as in 'displacing the dominance of the representational understanding of truth and thing',[41] Heidegger is in agreement with post-structuralism in its critique of those 'natural forms of reading' which traditionally presuppose a rather fixed understanding of the value of artworks and their claim to authenticity.

Yet Heidegger's essay on the origin of the work of art is careful to preserve a place for truth or authenticity in the sense that, as the philosopher puts it, art is truth setting itself to work:

> In a work, by contrast, this fact, that it *is* as a work, is just what is unusual. The event of its being created does not simply reverberate through the work; rather, the work casts before itself the eventful fact that the work is as this work, and it has constantly this fact about itself. The more essentially the work opens itself, the more luminous becomes the uniqueness of the fact that it is rather than is not. The more essentially this thrust comes into the open region, the more strange and solitary the work becomes. In the bringing forth of the work there lies this offering 'that it be.'[42]

For Heidegger, this 'disclosive' thrust-like dimension to art is one of the ways in which truth happens. Moreover, 'art is one of the ways in which history takes place' insofar as, as Bernstein puts it, for Heidegger 'whenever art happens – that is whenever there is a beginning – a thrust enters history, history either begins or starts over again'.[43] If we extend this sense of the originary power of artworks via the notion of exemplarity to the notion of great works and their continued epoch-making capacity to set truth to work, the questions that Heidegger raises clearly go to the heart of the formation of a literary tradition as an indeterminacy of disruptive settings.

To summarise, then, before moving on: the most effective adaptations are without anterior motive and as such they cannot claim to copy or 'lay hold of' an original. To conceive of adaptation as 'agreement with', imitation of, or depiction of something actual[44] is to treat adaptation as pre-scriptive in the sense of merely re-presenting a copy of what *is*, or to rehearse a restriction which, rather like textual revisionism of the worst kind, imposes a misplaced notion of fidelity on a unified original and thereby duplicates a 'logic of the same'. Most literary and cultural theorists would concur with this qualification and would agree that in this sense adaptation is fated never to measure up. Yet there is clearly a qualitative measure which distinguishes some adaptations from others and this relates directly to a conceptualisation of exemplary works as dynamically historical and notably successive. In this respect the event of adaptation can be locational (epoch-making even) in the difference that it makes. Indeed its sense of occasion could be said to disrupt and constitute a cultural history itself. In practice of course theatrical adaptation visits this disclosive, non-uniform, 'happening truth' potential of adaptation setting itself to work on an almost nightly basis, so that as Artaud puts it staging or setting becomes the 'starting point for theatrical creation':

> A performance that repeats itself every evening according to rites that are always the same, always identical to what they were the night before, can no longer win our support. The spectacle we are watching must be unique, it must give the impression that

it is unprecedented, as incapable of repeating itself as any action in life, any event brought on by circumstances.[45]

Crucially, as Artaud's comments suggest, insofar as the work of adaptation 'works' it is because the work of adaptation ungrounds itself on its own terms. What Heidegger might term the originary thrust of a work, its actualisation, is without antecedent even as it then ensures its own historical success as a measure without measure.

The play's the thing . . .

Thou art a scholar, speak to it, Horatio. (I. i. 45)[46]

In conceiving of a literary tradition as a form of discontinuous history, we are clearly far removed from traditional attempts to install a fixed or a priori distinction between 'one kind of writing and another'. In the very act of challenging our critical expectations exemplary works resist generalisation, and as such literary criticism is forced to confront the possibility that inheritance (literary or otherwise) is always already incomplete – a history only of located dislocation and partial assimilation – an experience which cannot be fully accounted for. Frustratingly, in the course of provoking thought and in making us think, this also ensures that literary texts are phantoms which finally resist critical appropriation. And no doubt this is partly because, in their own way, the questions of how we remember, of being and not being, knowing and not knowing, are themselves linked in intricate ways to the literary critical 'event'. For how can we 'know' that which simultaneously remains beyond our full comprehension? Or even (as Marcellus requires of the scholar Horatio) 'speak to it'?[47]

Hamlet of course stages this dilemma of critical finitude in some detail and in doing so opens with the most evidential of questions, 'Who's there?' (I. i. 1), while Francisco's response to Barnado's enquiry 'Stand and *unfold* yourself' (2) almost immediately directs us to the question of 'exposition' and interpretation.[48] In dramatic terms the staging of the Ghost during the opening scenes of the play effectively restages what Cavell might term a 'philosophical drama' insofar as we are confronted with an entity that does not fall within conventional bounds of 'naming', so that an audience is forced to reconsider 'that which one thinks one knows by the name of knowledge'.[49] Again of course it is precisely those more traditional or propositional modes of enquiry which attempt to establish an anterior or predetermined relation to the 'truth' that are immediately called into question here. The Ghost's arrival cannot be anticipated or prepared for. Indeed, in keeping with the best literary events 'it' appears quite literally without preamble *in medias res* (into the midst of things), and ironically, in doing so it interrupts Barnado's own 'Ghost story', so that, once again, any ordered sense of narrative sequence is further complicated and the boundary between the 'literary' and the 'fictional' is further blurred. As a result the apparition itself is more real than fiction, for as Barnado asks: 'Is not this something more than fantasy?' (I. i. 57). Again, the apparition is 'thing-like' insofar as it is referred to as an 'it', although 'it' is used interchangeably now with the antique form of he ('a') in Barnado's: 'Looks *a* not like the King?' (46). Here and in his preceding observation that the entity appears 'In the same figure like the King that's dead' (44), Barnado relies on a form of recognition that is also a form of *re*-cognition, i.e. a form of cognition that is based on comparison. Marcellus picks up the same comparison moments later, asking Horatio 'Is it not like the King?' (61). Yet Horatio's response to Marcellus, 'As thou art to thyself' (62), teasingly suggests that, insofar as an insistence on similitude or likeness depends upon a sense of difference, then it also constitutes a form of identification that is already split and divided against itself, insofar as it depends on a self comparing 'self' with self. It follows that the apparition throws any conventional sense of critical 'self-possession' or transcendent detachment into crisis, a situation Horatio (the most 'scholarly' and 'sceptical' of the observers) is unable to deal with. As a consequence, and as a mark of his confusion, Horatio the 'scientist' is now forced to swear a religious oath that he is witnessing something than cannot be, but somehow *is*: 'Before my God, I might not this believe / Without the sensible and true avouch / Of mine own eyes' (59–61). Insofar as Horatio's brand of scepticism relies on objective distance and proof the Ghost is clearly not susceptible to interpretation on these terms. In some sense, then, he and the others are unable to learn what Cavell characterises as 'the lesson of skepticism', namely that 'the human creature's basis in the world as a whole, its relation to the world as such is not that of knowing, anyway not what we think of as knowing'.[50]

Interestingly enough of course *Hamlet* – arguably the most performed of all Shakespeare's plays – itself pivots around the question of adaptation, in terms of Hamlet's staging of the play within the play. And here again of course, in more senses than one, succession and 'knowing' arise as the very nub of the problem, insofar as the act-event of Hamlet's own adaptation 'The Mousetrap' (III. ii) (with 'some dozen or sixteen lines . . . insert[ed] in't', II. ii. 535–6) is already an attempt to 'test' the 'accuracy' of the Ghost's testimony. In some respects of course Hamlet's problem here is analogous to the problem we have already faced, i.e. how does one stage what is apparently not there? Moreover the play-within-the-play once again highlights issues relating to interpretation and performance, insofar as it stages an audience on stage and a director (Hamlet) hoping to influence the outcome.[51] In some ways the failure of Hamlet's adaptation (his own attempt to stage the Ghost) is seminally instructive for those who attempt to direct theatre in anything other than an open-ended fashion – though, unsurprisingly perhaps, his own response during the play-within-the-play discloses 'a desire for certainty' and empirical evidence as he manifests the rage of the epistemophile who would pedantically 'piece out' and over-interpret every aspect of the story. As Ophelia observes, later on during the scene itself, 'You are as good as a chorus, my Lord' (III. ii. 240); while, for his part, Horatio assures Hamlet that nothing will escape his 'detecting' (III. ii. 89). Many literary critics have repeated the same mistake. And in some ways Hamlet's adaptation has become the editorial and interpretative crux of the play, as in trying to pin down the 'meaning' of Claudius's 'response' to the play-within-the-play generations of 'scholars' have effectively committed the same category error of attempting to preserve the 'veracity' of the Ghost 'at all costs'.[52] Yet in this sense, of course, in 'The Mousetrap' the 'burden of proof' is miscast and is the crux on which interpretation must founder, insofar as there can be no 'test' for testimony.

During the course of *Hamlet*, then, the attempted adaptation might be cast as an act of narration in which Hamlet the proto-intellectual will clarify the act of sovereign succession and rewrite the official history. Yet Hamlet's 'excessively goal-orientated consciousness' (in terms of theatre direction at least), ensures that both prior to and during 'The Mousetrap' itself, in casting himself as a 'minor' dramatist he unwittingly emerges as what Deleuze might term a 'despot of the invariant'.[53] Because Hamlet approaches adaptation from a homogenised perspective there is no allowance for the recursive 'catch' of 'The Mousetrap' or the surprise of the 'power of improvisation'. In brief, Hamlet anticipates a form of revelation or incarnation 'under the sign of presence' and fails to construe the non-originary origin of the event of disclosure. During his advice to the players, Hamlet condones an instrumentalist approach to the vagaries of performance that negates adaptation. In his desire for certainty he fails to allow for the fact that literary transformation is a form of what Heidegger calls 'preserving' – that is to say 'letting a work be' rather than attempting to restore it to what it once was.[54] One might say that the unfathomability of Claudius's response belongs to an abyss of the play's own making, as, however he tries to adapt or modify the conditions for its reception, it can never be Hamlet's play.[55] Rather like the ol' mole that burrows in at the beginning of the play, adaptation works its wiles in displacement. Following the play within the play, *Hamlet* necessarily reverts to the onto-theology of a deterministic universe. Or, as Francis Barker memorably puts it, the play effectively imposes military rule upon itself.[56]

As the creation of the other, adaptation is without motive, a relinquishment of self that is also a response to a provocation of the work's own making. It follows that there is no way of reincarnating the 'truth' or making such a world 'present to oneself'.[57] Ironically of course, in one further twist, Hamlet's failure to relate to his world in anything other than narrowly conceived terms of epistemic certainty is already exposed in advance of his attempted adaptation, during his initial response to the player's speech (a speech which itself of course also in some sense serves as a further prompt to stage 'The Mousetrap', cf. II. ii. 584–601):

> What's Hecuba to him, or he to her,
> That he should weep for her? What would he do
> Had he the motive and the cue for passion
> That I have?   (II. ii. 553–6)

In some ways Hamlet's 'own' mistaken sense here of not 'measuring up' finally returns us to the importance of the Kantian distinction between imitating and following, though we might say that he effectively refuses to put 'talent to the test' insofar as his response to the player is one of identification and 'self-possession' rather than an openness to alterity. As Gerald Bruns comments, generally speaking, 'Hamlet's desire for certainty . . . is continuous with his desire not to expose himself to the world around him'.[58] It follows then that despite his protestation of an aesthetic sensibility his own response to the player's speech betrays his inability to forego knowing for receptiveness, and in opting instead for 'authenticity' he chooses 'self-preservation' ahead of adaptation.[59]

Hamletism and humanism

> Thou art a monument without a tomb,
> And art alive still while thy book doth live
> And we have wits to read, and praise to give.[60]

With its talk of tombs and monuments, being and non-being, the question of literary succession is evidently entwined with what Derrida would term a 'logic of haunting', insofar as its surplus potential is not a matter of 'the meaning of an original' but is always already deferred and infinitely translatable, whether as a form of memorial or as a trace of a future-to-come. Again, for Derrida, it is important to stress the heterogeneity of this process. Moreover he does so in direct relation to Shakespeare: 'This is the stroke of genius, the insignia trait of spirit, the signature of the Thing "Shakespeare": to authorize each one of the translations, to make them possible and intelligible without ever being reducible to them.'[61] As Derrida suggests, there is evidently a claim here that is in a certain sense 'cognitive' but non-reducible – as such it is bound to prove unsettling for any humanist in search of authentic originality. Genius calls us to follow: not in any slavish sense of imitation but rather in the hope that we gather around the disjuncture that makes following a possibility.

In the case of *Hamlet*, as we have seen, the official history relentlessly imposes its own narrative on events and as such it construes the question of memory and related questions of intellectual inheritance in terms of a more reductive form of identification with the past. In doing so it underpins a regime which is based on vengeance and injustice – we might say that it belongs to the 'hegemony of the homogenous'. In this respect, of course, Hamlet's hyperbolic misidentification with the past is itself uncannily reminiscent of humanism's own nostalgic yearning for complete restitution. And in some part the progressive idealisation of Hamlet during modernity as a non-recuperable figure itself also caters to this nostalgia. In the process, 'Shakespeare's Hamlet' eventually emerges as a simplifying synecdoche for 'Shakespeare's genius', and by a further act of association quickly becomes the most readily identifiable representation of the liberal intellectual 'paralysed in will and incapable of action', yet still somehow possessing Hamlet's 'generalising habit' and thereby occupying the ethical and cultural high ground.[62] In short, we are presented with a version of intellectual life at a quasi-transcendent remove, though of course it is a living and an intellect that remains secure only in its inability to come to terms with what is in effect a productive melancholic entrapment with the past.

Yet the prompt provided by the example of Hamlet can be construed otherwise, for as Derrida observes: 'If right or law stems from vengeance, as Hamlet seems to complain . . . can one not yearn for a justice that one day, a day belonging no longer to history, a quasi-messianic day would finally be removed from the fatality of vengeance.'[63] The play's provocation, as Derrida rightly reminds us, is to pose the question without offering a solution that we can live with – unless, that is, we learn to live with ghosts.[64] In this sense the spirit of Hamlet exemplifies a non-foundationalist petition to justice that remains unfulfilled, yet it is difficult to see how a criticism which claims to be 'political' could refuse this call to justice. Again the ad-justment, the move towards justice, to 'put yourself in my place' remains a question of displacement rather than comparison: an act of adaptation that allows for the creation of the other. Yet in these terms alone exemplarity itself arguably always insinuates a reconceptualisation of the political.

Crucially, of course, in burdening himself with restitution at any cost, Hamlet fails to realise that memory itself is an ethical instant and an opening instance: 'O cursed . . . / That ever I was born to set it right' (I. v. 196–7). In this respect his misapprehension of his own legacy proves onerous. After all, one cannot expect a finite subject to think of all ethical obligations; such a legacy would be 'inhuman', though Hamlet's legacy to Horatio is precisely a form of inhumanity, as if to bequeath the full-bore canon of divine law – a type of madness. These questions go to the route of the problem of Hamletism: Hamlet the intellectual, the literary critic, the philosopher. The act of inheritance or witness, the aesthetic contract by which Hamlet and humanism seem bound, actually remarks nothing more or less than the inaugural aporia of intellectual life. As Derrida reminds us, 'the truth of the acolyte who follows without being fully present is [finally an analytic figure] who accompanies and does not accompany'[65] – a witness who must follow without following. This in turn also comes close to the freedom implied by Kant's theorisation of genius, without subscribing to its subjectivism.

Conclusion

In reconceptualising great works as 'successful' we might say that rather than adapt to circumstance, or adjust to new conditions, they (great works) continue to precipitate crisis on their own terms as well. It follows that some of the sharpest appreciation of the dislocationary potentiality of adaptation of great works comes from those who remain open to what we might term after Derrida the continued 'emergency' of adaptation, and who adopt a stance towards adaptation which is both interruptive and 'presentist' in terms of its critical orientation. In Walter Benjamin's 'Theses on the Philosophy of History', for example, adaptation ('blasting a specific work out of the lifework', etc.) surfaces as a recurrent preoccupation. Yet again, for Benjamin, we might say that, configured in these terms, the work of adaptation draws us together in a 'fitting' way only by being uniquely 'out of joint'. Opposed to the empty quantitative homogeneity of historicism his 'materialist historiography' is nonetheless based on an adaptive 'constructive principle' and as such it elicits a qualitative response, engendering what he terms elsewhere 'a unique experience with the past'.[66] In short, Benjamin's 'constructive principle' makes for an uncontainable 'presentist' type of moment which is no less fully historical for letting 'history happen' even as it marks a messianic cessation of happening.

For a range of theatrical adaptors of Shakespeare including Brecht, Artaud, Heiner Müller and many others, the ungrounding of adaptation aligns itself with the new aesthetic of a revolutionary theatre, which in its estrangement reactivates a 'political consciousness of the present' both in provoking an audience and in potentially transforming established modes of cognition. Yet it would be wrong to speak in terms of the motive or agenda or 'aim of adaptation', not least insofar as 'the political effects of such a theatre cannot be foreseen'.[67] Rather, in adaptation, as in Benjamin's sense of *Janzeit* or time of the now, we witness a teleology that undermines *telos* and where 'origin is the goal'. Maybe this is simply to say that, like history, adaptation works itself out behind the backs of the actors. This means that while successful revivals are name-making and epoch-making within the actualising thrust of adaptation itself, as Heidegger puts it, 'the artist remains inconsequential as compared with the work, almost like a passage-way that destroys itself in the creative process for the work to emerge'.[68]

Paradoxically, even while the most successful Shakespearean adaptations could be said to 'belong' to others – Brook's *A Midsummer Night's Dream*, Césaire's *Une tempête*, Müller's *Hamletmachine*, etc. – no one can 'own' the event of adaptation itself. Or at least one could say that adaptation stakes its claim for ownership in non-proprietary terms, or that if adaptations 'catch on' or are successful it is because they possess an 'originary governance', or again, that they are unmeasurable works which then measure future productions. Finally, as Hamlet teaches us, there is no setting it right. Adaptation implicitly conjures forth an ethical relation with an other in that it acknowledges an irreducible excess of things being out of joint. Yet how we negotiate, adapt or ad-just to the alterity of adaptation itself inevitably constitutes its own measure of creativity rather than following the rule. In this sense to adapt is also to *ad*-just – to move *towards* justice or rather to open up what Derrida might term the indeterminate future-to-come of justice itself. And in this latter sense, of course, there is no adapting to adaptation. As the 'creation of the other', adaptation is without motive, a relinquishment of self that is also a response to a provocation of the work's own making. In this respect just as the exemplary work measures its work as succession, then maybe adaptation could also be construed as the interval between adapted works. In fact we might say that the interval between works 'presents' itself as the non-determinable condition of adaptation itself, a summoning forth to further adaptation yet beyond the director's will.

Notes

1 See S. Cavell, 'Foreword', in J. J. Joughin (ed.), *Philosophical Shakespeares* (London: Routledge, 2000), pp. xii–xvi (pp. xii–xiii).
2 See S. Cavell, *Disowning Knowledge: In Six Plays of Shakespeare* (Cambridge: Cambridge University Press, 1987), p. 144.
3 See M. Fortier, 'Shakespeare as "minor theater": Deleuze and Guattari and the aims of adaptation', *Mosaic*, 29:1 (1996), 1–18. Fortier offers a provocative account of theatrical adaptation in the spirit of Deleuze and Guattari's concept of 'minor literature', as inducing 'a series of variations' which are not reducible to a unity. For more on the growth of 'adaptation studies' generally, compare D. Cartmell and I. Whelehan (eds), *Adaptations: From Text to Screen, Screen to Text* (London: Routledge, 1999), cf. esp. Whelehan, 'Adaptations: the contemporary dilemmas', pp. 3–19.
4 Cf. Timothy Gould, who makes an analogous distinction concerning the relation of 'original works' and their interpretative constituency in 'The audience of originality:

Kant and Wordsworth on the reception of genius' in T. Cohen and P. Guyer (eds), *Essays in Kant's Aesthetics* (Chicago: University of Chicago Press, 1982), pp. 179–93 (esp. pp. 179–80).

5 A quick additional word concerning my own use throughout the chapter of the word 'adaptation' is probably in order at this juncture. Many purists would insist that, strictly speaking, the term 'adaptation' should be restricted solely to productions which have substantially and distinctively new material inserted or added in advance. Yet this seems an overly formalistic and prescriptive way of understanding how adaptation actually works in practice and forecloses on understanding adaptation as a process which is itself open-ended. As Fortier and Fischlin remind us in their recent introduction to *Adaptations of Shakespeare: A Critical Anthology of Plays from the Seventeenth Century to the Present* (London: Routledge, 2000), the term adaptation is a helpfully flexible and wide-ranging one: 'Adaptation implies a process rather than a beginning or an end, and as ongoing objects of adaptation all Shakespeare's plays remain in process. . . . Adaptation as a concept can expand or contract. Writ large, adaptation includes any act of alteration performed upon specific cultural works of the past and dovetails with a general process of cultural recreation. More narrowly, its focus . . . is on works which, through verbal and theatrical devices, radically alter the shape and significance of another work so as to invoke that work and yet be different from it – so that any adaptation is, and is not, Shakespeare.'(pp. 3–4). I want to argue that, when it is construed as an 'expansive' concept, the theorisation of Shakespearean adaptation offers us a way of rethinking our encounter with exemplary works – as a dynamic, qualitatively variable and creative process which both is and is not 'Shakespearean', a process which Cavell labels a matter of Shakespeare's 'appropriability'. In other words the 'originary power' of adaptation/appropriability is not reducible to the more restrictively 'oppressive sense' in which (political) 'appropriation' has often operated in recent cultural criticism – usually to imply what Fortier and Fischlin themselves term 'a hostile takeover, a seizure of authority over the original in a way that appeals to contemporary sensibilities steeped in a politicised understanding of culture' (again see Fortier and Fischlin, p. 3).

6 I follow the lead here that is provided by J. M. Bernstein in his discussion of exemplarity in Heidegger as a 'generalized thinking' of the Kantian notion of genius, cf. J. M. Bernstein, *The Fate of Art: Aesthetic Alienation from Kant to Derrida and Adorno* (Oxford: Polity Press, 1992), esp. pp. 66–135. The extent of my indebtedness to Bernstein will be evident below; meanwhile, insofar as the paper draws on the work of thinkers like Bernstein and Bowie who have challenged the anti-aestheticism of recent cultural and literary theory and offered a reconceptualisation of aesthetic theory as fundamental to our understanding and experience of modernity, it could be classed as new aestheticist in terms of its critical orientation. It forms part of work in progress on a book-length study of Shakespeare and the aesthetic.

7 G. Bruns, 'Stanley Cavell's Shakespeare', *Critical Inquiry*, 16 (1990), 612–32, (pp. 630–1).

8 See Emmanuel Levinas, *Totality and Infinity: An Essay on Exteriority*, trans. A. Lingis (London: Kluwer Academic Publishers, 1991), and also again cf. Bruns, 'Cavell's Shakespeare', esp. pp. 619–20. This register of an openness to alterity is also widespread in the ethical turn of Derrida's work and is evident most recently in his development of the conceptual motif of 'hospitality', which begins with the 'unquestioning welcome' of that which 'is *given* to the other before they are identified'; see esp. *Of Hospitality*, trans. R. Bowlby (Stanford, CA: Stanford University Press, 2000).

9 See Cavell, *Disowning Knowledge*, passim; and again also cf. Bruns, 'Cavell's Shakespeare', esp. pp. 614–17.

10 See Cavell, 'Foreword', p. xvi.

11 See A. Bowie, *From Romanticism to Critical Theory: The Philosophy of German Literary Theory* (London: Routledge, 1997), passim.

12 See E. Young, *Conjectures on Original Composition* (London, 1759), pp. 78–80.

13 I am particularly indebted here and below to J. Bate, *The Genius of Shakespeare* (London: Picador, 1997), esp. pp. 26–30, and J. Bate, 'Shakespeare and original genius' in P. Murray (ed.), *Genius: The History of an Idea* (Oxford: Blackwell, 1992), pp. 76–97. Shakespeare was, of course, first and foremost an adaptor, a notorious Jack-of-all trades, an 'Upstart crow' who fleeced his competitors and lifted and reworked his best plots from the templates provided by English chronicles and Italian romance. For his part, in his own preface to Shakespeare's plays, Ben Jonson opts for a compromise formation conceding the fact that, despite Shakespeare's undoubted success in outshining competitors ancient and modern, when all's done and dusted 'a good poet's made as well as born / And such wert thou' (Ben Jonson, To the Memory of my beloved, the author Master William Shakespeare and what he hath left us, 1623, in 'Commendatory Poems and Prefaces 1599–1640' in *William Shakespeare: The Complete Works*, ed S. Wells *et al.* (Oxford: Clarendon Press, 1980), p. xliii). In short, the distinction between creating and making is eminently deconstructible and, from the very outset, a barely concealed rift begins to open up within any more narrowly conceived sense of a nature/art opposition which all too often imposes its own form of stable metaphysical binary in more traditional discussions of the playwright's work.

14 As Bate suggests, during this formative period other regular exemplars include Homer, Pindar and 'the sublime of the Old Testament prophets', cf. Bate, 'Shakespeare and original genius', p. 77.

15 See S. J. Greenblatt, 'What is the history of literature?', *Critical Inquiry*, 23 (1997), 460–81 (cf. esp. pp. 476–7).

16 See M. de Grazia, 'Shakespeare in quotation marks' in J. I. Marsden (ed.), *The Appropriation of Shakespeare: Post-Renaissance Reconstructions of the Works and the Myth* (Hemel Hempstead: Harvester Wheatsheaf, 1991), pp. 57–71 (p. 62).

17 *Ibid.*, p. 63.

18 See C. Norris, 'Post-structuralist Shakespeare: text and ideology' in J. Drakakis (ed.), *Alternative Shakespeares* (London: Methuen, 1985), pp. 47–66 (p. 49).

19 Even in France, despite an initial 'rationalised' resistance to Shakespeare, the exemplary status of the playwright's work begins to open up a productive faultline concerning native literary inheritance and the question of its legacy. By the second half of the eighteenth century Voltaire, originally one of the strongest polemicists for Shakespeare's 'strong and fertile genius' (though this was never a wholly unreserved endorsement), is nonetheless eventually dismayed at the consequence of his advocacy: 'it was I [Voltaire complains] who was the first to point out to Frenchmen the few pearls which were to be found in this enormous dunghill. It never entered my mind that by doing so I would one day help the effort to trample on the crowns of Racine and Corneille in order to wreathe the brow of this barbaric mountebank.' Cited in G. Steiner, *After Babel: Aspects of Language and Translation* (Oxford: Oxford University Press, 1975), p. 384.

20 See Bate, 'Shakespeare and original genius', passim. As Bate notes, along with an assortment of other British critics during this period Young was to prove extremely influential and key distinctions within his treatise on *Original Composition* help shape the aesthetics of Herder and others working in the same tradition, cf. esp. pp. 88–9.

21 See Steiner, *After Babel*, p. 401.

22 *Ibid.*, pp. 401–2.

23 *Ibid.*, p. 402.

24 For more on the philosophical context of the shift in the understanding of the function of language during this period and its connection to the 'wider issue of aesthetics' see A. Bowie, *From Romanticism to Critical Theory: The Philosophy of German Literary Theory* (London: Routledge, 1997), pp. 1–27 and cf. esp. p. 21.

25 See I. Kant, *The Critique of Judgement*, trans. James Creed Meredith (Oxford: Clarendon Press, 1991), pp. 168–9.

26 Again Young would concur: 'Genius is a Masterworkman, Learning is but an Instrument; and an Instrument tho' most valuable, yet not always indispensable. . . . For unprescribed Beauties, and unexampled Excellence, which are Characteristics of *Genius*, lie without the Pale of *Learning's* Authorities, and Laws', see *Conjectures*, pp. 25–6.

27 See Bernstein, *The Fate of Art*, p. 93.

28 *Ibid.*

29 *Ibid.*

30 See Kant, *The Critique of Judgement*, pp. 138–9.

31 *Ibid.*, p. 181, also cf. H. Caygill, *A Kant Dictionary* (Oxford: Blackwell, 1995), p. 213.

32 Cf. Bernstein, *The Fate of Art*, p. 94.

33 *Ibid.*

34 *Ibid.*

35 *Ibid.*

36 *Ibid.* and cf. Kant, *The Critique of Judgement*, p. 181.

37 See Bernstein, *The Fate of Art*, p. 94.

38 *Ibid.*, p. 8.

39 See M. Heidegger, 'The origin of the work of art' in D. F. Krell (ed.), *Martin Heidegger: Basic Writings* (London: Routledge, 1993), pp. 139–212, p. 165.

40 Again cf. Bernstein, *The Fate of Art*, p. 14, and pp. 66–135, passim.

41 *Ibid.*, p. 76.

42 See Heidegger, 'The origin of the work of art', pp. 190–1.

43 Cf. Bernstein, *The Fate of Art*, p. 84.

44 Cf. Heidegger, 'The origin of the work of art', p. 162.

45 See A. Artaud, *Selected Writings* (Berkeley: University of California Press, 1988), p. 157, also cited in Fortier, 'Shakespeare as "minor theater"', p. 3.

46 All quotations are from the Arden edition of *Hamlet*, ed. H. Jenkins (London: Routledge, 1990).

47 In this respect, as Stephen Greenblatt reminds us, our negotiation with old Hamlet's death is itself exemplary. Indeed in some sense it constitutes the *Ur*-scene of literary history itself, the singular act of witness and memorial whose ontological ambiguity continues to assure and maintain our literary critical life, for as Greenblatt puts it, 'It is the role of the scholar to speak to the dead and to make the dead speak: "Stay, speak, speak, I charge thee speak"'. See Greenblatt, 'What is the history of literature?', p. 479.

48 In this sense we also need to remember that Barnado's 'Who's there' already comes from a position offstage and outside of the frame of the play, so that even before we get to examine the question of apparition or who might be able to see what, we are invited to confront the dislocation of a hermeneutic encounter. In short, we are aware only of a question which comes from a place 'elsewhere' as one person speaks out of the void, enquiring about the identity of another. For further reflections on the ghost scene see my 'Pedagogy as event: *Hamlet* and hauntology' in P. Skrebels and S. Van der Hoeven (eds), *For All Time? Critical*

Issues in Teaching Shakespeare (Adelaide: Wakefield Press, 2002); the next two paragraphs owe a good deal to the argument developed there.

49 Cf. J. Derrida, *Specters of Marx: The State of the Debt, the Work of Mourning, and the New International*, trans. P. Kamuf (London: Routledge, 1994), p. 6. As Derrida reminds us, in theorising about a ghost or a 'specter': 'one does not "know" what it *is*. . . . *It is* something that one does not know, precisely, and one does not know if precisely it *is*, if it responds to a name and corresponds to an essence.'

50 See S. Cavell, *The Claim of Reason: Wittgenstein, Skepticism, Morality and Tragedy*, p. 241, also cited by Bruns, 'Cavell's Shakespeare', p. 616.

51 As a theatre director, of course, Hamlet insists upon a rather naive sense of the relation between 'theatre' and 'reality'. In advocating a form of mimeticism that would hold the 'mirror up to nature' (III. ii. 22) and a performance that would 'suit the action to the word' (17), he relies on an over-prescriptive sense of the distinction between the real and the unreal. Indeed, Hamlet evidently believes that events in a play can be conceived of in terms of their direct correlation to an anterior or predetermined reality, though at the same time it is precisely the improvisational unexpected 'event-like' nature of theatrical performance that he is forced to concede, complaining that 'clowns' are liable to speak 'more than is set down for them' (39).

52 See S. Cavell, *Disowning Knowledge*, p. 181 and cf. among others John Dover Wilson, *What Happens in Hamlet* (London: Cambridge University Press, 1967). As Gerald Bruns observes, 'It is no trouble to think of Hamlet's play-within-a-play, or indeed his whole effort of revenge, as a burlesque of Baconian method, since Hamlet experiences, without quite realizing it, the inevitable shortfall of strategic thinking with respect to the world' (Bruns, 'Cavell's Shakespeare', p. 616).

53 See Fortier, 'Shakespeare as "minor theatre"', p. 5.

54 As Bernstein notes, in Heidegger's sense of the term 'preserving' is to be contrasted with 'connoisseurship' or that which 'parries a work's thrust into the extraordinary'. See Bernstein, *The Fate of Art*, p. 88.

55 In an essay (which appears just as my own chapter goes to press) in *Shakespeare in the Present* (London: Routledge, 2002) Terence Hawkes makes an analogous point, along with the following acute summation: 'It's an interesting reflection of modern presuppositions concerning art, and especially drama, that this matter [the "Mousetrap" controversy] should be thought to constitute a "critical problem" or even a playwright's error. For it now seems reasonable to argue, to the contrary, that Claudius's null response represents another of those moments when the play, rather than one of its characters speaks. . . . Claudius's failure to respond to the dumb-show is not an "error" or a "mistake" made by Shakespeare. It's not something that goes "wrong". Or, rather, like Polonius's forgetting of his lines, it's the sort of "wrongness" that, once confronted, begins to reveal what our inherited notions of "rightness" conceal from us' (p. 73).

56 Francis Barker, 'Which dead? *Hamlet* and the ends of history' in F. Barker *et al.* (eds), *Uses of History: Marxism, Postmodernism and the Renaissance* (Manchester: Manchester University Press, 1991), pp. 47–75 (p. 52).

57 Again cf. Bruns, 'Cavell's Shakespeare', p. 616.

58 *Ibid.*

59 In teasing out the ethical implications of Hamlet's situation we might say that his failure to acknowledge the player's predicament in anything other than his own terms is clearly linked to what Cavell might term a fear of exposure of the self to the alterity of the other. And again there is an evident correlation here between Cavell and Levinas, especially insofar as

Levinas's own ethical turn substitutes 'What's Hecuba *to me*' for Hamlet's 'What's Hecuba *to him*', thus allowing for precisely the sense of hostage of self to other that Hamlet's response debars.

60 See Ben Jonson, 'To the Memory of my beloved', p. xliii, lines 22–4.

61 See Derrida, *Specters of Marx*, p. 22.

62 Or, as Coleridge puts it, 'I have a smack of Hamlet myself, if I may say so'; also cf. R. A. Foakes, *Hamlet versus Lear: Cultural Politics and Shakespeare's Art* (Cambridge: Cambridge University Press, 1993), p. 6.

63 See Derrida, *Specters of Marx*, p. 21.

64 Again cf. Derrida, *Specters of Marx*, p. xviii and also cf. his *Archive Fever: A Freudian Impression*, trans. E. Prenowitz (Chicago: University of Chicago Press, 1995).

65 Jacques Derrida during a question and answer session following 'Perjuries', a paper presented at the 'life.after.theory' conference held at the University of Loughborough, 10 November 2001. I am also indebted to Derrida for inadvertently suggesting the notion of the potential 'inhumanity' of a 'full remembering' rehearsed above a few lines earlier.

66 See W. Benjamin, 'Theses on the philosophy of history', *Illuminations*, trans. H. Zohn (London: Fontana Press, 1973), pp. 245–55, and cf. esp. p. 254.

67 Cf. Fortier, 'Shakespeare as "minor theater"', passim.

68 See Heidegger, 'The origin of the work of art', p. 166.

Critical knowledge, scientific knowledge and the truth of literature

Introduction: criticism has the character of knowledge, but it is not a kind of scientific knowledge

At the now-famous conference at Johns Hopkins University in 1966 that introduced both structuralism and what one could call, roughly, 'post-structuralism' to the USA, the critic Georges Poulet meditated about the nature of reading:

> a book is not shut in by its contours, is not walled up as in a fortress. It asks nothing better than to exist outside itself, or to let you exist in it. In short, the extraordinary fact in the case of a book is the falling away of the barriers between you and it. You are inside it; it is inside you; there is no longer either outside or inside.[1]

In the conversation afterwards, he said that 'criticism has the character of knowledge, but it is not a kind of scientific knowledge'.[2] The 'new aesthetics' – like all good names, a tag given to it by its enemies – seems to be an attempt to explore this position. In as much as it is a movement, it argues that the truth of art and the knowledge art generates are not the same as the truth of science and its knowledge. In turn, this reveals a mismatch between the way a text is experienced and how it is usually discussed by the disciplines that analyse it. These disciplines (forms of 'literary criticism') often, and usually implicitly, claim to offer a knowledge about the text that is true in the same way scientific knowledge is true: as if criticism *did* have the character of scientific knowledge. The 'new aesthetics' and its view of art are set against this claim. However, to take the argument a step further, if, as Bernstein, Bowie *et al.* argue, the character of art and of criticism is not scientific, what sort of knowledge can it claim? What are its characteristics? The 'new aesthetics' seems to leave hanging the question of what sort of knowledge criticism can have. The aim of this essay, then, is to explore the claim about truth that lies at the centre of the 'new aesthetics' and to see what it might be possible to know about art in a 'non-scientific' way.

Truth and art: truth as correspondence and *aletheia*

A significant strand in a range contemporary philosophy concerns the ways in which truth is to be understood. To simplify: there are two different conceptions. One

(Putnam calls it 'metaphysical realism'), is the belief that truth 'involves some sort of correspondence relation between words or thought-signs and external things and sets of things': the agreement or correspondence of a judgement, assertion or proposition with its object.[3] This is the 'common or garden' sense of truth, often identified with scientific understandings of the world. Assertions made under this way of understanding truth can, given the right circumstances, be proved or disproved. However, this model of truth – by far the most widely accepted and dominant model – seems to exclude much that people find of great value: visions of how the world was, is and ought to be, things that are core for people's personal and communal identity, feelings and judgements.

These are illuminated by another conception: another sense of truth which involves or invokes 'who we are and how things are in the world'. Some thinkers have argued that this 'existential' truth lies outside the realm of 'truth as correspondence' and is more 'true' to these concepts, ideas and feelings. This distinction is central to Andrew Bowie's work. Suggesting that 'many of the most important philosophical questions lead inevitably to issues connected to art',[4] he argues that, in the hermeneutic philosophical tradition at least, this understanding of truth is intrinsically involved with art

> via the claim that art reveals the world in ways which would not be possible without the existence of art itself – a version of this view can be ascribed to Schlegel, Novalis, Schleiermacher, Heidegger, Benjamin, Adorno and Gadamer . . . Truth here is seen in terms of the capacity of forms of articulation to 'disclose' the world.[5]

For Bernstein, too, 'art and aesthetics . . . appear as somehow more truthful than empirical truth . . . more rational than methodological reason, more just than liberal justice . . . more valuable than principled morality or utility'.[6] This is not to argue that art, and the world disclosed in art, are simply 'more true' than truth as correspondence, that 'art and aesthetics are true while truth-only cognition, say in its realisation in the natural sciences, is false'.[7] Rather, it is an attempt to think through 'what truth, morality and beauty (in its primary instance: art) are when what is denied is their categorical separation from each other'.[8] It marks, as far as I can see, an absolutely opposite position to Peter Lamarque's and Stein Haugom Olsen's work, seemingly on the same topic.[9]

Heidegger, perhaps, offers the strongest discussion of this view, principally in *Being and Time* and 'The Origin of the Work of Art', by arguing that truth is unveiling.[10] Dahlstrom argues that from the very 'outset Heidegger runs up against the logical prejudice of conceiving truth primarily as a property of a proposition. This prejudice abets and is abetted by the notion that theory and scientific knowledge, as so many systematic sets of true assertions, form the endgame of philosophy'.[11] Heidegger, in Section 44 of *Being and Time*, argues that truth as correspondence relies in turn upon a more primordial understanding of truth: the idea that truth is an uncovering or what he calls *aletheia*. Heidegger is not saying that 'truth as agreement' or as correspondence, or 'propositional truth', is wrong: his philosophy is 'not at odds with logic'.[12] Rather, he is arguing that the 'traditional' understanding of truth comes from and relies upon more primordial truth and, in turn, this 'being-true' is possible only 'on the basis of Being-in-the-world'. James Dicenso cites a very illuminating remark by Ortega y Gasset which predates Heidegger but captures his sense well:

> once known, truths acquire a utilitarian crust; they no longer interest us as truths but as useful recipes. That pure, sudden illumination which characterises truth accompanies the latter only at the moment of discovery. Hence its Greek name *aletheia*, which originally meant the same as the word apocalypsis later [did], that is, discovery, revelation, or rather, unveiling, removing a veil or cover.[13]

The question that arises, then, is this: what is revealed in this *aletheia*, this primordial revelation of truth? The answer to this is, in part, in Heidegger's essay 'On the Origin of the Work of Art'. Bernstein argues that this essay is not only central for understanding Heidegger but is a response to Kant. Very roughly, Bernstein argues that Kant separates the domains of understanding and reason – those that create assertion, truth as correspondence – from the domain of judgement – the faculty that appreciates beauty and art. It is this division that both formalises the separation of these two forms of knowledge and institutes the first as superior to the second. However, as Bernstein argues, this separation is complicated in Kant since judgement is entwined with 'commonality, communication and sensibility' and being 'capable of . . . judgement . . . and being human appear to be consubstantial'.[14] An 'attunement between us and things' is also 'an attunement between persons' and points to, or relies on, our being with others, our 'common' or 'communal sense' ('*sensus communis*').[15] Putting the 'traditional' conception of truth as assertion at the summit of philosophy is exactly the gesture Heidegger has been criticising, as it forgets Being. So, for Bernstein, the question the essay tries to answer is: what was 'art' like before this separation (of 'truth' and 'art') became taken for granted? Only by answering this can we see what the work of art is and does, and so, in turn, what is revealed in aletheia.

In 'On the Origin of the Work of Art' Heidegger argues that artworks do not simply represent reality as assertions do (although they do do this). More importantly and more fundamentally, they open up or 'unconceal' the world. A Greek temple 'opens a world', an artwork transforms 'our accustomed ties to the world'.[16] Art is able to break 'open an open place, in whose openness everything is other than usual' because of its nature as what Heidegger names 'poetry'.[17] It is 'poetry' because language is the paradigm of how all artworks work, since 'language alone brings what is, as something that is, into the Open for the first time'.[18] Thus, for Heidegger, the 'nature of art is poetry. The nature of poetry, in turn, is the founding of truth . . . art lets truth originate'.[19] An artwork reveals its – and our – world; it 'gives to things their look and to men their outlook'.[20] It reveals who and how we are, and how things are for us. It does this both by 'defamiliarising' what we take for granted in the world and so drawing attention to it but also, and in the same opening, drawing attention from 'the ordinary and particular to that which lets the ordinary and particular have their peculiar shape and meaning': the world.[21] There is no 'content' in a simple sense: truth reveals a world into which 'content' is put. This world, unveiled in an artwork, will vary from work to work: the world of a Greek temple is not the world of a Van Gogh painting nor the world of *Ulysses, Midnight's Children* or *Heart of Darkness*. Yet, this understanding of truth as unveiling a world cannot be reduced to truth as correspondence, but opens and shapes a world. As Heidegger writes later,

> Insofar as truth is thought in the traditional 'natural' sense as the correspondence of knowledge with being demonstrated in beings, but also insofar as truth is interpreted as the certainty of the knowledge of Being, *aletheia*, unconcealed in the sense of the opening, may not be equated with truth, rather, *aletheia*, unconcealment thought as opening, first grants the possibility of truth. For truth itself, just as Being and thinking, can only be what it is in the element of opening.[22]

That is, aletheia is the opening of a world on which truth as correspondence rests. First a world is established, opened, then truth claims in that world are made. This is a way of explaining philosophically the experience of art Proust describes:

> the original painter or the original writer proceeds on the lines of the oculist. The course of treatment they give us by their painting or by their prose is not always pleasant. When it is at an end the practitioner says to us: 'Now look!' And, lo and behold, the world around us (which was not created once and for all, but is created afresh as often as an original artist is born) appears to us entirely different from the old world but perfectly clear.[23]

A Matisse or a Picasso, or a poem like *Paradise Lost*, first opens a world before we can ask questions of this world. And it is the idea that art reveals or opens to a truth that is 'beyond' or different from 'truth-only cognition' that underlies the 'new aesthetics'.

The truth of art and ethics (and anxiety, irresoluteness, conscience, death)

The 'new aesthetics' seems to go further than this, though: both Bernstein and Bowie, drawing on Adorno, argue that it is through art, through this kind of revelation of truth, that an ethical critique can be made of the 'truth only cognition' characteristic of modernity.[24] Bowie argues that a conception of reason (and politics – I do not think the two can be separated) which fails to take account of aesthetics is potentially disastrous, as it is, for example, when the conception takes the form of contemporary scientism, or when it is unconcerned with the need to find ways of communicating rationality that will have a broad social resonance.[25] Bernstein writes that art 'is the critical self reflection of truth-only cognition and its conscience'.[26] In his recent book on Adorno, Bernstein describes what he calls 'Ethical Modernism': the radical claim that all the rational authority of modern moral norms and principles derives from fugitive ethical action and experience. Fugitive ethical experiences reveal the becoming modern of the ethical; by modern, I mean that conception of it which Adorno sees exemplified in modernist works of art. Thus, what is revealed by certain rare moments of ethical experience is an ethical modernism, that is, a fully modernist comprehension of the ethical.[27] Art here, in the form of offering a fugitive ethical experience, is, for Bernstein, one part of a source for 'a challenge to contemporary moral thought as well as a substantive alternative to it'.[28]

Although Adorno was opposed to Heidegger in many ways (illustrated by the first part of *Negative Dialectics*, for example), he shared some of the same philosophical trajectory, over the issue of truth at least. (Indeed, Bowie argues that Heidegger's concerns are not 'a total novum' and 'map onto the dominant concerns of Romantic philosophy and the history of Kantian and post-Kantian philosophy'; if so – and Bowie makes the case very strongly – this contiguity is hardly a surprise.)[29] Adorno writes of Benjamin that his

> writings are an attempt in ever new ways to make philosophically fruitful what has not yet been foreclosed by great intentions. The task he bequeathed was not to abandon such an attempt to the estranging enigmas of thought alone, but to bring the intentionless within the realm of concepts: the obligation to think at the same time dialectally and undialectally.[30]

That is, Benjamin's work, and the task Adorno takes up, is an attempt to bring into the 'realm of concepts' – philosophy – that which stands outside it (think of, for example, the role of the divine language in Benjamin's 'The task of the translator', or of the messianic in his 'Theses on the philosophy of history'). Bearing in mind the differences between Benjamin and this tradition, much post-Heideggerian thinking – including the hermeneutic tradition and the French phenomenological (and so, in part, post-structuralist) tradition – can be understood in an analogous way. In trying to explain the development of Heidegger's thought from Husserl (and not forgetting Heidegger's attempt cover up this influence, including his excision of his acknowledgement to Husserl in the fifth edition of *Being and Time* in 1941),[31] Dahlstrom writes that the

> young Heidegger sees something that largely escapes Husserl's intellectual radar, namely that the phenomena constituting religious experience, phenomena at the core of timeliness and historicity of human existence, do not readily admit, if at all, of a scientific comprehension. Just as importantly, he has – or better, comes to have – a conception of philosophy that would be imperilled if it either ignored these phenomena or attempted to secure them in a theory. The religious experience calls human beings back to such existential phenomena as anxiety, irresoluteness, conscience, death, not for the sake of theoretical closure but for the sake of opening human beings up to the disclosure of the original sense of these phenomena. So, too, philosophy, as Heidegger conceives it, must retrieve the phenomena for analogous purposes.[32]

Heidegger wants to bring these religious experiences ('anxiety, irresoluteness, conscience, death') into philosophy.[33] It seems to me that, although it may be a risk to invite these, and similarly unreasonable motivations (the desire to do good?), into philosophical thinking and certainly into how we understand literature, it is a risk well worth taking.[34] That this risks something worse seems to me to call for vigilance, not its elimination from thought.

The experiences of 'anxiety, irresoluteness, conscience, death' and the like that Heidegger and others sought to bring into philosophy are not, or are not only, or need not only be, religious experiences. They are also literary experiences, as thinkers about art, from Aristotle ('fear and pity') to the present, suggest. This is not to say, with so many, that religion and literature are the same (not, *pace* the highly significant and influential Newbolt Report of 1921, that 'literature is not just a subject for academic study, but one of the chief temples of the Human spirit, in which all should worship' and that the 'professor of Literature in a University should be . . . a missionary').[35] It is to say, though, that the literary experience also calls for 'anxiety, irresoluteness, conscience, death . . . for the sake of opening human beings up to the disclosure of the original sense of these phenomena': (this is surely one reason why religion and literature are often mistaken for each other). This is true of, for example, the Kafka aphorism about the need for books that, like axes, break the frozen sea within us or – in a longer analysis – Kermode's discussion of the relationship between death, apocalypse and literature in *The Sense of an Ending*. In this way, the 'new aesthetics' reveals – contra its defining critics Beech and Roberts – that how we conventionally discuss texts fails to take these profound experiences into account: *pace* Adorno on Benjamin, criticism fails to bring what is outside criticism into criticism. Being able to taxonomise Shakespeare's prosody or discuss his historical context is not the same as being moved by his plays – and it is the 'being moved' that we want to investigate. So this begs a question; indeed, from the point of view of the 'new aesthetics', it begs one of *the* questions.

'What is it about the art work that . . . ?'

If a work of art does offer a different sort of truth to what Bernstein calls 'truth-only cognition' – if the 'new aesthetics' is onto something – then *just what is it about the artwork that does this?* What sort of knowledge does this? What is it about, say, a picture of a pair of shoes (the painter's or a peasant's) or a day described in Dublin with adultery and an advertising canvasser that actually does this? And how might we discuss this without simply, say, presenting the artwork again?[36] (Is this a version of the question: what makes a great work of art great?) One thing that the 'new aesthetics' seems to reveal is the inability to answer these questions in conventional critical discourse. But does it offer any way of resolving this disjunction?

In one sense, clearly, 'what is it about the artwork that . . . ?' is a mistaken question that leads to a mistaken answer. (What thing in a novel reveals truth? The description of the freezing, starving army retreating from Moscow? The suffering of the main character? The adverbs? A banal and meaningless list.) Just as we do not feel molecules of air pressing against us, we feel the westerly wind, similarly we do not respond in this deep way to 'characterisation', say, or 'blocks of colour' or to 'metaphors' in a work but to the whole work as a whole work. Works of literature 'present' themselves and do not 're-present' themselves. To begin to break down an artwork ('character', 'plot', 'themes') in this way is already to treat it as an object of almost of 'natural science' to be looked at in a 'scientific' way: and so – while issues which we might call 'literary craft' might be more easily foregrounded in this way, and this is not unimportant – hoping to find the 'truth ingredient' in this way is mistaken.

The 'what is it about this artwork that . . . ?' question may also be a mistaken because it may be that each work of art reveals truth in a unique way which, if it allowed for any description, would ask for a unique description or act of criticism, one for which no rules of description or criticism, would fit. Perhaps only an innovation in critical language would be able to describe it. (This is perhaps what happened with Anglo-American literary modernism: the practitioners – Eliot, Woolf, Pound – had to be great critics as well as great artists in order to describe and think through what they were doing. Perhaps it is a pity that some of them – the racist and fascist Pound, for example – didn't think some more, or along different lines.) Yet can there be an altogether new language, let alone an altogether new critical language? Or perhaps no critical metalanguage could describe a work, leaving all 'criticism' to take place in new acts of artistic creation ('All serious art, music and literature is a critical act').[37]

But if this is a mistaken question, it seems we are left in a position where one would just present 'a great work of art' – to an audience, to a seminar, to a society – and let them appreciate it or not. It seems to me that learning to engage with art does not just happen in this way: that, rather, there is a process of *learning to attend to* art in certain sorts of ways. This does not mean that one could not develop other ways, or that there are not in fact numerous (and perhaps conflicting) ways of attending to an artwork. ('I was deeply moved by this novel even though I had to sit an exam on it'.) But it does mean that there are things to which one's attention can be drawn; this is one of things that teaching might be. There must (mustn't there?) be *something* about a great artwork that allows it to open towards, or to embody, or to be, this 'different sort of truth'. This 'something' is something we can talk about or, perhaps, talk *around* if we cannot name it directly (this is not an aesthetic mysticism). Stendahl's *The Red and Black* offers something other than (just) a history of France in 1830 or a satire on a conventional, generic *Bildungsroman* or a textbook on the psychology of love, ambition and hypocrisy or any other point of comparison.

Here an inadequacy in the language criticism uses to describe literature is made clear. This inadequacy is not at a 'surface' level: we all know what plot means, or metaphor. Nor is at the level of philology or literary history ('Hardy died in 1928'). This inadequacy is at the level 'before' these terms and on which these terms rely, the level of describing what it is about the work that grabs us. When somebody says they like a work because they identified with a character, or because of the 'way it was told', or because they like 'that sort of story', these are often thought of as naive reactions; in fact, they are the more primordial reactions. The (scandalous) inadequacy of much critical discourse is that we can't really do better than that: that while we use terms like 'identification', 'form' and 'genre' (to choose just three examples from many), and indeed base a whole critical industry on these terms and others like them, we don't have much of an idea what they actually mean or how they work. We take these terms for granted and so ignore them.

What does 'identification' mean?

For literature 'experts' (who are, exactly?), of course, reading is often considered to be much less 'naive' than 'identification', but I still think it apodictically true that for most people, and even for those employed to read and teach prose narratives, whether

'literary' or 'historical', identification is part of how and why we read: 'an embarrass-
ingly ordinary process', one so common and taken for granted that critics often
neglect to examine it, like the spectacles forgotten at the end of one's nose.[38] And, like
these spectacles (the sole joke in *Being and Time*, as it happens), it works best when it
is not noticed. When it is cloying, mawkish or over-heroic, or when readers find texts
sexist or racist or unacceptable ('Am I that name?') a 'dissonance' appears.[39] Yet, when
they work, as Diane Fuss writes, identifications

> are the origin of some of our most powerful, enduring and deeply felt pleasures . . . the
> source of considerable emotional turmoil, capable of unsettling or unmooring the pre-
> carious groundings of our everyday identities . . . Identifications are erotic, intellectual
> and emotional. They delight, fascinate, confuse, unnerve, and sometimes terrify.[40]

In her insightful book, *Psychoanalysis and the Scene of Reading*, Mary Jacobus
approaches these issues by using 'British object relations psychoanalysis, particularly
the version of object relations theory associated with contemporary post-Kleinian
thinking', aiming to explore 'the question of how things get, so to speak, from the
outside to the inside – simultaneously establishing the boundary between them and
seeming to abolish it'.[41] Yet the phenomenon is described as clearly in the high
Victorian idiom of Robert Louis Stevenson, who wrote that the 'plastic part of literature' is 'the highest and hardest thing to do in words'. Once 'accomplished', he continued, it 'equally delights the schoolboy and the sage . . . Compared with this',
Stevenson continues, 'all other purposes in literature . . . are bastard in nature, facile
of execution and feeble in result'.[42] These powerful moments are moments of identification, for 'we push the hero aside; we plunge into the tale in our own person and
bathe in fresh experience . . . Fiction is to the grown man what play is to a child; it is
there that he changes the atmosphere and tenor of his life'.[43] Both these in their different ways attest to the revelatory power of identification and to its centrality in the ways
in which an artwork reveals a world. Identifications are also complex, able to 'reverse
and disguise themselves, to multiply and contravene each other, to disappear and to
reappear years later'.[44] The process of identification is also part of how we think more
critically about reading: whenever a book or article discusses 'identity in such and such
a novel' it relies on the concept of identification with (say) characters, without explaining how that identification might arise in the first place. This is not to say that
accounts of identity formation (like Butler's basically Hegelian paradigm, for
example) are not accurate (if, for Butler, identity is constructed through parody of
texts – literary, living – this is to say identity is a sort of parody: but it does not explain
why or how it happens). It is to say that these sorts of accounts do not explain how
identifications work, how they get from text to subject, or how they have such power.
Indeed, for example, even in the discourse of psychoanalysis, the most likely place to
find such an explanation, Fuss finds that

> the psychoanalytic literature on identification is littered with taxonomic qualifiers that
> seek to identify, with greater and greater precision, modes and types of identifications:
> primary and secondary, feminine and masculine, imaginary and symbolic, maternal and
> paternal, idiopathic and hetereopathic, partial and total, centrifugal and centripetal,

narcissistic and regressive, hysterical and melancholic, multiple and terminal, positive and negative.[45]

Fuss goes on to suggest that this 'often incongruous proliferation of kinds of identification points to a theoretical difficulty psychoanalysis must routinely confront in laying hold of its object, a difficulty, that is in identifying identification'.[46]

And, yet, this thing we cannot identify or explain clearly is crucially important because, as Lacoue-Labarthe says, the

> term 'identification' is, however, borrowed from Freud, because it is ultimately the only one we possess to designate what is at stake in the mimetic process and, above all, because once eased out of its aesthetico-psychological context, in which it in fact remains problematical, it can be drawn into the stronger network of the proper (or own: *le propre*) and appropriating, of appropriation and de-propriation or disappropriation etc.[47]

That is, identification is the basis of politics ('*We*, the people . . .') and so is involved with art. What is at stake in the mimetic process is identification, which is what makes up the political (thus, the politics of deconstruction: 'an interrogation of the mimetologism and essentialism and hence of the metaphysics of presence').[48] Clearly the process of identification in reading novels is part of the revelation of 'how the world is for us' and part of the way that art changes the world. (How else was *Don Quixote* the 'novel that laughed Spain out of chivalry'?)

And yet, although it can be described, it cannot be, has not yet been, explained or defined. Perhaps, except for terms that are either vague (Stevenson's 'bathing', for example) or too precise to be useful outside a highly specific situation (Fuss's list of psychoanalytic taxonomies), there can be no strict definition, no one 'pinning down' of this fundamental experience that is part of reading, part of the revelation of truth in a work; but that does not mean that we should not talk about it. Indeed, to think that without a strict definition it is impossible to use this term, or discuss this experience, is the sign that criticism has misunderstood itself, and thinks that it is a (particular sort of) science, aspiring solely to 'truth as correspondence' and passing over the way that a world is revealed in artworks. Yet, identification is clearly centrally important in reading, in the way that literature opens up a different form of truth to 'truth-only cognition'.

What do 'form' and 'genre' mean?

The case of form and genre is more complex. Whenever a book or article discusses 'postmodern' or 'modernist' or 'realist' texts, or 'revenge tragedy', it relies on ideas about form and genre (and we can tell these apart and argue about what pigeonhole to put them in perfectly well: Beckett, modernist or postmodernist?) without explicitly understanding what form actually is. The rigorous attempts to split 'form' from 'content' (as in high structuralism, for example) only seem to reinforce the idea that the two are not really separate, save in our discussions of literature (as James said, 'the story and the novel, the idea and the form, are the needle and thread, and I never heard of a guild of tailors who recommend the use of the thread without the needle or the needle without the thread').[49] Clearly, form isn't simply 'how it's told' because – to choose just one example – the 'form' of a postmodern novel may include a rejection of narrative closure which will, clearly, involve 'content' elements. Form is how text and genre meet.

Peter Middleton and Tim Woods argue that genre

> is too often treated as a formalism, as if it were no more than a form of prosody that could be copied out of a manual. It is better thought of as a code of practise [*sic*] constantly under negotiation between texts and their readers, listeners, publishers, academics and reviewers, which advises them how they are expected to respond to the text.[50]

Indeed, for them, texts (which are all, in simple or in complex ways, perhaps, generic) and genre (which is, of course, textual) are the 'key sites of literariness . . . where literary production is not reducible to algorithms of language and cannot be dissolved into wider historical matrices'.[51] Even

> the most innovative writing presupposes many generic reading and distribution practices. Equally, the most production-line generic text may sometimes test the limits of genre and reformulate them tentatively, because genre is remade by every instance of its use. Like language, it exists only as practices, and its codes are no more than partially articulated recognition of its sedimented forms.[52]

Genre is not just a way of writing: it is a way of reading, too. It is where reading and writing meet. Genre – with all its signs, both textual and extra-textual – forms a horizon of expectations. Genre is the context of a work that both frames it and makes it comprehensible, as it were, 'externally' and gives it a shape 'internally'. Works – in their creation, in their reception – are suffused by context, by the language games they inhabit, and 'genre' is how context and language games are described for literature.

In the opening essay of *The World, the Text and the Critic*, Edward Said offers a way to understand how texts work in the world by discussing the interplay of 'filiation' and 'affiliation'. For him, roughly, filiation – the lines of descent – reflects how works influence and descend from each other, how, in T. S. Eliot's terms, the tradition of writing works. Affiliation reflects the text's relation not to the influence of other texts over time, but to the text's location in its own time, context and culture, a 'phenomenon in the world, located in a network of non-literary, non-canonical and non-traditional affiliations'.[53] I suggest that genre and form are a way of describing how these two meet at the point of any one text – a way of describing both the diachronic and synchronic influences on a text and on how that text is to be read. For example and to generalise, Said's work has generally concerned the affiliations of a work: his first book explored how Conrad's life and imperial experiences shaped his writing. Again, as with 'identification', there is no clear-cut definition of genre and to look for a general one is to think of criticism as a science, seeking to atomise both its concepts and its objects. Yet, even though these concepts are vague and changeable, they are vital in coming to terms with 'what is it about the artwork that' grabs out attention: that makes it great.

An example: *Heart of Darkness*

Of course, much of the 'new aesthetics' could be seen, as Beech and Roberts argue, as conservative and backward looking. However, this is not necessarily the case. If we assume that ideas about 'identification' and 'form and genre' are part of how a work reveals or uncovers a world, both can be seen as radically changing the way in which we understand literary texts. This is the case with *Heart of Darkness*, for example.

Eugene Goodheart writes that when he first encountered the novella in the 1950s, little mattered 'apart from Marlow's psychological drama on his African journey'.[54] Even in Hannah Arendt's account in *The Origins of Totalitarianism*, which uses the book as a way to discuss imperialism, the focus is on Kurtz as a European. F. R. Leavis wrote that the 'details of the journey to and up the Congo are presented to us as if we are making the journey ourselves' and Andrea White discusses the use of Marlow to 'control our response'.[55] These are questions of identification, of the way in which the European readings are identified through the European characters. However, quite famously, the study of *Heart of Darkness* was shaken up by another identification: from Chinua Achebe's point of view, Conrad was a 'bloody racist' (and so were Marlow and Kurtz).[56] From this – from this act which stemmed from a very different identification – a new way of seeing this novel has emerged: Conrad's Congo is not a psychic phantasmagoria, but the historically located site of an imperialist atrocity. The colonial exploitation is not the backdrop to the journey of a Western mind: rather, the 'vilest scramble for loot that ever disfigured the history of human conscience and geographical expansion' leads to the psychic collapse of the European narrator.[57] W. G. Sebald writes, with insight, that on the march to Leopoldville, 'Korzeniowski [Conrad] began to grasp that his own travails did not absolve him from the guilt which he had incurred by his mere presence in the Congo . . . he now regarded his original plan of taking up a command . . . with revulsion'.[58]

And this, too, leads to questions about genre, about how *Heart of Darkness* is read. Clearly, it is conventionally seen as a novel. However, what if it were seen not as a novel but as an act of testimony? Shoshona Felman and Dori Laub write of how testimony is 'pervasive, how it is implicated – sometimes unexpectedly – in almost every kind of writing'.[59] More than this, their discussion suggests that testimony is a different genre to fiction: 'the concept of the testimony . . . is in fact quite unfamiliar and estranging . . . the more we look closely at texts, the more they show us that, unwittingly, we do not even know what testimony is and that, in any case, it is not simply what we thought we knew it was.'[60] As Conrad's biographer Norman Sherry makes clear, Conrad and Marlow had different experiences and cannot be mapped onto each other. However, it is also true that there is no *cordon sanitaire* – as Achebe puts it – between the two.[61] Hawkins argues that *Heart of Darkness* was 'remarkably faithful to the facts of the Congo in 1890'.[62] And, while Ian Watt argues that the novella is 'no more a direct representation of conditions in the Congo in 1890 than it is of Conrad's actual experience there' he does concede that 'it is an expression of the essence of the social and historical reality of the Congo Free State as his imagination recreated it'.[63] If the genre of the book changes – if its context or genre as testimony is foregrounded

– then *Heart of Darkness* looks very different: an account of an unwilling perpetrator in the genocide (or at least, the mass murder) that characterised the Congo Free State during this period. Indeed, our view – our context – of this whole period has changed. In his second edition of *The King Incorporated*, a book discussing the Congo Free State, Neal Ascherson writes that

> moral reflection on the details and implications of the Nazi 'Final Solution' . . . has come to overshadow all assessments of our times. And the discovery that genocide is still with us, in Cambodia or Rwanda, has only made that shadow darker. This change of emphasis has altered perspectives on the history of the Congo Free State. What now seems most important is the sheer loss of life.[64]

Marlow and Conrad may not be analogous to Nazis, but they are certainly collaborators in atrocities (how far and how much, how real and how fictional are all questions to be asked). The unsettling effect that these suggestions have reveals that questions about identification, form and genre, in turn prompted by asking 'what is it about the art work that . . . ?', have led to a new vision of this text and the world it reveals.

Conclusion

In his much-praised book *Consilience*, which spreads from science to scientism, E. O. Wilson writes that the 'structuralist approach [to culture] is potentially consistent with the picture of mind and culture emerging from natural sciences and biological anthropology': to further improve our understanding, it needs 'a realistic connection to biology and cognitive psychology'.[65] (Indeed, much fascinating and insightful work has been done on literature following scientific advances, under the sign, as it were, of 'truth as correspondence'.)[66] However, at the core, perhaps, of the conference at Johns Hopkins on The Language of Criticism and the Science of Man, was an encounter between a scientific understanding of the truth of art ('truth as correspondence') and a different understanding ('truth as revealing'). In this encounter, and following Heidegger, it was not that either way of understanding truth was wrong, but that they were different, and one relied on the other. This is the centre of Derrida's contribution to the conference, which can be seen as a meditation on the relation between art and science. He writes of the 'two interpretations of interpretation': one 'dreams of deciphering a truth or an origin which escapes play and the order of the sign, and which lives the necessity of interpretation as an exile'.[67] This is interpretation understood as looking for propositional truth, truth as correspondence: the sort of truth which inspires the science that 'interprets' the world around us, believing that 'the world is orderly and can be explained by a small number of natural laws'.[68] The other form of interpretation, 'which is no longer turned toward the origin affirms play', the Nietzschean 'joyous affirmation of the play of the world' as it is revealed, somehow, before it is taxonomised.[69] Derrida goes on to argue – after Heidegger, again – that these two are 'absolutely irreconcilable, even if we live them simultaneously and reconcile them in a obscure economy' and that there is no question of 'choosing' between them.[70]

However, although there may be no question of choosing between them in how we live (that is, perhaps we are all hypocrites, relying day to day on both 'truth as correspondence' and *aletheia*, how the world is for us), there are choices in how we come to use these understandings of truth in criticism and the so-called 'human sciences' in general. The work of Michel Foucault, for example, stems precisely from the disjunction between these two as it explores, genealogically, precisely how, and with what contradictions and paradoxes, 'truth as correspondence' stems from 'how the word is for us', truth as revealed (another legacy of Heidegger). That is, for example, the discourses of 'how we are' establish the possibility of an identity on which power can be enacted – the 'Soul' Foucault calls it in *Discipline and Punish* – which acts both as 'the prison of the body' and as the site for further discoveries that could be in correspondence with this worldview – ideas about the science of criminology or of reformation.[71] Foucault 'is trying to show us how every culture lives, thinks, sees, makes love, by a set of unconscious guiding assumptions with non-rational determinants' ('how the world is for us') and how, in turn, these determinants are the basis for discoveries which have 'truth as correspondence'.[72] These two different forms of truth also seem to underlie ideas about communal and communicative reason. To change one's worldview, the truth as revealed to you, as you, is a *conversion*; that is why these moments are considered so important. It is a change that happens for many reasons – the experience of war or of religion, say – and those who champion Reason argue that Reason, too, can be central in these conversions.

However, the choices that the disciplines which deal with literature have made might be questioned. Putnam finds a 'certain scientism' not only obviously in logical positivism but also in the 'relativism' that reduces 'all there is to "rationality"' – to 'what your culture says . . . that [rationality] is simply defined by the local cultural norms is a scientistic theory inspired by anthropology'.[73] One could add in the case of literary studies, that structuralism, psychoanalysis, Marxism, nearly all forms of historicism (old or new) which rely on positivism all partake of this scientific positivism and make the same claim to 'truth as correspondence', a sort of truth that only offers one form of interpretation of an artwork. Perhaps criticism should eschew positivism and aim for a different aesthetic, informed by a philosophical tradition more in tune with literature, rather than simply plumping for an unspoken and often unrecognised scientism. The critical language in which we discuss artworks seems often to pass over the ways in which worlds are revealed in art and the ethical and political potential of this. However, there must be some form of discussion that can be held about artworks concerning what is worth attending to in them: what is it about them that . . . ? I have suggested that naive or undefined but widely used terms, such as identification, genre and form, might, in fact, be very useful and revealing when thought through more fully. They might be the grounding of some form of very provisional knowledge for criticism, different from scientific knowledge. In the case of *Heart of Darkness*, shifts that stem from these categories of understanding radically changed, in a politically challenging way, how the novel was understood. The 'new aesthetics' questions the positivist scientism that seems, often implicitly, to dominate intellectual enquiry.

Notes

1 G. Poulet, 'Criticism and the experience of interiority' in R. Macksey and E. Donato (eds), *The Language of Criticism and the Science of Man* (Baltimore, MD: Johns Hopkins University Press, 1970), pp. 56–88 (p. 57).

2 Poulet, 'Criticism and the experience of interiority', p. 57.

3 H. Putnam, *Reason, Truth and History* (Cambridge: Cambridge University Press, 1981), p. 126.

4 A. Bowie, *From Romanticism to Critical Theory: The Philosophy of German Literary Theory* (London: Routledge, 1997), p. 159.

5 *Ibid.*

6 J. M. Bernstein, *The Fate of Art: Aesthetic Alienation from Kant to Derrida and Adorno* (Cambridge: Polity, 1992), pp. 1–2.

7 *Ibid.*, p. 2.

8 *Ibid.*

9 See especially their exhaustive and rigorous work *Truth, Fiction and Literature* (Oxford: Oxford University Press, 1994).

10 At the same time, Heidegger's own Nazism reveals the worst that this idea can imply. For a longer discussion of this, in relation to the work of Hannah Arendt and Philippe Lacoue-Labarthe, see my forthcoming *The Holocaust and the Postmodern*.

11 D. O. Dahlstrom, *Heidegger's Concept of Truth* (Cambridge: Cambridge University Press, 2001), p. 17.

12 *Ibid.*, p. 1.

13 J. DiCenso, *Hermeneutics and the Disclosure of Truth: A Study in the Work of Heidegger, Gadamer and Ricoeur* (Virginia: University Press of Virginia, 1990), p. 67.

14 Bernstein, *The Fate of Art*, p. 54.

15 *Ibid.*, p. 55.

16 M. Heidegger, 'On the origin of the work of art', trans. A. Hofstadter, *Poetry, Language, Thought* (London: Harper & Row, 1971), pp. 17–87, 42, 66.

17 *Ibid.*, p. 72.

18 *Ibid.*, p. 73.

19 *Ibid.*, pp. 75, 78.

20 Cited in Bernstein, *The Fate of Art*, p. 84.

21 *Ibid.*, p. 88.

22 M. Heidegger, *On Time and Being* (New York: Harper, 1972), p. 69.

23 M. Proust, *Remembrance of Things Past*, 3 vols, trans. C. K. Scott Moncrieff and T. Kilmartin (Harmondsworth: Penguin, 1983), vol. 2, *The Guermantes Way*, p. 338.

24 Although there are parallels, the 'new aesthetics' is not aiming, as Martha Nussbaum does for example in *The Fragility of Goodness* (Cambridge: Cambridge University Press, 1986), to bring works of art into philosophy as an aid to philosophical reason (interpreting 'a tragedy is messier than assessing a philosophical example' Nussbaum writes; to 'invite such material into the centre of an ethical inquiry concerning these problems of practical reason is . . . to add to its content a picture of reason's procedures and problems that could not be readily conveyed in any other form', p. 14). Rather it is to suggest that the artwork itself is a ground for critique. Bernstein makes the point that, in modernity, we 'cannot return to judgement directly – the idle hope of modern neo-Aristotelians – since the conditions for it have been erased. Judgement now occurs only in and through self-reflection', *The Fate of Art*, p. 274.

25 A. Bowie, 'Confession of a "new aesthete": a response to the "new philistines"', *New Left Review*, 225 (1997), 105–26 (p. 108).

26 Bernstein, *The Fate of Art*, p. 5.

27 J. M. Bernstein, *Adorno: Disenchantment and Ethics* (Cambridge: Cambridge University Press, 2001), p. 38.

28 *Ibid.*, p. 39.

29 Bowie, *From Romanticism to Critical Theory*, p. 163.

30 T. W. Adorno, *Minima Moralia*, trans. E. F. N. Jephcott (London: Verso, 1978), pp. 151–2.

31 See H. Ott, *Martin Heidegger: A Political Life*, trans. A. Blunden (London: Fontana, 1994), p. 172ff.

32 Dahlstrom, *Heidegger's Concept of Truth*, p. 174.

33 Derrida, in contrast but also in parallel, aims not, perhaps, to bring these experiences into philosophy but rather to reveal what he calls in one place the 'exorbitant': 'the point of a certain exteriority to the totality of the age of logocentrism. Starting from this point of exteriority . . . a certain deconstruction of that totality which is also a traced path . . . might be broached'; J. Derrida, *Of Grammatology*, trans. Gayatri Chakravorty Spivak (Baltimore, MD: Johns Hopkins University Press, 1976), p. 162. If Heidegger and Benjamin want to draw in the 'unphilosophical' into philosophy, then Derrida wants to use the 'unphilosophical' to draw the limits of philosophy.

34 Certainly, it seems better than the opposite, which would mean excluding these things from our consideration and thought. Emmanuel Levinas writes that reason 'makes human society possible: but a society whose members would only be reasons would vanish as a society'; *Totality and Infinity: An Essay on Exteriority*, trans. A. Lingis (London: Kluwer Academic Publishers, 1991), p. 119. John Stewart Mill's life-changing revelation was that he would not wish to live in a utilitarian Utopia, that pushpin – prejudice aside – was not as good as poetry.

35 J. Giles and T. Middleton (eds), *Writing Englishness 1900–1950* (London: Routledge, 1995), pp. 149–60 (pp. 159, 158).

36 Have we all had conversations that go like this: 'To see why it's so good you just have to read it'; or '*Middlemarch* is fantastic. I didn't think so when I read it for my degree, but I think so now, and not because it meets these five criteria of "fantastic-ness"'?

37 George Steiner, *Real Presences* (London: Faber & Faber, 1989), p. 11. From the other direction, Hartman argues that 'literary commentary may cross the line and become as demanding as literature'; G. Hartman, *Criticism in the Wilderness* (New Haven: Yale University Press, 1980), p. 201.

38 D. Fuss, *Identification Papers* (London: Routledge, 1995), p. 1. An exception to this is Karl Morrison's '*I am You': The Hermeneutics of Empathy in Western Theory, Literature and Art* (Princeton: Princeton University Press, 1988).

39 See, for example, D. Riley, '*Am I that Name?': Feminism and the Category of 'Women' in History* (Basingstoke: Macmillan, 1988).

40 Fuss, *Identification Papers*, p. 2.

41 Mary Jacobus, *Psychoanalysis and the Scene of Reading* (Oxford: Oxford University Press, 1999), pp. 9, 19.

42 R. L. Stevenson, *The Essays of Robert Louis Stevenson* (London: Macdonald, 1950), pp. 355–6.

43 *Ibid.*, p. 361.

44 Fuss, *Identification Papers*, p. 2.

45 *Ibid.*, p. 4.

46 Fuss, *Identification Papers*, p. 4.

47 Lacoue-Labarthe, *Heidegger, Art and Politics*, p. 82.

48 Bernstein, *The Fate of Art*, p. 147.

49 Janet Adam Smith (ed.), *Henry James and Robert Louis Stevenson: A Record of Friendship and Criticism* (London: Rupert Hart-Davis, 1948), p. 70.

50 P. Middleton and T. Woods, *Literatures of Memory: History, Time and Space in Postwar Writing* (Manchester: Manchester University Press, 2000), p. 7.

51 *Ibid.*

52 *Ibid.*, p. 8.

53 B. Ashcroft and P. Ahluwalia, *Edward Said: The Paradox of Identity* (London: Routledge, 1999), p. 42.

54 E. Goodheart, *Does Literary Studies Have a Future?* (Madison: University of Wisconsin Press, 1999), p. 116.

55 F. R. Leavis, *The Great Tradition* (London: Penguin, 1962), p. 194; A. White, *Joseph Conrad and the Adventure Tradition: Constructing and Deconstructing the Imperial Subject* (Cambridge: Cambridge University Press, 1993), p. 75.

56 C. Achebe, 'An image of Africa', *Massachusetts Review*, 18:4 (1977), 782–94 (p. 788).

57 Cited in C. Watts, *Conrad's 'Heart of Darkness': A Critical and Contextual Discussion* (Milan: Mursia International, 1977), p. 61.

58 W. G. Sebald, *The Rings of Saturn*, trans. M. Hulse (London: The Harvill Press, 1998), pp. 120–1.

59 S. Felman and D. Laub, *Testimony: Crises of Witnessing in Literature, Psychoanalysis, and History* (London: Routledge, 1992), p. 7.

60 *Ibid.*

61 Achebe, 'An image of Africa', p. 787.

62 H. Hawkins, 'Joseph Conrad, Roger Casement and the Congo reform movement', *Journal of Modern Literature*, 9:1 (1981–2), 65–80 (p. 68).

63 I. Watt, *Conrad in the Nineteenth Century* (London: Chatto & Windus, 1980), p. 138.

64 N. Ascherson, *The King Incorporated: Leopold the Second and the Congo* (London: Granta Books, 1999), p. 8.

65 E. O. Wilson, *Consilience: The Unity of Knowledge* (London: Little, Brown & Company, 1998), p. 169.

66 See, for example, M. Turner, *Reading Minds: The Study of English in the Age of Cognitive Science* (Princeton, NJ: Princeton University Press, 1991) and *The Literary Mind* (Oxford: Oxford University Press, 1996).

67 J. Derrida, *Writing and Difference*, trans. A. Bass (London: Routledge & Kegan Paul, 1978), p. 292.

68 Wilson, *Consilience*, p. 3.

69 Derrida, *Writing and Difference*, p. 292.

70 *Ibid.*

71 M. Foucault, *Discipline and Punish*, trans. A. Sheridan (Harmondsworth: Penguin, 1977), p. 30.

72 Putnam, *Reason, Truth and History*, p. 160. Of course, the status of Foucault's work has always been in question; however, Foucault himself was first and loudest in eschewing its claim to positivism.

73 *Ibid.*, p. 126.

Melancholy as form: towards an archaeology of modernism

> When traditional aesthetics . . . praised harmony in natural beauty, it projected the self-satisfaction of domination onto the dominated.[1]

We can date the end of the novel precisely: the last novel ever written was Flaubert's *Sentimental Education*, published in 1869. It is sometimes said that Flaubert's work inaugurates the waning of the *Bildungsroman* and the inauguration of the novel of disillusionment. But that says too little. Can there be a *roman* without the *Bildung*? The unifying biographical form of the classical novel, paralleling the ambitions and trajectory of secularising modernity, chartered the formation, education, quest and achievement of identity and worldliness of its bourgeois heroes and heroines. What was previously narrative and adventure becomes in Flaubert a stutter, every appointment of learning a site for blindness, every posting of hope a tour of disappointment, each potential moment of formation a blank; the best there ever was, its protagonists conclude, is the memory of the adolescent visit to the local bordello – a visit, we should remember, which terminated in humiliation, mortification, and flight. The disillusioning of Frédéric portends the end of beauty: the semblance of wholeness or harmony through which narrative form raised the contingencies of empirical life into meaning; in Flaubert the semblance of wholeness devolves into nothing more than the movement of time.[2] One might claim that what Flaubert's novel projects is not so much the ruin of the ideal but the accommodation of bourgeois ideals to worldly reality, and hence a realism of maturity. The unfolding of modern fiction from Flaubert belies this easy synthesis of ideal and real; what transpires in modernist fictions is either the elaboration and continuation of Flaubert's stutter, *in extremis* in Proust, or, when even that seems no longer possible, an interrogation of those ideals as what themselves make life stutter and collapse, hence the affirmation of what is incompatible with those ideals as alone what might be required for their satisfaction.[3] Adorno pointedly expresses this conception of modernism: 'Rimbaud's postulate of the radically modern is that of an art that moves in the tension between *spleen et idéal*, between spiritualisation and obsession with what is most distant from spirit. The primacy of spirit in art and the inroads made by what was previously taboo are two sides of the same coin.'[4]

In order to begin prosecuting this conception of modernism, I will first sketch out the central lineaments of the dialectic of spleen and ideal as they are presented in Adorno's modernist philosophical aesthetics. These aesthetic claims inevitably raise a question: why consider the unfolding dialectic of forming-giving and decomposition, the immanent cancellation of form as modernism's most exacting aesthetic, hence formal demand as somehow a mode of resistance to the social world outside art, as not simply critique, but for Adorno the most salient and rationally coherent mode of critique? The long answer to this question, which I will not be pursuing here, would involve demonstrating the internal connection and necessary opposition between the development of the practical forms of bourgeois social life and those of autonomous modern art. My short answer will proceed through a discussion of Philip Roth's *American Pastoral*.[5] At first blush, this might seem a strange choice since Adorno's aesthetic theory is informed by the classic works of high modernism – Beckett, Kafka, Berg, Picasso – and it is the works of these artists that unquestionably best exemplify Adorno's thought. But it is less clear that reflection on these artists will illuminate the social question. On the reading of *American Pastoral* I will offer its representational content, the categories practically informing its representational world *themselves* undergo the dialectic of spleen and ideal, hence allegorically reinscribing the modernist dialectic as the truth content of empirical experience. To put the same thought another way: there is something uncannily 1869ish about *American Pastoral*, as if Seymour Levov is a very American Frédéric Moreau, as if Vietnam and the race riots contiguous with it were America's 1848, and hence as if in the narrating of that moment the necessity of modernism itself, the dialectic of form-giving and decomposition, were borne (again), or perhaps born in its American form, discovered as something not inherited from Europe and hence as a continuation of European art and history, but as intrinsic to the art practices of our place and time. *American Pastoral* can thus be conceived as performing an archaeology of American modernism, the spleen incumbent upon, or proper to, our ideals. *American Pastoral* narrates and represents the collapse of narration and representation, and the becoming of the self-reflexive, self-lacerating text whose relation to its world lies in its failure to be one with it.

Against beauty: categories

Adorno reconstructs the categories of aesthetics from the perspective of the achievements of high modernism, post-stutter so to speak. Modernist art is autonomous art, but autonomous art must always be understood as possessing a 'double character': 'something that severs itself from empirical reality and thereby from society's functional context and yet is at the same time part of empirical reality and society's functional context'.[6] Hence aesthetic phenomena are directly both purely aesthetic, phenomena that have their gravity and meaning as ingredients in an autonomous practice, and social facts, although these two aspects are never experientially simultaneous. In a gesture that will always strike his critics as intolerably fast, Adorno conceives of autonomy in art as categorially or formally setting art into opposition to society:

Much more importantly, art becomes social by its opposition to society, and it occupies this position only as autonomous art. By crystallizing in itself as something unique to itself, rather than complying with existing social norms and qualifying as 'socially useful,' it criticizes society by merely existing, for which puritans of all stripes condemn it. There is nothing pure, nothing structured strictly according to its own immanent law, that does not implicitly criticize the debasement of a situation evolving in the direction of a total exchange society in which everything is heteronomously defined. Art's asociality is the determinate negation of determinate society.[7]

It cannot be the simple fact of art's elaboration of its own immanent laws that explains how artistic autonomy resists social utility and heteronomy. Rather the specificity of art's immanent laws is that what they enable is the production of *particular* works whose claim to authenticity, art's form of rightness, depends upon nothing apart from their own internal complexion. Artworks are neither fungible things satisfying some antecedent end or idea nor empty universals that equate all the elements falling under them; as being lawful in its own right each work attains universality through particularisation.[8] Hence, it is only by means of particularisation that artworks epitomise the unsubsumable. An autonomous work is the semblance of a thing-in-itself, the semblance of something that is emphatically 'for itself' and not for another.

Because there are in fact no final laws of form, no laws constitutive of the novel or painting or music, then in each art form particularisation occurs progressively through the negation and departure from those formal requirements that have appeared to be constitutive of that form, its autonomy. Through a reiterative negation of features extrinsic to what enables a work to be a work of a kind, and the very work it is, modernist works seek a stringency of form in which their capacity to claim binding aesthetic attention is achieved wholly immanently. At this level of abstractness, there would seem to be little to separate this account of modernism from Clement Greenberg's, in which, in the case of painting, the representational or compositional demands of traditional painting are displaced by what can occur on and through dedication to a painting's surface – although Adorno's ascetic predilection for an intense muteness and silence as the terminus of this process would make Gerhard Richter's grey monochromes exemplary rather than the vibrant large canvases of Jackson Pollock. This difference, however, is more than a matter of preference or emphasis; for Adorno progressive autonomisation, the achievement of particularity, comes to possess the 'ideal of blackness'[9] since, as Kant anticipated, without the impoverishment implicit in this ideal artworks, however absorptive, would too easily lend themselves to consolation or a culinary sensuality, becoming thereby useful once more. But in order for this thought not to be an importation into art of a moralised asceticism (and art cannot make asceticism its norm[10]), there must be something more to the characterisation of the progressive achievement of autonomy than regression into immanent laws of working. The achievement of autonomy must be capable of being comprehended through the dialectic of ideal and spleen.

The collaborative antagonism between ideal and spleen is, in fact, but one of a number of pairs that function at different levels of analysis emerging from different conceptual spaces that Adorno employs in order to construe the core dialectic of modernism: beauty and ugliness, integration and disintegration, spiritualisation and fragmentariness, construction and expression, harmony and dissonance, art and anti-art. In Adorno's account the second term of each pair begins as the outside, the boundary, border or limit of the modern work, what compelling works normatively surmount or leave behind, and then in the reversal that makes modernist works the unavoidable fate of artistic autonomy becomes the condition through which the dominant or positive term is enabled to carry on functioning. It is then less a question of each artistic practice finding its own laws of form, its a priori (even its contingent a priori), and more an issue of each practice finding itself being required, simply as a matter of its forms being wholly and only secular, disenchanted, to fully acknowledge the diverse elements composing it, the material or given or elemental on which its form-giving works. And while in a wholly formalist way it would not be false to say that the second term of each pair represents the material condition of possibility that both must and cannot be wholly avowed by the positive term, this unduly normalises the dialectic. For Adorno, the reversal is more radical. As I read *Aesthetic Theory*, Adorno sees in the unfolding dialectic of modernism the emergence of a material logic of normativity. Hence, in the moment of disintegration and spleen what was formally excluded from the ideal, formally its material condition of possibility, becomes its stand-in and bearer: only in what fails the ideal is the authentic hope of the ideal to be found.

'Dissonance,' Adorno states, 'the seal of everything modern, gives access to the alluringly sensuous by transfiguring it into its antithesis, pain: an aesthetic archetype of ambivalence.'[11] Dissonance is the seal of the modern in the sense that it is that moment in which a work's illusoriness, its semblance character, is seen through and acknowledged; hence dissonance is a general term for the moment of negativity in modernist works in which their material or elemental substratum becomes manifest in divergence from their controlling formative elaboration (albeit necessarily only through and in virtue of that elaboration). Artworks, after all, are not real particulars, but only images or semblances of particulars; they exemplify particularity without being it. And they can appear as unique particulars, non-exchangeable thises, only on the condition that they remain enclosed in semblance. But this dialectic is only intelligible if we conceive of each form of autonomous art, each practice, as essentially the vehicle through which its elemental components, its material and practical givens and presuppositions, attain articulacy. Because, again, if nothing predetermines what is to count as a material component or elemental given, and nothing further predetermines what is to count as providing their articulation, then modernist works can assure themselves of their integrity only in their departures from eloquence.

According to Adorno the *stakes* of modernist art, then, are its material components, experiential givens, elemental presuppositions, all that is worked *up* in a modernist work. Or more precisely, in its unfolding modernist art discovers that works are the vehicles for their components, hence not the ideals operative in its form-giving but the materials formed become art's stake. One might conceive of this reversal as implicit from the outset in art practices that, by virtue of the rationalisation of modern social and political forms, have autonomy imposed upon them. The half-truth in this thought is that it is the unavoidability of autonomy that exposes modern art to the reversal that takes hold in modernism. But modernism progressively enacts a reversal, discovering and rediscovering it, only in the recurrent experiences of disillusionment, inside and outside art, with bourgeois ideals, experiences in which those ideals themselves are found to block the immanence and secularity they initially appear to promise and constitute. Spleen's obsession with what resists artistic forming is both a critique of aesthetic idealism and a reversal internal to autonomous art whereby its stakes are transformed from ideal to object, hence a demand for a bottom-up rather than top-down form of working. This thesis, if correct, would certainly lead to the monochrome and the readymade having a quite different significance than that usually offered. Equally, it is this reversal in which ideal is the vehicle for its spleenish other that gives Adorno's aesthetics its most peculiar inflection: art is the vehicle for and hence for the sake of non-art; artistic semblance is both the condition of articulacy and the prison house of its elements. This is the pathos of each modernist work: its fullest achievement can only be its failing – it is not the particular it longs to be but only a semblance. Dissonance as the determinate emancipation of the elemental from its integral setting evinces the aspiration to non-art in art; which, again, is why dissonance is the seal of everything modern.

There are many names for semblance in Adorno, but beauty is certainly the most insistent. Yet, Adorno contends that beauty is systematically elusive; it is indispensable in signalling an object's departure from the economy of self-preservation and utility, and hence in conveying the locus of a beholder's interest in an object beyond the practical, without it being possible to specify in what *its* transfigurative power consists. Beauty hence comes to function in *Aesthetic Theory* as the generalised equivalent or dummy term for the transfigurative mechanisms through which art raises its components to absorptive particulars. This is why, in the section dedicated to 'Art beauty',[12] beauty is almost never mentioned. The first two sentences of the section are emphatic in this regard: 'Nature is beautiful in that it appears to say more than it is. To wrest this more from that more's contingency, to gain control of its semblance, to determine it as semblance as well as to negate it as unreal: This is the idea of art.'[13] Modernist art is the practice of disenchanting beauty, secularising it without reduction or deceit. This thought anticipates the manner in which the modernist dialectic can perform a material logic of normativity: if beauty is the conceptual site of the more through which objects escape the sway of instrumentality, and hence the site of a meaning or normativity that eludes means-ends rationality, and art the disenchanting of that site, then art is 'the secularization of transcendence'.[14] That phrase encapsulates both the categorial ambitions of *Aesthetic Theory* and its guiding thought. Art, as much as any other modern practice, participates in the dialectic of enlightenment, albeit taking that dialectic in a direction different than what occurs outside art. In what, then, is art's secularisation of transcendence meant to consist? What counts as or reveals an artwork's accomplishment as one of secularising transcendence? Plainly, nothing other than work on and against illusory transcendence; and if beauty is a unique site of traditional transcendence, the unique site outside the domain of the practical, and art the field of disenchanting beauty, then only anti-art, only what spells the artwork as beyond the beautiful while remaining art can pronounce secular transcendence.

In art the most immediate conveyors of transcendence are unity, harmony, integration; through them artworks raise the elements composing them into intensive wholes. Art's power to raise the elemental, to give it a place within an integrated whole, make it, finally, beautiful, is art's power of transcendence. This is what the traditional prohibition on the ugly signified: there must be nothing that is not specific, not formed here and now. In traditional aesthetics the ugly was that element opposing the work's 'ruling law of form; it is integrated by that formal law and thereby confirms it, along with the power of subjective freedom in the artwork vis-à-vis the subject matter'.[15] Within a pre-modern metaphysics, art's integration of the ugly revealed the place of even the lowest within a world that was meaningful in itself, shot through with significance; even mud must have its form. In becoming autonomous the oldest philosophical truth about art becomes emphatic: artworks are not intensive wholes, true unities of the diverse, but semblances; their distance from the demands of praxis is both what enables them to unify the diverse, and what makes those unities illusory.

Art disenchants transcendence by revealing that its transfigurative power relies on nothing but its practical doings and the materials those doings work on.[16] But what is so revealed could not conceivably matter either inside or outside art, could not be a locus of mattering and concern, unless the materials worked on were somehow 'real', worldly, elements *not* belonging intrinsically to art in its traditional and formal self-understanding. Hence there is a material motive subtending the formal one in art's becoming autonomous. And it is this material motive which transforms the significance of the ugly, and by extension the meaning of the beautiful.

Formally, art disenchants beauty by making its practical activity and the elements worked visible, integral moments in a work's appearing. Because the 'utmost integration is the utmost semblance', modernist art comes to experience integration, previously the organon of art's truth content, as its antagonist. Artworks disillusion themselves by shattering integration, by mobilising a moment of disintegration and making that moment their truth content. Of course, 'the truth of such disintegration is achieved by way of nothing less than the triumph and guilt of integration'[17] – a thought we shall need to return to. Under the weight of the material motive the making of the disintegrative moment a truth content requires that what is so released be emphatically non-art. On the one hand, the generalisation of this requirement transforms the ugly into dissonance, which in Adorno's lexicon refers to whatever *in* a work materially and aesthetically exceeds its integrative structure. But this is equally to say that the moment of dissonance in modernist works materially bespeaks ugliness. On the other hand, then, the ugly is no longer what initially resists a reified conception of the harmoniously beautiful in order all the more to demonstrate spirit's omnipotence, but comes to stand for whatever cannot be illusorily integrated. But in a secular setting, what cannot be integrated is what secularising modernity has left behind in its spiritualising progress, what is so unworked and ruined in that progress that nothing can beautify it without utter deceitfulness[18] – remembering all the while that nothing is easier than that deceit. As the earliest practitioners of modernism knew perfectly well, and their successors often less so, the nauseating, the physically revolting, the sexually transgressive are not romantic embellishments but the site of the stakes of modern art. This is why Adorno is willing to affirm the prejudice that equates the ugly with the expression of suffering,[19] and hence espouse the dissonant transformation of sensuousness into pain. Which is not to deny that in being echoes of suffering, artworks diminish it: 'form, the organon of [art's] seriousness, is at the same time the organon of the neutralization of suffering'.[20]

Art's identification and obsession with what is incompatible with it reverberates onto beauty. Art cannot side with the ugly without at the same time coming to see in beauty a power that is antagonistic to that end. This thought has two fundamental moments. First, art's power of integration and closure comes to appear as precisely the espousal of the ideal above its materials; rather than the unification of the heterogeneous, beauty comes to appear as an act of totalisation which cannot acknowledge the heterogeneous within it without forfeiting its transfixing stillness, its power to compel. It is this thought Adorno has in mind when he states: 'In serene beauty its recalcitrant other would be completely pacified, and such aesthetic reconciliation is fatal for the extra-aesthetic. That is the melancholy of art. It achieves an unreal reconciliation at the price of real reconciliation.'[21] If once upon a time it was the glory of art to offer its contents a simulated eternity, the haunting stillness and immobility of the classically beautiful, its irresistibility, now appears to have an uncanny affinity with death. The affinity is more than a contingent association; it derives from 'the idea of pure form that art imposes on the diversity of the living and that is extinguished in it'.[22] Beauty, in its formal aspect, is utterly bound to pre-modern metaphysical ideality that opposes itself to the intransigently earth-bound; this is why from the space of the helplessly living, the overwhelming power of beauty appears as something deadly. If beauty nonetheless signifies an ideal of unity, call it presence, that we cannot forgo, then it is for the sake of the beautiful that modernist art sacrifices beauty: 'because it is no longer beautiful'.[23]

Secondly, the idea and appearing of beauty could not have this aporetic character unless it was integral to the practice of making artworks, the activity of forming and integrating; and this compromises even those art practices that aim for a wholly secular transcendence. Obsession with the ugly and the cruel do not belong solely to art's antithetical subject matter:

> art's own gesture is cruel. In aesthetic forms, cruelty becomes imagination: Something is excised from the living, from the body of language, from tones, from visual experience. The purer the form and the higher the autonomy of the works, the more cruel they are . . . If in modern artworks cruelty raises its head undisguised, it confirms the truth that in the face of the overwhelming force of reality art can no longer rely on its a priori ability to transform the dreadful into form. Cruelty is an element of art's critical reflection on itself; art despairs over the claim to power that it fulfills in being reconciled. Cruelty steps forward unadorned from the artworks as soon as their own spell is broken.[24]

At least for the time being, art cannot endeavour even the least act of forming without that forming bearing the stigmata of surgical abstraction, even if the point of the abstraction is to give a second-order life to what has been deprived of life empirically. Hence, the disintegrative moment of modernist works is ironically the same moment in which they, implicitly or explicitly, confess their cruelty, confess the violence in which forming is implicated and the impotence of that forming. But this is equally to say that beauty does not end or die; it lives on, practically, in the cruelty of artistic forming, in the violence that severs the aesthetic from purposiveness, and formally, ideally, in the rebarbatively dissonant that eludes that forming. Even as a world apart from empirical experience, art belongs to the social world it opposes; its oppositional stance does not free its forms of acting from complicity. When, in *Minima Moralia*, Adorno states that 'Every work of art is an uncommitted crime',[25] a murder, say, he is not proclaiming art's innocence, but on the contrary asserting its utter proximity to what is violently criminal without as yet being it. In art so-called humaneness only signifies a lack formal rigour.

Categorially, and it is nothing other than a train of categorial thought that we have been tracing, Adorno's contention is that modernist art in its dissonance, cruelty and self-implicating reflexivity rehearses a material logic of normativity, and hence an envisioning of secular transcendence. But that this rehearsal and envisioning has fallen on art to perform only makes sense if it has failed to occur in the social world outside art. What counts as transcendence outside art is not yet secular, not yet at one with a world that is irredeemably temporal and natural. But this claim *for* art can only be made binding *in* art, otherwise the characterisation of secular transcendence would be available wholly independently of art, and art's autonomy, its specific forms of practice, would not be categorially the bearer of another form of praxis bound to another conception of transcendence. Reiteratively, even the claim for art being bindingly available only in art can be made only in art. While true, that claim is still about the relation of art to empirical social norms. Tracing the fate of secular normativity as integral to the character and meaning of aesthetic normativity is very much the burden of Roth's *American Pastoral.*

'Beauty itself must die!' (Schiller)

The task of art today is to bring chaos into order.[26]

With a flat Jamesian irony and allegorical cruelty Roth names the protagonists of his novel Seymour, Dawn, Merry, since calling them too quickly by their true names, Blind, Dusk, Despair, would empty their lives of what makes those unspoken names fit, hang over them like an unendurable fate. Not immediately knowing that fate is all that allows the novel, or a life, to begin. Ten years after bumping into him at a Mets game, Nathan Zuckerman, Roth's long-time fictional alter ego, receives a letter from his childhood hero, Seymour, the Swede, Levov, asking him to help write a tribute to his father. Zuckerman recalls the moment in which he became forever caught in the Swede's orbit. It is a chill fall afternoon in 1943, Nathan is standing beside a practice pitch watching as the Swede is slammed into the ground after catching a pass. The whistle blows, the practice is over. The Swede rises up flexing a bruised elbow, and begins limping off. Then, spotting Nathan among the gaggle of his admirers who have been gazing at his performance, he calls out to him, 'Basketball was never like this, Skip.'[27] For a brief moment, but one indelible in his life, Nathan participates in the 'glory' that is the Swede. It is not simply a matter that 'The adored had acknowledged the adoring',[28] but the manner of that acknowledgement: gracious, easy, generous, self-mocking, all the abundant self-pleasure and modesty of the athlete for whom 'there were no obstacles, who appeared never to have to struggle to clear a space for himself'.[29] What Nathan is overwhelmed by is the Swede's perfect grace at that moment in our history when an athletic performance could still be the repository of an immigrant community's hopes,[30] when athletic virtuosity was still an icon, a symbol not only for the morally good or the virtuous life, but something that while partaking of those is more specific; call it the American dream.

The Swede physically embodies, believes, will live the American dream. So complete is Seymour Levov's assimilation that it has crept into his genes: six foot three, blond hair, blue eyes, possessed of unsurpassable style, a so 'unconscious oneness with America'[31] that Zuckerman wonders where the Jew in him is – where is the wayward temptation, the guile, the artifice, the doubleness; indeed, what does he do for subjectivity? Still, in the case of the Swede this unconscious oneness really does adumbrate a life: after high school he will join the Marines, go to college, marry a former Miss New Jersey (who almost became Miss America), he will master the intricacies and the lore of his father's leather glove business, become wealthy, buy the gorgeous stone house in Jersey countryside. But these external trappings, as everything we come to learn will confirm, are not external goods, but ingredients in a life dedicated to the liberal virtues of decency, tolerance, hard work, fairness, responsibility, concern. The Swede is 'blessed with all the attributes of a monumental ordinariness';[32] he is 'The philosopher-king of ordinary life'.[33] Even the Swede's narcissistic, cynical brother will conclude: '"My brother was the best you're going to get in this country, by a long shot."'[34]

I can think of no better way of characterising the distinctly secular, egalitarian vision of America than through the synthesis of material aspirations, prosperity and liberal virtues that transform ordinariness into something monumental. The American dream figures this synthesis, turns its discrete elements into a vision. It is again this dream that has crept into Seymour Levov's genes and imagination, naturally, spontaneously governing all he believes, does, hopes for himself and those around him. What, then, finally moves Seymour Levov, compels him and makes his life compelling is a vision of beauty, first, metonymically, the beauty of a stone house and a girl on a swing glimpsed during a high-school outing,[35] later the almost paralysing beauty of the Miss New Jersey to be,[36] but in all beauty; beauty not as an empty image but as the promise and hope of American ordinariness, monumental ordinariness. *American Pastoral* is a novel about the meaning of beauty, democratic beauty, truly demotic beauty, about the end of beauty. The beauty in question is the beauty of the American dream for it is only *as* beautiful that the complex set connecting industriousness, prosperity and liberal virtues have their *truth* as ideals both worthy and capable of orienting a life. The beauty of the American dream as exemplified by

Seymour Levov physically and practically is the charismatic authority of 'America', the idea of America.

While for the still not quite fully assimilated Jews of Newark the young Swede was like an 'Apollo'[37] or 'Zeus',[38] these signify only the pagan and secular nature of the ideal. Seymour Levov is not a god or a saint, not a noble hero or a hopeless innocent; he is simply unshakeably decent, monumentally, which is to say visibly, beautifully decent. *American Pastoral* is about beauty because only in so being can it be about what, arguably, is 'the best' America has to offer, what is truly American, and hence record our true story. From the outset Seymour Levov 'was fettered to history, an *instrument* of history'.[39] If there is a history to be told about America from the end of World War II – 'No more death and war!'[40] – to the present, a history which probes the meaning of America through the values and ideals that moved the generations of immigrants that flanked the war on either side, it must be a history of beauty; the *normative* history of the past half century is the history of this beauty, its fate.[41] And the question being interrogated must be about the normativity of the norm, about the intrinsic meaning of that normativity. But the intrinsic meaning of a wholly secular ideal cannot be something separate from its history, the realisations and failures of the idea in practice as events belonging to it.

This, at any rate, is Roth's claim. And it is the explanation of why this novel is Roth's least reflexive, least playful in its exchanges between art and life, least modernist and spleenish since *Portnoy's Complaint*. It is no accident, I think, that this novel follows on the heels of *Sabbath's Theater*, whose ambitions were not that different from *American Pastoral*, to summon up and make a judgement upon the past half century of American life, but which is Roth's most spleenish work to date, full of vituperation, sexual excess, vulgarity and a sour anger that repels and attracts in equal measure. Mickey Sabbath exuberantly exemplifies 'all the crudeness it takes to stay alive'.[42] How one judges that crudity is here beside the point; for what is missing from *Sabbath's Theater* is any convincing account of what all the anger is about, and hence something that would make intelligible why an art of spleen, an extremist art embracing all that is base, is called for and necessary in order to pass judgement on our history; why its celebration of vulgarity is not sheer spectacle or a pleasure in shocking or a relish in what American hygienic hypocrisy would prefer to forget, but demanded as a condition of aesthetic rightness and authenticity, what novel writing *must* here and now take on board. What makes *Sabbath's Theater* fail in its highest ambitions is that its excesses remain unmotivated, disconnected from the judgement it wants to pass and the lament it means to offer. In the consideration of Seymour Levov, in his iconic beauty and in the beauty that moves him, Roth finds an answer. The role of beauty *in* history, its failure, to state the thought at its weakest, is the condition for an art of spleen, for American novelistic modernism. *American Pastoral* is thus not only an attempt at construing the normative fall of America, in so doing it means to provide an archaeology of the very modernism Roth has been practising throughout his career; the fall of the dream is, at the same time, the undermining of the *forms* of representation of the realist novel as providing the epic of the modern world. If dissonance, formally, is to become the bearer of a secular ideal, then its claim must be about the relation between collapsing ideality without and within the novel. Only working outside in, from the representational order to the order of representation, can establish this internal connection. Thus in order to succeed in the archaeological project, to locate the necessity of modernist spleen in history, Roth must withdraw from high modernist excess, dampen the transgressive brio of his 'alter id'[43] Zuckerman with prostate cancer, impotence and incontinence in order to clear a compelling space for the beauty of the Swede's America and for history's own introduction of chaos into order. Roth can only reveal the ultimate meaning and validity of a lifetime of pyrotechnic performances by gently bracketing the inevitable performance his novel is.[44]

At the dinner meeting with Seymour in order to discuss the writing of the tribute, the project is not mentioned. So insistent is Seymour on the bland ordinary goodness of his life, so without side is his talk, that Zuckerman wonders if he is mad. Maybe. Or maybe he is just happy. Maybe 'Swede Levov's life . . . had been most simple and most ordinary and therefore just great, right in the American grain'.[45] A few months later, whilst attending his forty-fifth high-school reunion, Zuckerman runs into Seymour's brother Jerry and learns of Seymour's death. Zuckerman also learns that Seymour's life was not simple or great. He had had a daughter, Merry. In 1968 Merry, age 16, at 5 a.m. one morning, in protest against the war in Vietnam, had bombed the village post office, inadvertently killing the local doctor. She had then disappeared. 'The monster *Merry*'[46] had detonated the Swede's life, ruined it utterly. Why had she done it? How could a child of the unutterably decent Seymour and his beautiful wife living their unutterably decent lives become a maddened bomber? What makes Merry, if anything, the outcome of that life, its ruination? How can we hold together in one thought, one narrative, those decent lives and what explodes them? What is the line connecting the longed-for American pastoral and 'the fury, the violence, and the desperation of the counterpastoral – . . . the indigenous American berserk'?[47] There are no ultimate facts of the matter here: the Swede is dead, and what Zuckerman gets from Jerry are but brief, angry fragments from a mourning brother. So Zuckerman, the novelist to his core, will need to dream a 'realistic chronicle',[48] he will need to invent the exact history which holds together the man of monumental ordinariness, the beautiful wife, and the monster daughter exploding it all in 1968 in protest against an unjust war only a year after the Newark race riots that had almost burned away the glove factory, and did spell the demise of Newark, 'the worst city in the world'.[49] Why this history must be invented, a novel, is a matter I shall return to.

Throughout the course of the novel numerous answers to the question 'Why?' are proffered, some by Seymour himself, most by other characters: because the American dream is only a fantasy and the real world is the violent chaos that Merry makes visible; because the truth of America is capitalist greed and imperialist rapaciousness that decent liberalism colludes with rather than truly ameliorating; because, in fact, meaninglessness exists and cannot be indefinitely hidden from; because her parents are so respectable, decent and tolerant, that in order to separate from them, as any child must from any parents, Merry must go to the extreme; because as part of the natural history of nations and peoples, the time for the fall of American has come. We know all these explanations, left, right, political, apolitical, and they are not altogether wrong; but what none of them accounts for, what makes each so partial and slanted, is that they leave out the most puzzling and significant piece of the picture: American beauty, the Swede himself and all that he stands for. What none of the explanations will allow is the actual beauty and hence the actual rightness of the American dream. Hence each makes Merry an instrument of unveiling: beneath the veil of the dream, just outside the enclosed rural pastoral is the truth, the fact of the matter: the urban decay that is the final legacy of American racism, material greed, national power, existential chaos, or just the ordinary psychological yearnings of an adolescent girl going through a stage she would have grown out of if . . . Whether in terms of false consciousness or, what is nearly the same, the discovery of some explicit transgression and hence injustice, what each of these accounts yearns for is some ultimate fact of the matter, some fact or flaw that will finally explain, and so explain away, Merry.

The most desperate and pathetic of these, and hence standing for all of them, is Seymour's own. He thinks he must be to blame, he is the father and so he must be responsible for what happened, and hence surely there is something he did that will explain it all, some moment, some act that working like a virus on Merry's psyche drove her to become the mad bomber of Old Rimrock. Achingly, Seymour imagines that the cause of it all was a fumbled impassioned kiss as he and 11-year-old Merry drove home sun-drunk from the beach on a hot summer's afternoon. '"Daddy, kiss me the way you k-k-kiss umumumother,"'[50] his 11-year-old begged; and after he coldly rebuked her, and she, humiliated by the rebuff, in desperately trying to withdraw her request got caught in another long stutter, Seymour became overwhelmed with frustration and guilt and pity and compassion and love and so covered her stuttering mouth with his own. Is this the transgression, this crack in the etiquette of the family romance, that explains it all? As the years pass after Merry's disappearance and Seymour hallucinates kitchen-table conversations with Angela Davis explaining to him the brutality of American imperialism at home and abroad and Merry's political heroism; as he imagines Merry coming under the influence of the Weathermen in the person of the messenger between him and Merry, the malevolent, dark angel Rita Cohen (whom Merry will deny ever having known, and who hence may or may not have ever existed); as he considers the anger, envy and resentment others might well feel toward him and his life; as he rehearses over and over again the politics and the everyday of Merry's young life, searching for the cause, he keeps coming back to the kiss.[51]

And in a sense the kiss is a more accurate representation of the fall than any of the other explanations offered, not because it is transgressive, not as the emblem for a breach in morality and justice that is Seymour's and America's tragic flaw, a particular wrong for which remorse would be possible, and which, if the mark of a larger wrong, would be put right; but because the kiss is an emblem of his love and tenderness and compassion and sheer hopeless decent ordinariness.[52] As Seymour places his mouth over the mouth of his stuttering daughter he is re-enacting his entire life: let this impassioned and innocent kiss heal and transform this gross brokenness, these words blasted into meaningless fragments of noise, these flying bits of pained sound, of speech become pain. Merry's stutter in miniature is the remnant of liberal fluency, its excess, what it leaves behind in its ascent. So to imagine the kiss as the cause of Merry's pain is to imagine that it is, precisely, the actual beauty of Seymour Levov and his life that produces the monster Merry. It is beauty itself that is evil and hence the very beauty of the American dream that is the cause of the fall. Although we have already, implicitly, worked through this claim in tracing out the categorial dialectic of ideal and spleen, as it imposes itself in the representational discourse of Roth's novel its difficulty and complexity becomes palpable. He cannot be thought to be urging that the immediate cause of Vietnam and the race riots and Merry's bombing is the beauty of the American dream, although he does want to say that this beauty is evil, murderous, and that the inability of America to really be a melting pot, to truly trans-form its heterogeneous mass into fully American citizens in which Thanksgiving might be the celebration of the American pastoral,[53] its antithetical pursuit of war and power *are also* all correlates of beauty, its inevitable detritus. Beauty produces these monsters because its ideality, its mode of transcendence, is insufficiently immanent, not yet a form of truly secular transcendence. The American berserk is the exact cor-ollary of the American pastoral. American beauty is cruel, and in its cruelty evil.

This is why the overwhelming focus of the novel is not on Merry, as one might have expected, but on Seymour. He is a mystery darker than Merry because conceiv-ing of him must be a conceiving of liberal decency somehow being evil in itself. To conceive of him is to conceive of how 'a kiss could make someone . . . criminal',[54] not as transgression, but as kiss. Hence what can appear on first reading as a relentless charting of Seymour's overwhelming decency – his sixty-seven endlessly patient dis-cussions with his rebellious daughter about her life and politics;[55] his dedication to his work like that of a traditional craftsman to his; his loyalty to the Afro-Americans who work for him and hence to Newark well after the rest of the business world has left them and it behind; his tender nurturing of his despairing wife as their world col-lapses around them – all this unexciting and undramatic stuff is the stuff of ordinari-ness and decency and hence what must be shown if the beauty of the American dream is to be something other than a myth or a fantasy.[56] '"Decency?"', a voice not unlike Zuckerman's own on other occasions cavils, '"Much overvalued, wouldn't you say, the seductions of decency and civility and convention? Not the richest response to life I can think of."'[57] So one burden of the novel is to show the seductions of decency, its beauty. The other burden, of course, is to show how the pursuit of beautiful ordinari-ness is cruel.

Consider this in small. From the outset Dawn is ambivalent about her role as Miss New Jersey since she senses that there is something about the beautiful that is danger-ous and deforming, just as, in retrospect, she senses that there has been something dangerous and deforming about Seymour's pursuit of beauty, his having to have her, the beautiful, and to create their life of beauty:

'I was trying to help out at home! But then you arrive. You! Those hands! Those shoulders! Towering over me with your *jaw!* This huge animal I couldn't get rid of! You wouldn't leave me be! Every time I looked up, there was my boyfriend, gaga because I was a ridiculous beauty queen! You were like some *kid!* You had to make me into a *princess.* Well, look where I have wound up! In a madhouse! Your princess in a *madhouse!*'[58]

Both Seymour's own Apollonian beauty and his pursuit of it have now become unbearable. What is trivially and obviously unbearable about this beauty is that it denatures, squeezes the life out of all it touches. So Dawn continues her diatribe in recollecting how when she won the Miss New Jersey contest she was still introvert, awkward, unpolished. Hence in preparation for the Miss America pageant they would teach her how to sit, stand, listen and above all walk. Walking, ordinary walking, was not good enough; you must not swing your arms too much, but not keep them stiffly by your side either; you don't just walk, you must somehow glide. Ideal walking, Miss America walking, the ordinariness of walking become monumental, makes impossible one thing: walking – '"All these little tricks of the trade made me so self-conscious I could barely *move!*"'[59]

Beauty, the very beauty that transfigures the ordinary into a secular ideal, making the ordinary into a form of life worthy for its own sake, kills the ordinary. We can press this thought further and ask what of walking is left over when it is transformed into gliding? What of everyday speech is left over when it is transformed into the fluent reasonableness of liberal tolerance? What of the human body is left over after it has been idealised into the perfections of Dawn and Seymour Levov? Only one answer seems possible: the six-foot, fat, angry, stuttering monster Merry. Merry is perhaps 'The ugliest daughter ever born of two attractive parents'.[60] Her ugliness is not the raw stuff of nature that beauty has yet to work its magic on, but what is left behind of the human after democratic beauty has done its work. And we are meant to find that image of Merry's ugliness compelling because we are meant to see it as a direct inflection and intensification of Dawn's beauty. For Dawn, her own beauty and the beauty of her life progressively develop from being a threat to mobility, to an immobility escaped from only in sex and in caring for her herd of cows, that is in escapes from form and endeavour into intentionless nature, to, finally, madness. A natural history of American beauty. But this is Merry's mother, and her ambivalence is how she loved her daughter. Despite herself, her intense ambivalence is all she can pass on to her daughter; hence the ironic justness of Merry's rage against her. Merry is beauty's stutter.

What kind of account or explanation of Merry or the fall of America is this? What do we know of Merry as yet other than her stuttering and her bombing, her small and large exploding of the fluency of American life? Five years after the bombing Seymour receives a letter from Rita Cohen saying that Merry is working in an old dog and cat hospital in Newark. What he sees walk out of the building in one of the most derelict bits of the city is unrecognisable, a scarecrow figure, stick thin, a veil made of the ragged foot off an old nylon stocking covering her mouth and chin. Her speech now fluent, she tells him she has become a Jain: she wears the veil so as not to harm microscopic organisms, reveres all life, does not wash so as not to harm the water, eats as little as possible. And there is a story to tell. Fluently, quietly, with insane clarity she tells it: wanderings and hidings, four rapes, other bombs made, three more dead, and then the discovery of Jainism. Of course in the centre of the conversation between father and daughter is the recurrent question, 'Why?' After some limp armchair psychological accounting by Seymour, Merry objects: '"You can't explain away what

I've done by motives, Daddy. I certainly wouldn't explain away what *you've* done by motives."' Seymour replies that he does have motives; everyone has motives. Merry: '"You cannot reduce the journey of a soul to that kind of psychology. It is not worthy of you."'[61] Motives might explain this or that action, but they cannot explain a life; rather it is the shape of life, its form, that makes its motives intelligible. Is not American beauty the fundament of Seymour's life, the condition of its intelligibility, and hence what shapes his motives here as elsewhere?[62]

For exactly the same reason, trying to understand Seymour's and Merry's lives through freedom and unfreedom, reason and unreason will misfire. Seymour accuses Merry of not thinking for herself, of being tyrannised by a revolving set of extremist ideologies, of letting other people do her thinking for her; if only she would think for herself, become autonomous, she would see the wrongness of her ways. But how can he, Merry objects, who is conformist to his bones, who does exactly what the world expects of him, accuse her of not thinking for herself?[63] At this level of concreteness, can we distinguish between what is autonomous and what is heteronomous? Apart from psychological and social extremes, can we label anyone's thinking as either one or the other? Are not acting in accordance with the norms of liberal decency and acting against them (but for their sake) both potent images of autonomy belonging to its full expression? And conversely, will not social conformity and transgressive action both always raise the possibility of heteronomy? Neither her radicalism nor his conformism is either obviously autonomous or heteronomous. Nothing will shift the stalemate here.

But these two possibilities, explanations in terms of motive, on the one hand, and through either reason or its determinate failure on the other, can legitimately be regarded as exhausting the possibilities of comprehending these lives conceptually. Conceptual understanding is going to be deficient because for it ideal and fate, value and fact remain separate; to be sure, related to one another (facts can be adequate or inadequate instantiations of the value, better or worse applications), but nonetheless distinct. To think that the modes of failure are to be understood through contradiction (in the concept), causal interference, or via simple not measuring up is already to have departed from the immanence of secular life. Conceptual understanding will fail here because ingredient on both sides of the equation, with respect to father and daughter, is the material embodiment of an idea which, in being so embodied, is constitutive of it. Tracking the fate of the idea is tracing its material transformations. In order to comprehend Seymour, his ordinary beauty, we must see Merry's ugliness as its catastrophic fulfilment. And hence we understand Merry fully not through all the perfectly good psychological reasons for her explosion, but through seeing those reasons as beauty's regurgitated other. Roth's discretion in *not* providing Merry with a subjectivity worth noting, of letting her be solely the *figure* of her life, is the condition for seeing it as a *life*. Only then in the telling and narrating of these lives, only in the finding of a *form* of telling that is responsive to what they demand, can they become perspicuous. So the binding relation between Seymour and Merry is not psychological or causal but formal, a matter of form.

As stated, even this is too quick and undiscriminating. For what is at stake in this

novel is the informing power of beauty, the power of form to render the secular everyday intelligible. Or, again, the issue is what the American form of beauty enables and
destroys. It enables the life of Seymour Levov and destroys his daughter. So the fate
of a certain form (of life) will be the *informe*, if you will, ideal life disintegrating into
its components, bare life. Finally, in despair and frustration at Merry's insane reasonableness and his inability to puncture it or find a reason he can understand for all that
she has done and become, in a wild and manic attempt to get at the truth he tears the
veil from her face and orders her to speak. Greeted with nothing but silence Seymour
deserts the last shibboleth of liberal decency and, in remembrance of a kiss, violently
pries her mouth open:

> 'Speak!' he demanded, and at last the true smell of her reached him, the lowest human
> smell there is, excluding only the stench of the rotting living and the rotting dead. . . .
> [W]hat he smelled now, while pulling open her mouth, was a human being . . . a mad
> human being who grubs about for pleasure in its own shit. Her foulness had reached
> him. She is disgusting. His daughter is a human mess stinking of human waste. Her
> smell is the smell of everything organic breaking down. It is the smell of no coherence.
> It is the smell of all she's become. She could do it, and did do it, and this reverence for
> life is the final obscenity.
>   [. . .] A spasm of gastric secretions and undigested food started up the intestinal piping
> and, in a bitter, acidic stream, surged sickeningly onto his tongue, and when he cried
> out '*Who are you!*' it was spewed with his words onto her face.[64]

When Merry first emerges from the dog and cat hospital and she and her father
embrace like any passionate father and daughter might embrace, crying in one
another's arms, it is an embrace, we are told, between 'the dependable father whose
center is the source of all order . . . and the daughter who is chaos itself'.[65] As Seymour
in body and belief is American beauty, so Merry in body and belief is the repository
of all that is incompatible with beauty. Seeing her thus is all. Beneath the veil, the
slightest art that allows Merry her fluency, is indeed the truth about her: she is all and
exactly what cannot be rendered beautiful; she is all and exactly what has been left
behind in the forming action of America; '[she] was his daughter, and she was
unknowable'.[66] If one wants a name for this moment, call it 'self-recognition in absolute otherness', but Merry's unknowableness reverses the meaning of that philoso-
pheme. Beauty finds itself in its opposite, in the decomposing rancidness Merry has
become. Merry is life decomposing, beyond incorporation or forming; but she is this
as being her father's daughter, as if in the tearing of the veil he all unknowingly
becomes the artist renouncing his forming capacity, decomposing his work in order
that its elemental being can appear. Ordinariness cannot be ordinary if it leaves no
room for walking. But the ordinariness that immobilises life leaves decomposing
Merry in its wake. She is the stakes of ordinariness, she is the repository of what beauty
cannot tolerate, and hence as its failure its ideal future. Merry's Jainism, its reverence
for the ordinary even in its microscopic incarnations, is crackpot and chillingly
knowing.

The unveiling which transforms the artist's fluency into vomit at the sight of
what cannot be seen, however shocking, is and is not a moment of dissonance; it is

not dissonant because it falls squarely within the representational order of the novel; but in its representation of sublime, grotesque unknowability it devours form, blinding it, leaving only the smell of incoherence and vomit in its place. In place of the judgement of beauty, but as a consequence of it, we, formally, find ourselves making a judgement of disgust, revulsion, horror. But this is a judgement (the smell of decay is not literal, after all), the way in which we experience the entanglement of beauty and decomposition. This is the end of American beauty. This is the origin of modernism. Every effort of art from now on and in remembrance of this moment will find its authority dependent upon what it can neither enliven, beautify, nor forget (since forgetfulness, aesthetically, is just sentimentality, entertainment, the culture industry). Dissonance, sublime unknowability, is the aesthetic (non-)representation of the undead.

Near the beginning of the novel this climatic moment is anticipated as Zuckerman reflects on how everyday life depends on our trying to understand those people around us and how, no matter how careful, judicious, patient, attentive our efforts, we get it wrong: 'You get them wrong before you meet them, while you're anticipating meeting them; you get them wrong while you're with them; and then you go home to tell somebody else about the meeting and you get them all wrong again.'[67] As temptingly modest as it sounds, Roth cannot quite mean this literally; is not the gamble of his novel that he will get Seymour, Dawn and Merry Levov right? But then, perhaps, wrongness is not wrongness. Zuckerman continues: 'The fact remains that getting people right is not what living is all about anyway. It's getting them wrong that is living, getting them wrong and wrong and wrong and then, on careful reconsideration, getting them wrong again. That's how we know we're alive: we're wrong.'[68] The great and impossible task of the novel is to know the other; but the other that is to be known now is the life without *Bildung*, the life that is from the first a stutter. In this casual reflection on the problem of other minds, I hear the emergent dialectic of ideal and spleen in which the attempt to get people right is the business of form-giving, of beauty, and getting them wrong the release from form-giving that enables life in its broken concreteness to appear. Only in the wrongness that transpires through efforts of right-making can we *know* we're still alive, or rather know the extent of our lack of life. The crescendo of 'wrong' in this reflection is normative not factual; and the issue is one of knowing what being alive was. We can come to knowledge of being alive, that someday we might just walk, only via the systematic escape from rightness. Modernist art, the art of wrongness and dissonance, is the condition for us knowing of life, death and what lies between.

If the scene of decomposition, the revolting image of revulsion, is the pivot of *American Pastoral*, if it is the formal centre of the novel, it is neither its meaning nor its end. Even what is without form, what cannot be formed, must be transmitted, hence is related to form, so in another way formed. The remainder of the novel must unpack that image not through interpretation but through uncovering the *durée* appropriate to it. Seymour's life continues, or if that is too strong, becomes a certain kind of stutter; or rather, he must learn stuttering as a way of continuing. What Seymour must learn is that he cannot reclaim, enliven, protect or save Merry. It is a hard lesson that he initially avoids by focusing on the fact of the four rapes as identifiable failures of his power to protect. But there is guilt here too, since what he truly could not protect Merry from is himself, in small his violently prying her mouth open, the rape Merry always suffered. If Merry was '"*always* a defenseless girl"',[69] she was also always without protection, vulnerable and ruined. And it continues. Seymour cannot reclaim or enliven Merry, but he cannot leave her behind, mourn her, either. There is a temptation to mourning, a temptation to think that all the crudeness it takes to stay alive is a matter of leaving the dead behind, letting them go – letting the dead bury the dead. This temptation is voiced continuously by Jerry; he is nothing but that voice. But his hysteria, masquerading as egomania, underlines how illusory the escape from the undead is. Merry is not quite dead; and because she has never been fully alive either, she cannot die, and so cannot be mourned, ever. Seymour in and through his decency knows he is bound to her, bound to her undeadness, her decaying life. Finding what might count as acknowledging and sustaining a relation to the undead is Seymour's conundrum. If Merry was always the undead, the not yet living, and Seymour always her executioner and her protector, the order of her disorder, then the mystery of Seymour is, finally, the mystery of *that* relation.[70] But it is a mystery that cannot be lived or take shape as a life – a certain crudeness, life's insistence, does always intervene in a life to de facto separate what cannot be separated. And this is what Seymour, in the midst of being relentlessly, crudely, moved forward through attachments to a second wife and new children, must have implicitly sensed in approaching Zuckerman in the first place. Doing *justice* to Merry is nothing he can accomplish, something that nothing in life can accomplish although it is the meaning and failure of his life.

To say that nothing in life can do justice to Merry is hence equally to say that what doing justice to her amounts to is something that cannot be represented. Hence doing justice to Merry is what drives the novel back into itself, drives representation into figure and form. This is the ultimate reason why this so-called realistic chronicle is not a work of representation, finally, but of exactly imagining; why a work at moments relentlessly realistic must, finally, withdraw its power to depict as its ultimate authority. Zuckerman's realist chronicle is, well beyond realism and disillusionment, the non-narrative form of Seymour's loss, America's loss. At its furthest extreme, *American Pastoral* is, formally, first the discovery that the requirement of doing justice to the undead is its condition of possibility, both the space between and what connects each name with its allegorical actualisation; thus, secondly, the self-reflexive or internal *becoming* of the form which transmitting the undead takes. Its discovery of itself *as novel* is nothing other than its conveying of the undead, the movement whereby it narratively transforms realist chronicle *into* melancholic form, its form being the emergence of modernist form as not representation but refuge, the almost painterly figure of the grotesque embrace of order and disorder. Thus all the modernist novel is now, perhaps was always, is affirmative melancholy, impossible mourning, the narrative mechanism through which melancholy becomes affirmative or mourning becomes permanent, the reiterative undoing of itself before all that it fails, its form a mode of embrace of the undead.[71]

And is not this form of protection of the undead precisely what the *idea* of secular transcendence now comes to, the idea or possibility or hope of binding meaning being located in the transmission, through form, of the undead – the *art* of stuttering? Not the monumental ordinariness of the American dream, but the affirmative melancholy of its dissolution now spells secular transcendence. What could be more emphatically secular, as bound to the materiality of human lives and yet transcendent, than that gesture which, here and now, prevents the undead from being left behind? Which here and now repeats their loss as the intolerable itself, the unjust itself? To be sure, there is something exquisite here, nearly beautiful. There can be no transmission of the stuttering without form, thereby mitigating its pain. But the seal of the novel's authenticity is that, finally, it is only life in its brokenness that is transmitted, just the most minimal *holding* of ruination. Nothing else is possible. And even that, of course, nothing but semblance.

American Pastoral ends with a débâcle of a dinner party in which Seymour discovers his wife being dry humped by the family architect; where the focus of conversation is the new popular pornography in the person of Linda Lovelace in *Deep Throat*; and where his father is nearly blinded in a fork attack by the architect's drunken wife. Marcia, a New York intellectual, at the sight of this final indignity finds herself convulsed with laughter and delight: these pillars of society are going down, their decorum now truly only facade, their life not robust at all, but enormously assailable and frail. Is not this laughter the one Roth himself has encouraged for a lifetime? Not quite, for although it is true that the dream is over and cannot be recovered still he queries: 'And what is wrong with their life? What on earth is less reprehensible than the life of the Levovs?'[72] In his review of *American Pastoral* Michael Wood complains about these final sentences that 'they still seek to moralise the wreck of a world, as if Zuckerman had never heard of Job, as if the Levovs' virtue ought really, after all, to have been a protection for them, rather than an invitation to damage'.[73] This seems to me quite wrong; almost the first thing we can be sure of is that this novel is going to be the adult version of the adolescent Swede's favourite book, John R. Tunis's *The Kid from Tomkinsville*, a baseball 'boys' Book of Job'.[74] The stakes of the final passage are not the question of protection,[75] but of rightness. Intrinsically, American beauty which has liberal decency as one of its fundamental components is evil. Roth's further and darker thought is the query, the wonder whether nonetheless 'on earth' this is not the least reprehensible of lives? One might think that showing how normative beliefs themselves produce evil outcomes demonstrates their falsity. The shape of Roth's novel throws this comforting belief into question. Would not any form of life capable of sustaining a vision of transcendence have to partake in the beautiful as condition for it figuring something desirable, something capable of inspiring and moving human beings? Is the idea of a post-charismatic form of life capable of sustaining transcendence intelligible? Is not beauty the very thing which internally connects normative ideals with human sensuousness? And hence is not the raising of ordinariness to monumentality as encapsulated in the American dream the furthest reach of secular transcendence? In showing the decency of Seymour Levov to be evil, has it been shown that he is anything other than unutterably decent? Beauty has stopped being beautiful and become grotesque, evil. But only nihilistic laughter would think this means that there is no longer beauty or that beauty is not the ultimate stakes of non-beauty.

Secular transcendence transpires in art; but since art is semblance even in its furthest disintegrative reach, it transpires only as a material idea. Consider the notion of material idea as what modernist art adds to the inventory of modern social experience and epistemology. Secular transcendence can be integrally conceived, that is become binding for us, nowhere else than *in* art as material idea, since otherwise it would forsake the necessarily bottom-up movement which makes secular norms truly secular. For the present, at least, Roth is contending that the immanence of ideality is sustained in an integral and not negative dialectic of ideal and spleen, in a movement in which the wrong carries the burden of the right without as yet falsifying or eliminating that very right, and hence in the elaborated figure of the crying embrace between the father whose centre is the source of all order and the daughter who is chaos itself. That is the material idea of this life. So being is the social significance of art. But that significance is politically idle. Art can be the bearer of the knowledge of this life only as art, as semblance. Art's autonomy ensures its practical harmlessness. That is not an objection to art, but to the world in which beauty survives, when it does and probably for not very long, as also emphatic evil.

Notes

1 T. W. Adorno, *Aesthetic Theory*, trans. R. Hullot-Kentor (Minneapolis: University of Minnesota Press, 1997), p. 159. Hereafter abbreviated AT.

2 The thought is G. Lukács's, *The Theory of the Novel*, trans. A. Bostock (London: Merlin Press, 1971), pp. 112–31. For an elaboration of it, see my *The Philosophy of the Novel: Lukács, Marxism, and the Dialectics of Form* (Minneapolis: University of Minnesota Press, 1984), ch. 4.

3 One might aver that since the novel is formally nominalist and open in the sense that it must be responsive to the contingencies of empirical experience, then from the outset decomposition as a principle of formation belongs to it. By itself, this will only minimally mitigate the apparent hyperbole of the 'end of the novel' thesis since one must still account for the stutter and reversal of orientation – from synthesis to decomposition – that commences emphatically with Flaubert (and by implication with the defeats of 1848 – the bourgeois revolution is over). The thesis that the novel ends with Flaubert and James was, of course, first pointedly made by T. S. Eliot in '*Ulysses*, order and myth', in T. S. Eliot, *Selected Prose*, ed. F. Kermode (London: Faber & Faber, 1975), pp. 175–8.

4 AT, p. 93.

5 P. Roth, *American Pastoral* (New York: Vintage Books, 1998). Hereafter abbreviated AP.

6 AT, p. 252.

7 *Ibid.*, pp. 225–6.

8 Cf. *ibid.*, p. 83.

9 *Ibid.*, p. 39.

10 On the contrary, for Adorno the black and grey of recent art, its asceticism, is 'the negative apotheosis of color' see AT, p. 135. But, then what else could it be?

11 AT, p. 15.
12 *Ibid.*, pp. 78–100.
13 *Ibid.*, p. 78.
14 *Ibid.*, p. 29.
15 *Ibid.*, p. 46.
16 It is part of Adorno's stringent conception of aesthetic immanence that unless the materials are at least co-equals in this endeavour, then what is produced will be nothing more than a mirror of our power of freedom, with the emphasis on power, and hence illusory once more. Adorno thus conceives of the form of late works as emerging from their materials (which of course includes inherited forms), so to speak; hence the relevant notion of freedom, in both production and reception, is openness to the 'object'. This is important metaphysically – it enunciates why this is a wholly secular conception of transcendence – but unsurprisingly appears only obliquely in the consideration of the linguistic arts.
17 AT, p. 45.
18 Underlining thus, again, the way in which dissonance as the failure of integration becomes the seal of the modern, the marker of authenticity.
19 AT, p. 49.
20 *Ibid.*, p. 39.
21 *Ibid.*, p. 52.
22 *Ibid.*
23 *Ibid.*, p. 53.
24 *Ibid.*, p. 50.
25 T. W. Adorno, *Minima Moralia: Reflections from Damaged Life*, trans. E. F. N. Jephcott (London: New Left Books, 1974), aphorism 72, p. 111.
26 *Ibid.*, aphorism 143, p. 222.
27 AP, p. 19.
28 *Ibid.*
29 *Ibid.*
30 *Ibid.*, p. 4.
31 *Ibid.*, p. 20.
32 *Ibid.*, p. 81.
33 *Ibid.*, p. 69.
34 *Ibid.*, p. 66.
35 *Ibid.*, pp. 189–90.
36 *Ibid.*, p. 191.
37 *Ibid.*, p. 4.
38 *Ibid.*, p. 17.
39 *Ibid.*, p. 5.
40 *Ibid.*, p. 209.
41 For naive sociological accounts of the beauty of the American dream, for which Roth's novel is the necessary corrective, see R. Bellah *et al.* (eds), *Habits of the Heart: Middle America Observed* (Berkeley, CA: University of California Press, 1985); and A. Wolfe, *One Nation, After All* (New York: Penguin Books, 1999).
42 AP, p. 36.
43 The phrase is from M. Wood's review of *American Pastoral* in the *New York Times* (20 April 1997), Section 7, p. 8.
44 Zuckerman discreetly disappears from the novel on p. 89.
45 AP, p. 31.

46 *Ibid.*, p. 67.
47 *Ibid.*, p. 86.
48 *Ibid.*, p. 89.
49 *Ibid.*, p. 24.
50 *Ibid.*, p. 89.
51 *Ibid.*, p. 174.
52 In the convolutions of my phrasing here I am aiming to suggest that *American Pastoral* belongs to the collection of works which operate in accordance with the idea of 'moral perfectionism' as argued for in the writings of S. Cavell, especially his *Conditions Handsome and Unhandsome: The Constitution of Emersonian Perfectionism* (Chicago: The University of Chicago Press, 1990). In Cavell's tight phrasing of the idea, the field of moral perfectionism is one 'on which moral justifications come to an end, and justice, as it stands, has done what it can, specific wrong may not be claimable; yet the misery is such that, on the other side, right is not assertible; instead something must be shown' (p. 112). Part of the burden of *American Pastoral* is the attempt to institute just this kind of space of reflective judgement.
53 AP, p. 402.
54 *Ibid.*, p. 92.
55 *Ibid.*, pp. 104–13.
56 Which is not to deny that the American dream participates in myth and fantasy. The most endearing element of this is Seymour's worship of Johnny Appleseed, striding along the countryside tossing out his seeds as he goes; an event the Swede could not resist enacting during his walks to and from his home and the village of Old Rimrock. The masturbatory character of the image of the Swede 'making love to his life' (AP, p. 319), is enough to indicate that the fantasy is not altogether innocent.
57 *Ibid.*, p. 360.
58 *Ibid.*, p. 178.
59 *Ibid.*, p. 180.
60 *Ibid.*, p. 243.
61 *Ibid.*, p. 251.
62 Does this include unconscious motives too? It must. To be sure, both Seymour and Jerry suffer differently from their overbearing father, and hence the lives of both can be viewed as either living up (Seymour) or rebelling against (Jerry) their father's relentless authority. The terrible business of fathers and sons does not disappear. But throughout the novel, and this is its delicacy, Roth works through the difficult Hegelian thought that while of course everyone has motives (and every hero his valet), motives are not the ultimate explanatory key to these lives. Said another way, the implosion of patriarchal authority belongs to a story about the collapse of the unique kind of traditional authority embedded in the American dream itself; which is to assert that the pathology of tortured oedipal relations is to be understood through the grid of the collapse of the complex symbolic, the American dream, which was originally the source of their resolution. Ignoring the symbolic stakes at work in the collapse reduces fates to case histories. Hence, part of the reason that *American Pastoral* remains in the mode of the nineteenth-century representational novel is because its narrative structure presumes, in almost a Balzacian way, that narrative careers are emblems of social forms.
63 Cf. AP, p. 241.
64 *Ibid.*, pp. 265–6.
65 *Ibid.*, p. 231.

66 *Ibid.*, p. 266.
67 *Ibid.*, p. 35.
68 *Ibid.*
69 *Ibid.*, p. 378.
70 The failure of empirical experience to tolerate whole lives is, Adorno contends, the source of modernist works' inability to end: 'What Lukács once called the "discharge of meaning" was the force that allowed the artwork, once it has confirmed its immanent determination, to end on the model of one who dies old, having led a full life. That this is denied [modernist] artworks, that they can no more die than can the hunter Gracchus, is internalized in them directly as the expression of horror' (AT, p. 147).
71 The idea being expressed in these final few sentences I owe, in whole, to Gregg Horowitz. For a full elaboration of it see his *Sustaining Loss: Art and Mournful Life* (Stanford, CA: Stanford University Press, 2001). Using his interpretation of the installations of Ilya Kabakov as a guide, it might be said here that in the unfolding of his narrative Roth transforms realist chronicle into lament.
72 AP, p. 423.
73 See note 43.
74 AP, p. 9.
75 This is not to deny that the question of assailability as a component of the American dream is something Roth is interested in throughout the novel. Part of the American dream is feeling 'grateful', 'lucky' for the goods it provides (AP, p. 86); which is to say, desert is too abstract a notion to capture the relation between empirical flourishing and endeavour. But if so, then being reminded of how assailable life is belongs to the full idea of the American dream, which Roth indeed says: 'Who is set up for tragedy and the incomprehensibility of suffering? Nobody. The tragedy of the man not set up for tragedy – that is every man's tragedy' (*ibid.*). This is not to moralise assailability, but to provide it with the pathos appropriate to it. Since this is a very old idea, the idea of tragedy itself, Roth cannot be thought to be attempting to reverse secularity by making being assailable somehow cosmically unjust. Moral luck, good and bad, belongs to morality while being, precisely, the point at which all effort fails and chance, contingency, accident, enters.

Part III

Reflections

Kant and the ends of criticism

Since the beginning of the 1990s there has been a marked revival of interest in both Kant and aesthetics.[1] This revival has been accompanied with a move beyond the theoretical positions that sought to displace the notion of aesthetics and often requires a rethinking of the relationship between criticism and philosophy. I wish to present here an account of Kant's 'invention' of aesthetics that allows its terms to become both operative within and yet also transformed by the practice of critical engagement with literary and visual works of art. It is important to mention however that the context for this reinvention of an aesthetic criticism is one that should embrace the different kinds of artworks, as an exclusive focus on the literary tends to reduce the discussion of art to an account of language, a reduction partly responsible for the prior tendency to dismiss aesthetics.

Alongside this attentiveness to the distinction between literary and visual works should also come a challenge to the attempt of many thinkers to dismiss aesthetic considerations in favour of historical readings. The historicist orientation in criticism has had a long vogue despite the general recognition of the real problems that such concentration has, not least in accounting for its own conditions of possibility.[2] The real reason for the continuing production of works that present an opposition between 'contextual' reading and aesthetics is a wide acceptance that aesthetic accounts of works do not involve historical considerations.[3] I would like therefore here to present an account of aesthetic criticism that makes clear the nature of its historical purchase. This account of a Kantian aesthetic criticism will be presented by first making clear the expansive sense the term 'aesthetics' has for Kant, secondly arguing for the vital importance of understanding Kant's decision to discuss the critique of taste in the same work as he presents a critique of teleology, thirdly describing the 'ends of criticism' and fourthly setting out the type of criticism that can be produced by the approach that thus emerges.

The multiple senses of 'aesthetics' in Kant

It is not generally noted that each of Kant's three critiques contains a discussion of something termed 'aesthetics'. I will here briefly revisit the three distinct senses given to the term 'aesthetic' in Kant's three critiques, suggesting thereby an agenda for an expansion of the term beyond the restricted notion which presently is the major one accepted.

Kant's *Critique of Pure Reason* opens with a section entitled the 'transcendental aesthetic'. In this part of the work Kant treats of the contribution to knowledge provided by sensibility. The use of the term 'aesthetic' to describe the notion of sensibility was widely accepted at the time Kant wrote the first critique and Kant uses it in this work to discuss an 'immediate' relationship between cognition and an object as opposed to a mediated relationship between the two, as is provided by concepts and judgements. The reason why Kant here is not just presenting an account of sensibility *per se* is his transcendental purpose. As Kant puts it:

> Since that within which the sensations can alone be ordered and placed in a certain form cannot itself be in turn sensation, the matter of all appearance is only given to us *a posteriori*, but its form must all lie ready for it in the mind *a priori*, and can therefore be considered separately from all sensation.[4]

The way in which sensations are presented to us in their specific vividness is what Kant terms a *matter*. This *matter* is contrasted with that which permits us to receive this matter as such, and this is termed by Kant *form*. Since Kant identifies the matter here with the term 'sensation' itself we need to separate sensation from that which makes us capable of receiving its inputs, and this we can term 'sensibility'. If there is something that organizes and permits reception of sensation then the enquiry into this must be an enquiry into something that is not derived from experience and is hence *a priori*. Since we are here enquiring into sensibility we are forced to the view that there is such a thing as *a priori* sensibility.[5]

We will see that this notion of *a priori* sensibility is important in reviewing Kant's other enquiries into something termed 'aesthetics'. In the second critique sensibility is approached not in terms of the capacity of receipt of sensation but rather in the sense of 'feeling'. Here what Kant wishes to suggest is that there is a ground for thinking of feelings in a non-empiricist manner. The ground for this second sense of the term 'aesthetic' is that Kant has uncovered within this work the pure basis of morality. This argument leads him to consider the relationship between the moral law and motivation to act in accordance with it. The examination of this latter must turn on the question of an *a priori* feeling, otherwise we would be faced with the irresolvable paradox of a pure law and a merely pathological motivation. So, if the argument about the purity of morals is to carry conviction it is essential that Kant should demonstrate that there are pure feelings. Given that the moral law acts as a counter to the demands of sensuousness the first feeling that it produces in us is humiliation. But humiliation has also a positive correlate in the form of respect for the moral law, a feeling 'produced by an intellectual cause, and this feeling is the only one which we can know completely *a priori* and the necessity of which we can discern'.[6] Further, respect is not a 'drive' to morality but rather 'morality itself, regarded subjectively as a drive' and which is produced in us by the example of another person following the law.[7]

The basic notion of intellectual feeling given in the second critique is made much more intricate in Kant's subsequent works, particularly *Religion within the Limits of Reason Alone*.[8] But whilst these works suggest that the picture given in the second critique requires further elaboration they do not present reasons for rejecting the basic notion of the 'aesthetic' of this work. The reason for describing the discussion of pure feelings as an 'aesthetic' is not merely because Kant does this himself.[9] It is also the case that many contemporary moral theories also relate the importance of thinking of feeling in morality and, indeed, so did theorists in Kant's time.[10] That the term 'aesthetic' should include a clear reference to 'feeling' is a crucial development in the second critique and connects it to the demonstrations of the third critique. It is essential however to be clear that 'feeling' should be understood not merely as a reference to a set of empirical states but, if we are undertaking to set out a description of feelings which we characterise as 'aesthetic', that these feelings should be understood to be pure in nature.

It is in the third critique that Kant turns to examining the credentials of a 'critique of taste' to be entitled an 'aesthetic'. In section VIII of the first introduction to the work he described how the connection between the presentation of an object and a feeling of pleasure or displeasure has come to be termed an 'aesthetic' relation even though in this relation we do not find a cognition presented (as is the case with the intuitions discussed in the transcendental aesthetic). Rather, what is occurring in the relation in question is that we have given to us a presentation of intuition to which no concept corresponds and this lack of correspondence can take the form of either pleasure (as is the case when we describe something as beautiful) or displeasure mixed with pleasure (as when we describe something as sublime).

It is important for Kant to distinguish between the aesthetic judgements that are thought of as involving only particular sensations and those which affect the basic judgement itself in its intrinsic nature. The former type of relation to an object does not fall within the province of a transcendental enquiry as it concerns only things found, contingently, to be 'agreeable' whilst a transcendental enquiry is concerned with that which seems to us to involve a *necessary* relation to pleasure and displeasure. So, just as the description of 'feelings' as aesthetic in the second critique only applied to pure feelings, here it is also the case that not all types of relation to an object that involve pleasure or displeasure are included in the province of an 'aesthetic', only those that involve a *necessary* relationship.

The *Critique of Aesthetic Judgement* concerns itself with the two forms in which there is an experience of the essential nature of subjectivity, in relation to the beautiful and the sublime. The experience of the beautiful harmonises a relation between the subject and what it relates to such that the beauty perceived and the one perceiving it appear to be intimately united, which is why beauty provokes a 'lingering' and a feeling of peacefulness that we term 'taste'. The experience of the sublime is much more violent and entails a conflict involving alternate feelings of attraction and repulsion, which is why Kant does not address the sublime under the heading of 'taste' but rather places it in close proximity to moral feeling by describing the feeling of the sublime as an 'intellectual feeling'.[11]

The distinction between taste and intellectual feeling parallels the distinction between the relation to nature in terms of law and the relation to morality in terms of law. Just as the comprehension of the world as ordered is productive of pleasure and a feeling of relation between perceiver and perceived, the experience of the beautiful involves a sense of the connection between the one experiencing something as beautiful and that which is so experienced. Similarly, the relation to the moral law involves a mixture of feelings, as is evidenced in the attraction and repulsion of humiliation and respect, an admixture given a clear parallel in Kant's description of intellectual feeling in the case of the sublime. These parallels should help us to see that there is, on the one hand, a connection between the experience of beauty and the thought of purpose and, on the other hand, a notion of the necessity of a conflict involved with our relation to morality that is paralleled in some of our aesthetic experiences.

These parallels between the discussions of the *Critique of Aesthetic Judgement* and Kant's other critical works indicate the systematic placing of the former. They also suggest the dependence of the whole critical system on an expanded notion of 'aesthetics'.[12] The relation between the three forms of enquiry Kant terms 'aesthetic' can now be summarised. The transcendental aesthetic explicates the a priori conditions of sensibility, the second critique provides us with reasons for thinking that there are pure feelings and the third critique details the relationship between pleasure and displeasure and necessity. All three forms of 'aesthetic' therefore reveal the non-sensuous grounds of sensuousness.

The unity of the third critique

The *Critique of Judgement* is concerned to describe the relationship between the general structures of law outlined in the first critique as the basis of a nature in general and the laws that contingently prevail in the world we happen to inhabit. In other words, the question arises, given the demonstrations of the first critique, of why we describe such things as the law of gravity as laws when the operation of them in our world seems contingent and the notion of law itself is intrinsically necessary in its thought. In order to treat of this question Kant finds it necessary to return to the topic of how 'judgement' should be described.[13] Whilst the importance of the topic of 'judgement' in the first critique is undeniable (the understanding itself is described there as a 'faculty for judging' and the discussion of the notion of schematism is given as part of the doctrine of judgement), the 'reflective' aspect of judgement is relegated to an appendix to the transcendental analytic.[14] Since reflective judgement deals not with the nature in general that is at issue in the first critique, but rather with the contingencies of the world we happen to inhabit, it must address the problem of relating the 'laws' we discern in this world to the thought of law presented in the first critique. So this type of judgement cannot rely on the understanding to provide it with laws but since it is dealing with nature (and not freedom) it also cannot rely on reason. Therefore there is, for this type of judgement, no pre-given mode of operation. It thus has to deal with appearances '*artistically*, in terms of a principle that is universal but also indeterminate', which is 'a purposive arrangement of nature in a system'.[15]

In order to justify the principle of purposiveness what Kant has to do in the third critique is to show how the concept of 'art' (or *techne*) arises and what the connection is between 'art' and the cognition of nature as possessing laws. Once we have described the task of the third critique we can begin to see why it contains both a critique of aesthetic judgement and a critique of teleological judgement. What Kant is treating in this work is a logical purposiveness in nature (a *teleo*-logic) and an aesthetic purposiveness in nature, and the division between logical purposiveness and aesthetic purposiveness repeats the division in the first critique between a transcendental aesthetic and a transcendental logic.

This description also helps us to grasp the notion Kant has of the term 'art'. The connection between the terms is clear in the sense of a 'making' that is the product of a form of cultivation. This suggests that the question of 'culture' will be of some significance in grasping the manner in which Kant describes art and that it will also be the key to a criticism of works of art. It should be remembered however that Kant is also describing the capacity of our judgement to 'make laws' as itself 'artistic' due to the fact that this reflective capacity involves a use of universal but indeterminate concepts. Kant refers to the universal but indeterminate concepts through the principle of 'purposiveness'. It is the principle of purposiveness that enables us to treat the regularities of experience through the notion of law. Similarly, there is such a principle in operation in both creating and judging works of art.

Kant and fine art

The manner in which Kant treats the work of art in the *Critique of Aesthetic Judgement* has rarely been regarded with much enthusiasm.[16] One of the reasons for this is that it has been thought, perhaps under the influence of Hegel's account, that Kant has less interest in works of art than in natural beauty. There is a passage where Kant refers to the 'superiority' of natural beauty over artistic beauty, but it is worth noting that the place where Kant states this is during a discussion of the 'intellectual interest' in the beautiful before he has set out the distinction between fine art and the thought of art in general.[17] When Kant turns to discussing 'fine art' he describes its purpose as involving the standard of the 'reflective power of judgement'.[18] This involves fine art in an intimate relationship to nature as its artistry is dependent for its effect on a certain type of self-effacement that involves us in looking upon it as 'natural'.

The manner in which this impression of a natural power is conveyed to us by fine art is through the rule that is responsible for its production, a rule that Kant terms 'genius'. Just as the ability to perceive nature as purposive requires a relationship to take place between the presentation of a regularity and a reflective giving of law, so the production of an object after the rule of genius requires a self-renunciation of determinate results in favour of simple attention to the act of creation as such. This attention relates, however, in the production of fine art, to the 'material' that is worked on whilst the active *formation* of this material 'requires a talent that is academically trained, so that it may be used in a way that can stand the test of the power of judgement'.[19] The relationship between the talent that is required to make formation artistic and the genius that is required to find the material worked on exacting is an intricate one that parallels the relation between receptivity to sensation as such and the active formation of sensibility in the provision of our formative role in placing sensuousness within its conditions.

The creation of a type of beauty that is the product of the combination of cultivation with intimate receptivity is responsible for a 'superiority' that fine art has over natural beauty, namely, the beautiful description of things that we would find ugly in nature itself. To be able to exhibit things in this manner is what requires genius, but genius itself is based on the possession of 'spirit' (*Geist*). Kant terms this 'the animating principle in the mind' and states that it is 'the ability to exhibit *aesthetic ideas*'.[20] An aesthetic idea is a presentation to which no concept is adequate, 'so that no language can express it completely and allow us to grasp it' or, in other terms, an intuition that exceeds the powers of a concept to govern it through the rules of understanding (which is why Kant also terms this type of idea a presentation 'of the imagination').[21] This involves a relation to the understanding, but one which is expressive of an idea rather than a concept.

Whilst the discussion of 'genius' gives us a clear clue to the production of a work of art, it is only the combination of this with 'taste' that allows us say that we have '*fine* art'. If genius is governed by the imagination in its freedom, then taste requires the introduction of a lawfulness that tempers the fertility of reference to aesthetic ideas and gives them form. Because of this, taste, like judgement in general, 'consists in disciplining (or training) genius'.[22] Before looking further at the conditions for this training, conditions which will lead us beyond the *Critique of Aesthetic Judgement* and to the *Critique of Teleological Judgement*, it is first necessary to look in more detail at the very notion of 'fine art' itself, as so doing will help to defuse the notion that an aesthetic criticism is one that is blind to history.

The fact that the opening sections of the *Critique of Aesthetic Judgement* concern a discussion of 'pure judgements of taste' has led to a misleading reading of Kant's account of fine art. Whilst the notion of a pure aesthetic judgement is outlined by Kant to be 'disinterested', this term is not applicable to his account of works of art. Kant explicitly states this when he writes that judgements that concern works of art 'have to assess the thing's perfection' and that this entails that they are not purely aesthetic judgements.[23] Rather, the judgements of works of art approximate to the Ideal of Beauty described in the Analytic of the Beautiful rather than to the pure judgements of taste accounted for there. Because of this a relation to a concept is at work in judging *and producing* works of art. The incorporation of conceptuality into the production of works of art is described in the notion of 'aesthetic ideas' – presentations of the imagination which prompts much thought but to which no concept can be adequate, which is why 'no language can express it completely'.[24] But the incorporation of such aesthetic ideas into the production of a work, which is the work of genius, can only be given through the training that results from taste. This training requires an essential involvement of the artist with history. To understand this involvement of the work of art with the history of art is integral to the act of criticism and this shows the centrality of a historical purchase for an aesthetic criticism. It is this notion of a discipline or training that requires an effective step beyond the account of the *Critique of Aesthetic Judgement* towards the *Critique of Teleological Judgement*. The reason for stating this is that the production of forms of an exemplary kind involves a clear relationship to the history of the production of artworks and, with this, an account of the conditions of *culture*. Kant describes culture as the production in a rational being of 'an aptitude for purposes generally'.[25] This production requires two conditions.

Kant terms these conditions two forms of culture, though in fact they are part of the unitary complex that culture itself constitutes. The first is what he terms a culture of skill and this is required for the promotion of purposes at all, but its condition is the development of a culture of discipline which is necessary in order to free us from the 'despotism of desires'.[26] The fact that it is within the discussion of the *Critique of Teleological Judgement* that we are led to this idea of discipline as a precondition for the exercise of freedom is in itself very instructive about the unity of the whole third critique.

Whilst the most obvious sense of teleology is in relation to the understanding of organisms it is also the case that Kant's key example of final causation is a cultural relation involving the notion of 'rent'.[27] The recursive logic of final causes operates in culture through the production of inequality and conflict in history, a production that ensures competition and distortion, a process which we could term a 'cunning of nature' or to use Kant's own expression 'a deeply hidden and perhaps intentional endeavour of the supreme wisdom'.[28] This 'deeply hidden' endeavour directs the conflict within which the history of humanity is found to an overall goal of further production of culture and is the prime means of 'discipline' for nations as inequality is the means of disciplining individuals. This important set of claims is key to the understanding of what discipline is involved in taste. Taste is analogous in its action on the work of art during its production and in the course of its judgement to the cruel and vigorous elements of culture itself. A final way of putting the relationship into focus is through Kant's contrast between mechanism and teleology. Just as 'mechanism' involves only a linear causal relation as opposed to the recursive causality of final causes and this leads the former to produce only limited operations incapable of 'spirit' (because of lacking life), so also the interaction between the artwork and its criticism is one of connection between that which is filled with life and the fixity that produces death. Criticism's ends can include the destruction of a work just as easily as its perpetuation and reproduction.

The ends of criticism

To describe the implications of the agenda for criticism that emerges from this account of Kant requires revisiting the notion of 'ends'. There are four types of 'ends' that need to be distinguished: we can think of an 'end' as the limit of something; we can describe an 'end' as something's purpose; we can think of an 'end' as a conclusion or destination; finally, we can think of an 'end' as an 'affinity' between elements or as a notion of 'co-determination' of parts. Whilst the notions of limit and purpose are closely interconnected for Kant, as to think of a purpose of something is limit our comprehension of it to the terms of that purpose, these elements of 'end' are still analytically distinct.

The limit of the criticism of a work should be given in terms of the relationship between setting rules for its comprehension in a lawlike manner and recognising that this law has to be referred to the nature of the work itself and not simply pre-set. Hence, the act of criticism has to involve a *reflective* judgement, which uncovers the law within the work and relates the law 'of' the work to the thought of law in general. This limitative element of the 'end' of criticism is connected to the purpose of criticism itself, this purpose being one of relating the work to the formation of culture. The purpose of criticism in other words is to further sharpen the process of relationship between the elements of skill and discipline within a culture, providing conditions for 'disciplining' the work in the process of inaugurating its entry into the historical network of works. This disciplinary aspect of criticism is both its promise and its danger. The promise of criticism at this level is that its introduction of the work assessed into the network of works will permit new reflection on the corpus of works already assessed; the danger is that it will simply kill the work and permit no new growth to emerge from it.[29]

Whilst the danger of criticism's foreclosure of a work is one sense of the understanding of 'end' as destination the real sense of this notion of criticism is its relationship to the Idea of the work, an Idea which we can grasp as contained within the possibility opened by the work and which is not a destination in the sense of a finish but an infinite possibility that permits further critical reaction and the elaboration of an embedded presence of the work within culture as part of its own criticism. This notion of a 'destination' indicates the infinity of criticism and the way in which criticism lives through its own history. This aspect of criticism is another element of the negotiation that an act of criticism involves, as without a relation to the history that has made possible its intervention in relation to the work the criticism produced has the tendency to be merely a 'view' or opinion which does not itself have any 'spirit'. For criticism itself to possess 'spirit' is for it to be involved with the 'life' that is its own historical condition. However, this relation is again something that requires a *reflective* negotiation, as a determinative relation to the history of criticism reduces each critical act to a mere repetition and does not permit the reopening of the engagement with the work that will allow the conflict that is the life of culture. Hence, there is the same danger and the same opening for each act of criticism in relation to its own history as there is for this criticism's relation to the possibility of the work confronted, and the case is further complicated when we include discussion of the criticism directed upon the particular work, a relation which soon involves considerable complexity.[30] Hence, not merely the production of the work and a recognition of its entry into the set of works is an historical act but the critical relation to the history of the criticism of a work is a further historical act, and these twin historical conditions require thinking in relation to their own possibility, a thinking that has precisely been ruled out by recent forms of historicism.

The notion of 'end' as affinity or co-determination involves assessment of the work criticised in relation to its conditions of production and is often the most decisive element of the critical act, not least because there are many conditions of production for a work and the relation of the work to the different elements of culture can again enrich relation to the work or simply produce a reductive response to it which permits no new invention. Understanding the conditions of the work involves grasping the strife of which it is part and negotiating a relation between the work and this strife, without either ceasing prematurely to close the strife or simply articulating this strife as exterior to the work's immanent sense.[31] This relationship to the work involves not a simple rendition of 'contexts', as is all too common, but rather seeing the work as emerging from a medium that is specific to itself and grasping this medium not simply as a sociological or historical given but as marking an originary irruption and thus as saturating any 'context'. Grasping the nature of this irruption clearly involves a sense of what makes the originary work possible. This is endless work as there are no definable 'facts' that could close this accounting; hence the accounting should overflow the arena of facts and reshape them. In other terms, this grasp of the medium that permits the work's emergence is one that should reshape the work's 'backgrounds' in the work's image instead of fashioning the work in the image of the circumstances of its arrival.

The listing of the thoughts of end and the thinking through of how they relate to acts of criticism should help us to see that Kant's notion of aesthetic judgement is not intended either to freeze works within some straitjacket of formal beauty or to foreclose a relation to history as integral to the comprehension of their aesthetic import. The key element underlying all these disparate considerations, however, is the relationship between art and life, culture and the reproduction of its conditions through a reference of both to law and its reflective comprehension. The combination of these considerations suggests strongly that works are engaged in the same difficult negotiation with death that is, in fact, a condition of life itself. It is this ultimate relationship between life and death, work and its destruction, that is involved in the critical relationship to works of art.

Practical exemplifications: Wyndham Lewis and Robert Mapplethorpe

The works of Wyndham Lewis provide us with a case study for the application of this view of criticism to the understanding of artistic productions. Lewis's work has been subjected to the same range of assessments as most other authors, from the classic description of it in terms of certain types of basic writing patterns to the relation of it to psychoanalytic or Marxist categories.[32] If we turn to the novels of Lewis from a Kantian direction, however, we can see the vital character of his work as consisting precisely in its negotiation with the characteristics of life itself. This is clearly seen in such a work as *The Revenge for Love*, a work in which description of the political struggle engaged in by the leftist artists and writers of the 1930s against the backdrop of the Spanish Civil War is set out as involving a struggle between the engagement with life and the surrender to the forces which mechanise life. This can be seen in the passages where the characters are given lucid moments, as when Margaret, at a party, is driven to reflect on those around her as being 'big portentous wax-dolls, mysteriously doped with some impenetrable nonsense, out of a Caligari's drug-cabinet, and wound up with wicked fingers to jerk about in a threatening way – their mouths backfiring every other second, to spit out a manufactured hatred, as their eyeballs moved'.[33]

This vivid description, which involves references to drugs, the cinema and wax-dolls, conjures up an image of the various forces that are included in the mechanical reproduction of modern humanity and is one of the characteristics that stamps Lewis's work as a whole and the narrative of *The Revenge for Love* in particular. Within the space of this work there is the perception, stated by Margaret, but involving the consciousness of the majority of the characters, that living is a 'fever' and that the characters are merely 'all ghost-persons together'.[34] This collapse of the vitality of the characters is orchestrated within the work as part of the elemental struggle with the condition of their own life, a condition that is shaped by impersonal forces that are mechanising existence.

This sense of a struggle between mechanism and life is Lewis's version of the relationship between teleology and mechanism elaborated within Kant's *Critique of Teleological Judgement*. Just as Kant reveals the 'deeply hidden' intention of cultural history to be the reproduction of conditions of strife that constantly endanger life itself, so Lewis sets out the intensification of this conflict within conditions of mechanical modernity. The depth of Lewis's engagement with this difficulty in his novels encompasses a whole range of different types of situation from the isolation described by him in *Self Condemned* to the eschatological involvement of *The Human Age*.

The fact that Lewis's work can be addressed in this manner is itself a tribute to the type of criticism that is possible from a Kantian position. If, however, it were simply the case that the assessment of a work, whether by Lewis or anyone else, was an application of a pre-set notion of criticism and did not involve an alteration of the terms of that criticism, we would not have described a *reflective* criticism at all. The engagement with works has to alter the terms of the criticism otherwise the immanence of the law of the work has been missed. In the case of Lewis we can note a continuous setting out of instability in the relation between life and death, automation and humanity.[35] The introduction into the terms of the criticism of what is required by the nature of comprehension of the work offers a living futural character to criticism as it enables it to engage with its own conditions of possibility and articulate its own methods in a manner that consistently requires invention.

Whilst Lewis's work, as a literary work, reveals its effects through a process of linguistic display, it relies heavily on the relationship modern literature has to mechanised production of images. The arrival of cinema and photography as contemporary means of production altered the condition of literature in terms of both its production and its criticism. The quotes from Lewis that refer to cinema directly are only the most obvious sign of this intrusion of visual art into modern literature. The writing that Lewis produces is in fact much more heavily involved with modern images than this suggests. Lewis understood his work to be based on tracing an 'external' relationship to character in which behaviour and physical appearance become the source for understanding rather than an appeal to a deep 'inner' self. This understanding of the nature of the character in terms of a fixity that is grounded in their physicality emerges from the nature of figures that are given to us statically in photographs and through a kinetic procession in cinema. This behavioural engagement with personality is part of the increasing becoming-artificial of humanity.

In conclusion therefore it is worth looking at the placing of literature in relation to visual art and to tracing out the connection between the two required for an aesthetic criticism as well as indicating something of the distinction between them. The photographs of Robert Mapplethorpe are a reference of some import for discussing the nature of visual media. In the posthumously published collection *Pictures* the most explicitly erotic of Mapplethorpe's photographs are presented together.[36] There is for example the four-picture sequence *Helmut and Brooks* (1978), *Fist Fuck* (1978), *Double Fist Fuck* (1978) and *Fist Fuck* (1978). These works caused considerable controversy and have been at the centre of battles about censorship. The point of discussing them is not to revisit this debate but to suggest, in agreement with Arthur Danto, that a defence of these works cannot be based on a 'formalist' discussion of them as 'figure studies'.[37] I do not accept that such a purely 'formalist' reading of the works is Kantian. Rather, a Kantian appreciation of these works has to begin from assessing them reflectively in terms of the type of entry they have into the world of works of art. As a fourfold sequence they make a powerful collective statement, but it would not be 'formalist' to relate them to the conditions of their framing, conditions always of central significance to Mapplethorpe. Hence *Helmut and Brooks* displays the action it portrays through a geometric spacing of the figures that places the apex of the buttocks central to the composition, a centring that ensures the eye follows a curve upwards to the back of the chair and downwards to the inserted face with a smoothness that is clearly classical. Similarly, the first *Fist Fuck* places a figure's profile in full view, albeit with a backwards vision that permits a sliding portrayal of the man on the floor and allows a graceful upwards movement of the eye towards the point of the fist's insertion. *Double Fist Fuck* by contrast offers a foreclosure of its subject which places its elements in a bare relationship that simply and compellingly allows the connection between the limbs involved to be presented. Of the four, only the second *Fist Fuck* might be thought to be unsuccessful in terms of the relationship the tableau has to the history of visual works. Here the figure that is entering is presented standing, with a forward thrusting movement that prevents a clear focus on his form and renders the composition less harmonious.

This limitative criticism of these works, which places them within the conditions of their talented production, is only the first part of their appreciation. The purposive orientation of the works and their criticism is to alter the way in which the conventions the work has utilised can be understood and this involves the fact that the shapes of the presentations given affect much other subject matter that is governed by the same rules of portrayal. We can see this in relation to Mapplethorpe's own work, where portraits of film stars and pictures of flowers cannot be viewed without a sense of how their portrayal partakes of the eroticism of the works just referred to, and in relation to works of other photographers who use or abjure these conventions. Cultural awareness of the works and the intertwinement between their compositional possibility and the subject they present affects the comprehension of Renaissance paintings of angels as much as it does the history of photography.

A criticism of these works that has 'spirit' will relate them in unexpected ways to the history of which they are part and will in the process ensure that this history bears the traces of its effect. As for example Thierry De Duve has ensured that it is now part of the history of thinking of Duchamp that we think also of Kant, so also this reading has ensured that Kant's name is now connected to that of Mapplethorpe. The 'medium' of production of Mapplethorpe's work is not simply photography but the place of photography in relation to the arts as these are placed after the invention of photography. This placement requires the comprehension of this history as one of a displacement that constantly requires an invention of criticism, an 'invention' that pretends neither to collapse the appreciation of works into the form of one type of art (as is done with semiotic criticism) nor to suggest that distinct art forms are not integrally related. This double vigilance, attending both to the specificity of a medium and grasping its emplacement in a wide history that it alters due to its originariness, is key to a futural criticism.[38]

This involvement of criticism with its own invention is the condition of criticism having a future at all. The involvement of aesthetics with teleology in a unitary relation that comprehends works as parts of a 'culture' that they both continuously create and are judged by is a recursive process and hence part of what the third critique has enabled us to recognise. For criticism to become reflective concerning itself is for it to live up to the challenges of the transcendental conditions of its own possibility, a challenge Kant himself did not feel he was in a position to meet.[39] In suggesting that the resources for criticism to meet this challenge are certainly available I wish to propose a new future for aesthetics as integral to the criticism of works, a future that will enable a different type of criticism than is generally practised, a criticism that will remain open to its own conditions of transformation.

Notes

1 The range of works that deserve mention here is very wide indeed. Works that discuss both Kant and aesthetics include: J.-F. Lyotard, *Lessons on the Analytic of the Sublime*, trans. E. Rottenberg (Stanford, CA: Stanford University Press, 1994); H. Caygill, *The Art of Judgement* (Oxford: Blackwell, 1989); R. Makkreel, *Imagination and Interpretation In Kant: The Hermeneutical Import of the Critique of Judgement* (Chicago: University of Chicago Press, 1990); T. De Duve, *Kant After Duchamp* (Cambridge, MA: MIT Press, 1996). Works that highlight the interest of aesthetics in contemporary terms that are based on accounts other than Kant's include A. Bowie, *From Romanticism to Critical Theory: The Philosophy of German Literary Theory* (London: Routledge, 1997) and I. Armstrong, *The Radical Aesthetic* (Oxford: Blackwell, 2000), the latter of which makes interesting use of the work of Gillian Rose.

2 The reflexive problematic that historicism is caught in is described well by Fredric Jameson at the opening of his book *The Political Unconscious: Narrative as a Socially Symbolic Act* (London: Routledge, 1981): 'Always historicize! That is the transhistorical imperative.' The

fact that a work could begin with such a slogan with no apparent sense of irony is an index of the degrees of absurdity historicism very quickly reaches.

3 A classic sign of unease about this view within Marxist circles was, however, expressed by the publication by New Left Books (ed.), *Aesthetics and Politics* (London: Verso, 1977), in which Rodney Livingston, Perry Anderson and Francis Mulhern introduced and contentiously discussed texts by a range of authors classified as 'German Marxists' (and including the Hungarian Georg Lukács). More recently T. Eagleton, in *The Ideology of the Aesthetic* (Oxford: Blackwell, 1990), attempts to retrieve a relationship to the history of aesthetics but does so whilst multiplying reservations about the discipline and indicating very little grasp of its conceptual history, a fact he puts down in the preface to the book to the fact that he is 'not really qualified to write the book'.

4 Kant, *Critique of Pure Reason*, trans. W. S. Pluhar (Indianapolis: Hackett, 1999), A20/B34.

5 For a more extensive account of the transcendental aesthetic and its relationship to the other forms of 'aesthetics' in Kant see G. Banham, *Kant and the Ends of Aesthetics* (London: Macmillan, 2000).

6 Kant, Ak. 5: 73. All references to works other than the first critique in this chapter are to the standard edition, the *Akademie* edition of *Kants gesammelte Schriften* (Berlin: Königlich Preussische Akademie der Wissenschaften, 1908–13), and are cited as Ak. volume: page number.

7 Kant, Ak. 5: 76.

8 See Banham, *Kant*, ch. 10 for a fuller account of the later works in which Kant treats of moral feeling. I am currently working on a sequel to this book in which I will set out the density of Kant's moral psychology in much more detail than can be attempted here.

9 Kant uses the term 'aesthetic' at Ak. 5: 90 but indicates that the term is used by 'analogy'. It is rare to discuss the 'aesthetic' of the second critique although there is the important precedent of L. W. Beck. See Beck, *A Commentary on Kant's Critique of Practical Reason* (Chicago: University of Chicago Press, 1960), ch. XII, and for an account of the reasons for its particular place in the architectonic of the second critique see Banham, *Kant*, ch. 1.

10 It is almost a commonplace for contemporary critics of Kant to suggest that he has little room for feeling in his account of moral motivation, an accusation that seems to me quite false. For a critical assessment of Kant's position see N. Sherman, 'The place of emotions in Kantian morality' in O. Flanagan and A. Rorty (eds), *Identity, Character and Morality* (Cambridge, MA: MIT Press, 1990), pp. 149–70 and for a more positive assessment see A. Reath, 'Kant's theory of moral sensibility: respect for the law and the influence of inclination', *Kant-Studien*, 80 (1989), 284–302. The most influential current criticism of Kant on feeling is B. Williams, *Moral Luck* (Cambridge: Cambridge University Press, 1981), to whom C. Korsgaard replies in *Creating the Kingdom of Ends* (Cambridge: Cambridge University Press, 1996). For clear historical accounts of the background of Kant's ethics see J. B. Scheewind, *The Invention of Autonomy* (Cambridge: Cambridge University Press, 1998), and contrast this with the more reliable K. Ward, *The Development of Kant's View of Ethics* (Oxford: Blackwell, 1972).

11 Kant, Ak. 5: 192.

12 For a discussion of the notion of a 'general aesthetic' as underlying and uniting the disparate forms of aesthetic that Kant discusses see Banham, *Kant*, particularly chs 1 and 10.

13 For a fascinating and elaborate treatment of the place of 'judgement' in the first critique see B. Longuenesse, *Kant and the Capacity to Judge: Sensibility and Discursivity in the Transcendental Analytic of the Critique of Pure Reason*, trans. C. T. Wolfe (Princeton: Princeton University Press, 1998), and for a treatment of the history of the role of judgement

in modern philosophy see H. Caygill, *The Art of Judgement* (Oxford: Blackwell, 1989). Longuenesse presents a compelling argument for the importance of 'reflective judgement' in the first critique, an argument similar to that given in Lyotard, *Lessons on the Analytic of the Sublime.*

14 The second part of the transcendental analytic is described by Kant as the 'analytic of principles' or 'doctrine of judgement' and comprises an immense part of the work: A130/B169–A292/B349. The relationship between this notion of judgement and the key notions of transcendental psychology treated within the work, such as the transcendental imagination, would be worth extensive analysis given the immense richness of the questions involved. I will undertake this work elsewhere.

15 Kant, Ak. 20: 214.

16 The treatment of Kant's aesthetics rarely accords much space to his treatment of art. For a significant exception see S. Kemal, *Kant and Fine Art: An Essay on the Philosophy of Fine Art and Culture* (Oxford: Clarendon Press, 1986).

17 Kant, Ak. 5: 301.

18 Kant, Ak. 5: 306.

19 Kant, Ak. 5: 310.

20 Kant, Ak. 5: 314.

21 *Ibid.* Kant is very cautious in setting out the reason for calling these presentations 'ideas', a terminological choice which is as interesting in its way as his gradual extension of the term 'aesthetic' as it indicates a correlation between the imagination and reason (the latter involving the production of 'ideas' as described in the first critique).

22 Kant, Ak. 5: 432.

23 Kant, Ak. 5: 311.

24 Kant, Ak. 5: 314.

25 Kant Ak. 5: 431.

26 Kant, Ak. 5: 432.

27 For a description and discussion of this example within a general account of the 'artificiality' of teleology see G. Banham, 'Teleology, transcendental reflection and artificial life', *Tekhnema: Journal of Philosophy and Technology,* 6 (2000), 52–17.

28 Kant Ak. 5: 433.

29 Walter Benjamin vividly presents this danger when he describes criticism as 'the mortification of the works'. This description takes place in the discussion of 'allegory and *trauerspiel*' in W. Benjamin, *The Origin of German Tragic Drama,* trans. J. Osborne (London: Verso, 1977), p. 182. For a discussion of this work in relation to reactions to it by both Jacques Derrida and Gillian Rose see G. Banham, 'Mourning Satan' in Banham and C. Blake (eds), *Evil Spirits: Nihilism and the Fate of Modernity* (Manchester: Manchester University Press, 2000), pp. 7–21.

30 This relation is again the subject of intriguing and very important reflections by Walter Benjamin, both in the aforementioned study of the *trauerspiel* and in W. Benjamin, 'The concept of criticism in German Romanticism' in Benjamin, *Selected Writings, Volume 1: 1913–1926,* trans. D. Lachterman, H. Eiland and I. Balfour (Cambridge, MA: Belknap Press, 1996).

31 Although there are considerable differences between the approach advanced here and that of Gillian Rose, the notion of keeping the middle 'broken' and not attempting to 'heal' it is one with which I am in fundamental accord. Cf. G. Rose, *The Broken Middle* (Oxford: Blackwell, 1992).

32 For a classic type of analysis see J. Meyers, *Wyndham Lewis: A Revaluation* (London:

Athlone, 1980) and for the application to Lewis's work of psychoanalytic and Marxist thought see F. Jameson, *Fables of Aggression: Wyndham Lewis, the Modernist as Fascist* (Berkeley: University of California Press, 1979). The outline I am merely sketching here of an alternative type of criticism of Lewis to those in these works has been set out at much greater length in Banham, 'The uncanny purposes of machines', *Wyndham Lewis Annual 1996*, 20–30.

33 Wyndham Lewis, *The Revenge for Love*, ed. Reed Way Dasenbrock (Santa Rosa, CA: Black Sparrow Press, 1991), p. 153.

34 Lewis, *Revenge*, p. 163.

35 This involves the addition to the vocabulary of Kantian criticism of the 'uncanny' and the 'diabolical'. For an illustration of the necessity of these terms and an illustration of their appreciation see Banham, 'teleology, transcendental reflection and artificial life', 'The uncanny purposes of machines' and 'Mourning Satan'.

36 R. Mapplethorpe, *Pictures*, ed. D. Levas (New York: Arena Editions, 1999).

37 A. Danto, *Playing with the Edge: The Photographic Achievement of Robert Mapplethorpe* (Berkeley: University of California Press, 1996). This 'formalist' defence was at the centre of an obscenity trial provoked by the photographs.

38 For a more extensive engagement with Mapplethorpe in relation to Kant and Duchamp see Banham, 'Mapplethorpe, Duchamp and the ends of photography', *Angelaki: Journal of the Theoretical Humanities*, 7:1 (2002), 119–27. This whole issue is devoted to the relationship of aesthetics to the appreciation of works of art.

39 'Since this enquiry into our power of taste, which is the aesthetic power of judgement, has a transcendental aim, rather than the aim to [help] form and cultivate taste (since this will proceed, as it has in the past, even if no such investigations are made), I would like to think that it will be judged leniently as regards its deficiency for the latter purpose' (Kant, Ak. 5: 170).

Including transformation: notes on the art of the contemporary

Central to any understanding of contemporary art and therefore central to any engagement with a contemporary politics of art is the question of the nature of the contemporary.[1] Even before definitions of art and politics are offered it is the contemporary that emerges as the more insistent problem. While any attempt to pursue the contemporary in a detailed manner must become, in the end, an engagement within the philosophico-political problem of modernity, here, in this context, a form of abbreviation needs to be found. A shortened yet insistent staging of the issues involved in a sustained investigation of the contemporary will stem from a consideration of the terms 'transformation' and 'inclusion'. As will be seen, their positive and negative determinations can be taken as defining an opening in which the art of the contemporary can be located.[2] Prior to pursuing the detail of these terms their initial field of operation needs to be identified. They stage a number of different possibilities.

The term 'transformation' marks the presence of a contested argument. Without, at this stage, commenting on its viability, its opening move involves the claim that the term 'transformation' identifies a political possibility that is taken to pertain no longer.[3] The argument continues in this vein. Projects of political transformation have been replaced by strategies either of adaptation or of denial. Art that was linked either directly or indirectly to transformation has, from within the purview of this argument, failed to note the move away from strategies of complete social transformation. To the extent that certain artistic practices identify with this conception of transformation, that act of identification constrains art to oscillate between a series of carefully identified positions. Art that seeks to be directly political can be viewed as either utopian or outmoded. Work that attempts to resist incorporation and thus allow for an opening up of transformation because of the autonomy entailed by such work, suffers the charge of elitism. The direct or indirect politicisation of art can be dismissed therefore because of its failure to address the contemporary. Such would be a 'contemporary' view of art. Any engagement with this position cannot take place merely on the level of the work of art. The locus of engagement is that specific conception of the contemporary within which art is taken to announce the impossibility of transformation. The work of art becomes the site of that engagement.

'Inclusion' is a term that can be taken as working in relation to the oscillations already identified within the domain opened up by any consideration of transformation. There are two different senses of inclusion. The first is a conception of inclusion in which there is a shared agreement – or at least the assumption of such an agreement – concerning the conditions of inclusion and exclusion. Without being immutable such assumptions are already in place. In this instance inclusion is dictated by a commitment to a reiteration of sameness. Within the confines of this argument, sameness is the refusal of transformation. Allowing this conception to dictate how the contemporary is understood means that all works of art, even in being different, are the same. What makes them the same is their implicit recognition of the impossibility of there being a transformation. This recognition is linked as much to works that are explicitly connected to the social as to ones whose relationship is always to be established. Once art is defined beyond any link to a project other than the one provided by its content, what remains is a proliferation of styles without end. There is however a second sense of inclusion. Here, rather than the assumption of sameness as underlying relation, there is the presence of difference. Difference, rather than being an effect of sameness, is already present. Difference and thus the problem of relation are at work *ab initio*. (This accounts for why sameness and difference do not form a simple opposition.) From this perspective inclusion becomes a form of negotiation where the accepting and the 'housing' of the different has to allow for strategies that maintain the different as such. This will have an eventual transformative effect on the site in which the different is housed. The question that will have to be pursued concerns the way this possibility is registered.

Having sketched some of the issues at work within these terms they now need to be developed. In the process both the contemporary and the art of the contemporary will be able to figure. What will emerge is that the nature of the contemporary and the presence of contemporary art demand that the site of intervention be linked to the act of criticism. In other words, art will not be able to intervene without the assistance of criticism. While criticism can always be presented such that it reiterates the position in which difference is the work of an unending sameness, criticism cannot be equated absolutely with a presentation of this nature. There is another possibility. It arises precisely because it is equally the province of criticism to allow art to interrupt that perpetuating similitude. To allow for that interruption is to allow for the structure of transformation. Moreover, not only will criticism emerge as central, of equal importance is the fact that it is the nature of the contemporary – its particular determinations – that demands this exacting role from the critic.[4]

Transformation

The argument against the possibility of transformation and thus for a version of the equation in which realism equals political conservatism warrants a detailed analysis.[5] The position contains a fundamental flaw. While it may be the case that direct causality no longer pertains such that it is not possible to argue that a series of political actions or even artistic actions will have necessary effects, it does not follow that arguments for a politicisation of art are themselves no longer possible. (Politicisation, in this context, involves the affirmed retention of transformation thought in terms of an interruption of the repetition of sameness.[6]) In the absence of causality the question that emerges concerns how art is to be political. To allow for this question is to resist the claim that the only way in which art can interrupt a consensus concerning the impossibility of transformation is by being directly political. Indeed it may be the case that allowing the political to be coextensive with that which is literally 'political' is allowing such art to be dismissed as simply unrealistic. Fundamental to the problem of the literal is the belief that the desired end can be achieved by art alone. Not only is such a view of art heroic, it is also false.

If the contemporary is the site of contestation concerning the possibility of transformation, then the claim that transformation is impossible cannot be met with the counter-claim of its possibility. After all, the copresence of both positions is that which defines the contemporary. What is significant is that its possibility can no longer be assumed and that therefore what counts as a response to the art of consensus is left open. And yet, it is the presence of that opening that provides the way of taking up what looks to be an aporia at the heart of transformation. The aporia is simply that there would seem to be no way out of the setting in which art is positioned as no longer having the capacity to stage an interruption and that this positioning cannot be overcome by the direct politicisation of art. Art as a practice cannot be straightforwardly politicised while at the same time remaining art. To allow for the aporia, which in this context is to identify contemporary art with an unending proliferation of styles, is to reduce art to no more than a register of decoration articulated within the cult of personality as well as the temporality of fashion. Any move beyond the aporia will have already signalled holding fashion and personalities in abeyance. How is the holding to be done? In what name is it to be undertaken?

The initial answer to these questions is 'art'. Art is that which escapes the hold of fashion and therefore of differing forms of complacency. Its escape is undertaken in the name of art. Once again such a response is circular. And yet, within that very circularity there lies another possibility. If art can be interpreted as no more than part of an endless proliferation of possibilities; or if art is able to be reduced to the staging of the 'personality' behind its production – and there will be other examples – then the truth of art does not lie in the particular interpretation or reduction but in the fact that art is able to lend itself to such possibilities. Art's truth therefore lies in its capacity to bear different and conflicting interpretations. What this means is that art is able to function as the locus in which the contestation concerning the contemporary is able to be staged. While one interpretation of art's work will support claims concerning the impossibility of transformation, since the evidence for such claims is that the practice of art is the continuity of difference where difference is always that of the same, it is equally the case that this 'evidence' can also be marshalled within arguments and interpretations that resist this particular conception of the contemporary. As such what is also changed is that for which art functions as evidence. Given that art's truth is its interpretive instability, what that truth demands is criticism as integral to art's work. Criticism – now understood as an inseparable part of art's truth – is, in this context, best approached under the heading of 'inclusion'.

Inclusion

As has already been intimated, there is an ineliminable divide within the space marked out by this term. In the first instance, once it is assumed that art is no more than a collection of different permutations of a generalised problematic, then all art is potentially able to be assimilated and therefore included. Part of the strategy of an avant garde was to create works of art that resisted assimilation. The museums and traditional gallery spaces would have been unable to house such interventions. That this is not the case means that on the level of literal inclusion the museum has yet to be challenged. If the price of inclusion is a certain homogeneity – and this is often the case even for those works that seek forms of differentiation – then does this not mean that art is, in fact, the site of an unending conformity to the given in which the possibilities of interruption and transformation are necessarily excluded?

Answering this question involves a twofold move. In the first instance an analogy is necessary. If the incorporation or inclusion of new work (or even works that had been thought to have been incorporated, assimilated and thus rendered familiar) parallels a version of citizenship, then the argument would be that a certain conformity to expectation is the price of admission. And yet the site of incorporation seems to be infinitely expandable and thus able to incorporate all possibilities. In the case of citizenship the incorporation of the outsider – be it immigrant, refugee or even home-born person – will be the inscription of the outsider within a process of homogenisation. Marginalisation becomes the cost and possibility of a resistance to that process. The limits of tolerance within contemporary democracies can be located within the terms set by this process and the way it operates in given contexts. The contemporary problem of the refugee tests the system precisely because the inclusion of refugees may have a transformative effect on the site that absorbs them. Holding to a liberal doctrine of tolerance while at the same time resisting the cost of absorption is the contradiction within government policies dealing with refugees. The task of intellectuals in this regard is to argue that inclusion has an effect and that the effect contains real potential for development and change (perhaps the only such potential within the European context).[7]

The analogy with art emerges at this point. However, the analogy is not between the work of art and the citizen (or would-be citizen); it occurs at the locus of reception. The problem posed by the refugee is that inclusion could interrupt the repetition of sameness. For the work of art there is a conflict – even if it is unstated – between that form of reception in which the work is easily assimilated and the form that works to identify and maintain a significantly different conception of assimilation, one present in terms of the continuity of negotiation. There will always be forms of assimilation. However, art's capacity to transform or to maintain forms of criticality can always be muted by, for example, a concentration on the cult of the artist. In such an instance a consideration of the work is deferred by the emphasis on the artist. Assimilation can only take place by refusing the work in the name of the artist.[8] The capacity for the work to have a transformative quality is stilled not by the work in and of itself but by its reception. Assimilation is necessary in order that the repetition of sameness be maintained. The new can only be incorporated if such an act is not the occasion where this repetition is interrupted. The threat of the refugee is the potential staging of such an interruption. Once art and criticism are interarticulated, art is able to maintain the same position. Consequently, while it is possible to include most works, because of the nature of the artwork such objects bring with them the power to maintain themselves as sites of contestation and therefore as sites of potential transformation. The potential lies not in the work of art in itself but in the question of its reception. That question is the province of criticism.[9]

To the extent that the refugee is allowed to maintain difference as the determination guiding inclusion, then housing the refugee necessarily becomes a form of negotiation with that difference. While it will always be possible to demand of the refugee that conformity to expectations such that inclusion is undertaken in the name of sameness, there is this other possibility. What matters with the refugee is the policy guiding inclusion. Different directions and therefore different avenues of government policy emerge with an inclusion structured by the maintenance of sameness than would emerge in allowing for the continuity of negotiation. The latter is a form of inclusion that allows for the potential endlessness of negotiation within a community structured as much by continuity as by discontinuity. The divisions concerning the reception of the refugee are reiterated within the activity of criticism accompanying the reception of the work of art.

The point that needs to be argued therefore is that the divisions within reception, and therefore the presence of at least two different modes of inclusion, are inextricably bound up with what has been identified above as the truth of the work of art. It is this point that needs to be developed. Moreover, it is only in recognising this 'truth' that it becomes possible to address the question of policy in relation to the production of works of art. The claim here therefore is that the only way that it is possible to take up questions of policy in relation to art, the production of art and finally the reception of that production is within the terms set by the nature of the artwork itself. Furthermore, because there is no such entity as the work of art in and of itself, what is essential is that the art of the contemporary be given its appropriate setting; namely that it be given an account that takes the present – the contemporary – as a necessary component within art's work. That necessity arises precisely because there cannot be any real separation of the work from the activity of criticism – the activity that identifies the work, thereby allowing the work to become a site of contestation.

From truth to policy – the name of criticism

The obvious counter to the argument that policy depends on a decision concerning the truth of art is that such a position overstates the needs of policy makers and confuses philosophical argumentation with the 'hard-nosed' practice of decision making. The are many ways of responding to this claim. The most germane for this argument concerns the nature of a decision. What is it to decide? What is a decision?

A decision in this context is linked to the truth of art. That truth is simply that fundamental to art's work is the impossibility of there being any form of finality concerning the nature and thus meaning of the work. The absence of interpretative finality is neither relativism nor semantic undecidability. It is a direct consequence of the ontology of the artwork. What absence opens up here is the necessity for a decision concerning the work of art. Interpretation – and this will be the case whether it is recognised or not – has the structure of a decision. While what is at stake in the practice of criticism is the decision, the question that has to be asked concerns the relationship between this formulation of criticism and policy. Answering a question of this nature involves tracing the move from the nexus made up of artwork/criticism/decision to the domain of policy. Policy cannot be self-justifying. Implicitly it maintains a conception of this nexus even if it is a banalised one. Given this nexus, policy can work in at least two different directions.

In the first instance policy will stem from the position that holds to the impossibility of transformation and therefore from the description of artistic practice taking place in terms of a proliferation of styles. Within this set-up such a proliferation has to be maintained. Consequently, what will have to be excluded are artworks which seem to question the likelihood of inclusion. In this context that questioning will not be ostensibly 'political' artwork. Indeed, such works can always be included in the name of tolerance. Exclusion will be linked to difficulty. And yet, this position is more complex than is allowed for by a simple evocation of difficulty. Within the domain of contemporary art the work that is apparently the most difficult seems to find a place. Inclusion, for the most part, is an ineliminable possibility. Indeed, that is the point. The question therefore has to concern what it is that would make work difficult. Prior to pursuing this question the other eventuality for policy needs to be noted.

If, rather than linking policy to a reiteration of sameness – a position guided by an interpretation of contemporary art that refuses it a transformative power – the strategy behind policy is the refusal of that reiteration, then a more demanding question emerges. What would it be like to decide that there is another possibility for art and that the realisation of that possibility should be the result of decisions made by government and public funding bodies? The answer to this question involves a similar policy response as one that would be made to the refugee. If the refugee is encouraged and accepted on the basis that inclusion will have a transformative effect on the site of inclusion, then policy has to be linked to realising that end and thus allowing for a mode of acceptance articulated in terms of negotiation. What this yields is a redescription of the site of inclusion as one of negotiation. If the work of art is allowed a position in which its presence is mediated by negotiation, this gives rise to two specific openings.

The first opening stems from the recognition that this mediation has always taken place. In many instances it was unstated. In such instances inclusion was always unproblematic. Where there was a potential problem then either curatorial practice or criticism effected inclusion by operating in ways that overcame any potential difficulty. However, to allow for the presence of explicit negotiation is to allow for work by curators and critics whose task is to stage an explicit negotiation. There is a need here to insist on the term 'negotiation'. Explicit negotiation precludes both the didactic and the prescriptive. Once negotiation is taken as central, policy becomes linked to staging a set-up in which what occurs, and therefore the event that will happen, are not inscribed, directed and ordained in advance. And yet, the retention of the term 'negotiation' does not mean that anything is possible. Explicit negotiation only ever occurs from a position. Here, what is being suggested is that this position sustains negotiation. (It will be in terms of the continuity of negotiation that 'difficulty' will come to be reworked.) The necessity that there be a position is a consequence of the ineliminable presence of the decision. Negotiation, in this sense, cannot be thought other than as the result of a decision.

The second opening occurs once explicit negotiation is allowed a central role, one where it works as a motif for reception. From the start such a position is actually closer to what has already been identified as the truth of art. This proximity does not guarantee the approach. Rather, it reinforces the necessity of holding to the nexus of artwork/criticism/decision as integral to activities undertaken in the name of art.

When used in a number of contexts the term 'negotiation' brings with it a specific goal. Negotiation can envisage a particular end. Once that end is reached, the negotiation is over. While the term needs to be retained, it has to be given a different temporal description. In this context the importance of a negotiation lies in the continuity of its being maintained. In other words, the term designates a specific strategy of reception in which the conditions for the reception of given works resist automatic assimilation, such that the question of how such works are to be included becomes the question to be pursued. Pursuing such a question is not an activity that pertains to the work alone. It involves curatorial decisions as well as the practice of criticism. Indeed, the work of art on its own cannot sustain a negotiation concerning its own reception. The recognition of the work's limit – a recognition that is, on one level, no more than a redescription of the nature of the work of art – reinforces the central place of criticism. Difficulty describes the predicament in which a work resists automatic assimilation. Part of that resistance is that the work – and here work now has to involve curatorial practice and criticism – comes to set the conditions of its reception. It is in the attempt to set those conditions that there is a potential conflict with the reiteration of sameness. The conflict occurs precisely because such an attempt would, almost of necessity, interrupt that reiteration.

Within this framework policy is defined by the retention of difficulty and the maintenance of sites of negotiation. While this is an abstract formulation, its force lies in the recognition that its site of application is always strategic. In other words, abstraction is always resolved by the decision. The immediate counter to the retention of even a reworked conception of difficulty itself coupled to the affirmation of a conception of negotiation marked by the problem of resolution rather than its inevitability, is that it re-establishes boundaries and therefore makes access to work more exacting. Such work will only appeal to a privileged few. This is of course a highly charged description of what would occur. Another description is that holding to difficulty and negotiation opens up the work of art as a site of engagement – an engagement which is constrained to take place in the name of art. Once inclusion is uncomplicated, and any negotiation is only even implicitly present – present almost to the point of its own disappearance – then art slides into mere entertainment and thus loses its capacity to function as art.

Allowing for difficulty means that judging policy, devising policy and implementing policy take place in relation to the nexus comprised of artwork/criticism/decision. The question that always needs to be addressed is straightforward: what, here, is to be negotiated? In the case of new work the challenge resides in allowing that work to be criticisable. The task of criticism therefore cannot be foreclosed in advance. In the case of already existent, if not canonical work, the task is to reactivate that potential. In both instances what allows for such strategies is the ontology of the work of art. As has already been indicated, it is an ontological set-up that allows for the nexus of artwork/criticism/decision to define the work of art. Finally, therefore, criticism is not an extra element that can be either added or subtracted. Nor, moreover, is criticism necessary because art no longer has a sustained philosophical basis. Indeed the contrary is the case. The inescapability of criticism – its need – lies in the ontological nature of the work of art. The truth of art is its work.

As a conclusion it is vital to pursue, albeit schematically, this relationship between art and truth. The argument developed here has, given the ineliminable presence of the present having a determining effect on the activity of criticism, two central tenets. The first is that art depends on criticism, since the concern of criticism is to establish the way art works as art. The second is that the predicament of criticism is that even though acts of criticism take the form of a decision, that decision cannot stem other claims – critical claims – about either particular works of art or art in general. To opt for the centrality of ontology is not to define ontology within the terms provided by any prevailing claims about the ontology of the work of art. What the term 'ontology' is intended to designate here is the mode of being proper to art being art. While it is possible to approach ontological considerations in terms of arguments concerning art itself – and this designates a task to come – these concluding comments will concern particularity.[10]

The particular work of art has a twofold reference. It is articulated within and criticisable because of this referential set-up. The two types of reference are, firstly, that any particular work of art refers to the genre of which it forms a part, and, secondly, that it refers within a space which will be interrupted by the decision. Modes of reception that take the form of a decision need to be linked to particularity. As particularity will always involve distinctions in terms of style and value, reception needs to be governed by the question of how particularity is to be maintained. Maintaining the presence of the particular and thus paying attention to its detail should not be thought a type of interpretive empiricism. Such a position would be constrained to deny what was identified above as the referentiality that is integral to art's work. Holding to the particular orientates the concerns of criticism towards the presence of the particular as art. The argument is that the particular should be judged *not* in terms of the ways it evidences art but in terms of the way it is art. The distinction is vital. Concentrating on particularity takes the particular as the work of art. The artwork is such that it sanctions an interpretive conflict without end. And yet it is a 'without end' that is interrupted by the specific act of criticism.

The differing possibilities for the way the artwork is received all underlie the fact that the work of art is a complex within which an interpretation – understood in the widest sense – is an act of individuation that does not deny the inherent plurality of the work; rather it depends upon it. Recognising that as the state of affairs that allows for criticism will give it a particular direction. Refusing it and insisting on the singularity of the object – whether that singularity is thought historically, politically or philosophically – reduces criticism to an informed description and as such the challenge the work may have presented is eliminated from the start. To allow for difficulty and thus for whatever overlap art and politics may have is to sustain criticism. The challenge for criticism is to return to the work of art.

Notes

1 The term 'art' is used here with great generality. It goes without saying that any detailed act of criticism has to engage with particular works. Furthermore, the use of the term 'contemporary' forms part of a general philosophical project which takes as its object the development of a philosophical understanding of the present. I have begun to develop this position in a number of different places; see in particular *Present Hope* (London: Routledge, 1997).

2 For an extremely valuable and persuasive discussion of 'inclusion' as both a political and an aesthetic term see G. Hartman, *The Fateful Question of Culture* (New York: Columbia University Press, 1997), pp. 166–203.

3 The form this argument takes is that the emancipatory programmes linked to Marxism and even to socialism neither have an explanatory force let alone a programme for the future. As such the present becomes the site marked by the necessary impossibility of emancipation and thus differing forms of transformation.

4 By extension such a set-up also delimits the necessity for, as well as the task demanded of, intellectuals.

5 A fundamental part of that analysis has been undertaken by Perry Anderson in *The Origins of Postmodernity* (London: Verso, 1998).

6 'Sameness' is a complex term. From one perspective the proliferation of styles marking the present state of art while allowing for individual differences between works establishes a reign of the same once it is also assumed that integral to the practice of interpretation is the elimination of the possibility of transformation. Interrupting the endurance of this conception of the same becomes an activity that need not demand other works – though their presence is not being precluded; rather what is demanded is a different strategy of interpretation and therefore of critical practice.

7 The way in which the refugee is able to be excluded is in terms of a refusal of this process. Claims that a given group is too different are generated from a position in which inclusion is the consequence of a process of inscription. One of the most philosophically acute and politically alert studies of the impact of the refugee on how inclusion is to be thought is M. Dillon, 'The scandal of the refugee: some reflections on the "inter" of international relations and continental thought' in D. Campbell and M. J. Shapiro (eds), *Moral Spaces: Rethinking Ethics and World Politics* (Minneapolis: Minnesota University Press, 1999), pp. 92–124. While pursuing a different direction, Giorgio Agamben is also concerned with the way the refugee functions as a limit concept. See *Homo Sacer: Soverign Power and Bare Life*, trans. D. Heller-Roazen (Stanford, CA: Stanford University Press, 1998), pp. 131–2.

8 It is in these terms that it would be possible to begin an interpretation of Tracy Emin's work *Bed*. Whatever force the work may have had was quickly muted by the nature of its

reception. The fact that the artist was in some sense complicit in this reception only reinforces the claim that the capacity for transformation lies in the possibility that the work can be interpreted as having that quality. While there may not be unanimity concerning how that quality is to be identified and thus named, what is essential is that criticism is able to win the work of art from the hands of 'biographers' (and 'autobiographers').

9 While it cannot be argued for in detail, what this claim amounts to is a reassertion of the position identified by Walter Benjamin as central to Romanticism, namely that criticisability is integral to an object being a work of art. Criticisability cannot be separated from the truth of art. This position is developed by Benjamin in 'The concept of criticism in German Romanticism' in W. Benjamin, *Selected Writings Volume 1*, ed. M. Bullock and M. W. Jennings (Cambridge, MA: Harvard University Press, 1996), pp. 116–200.

10 I have given a detailed account of the argument concerning particular and universal in my 'Perception, judgement and individuation: towards a metaphysics of particularity', *Pli*, 14 (2001).

13 *Joanna Hodge*

Aesthetics and politics: between Adorno and Heidegger

Antinomies of reason

The alignments of T. W. Adorno to the protracted, difficult process of coming to terms with a broken Marxist inheritance and of Martin Heidegger to the Nazi politics of rethinking the human might seem to leave them at opposite non-communicating poles of political difference.[1] Their views on aesthetics seem similarly starkly opposed, in terms both of judgements and of the place of aesthetics within the philosophical pantheon. Aesthetic theory for Adorno marks out a domain of experience relatively immune from the impact of the banalisation of evil, indicated by Hannah Arendt to be distinctive of the latter part of the twentieth century.[2] Heidegger conversely seeks to build the movement of presentation and withdrawal of art in artworks into a central place in his dangerous affirmations of a fatal twentieth-century and specifically German destiny.[3] With his mythologising hope for a distinctively German word for holiness, spoken by that distinctively German poet Hoelderlin, Heidegger displaces aesthetics as analysis of sensibility and judgement, with universal scope, in favour of affirming a transformative power of poetic naming within a quite specific linguistic register: German. The differences between Adorno and Heidegger, then, concerning politics and language, aesthetic analysis and its philosophical significance are clear cut. This essay will however suggest that taking their positions as two halves of a divided exposition, rather than as competing accounts of art, gives a clue to the paradoxes of the relation between art and politics, which have caused much perplexity in the twentieth century. While Adorno and Heidegger give different philosophical responses to these paradoxes, they are in agreement about the importance of an analysis of artworks in assessing what philosophy can contribute to an understanding of epochal change and world crisis.[4]

This epochal change and world crisis Adorno analyses in conjunction with Horkheimer, in 1944, as an irresolvable dialectic of enlightenment, Heidegger in terms of a dangerous domination of human endeavour by technology.[5] Adorno goes on to read Heidegger critically in *Jargon of Authenticity: On German Ideology* (1964) and in the even more demanding *Negative Dialectics* (1966), from which the former text was separated off.[6] The proposal here is to read Adorno and Heidegger as presenting two apparently incompatible halves of one argument, two halves of what Gillian Rose has called a 'broken middle' or an unresolved antinomy of reason.[7] The key to the commonality in their analyses is to identify the role of time and of temporality in their respective accounts of enlightenment and reason, of technology and authenticity. The notion of antinomy has a complex origin in the writings of Kant.[8] It is also deployed distinctively by Adorno, in his analysis of artworks.[9] In this context, however, its development as a technique for thinking about specifically twentieth-century conditions in the writings of Benjamin is more significant. For Benjamin, in his address to the Institute for the Study of Fascism, 'The Author as Producer' (Paris, 1934), the antinomy is between the necessity to align artistic activity with the exigencies of political transformation and the constraint of artworks providing their own standards of excellence.[10] The task is to show how both lines of determination can be shown to be true and compatible one with the other. It is thus Benjamin's version of antinomy which is to be evoked here, for both Adorno and Heidegger work in philosophy for its own sake but also with an eye to a political transformation.

Notoriously Heidegger thought for a while that the destiny of the German people had a promising future under the leadership of Hitler and his Nazi party. Of course Heidegger was not alone in this, and was not alone later both in claiming to recognise the enormity of the error and in failing to give an account of it. This, however, is not the topic of the current essay, as the literature discussing Heidegger's Syracuse is too vast to permit of easy summary.[11] Instead this essay gives an account of Adorno's critique of Heidegger's notion of authenticity, in his book *Jargon of Authenticity: On German Ideology*, in order to argue that this emphasis on authenticity, aligning Heidegger with existential philosophy, conceals a more challenging engagement between Adorno and Heidegger on the nature of history and time, and on the relation between historical conditions and concept formation. Indeed it will become clear that had Adorno discussed Heidegger's concept of historicality at greater length, perhaps even making it and not authenticity the focus of the title, the encounter would have been more clearly delineated. For what Heidegger shares with existentialism is less significant than what he shares with Adorno: a dispute for the inheritance of the Western philosophical tradition. Adorno reads this tradition as culminating in negative dialectics, because philosophy, 'which once seemed to have been overtaken, remains alive since the moment of its realisation was missed'.[12] Heidegger reads that history as culminating in devastation and destitution, as a consequence of a retreat of being behind its emanations in historical circumstance. This retreat of being behind its historical instances leads to a flattening out of the presentation of being in history as no more than what is simply present, erasing both history and being. Heidegger reads artworks not as sites for a restricted exploration of sensibility but as showing how more generally in what presents itself to an observing subject, there is an emphasis on what is present, in which its mode of presentation goes missing. For Heidegger this mode of presentation as concealment conceals within it, and thereby obscures, the moment of being as how there comes to be what there is; and it conceals its historicality and its relation to time.

For Adorno there is a determination of time as the no longer of political hope; for

Heidegger there is both a no longer, in a loss of an understanding of being, and a not yet of a return of being, arising out of this distorting emphasis on the now of presentation. For both, different historical epochs present different possibilities for philosophy. This sets up a difference between history as a sequence of events of history, ordinarily understood, and history as transcendental condition for the occurrence or non-occurrence of philosophy. A focus on Heidegger's notion of historicality then permits the differences between these two responses to the history of philosophy to emerge and permits a thinking of the differences between them on the no longer of hope and the not yet of its retrieval. Adorno's allegiance to Marxism indicates his recognition of a relation between historical process and its role in forming what can be thought. Heidegger's notions of authenticity and historicality provide a challenge to the apparently dehistoricised notions of politics and aesthetics, which are in fact burdened with an unthought-through reception of the Greek notions of order and community. The notions of aesthetics and of politics in their Greek origins contain implicitly a presumption concerning a continuity between divine and human faculties, and a hierarchy of human competencies, with some included and some excluded both from the processes of deliberation about collective goals and from engagement in artistic activity. This continuity and hierarchy is broken by Heidegger in his insistence on an analytic of finitude, and, less directly, in Adorno's identification of the negativity of dialectics.

Heidegger displaces the temporally unrestricted notions of aesthetics and politics in favour of the temporal relation set out between authenticity and historicality. This temporal relation describes the situation of determinately existing being, Dasein, in its relation to history. Dasein is Heidegger's technical term for an analysis of the human situation, whereby a human determinacy in space and time, its Da, and its relation to being, Sein, can be held out for analysis.[13] Authenticity and historicality then pick out what is distinctive about one and the same structure of Dasein, as where it happens to find itself, but viewed from two radically distinct stances. Historicality is the condition viewed from the outside, in advance of any determinate existence actually acquiring an understanding of itself as historical. Once this abstractly viewed historicality is appropriated as true for an actual existence, it becomes authentic, viewed from within, as following on from that actual existence. Thus Dasein is first of all abstractly historical, inheriting a condition, but it is then able to take up a relation to that condition and make it its own. These determinations of Dasein bear in them temporal indices of a before and an after, as lived processes of growing self-understanding, in conflict with and as challenges to the inherited philosophically established notions of the a priori and the a posteriori, that which comes before experience and that which comes after experience. For the notion of experience has been displaced by Heidegger in favour of an analysis of Dasein as being in the world and as being in time. This structure marks a definitive break, cutting the finitude of human reasoning free from the idealisation of a divine wisdom. The key contrast here for Heidegger is that between the supposed timelessness of a concept of eternity and the temporality concealed in any human thinking of time.[14]

For Adorno, time and history pose the problem of the continuing availability and adequacy of inherited notions of categories and concepts for the task of philosophy. It is this problem which poses for him the necessity of rewriting Hegel's dialectics as negative, as no longer providing their own completion in real lived relations. Emphasising Heidegger's innovation in his analytic of finitude and analysis of historicality as authenticity focuses discussion between them. It makes room for the thought that there is a more subtle critique of Heidegger available to Adorno than the emphasis on authenticity in *Jargon of Authenticity*. This critique concerns the relation between concept formation and a thinking of time. Heidegger introduces a notion of existentials through which what is distinctive about Dasein is articulated. These existentials are not neutrally ascribable to entities from the outside, but must be owned and lived through as the structure of an actual existence. Thus they undercut any distinction between concept formation and thinking about time, since the concept formation concerning existentials takes place in the time of an actual living being, Dasein, stretched out between a quite specific date of birth and a quite specific time of death. For Adorno this renders the meaning of existentials irreducibly contaminated by contingency and by arbitrary determination of meaning, not least by their inventor, Martin Heidegger. Adorno by contrast supposes there to be an all-important break between the possibilities of thinking and the constraints imposed by actual historical and political context, which are traced out by the notion of negative dialectics, the non-matching between thought and its context.[15]

Both Adorno and Heidegger pose a challenge to the analysis given by Kant in the transcendental aesthetic of the first critique about time, space and the place of thought.[16] Kant's transcendental aesthetic appears to give a single universally applicable account of the relation between time and space in human reasoning and experience, whereas Adorno and Heidegger give historically, temporally and spatially specific accounts of the structuring of human experience by space and time, responding to the specific conditions in which human beings find themselves: Adorno in terms of dialectics, Heidegger in terms of a developing relation between technology and nihilism. Adorno and Heidegger in developing further the relations between time, temporality, philosophy and history continue a line of discussion suggested by Kant, while displacing some of his key concepts. For Adorno, the nineteenth-century emphasis on historical progress and cumulative human emancipation is a delusion, and a political thinking of time and history, in relation to a less problematic notion of space, must give way to an aesthetic thinking of a more highly problematised notion of space in relation to a notion of time, as no longer the arena of change. This permits a critique of the idea of progress, in the name of which philosophy is not realised in a just society but abolished in favour of positivity.[17] For Heidegger the sendings of being are in each epoch distinct, but have culminated in the twentieth century in a triumph of technicity in which thinking and being have been almost entirely erased.

The discussion between these two is here held in place not only by reference to a reception by Benjamin of the Kantian notion of antinomy of reason but with respect to Kant's analyses of imagination, time and judgement in the first and third critiques. Adorno repeatedly returns to the critical philosophy of Kant and especially the analyses of the third critique, reading the division between aesthetic judgement of artworks and teleological judgement of natural processes as concealing the possibility of a thinking of the processes of history as an elided combination and subversion of the difference between these two. Heidegger, in his study, *Kant and the Problem of Metaphysics* (1928), concentrates on the first edition of the first critique, where imagination is to be shown to be the condition of possibility for the inauguration of new orders of experience and community, not just as a condition for historical change but as the structure of temporality itself.[18] The contrast between the directions of these readings could not be more extreme and yet the concerns are similar: the question of the place of a thinking of time and history.

This essay has two further sections. The second part is called 'Aesthetics and politics: beyond and behind'. The third part is called 'Once more a question of translation'. They seek to retrieve Heidegger's thinking of authenticity as a thinking of historicality from Adorno's attempted demolition. This opens the possibility of rethinking history as neither linear, held in place by chronology, nor catastrophic, held in place by irretrievable break points. It proposes a notion of elliptical history. This rethinking takes the form of a movement of ellipsis, a destabilised oscillation around the two points, variously Adorno and Heidegger, aesthetics and politics, and artworks and political history.[19] An ellipsis in time traces a movement where what is left out at an earlier point in a sequence returns to disrupt the linearity of that sequence at a later stage; and whereby the appearance of standstill turns out to be not an irretrievable break but rather a turning point. This third movement, neither linear nor catastrophic, is held in place by the structures of antinomial reasoning, concerning aesthetics and politics, and concerning the temporalties of the no longer and the not yet. The paper thus presents a thought experiment under the titles 'antinomy ' and 'ellipsis'.[20]

Aesthetics and politics: beyond and behind

It is possible then to read the enquiries of Adorno and Heidegger as cumulatively moving beyond Kant. Instead of the Kantian project of determining the scope of concepts and categories, irrespective of historical and linguistic conditions and constraints, they affirm the possibility of a historically and politically determinate context of conceptual determination. This then poses the problem of historicism. By reading Kant, Adorno and Heidegger explicitly in terms of the historical and temporal conditions of possibility, making their thought comprehensible, it becomes possible to develop an account of the historicality of thought, of concepts and of categories. This sets up an oscillating move between conceptual determinacy and historical specificity, between occasion for thought and conditions of possibility, understood as historical conditions. This oscillation becomes a movement of ellipsis since the thinking of both Adorno and Heidegger is pulled off course by the gravitational force exerted by the Kantian system on the one side and by its disaggregation in the writings of Benjamin on the other. The Kantian system is no less important to Benjamin than it is to Adorno, and Benjamin develops three quite specific challenges to it: a challenge to the modal notions of possibility, actuality and necessity presented in the first critique, a challenge to the notions of virtue and happiness in the second critique, and a challenge to the distinction between art and nature in the third critique, affirming instead the notions of ruination, destruction and technique, which are simultaneously modal and critical. This permits Benjamin to recast conceptual determination as always marked by an historical index and as temporally unstable, thus radically displacing the neutralisation of history and time in philosophy.

Benjamin's relation to Adorno is highly contested. His critique of Heidegger is severe, and he would see the attempt to separate the judgements of the man from the philosophical task as spurious, since there is one and only one sensorium, which in failing to think the specificity of its situation fails to perform politically, and fails to do justice to the twin claims of time and truth. Important here is a transformation at work in Benjamin's analyses, from a notion of a logical contingency, subordinate to a notion of necessity, completabilty and perfectibility, placed within the hierarchy of Kant's categories of modality, into a notion of a necessity subordinated rather to a principle of radical non-identity. The temporalities of anachronism, delay and destruction take over from those of Kant's analogies of experience, permanence, succession and coexistence, and completed works are to be thought of as death masks, not as fulfilments of their conception. This is alluded to in the thirteenth thesis on the technique of the writer, in *One Way Street and Other Writings*: 'The work is the death mask of its conception.'[21] From an innovation in the order of things, the artwork through its reception becomes domesticated and subordinated to generalising accounts of the relation between time and art, from which it has to be again wrenched free, to reactivate its moment of disruption. By contrast to a limited notion of the contingent, which could be otherwise, could be corrected and completed, there is here a radical contingency, which is necessarily incomplete in the form in which it is, as a matter of fact, found. This is the ruination brought to our attention by Benjamin's preference for the irresolutions of Renaissance and Baroque mourning plays over Greek tragic resolution, as discussed in *The Origins of German Tragic Drama* (1928).[22] This notion of ruination, like the notion of ellipsis, is also remarked by Heidegger in his lectures on Aristotle from 1921–2 and is subsequently developed in *Being and Time* into the notion of Dasein's condition as *Verfallen*, the movement of absorption in everydayness.

A link between this notion of contingency and a recasting of the notion of contemporaneity has implications for the relation of theorists to their own context: 'if the perspectives of the philosophy of history should prove to be an essential part of a theory of tragedy, then it is clear that the latter can only be expected from research which shows some understanding of its own age', Benjamin wrote in 1925.[23] The challenge is to construct a philosophy of history, of politics and of historicality, which resists the banalisations of relativism, scepticism, historicism by affirming a notion of necessity which is not reappropriable into the historical neutrality of its insertion into the Kantian system under the sign of completability and perfectibility. The three levels of Benjaminian disaggregation consist in an affirmation of a relation to contemporaneity as the basic historical determination; a recasting of any philosophy of history in such a way as to respect this priority; and a rethinking of modality as radical contingency, not to be subverted by a presumption that all the same there is a City of God, by contrast with which human imperfection and fallibility may be measured. Through these moves Benjamin's notion of antinomy can be set apart from those of both Adorno and Kant. Even antinomy is not generalisable, and is to be performed on each occasion in relation to a reading of specific texts in terms of discrete, determinable topics and topologies. This is Benjamin's innovation in aesthetics.

While Adorno seeks systematically to set out a separateness of aesthetic experience, Heidegger tears up the customary subdivisions of philosophy and indeed discards the protective shield of universalism and abstraction, plunging the philosophical inheritance into the maelstrom of political culpability. For Adorno, the separability of aesthetics from the accommodations of epistemology and metaphysics, which substitute exchange value for use value, permits aesthetics still to trace out the registration of an experience not yet appropriated by that which it experiences: 'Kant shall have the last word on aesthetic hedonism.' Adorno writes at the end of the first section of *Aesthetic Theory*: 'In his analysis of the sublime, which is set apart from art, Kant wrote that happiness in relation to works of art is the feeling they instil of holding one's own, of resisting.'[24] Aesthetics may for Adorno have become the necrology of art; nevertheless, it is the only living aspect of philosophy. For Heidegger, by contrast, the destruction of these internal divisions between philosophical specialisms is the only route to retrieving the initial and sole source of philosophical energy: an uncontaminated, uncoerced wonder in response to what there is. He makes this clear in the *Letter on Humanism* (1946), but the thought is already in evidence in *Being and Time* (1927) where the customary division between epistemology and metaphysics, between ethics and aesthetics, is not to be found.[25] Where Adorno resists the question of origin and genesis, of art, of sensibility, indeed of what there is, for fear of some coerced complicity in an inhuman totalisation, for Heidegger there is one question, and one question only, in pursuit of which all and everything may and must be sacrificed: why is there something rather than nothing?

In his essay 'The origin of the artwork', Heidegger pursues this ontogenetic question through the inflection 'how is there something rather than nothing?'[26] Not only is the question of the origin of the artwork thereby to be resolved but also that of the origin of there being a world in which human being can question itself and its relation to being as destiny. Heidegger makes three moves. 'Art is truth setting itself to work', he says; 'To be a work means to set up a world'; and then:

> World is never an object that stands before us and can be seen. World is the ever non-objective to which we are subject as long as the paths of birth and death, blessing and curse keep us transported into being. Wherever those decisions of our history that relate to our very being are made, are taken up and abandoned by us, go unrecognised and are rediscovered by new inquiry, there the world worlds.[27]

He goes on: 'A stone is worldless. Plant and animal likewise have no world; but they belong to the covert throng of a surrounding into which they are linked.' This provides the background for Heidegger's claim that the happening of truth is historical, in the double sense, both as calling history into existence and as grounded in historical specificity. There is then an internal consistency to his insistence that art culminates in poetic composition and the imposition in poetry of linguistic specificity. For linguistic specificity, the languages of human beings, by contrast to language as such, is inseparable from the occurrence of history and from historical specificity.[28] This line of thought puts in question the presumption that what is at stake in aesthetics and in philosophy more generally is the status of universalising judgement. For universalising judgement presumes the availability of a single theory of judgement true for all times, whereas Heidegger supposes that judgement arrives differentially in different specific human contexts, in accordance with current understandings and misunderstandings of their positioning in time and history. As Heidegger puts it, even a refusal of time and of history is a relation to history, if of a deficient kind.

Heidegger links the analysis in 'The origin of the artwork' back to that of *Being and Time* by citing the notion of resolution, *Entschlossenheit*, and by replaying the disjunction, thrown projection, discussed at length in *Being and Time*, in the following manner: 'Truth is never gathered from objects that are present and ordinary. Rather, the opening up of the Open and the clearing of what is, happens only as the openness is projected, sketched out, that makes its advent in thrownness.'[29] There is no determinacy of truth given in advance of thinking and time, but rather truth takes shape and arrives as a result of specific efforts to think and to understand the relation between thinking and the passage of time. Heidegger draws his reflections together in the last pages of the essay thus: 'The origin of the work of art, that is the origin of both the creators and the preservers, which is to say of a people's historical existence, is art. This is so because art is by nature an origin: a distinctive way in which truth comes into being, that is, becomes historical.' When art happens, according to Heidegger, there is a beginning in history, a departure for history, an emergence in history of what is historical, which can then be preserved or abandoned. The crucial sentences are:

> Whenever art happens, that is, whenever there is a beginning, a thrust enters history, history either begins or starts again. History means here not a sequence in time of events of whatever sort, however important. History is the transporting of a people into its appointed task as entrance into that people's endowment.[30]

The double challenge here is: how to think this endowment, inflected as it must be through the implicit hope for a German collectivity under the sign of brown shirts. This endowment (the German is *ein Mitgegebenes*), is also challengingly a transposition of the Kantian task of reason, *die Aufgabe der Vernunft*, as *Aufgegebenes*. The task of reason takes thinking away from this historical specificity, whereas the happening of art takes place nowhere but in specific historical conditions and contexts, and is responded to or ignored by the people who are exposed to it. Despite the specificity of the linguistic connection, however, it would be a mistake to think that each, the collectivity of brown shirts and the task of reason, can be thought to be specifically German destinies. For Heidegger, it is art, not Germanness which, as founding, is essentially historical and grounds history; and this notion of the essentially historical takes up from *Being and Time* the theme of historicality, as a translinguistic category, or as Heidegger there calls it an existential.

For Adorno the notions of resolution, of thrown projection, of endowment and of essential historicality are empty abstractions, and in *Jargon of Authenticity* he emphasises his differences from Heidegger on the use of the language. They are thus in battle not just for the inheritance of the philosophical tradition but also for its articulation in German. There is a remarkable asymmetry between the registers and range of reference for Heidegger and for Adorno. Heidegger in 'The origin of the artwork' seems quite deliberately to constitute a series of works with the hallmark of simplicity, with no irony and no gesture of delimiting critique. The series, the temple, the thing poem, 'The Roman Fountain' by Meyer, and the Van Gogh painting, could be linked together under the title unsophisticated primitivism. By contrast, Adorno prefaces *Jargon of Authenticity* with the following epigraph from Samuel Beckett: 'It is easier to raise a temple than to compel the object of the cult to descend into it.' This, with its resonance of Voltaire, and its obvious edge against exactly Heidegger's invocation of the temple in the artwork essay, has the effect diagnosed by Benjamin: 'Quotations are the muggers of literary work, leaping out armed to relieve the unwary of their convictions.'[31] For Adorno the exemplary artworks are Berg's *Wozzeck*; the writings of Samuel Beckett, abstract minimalism, and he has no time for a theorising of art irrespective of historical context. Thus for Adorno it makes no sense to align a continuity and contrast between the absence of the gods in the Greek temple and Hoelderlin's diagnoses of the departure of the Greek gods in his hymns on the German reception of Greek thought; and to contrast this then to the enigmatic presentation of a pair of shoes in Van Gogh's paintings.

The figure against whom Adorno and Heidegger turn, with shared venom, is Lukács. Adorno, in his essay 'Reconciliation under duress', wrote witheringly of Lukács's theory of a necessary reconciliation to the order of what there is, when Lukács took on the role of apologist for the State Socialism of Hungary.[32] Heidegger implicitly denounces Lukács in the *Letter on Humanism*, in the critique of deployments of the categories of rationalism and irrationalism. There are no consolations of philosophy for Adorno and Heidegger: Adorno regrets the moment of the failure to realise philosophy in Marxist revolution. Heidegger, similarly regretful but addressing the lost hopes of Hoelderlin and Nietzsche, rather than Marx and Engels, observes in 1962: 'Only a new god can save us now.'[33] While for Adorno philosophy has moved from the possibility of political engagement back into an autonomous articulation, for Heidegger the movement goes the other way, from a long history of separateness into a political alignment made necessary by the globalisation of technical mastery of natural processes and the concomitant nihilism with respect to values higher than those of mastery and calculation. The notion of an elliptical history then is one in which there is an oscillation both between the orientations of Adorno and Heidegger with respect to politics and to aesthetics and between a supposedly irretrievable past possibility and an undesirable because still not emancipatory future.

Lacoue-Labarthe argues in *Heidegger, Art and Politics: The Fiction of the Political* (1990) that Heidegger's political affirmation fictionalises politics, under the aegis of Hoelderlin.[34] It is a fiction, in the sense of composing, *Dichten*, in which there are no longer external standards of good and bad, human flourishing and human evil: in a moment of caesura, a break in the linear development of the line, of meaning and value, and of time, a term borrowed from the technical performance of Hoelderlin's poetry, a standstill makes way for the invention or arrival of order. As Lacoue-Labarthe puts it, concerning holocaust: 'That is why this event – Extermination – is for the West the terrible revelation of its essence.'[35] However, there are no controls over what may arrive in the moment of standstill, with its implied condition of destitution. Thus for Lacoue-Labarthe, Heidegger's much disputed silence after Auschwitz is required by the nature of that event, and is not to be read as the inadequacy specifically of Heidegger's political judgements.[36] Adorno too, perhaps no less inadequately, announced in 1949: 'Cultural criticism finds itself up against the last level of a dialectic between culture and barbarism: to write poetry after Auschwitz is barbaric and this also eats up the cognition which expresses why it became impossible to write poetry today.'[37] He subsequently came to modify the claim in his *Aesthetic Theory*, for which aesthetic activity seemed the only possible form of insurrection or indeed self-protection against the impact of a controlled controlling world. Each stance, that of Adorno and that of Heidegger, is open to trivialisation and misrepresentation; for each the extremity of disaster brings poetry and writing, and thinking and philosophising, to a standstill, in a realisation of Hoelderlin's caesura.[38] According to Lacoue-Labarthe this 'counter-rhythmic suspense' leads to a turn into a better understanding of the 'law of finitude', first set out by Heidegger in the 1920s. In the writings of philosophy, this must lead into an affirmation of the radical contingency of philosophical order, which would appear to suggest that there is no philosophical inheritance for Adorno and Heidegger to contest. Adorno accepts and Heidegger rejects Kafka's diagnosis: an infinity of hope, but not for us. Adorno is willing to wait for another turn in the awkward asynchrony between historical time and human fulfilment. Heidegger affirms the more distant Nietzschean, Hoelderlinian hope for a new god. Thus Heidegger accepts and Adorno rejects Nietzsche's affirmation of Heraclitus: that if a human being has character, there is an experience which constantly recurs. Their responses to the twentieth-century political and aesthetic exigencies are quite distinct, one affirming Nietzsche's eternal return and the other Kafka's surrender, but there is demonstrably in the conjunction of their writings a shared moment of inarticulacy in response to Auschwitz.

Once more a question of translation

The strategy here, then, is to take Heidegger's notions from *Being and Time*, *Geschichtlichkeit*, variously translated as historicity and as historicality, and *Eigentlichkeit*, usually translated as authenticity, and to retranslate them, in order first to reveal their interconnection in delineating the move from fallenness, as absorption in everydayness, into a self-transparent historically given human existence. It is then possible to show how as a pair they make available a distinctive construal of the relation between human sensibility, the present, the opening of the future and the retrieval of the past. This opens out a question to the self-evidence both of the meaning of these two terms and of the meaning of the notions of aesthetics and politics. Each set of terms then is to be deployed in order to unsettle the sense of obviousness and meaning of all three conjunctions: Adorno and Heidegger, aesthetics and politics, authenticity and historicality. By translating *Eigentlichkeit* as appropriation, it is possible to underline the manner in which *Eigentlichkeit* sets up the challenge of coming to terms with an occasion for thought, in excess of a capacity for thought. This involves thinking in a context determined by forces above and beyond the compass of any given cognitive ability, presentation or evidence. The cognitive ability develops or not as the case may be only as a response to the challenge. This is a thinking, which must almost necessarily impose distortions on what is thought, but in such a way as to constitute the identities of the thinkers themselves. This, then, is no idle distortion but one constitutive of human identities and future possibilities.

In authenticity or appropriation, there is a projection of an identity and a future as a horizon for meaning and activity. This is framed by what it responds to, and this is the play of *Geschichtlichkeit*, which in parallel with thrownness predisposes a certain way of appropriating what arrives. It is tempting, then, to translate *Geschichtlichkeit* as aptitude, playing up the connection to the cognate notion, *Geschicklichkeit*, ability, facility or fatality, for it was one of Benjamin's self-deprecatory complaints that he was ill-equipped, or indeed not fated, *ungeschickt*, to deal with twentieth-century conditions. However, more promising for an understanding of Heidegger's text is the translation of *Geschichtlichkeit* as the conditions of possibility for appropriating history, given on each occasion differently to Dasein in its pre-theoretical understanding of both time and being. This displaces any alignment of *Geschichtlichkeit*, as straightforwardly historical or political category, rendering it rather a question of aesthetic sensibility and attunement. There is then the correlative possibility of relocating *Eigentlichkeit* as nothing like an ethical category of moral worth nor yet an aesthetic category concerning a refinement of self-awareness, but much more as the condition of being human, as constrained by specific historical and political contingencies. It is the manner in which human beings come to terms with circumstance, as a result of which certain individual and collective trajectories might or indeed might not be set out. It is the occasionality of this condition that goes missing in Adorno's reception of it, as does the specificity of Heidegger's question to the continuing relevance of the distinction between, and indeed the validity of the very categories, politics and aesthetics.

In 1964 Adorno published his *Jargon der Eigentlichkeit*, separately from and in advance of *Negative Dialectics*, as a response to the emergence in the pre-Nazi and Nazi years of the strand of philosophising called existential philosophy, in the writings of amongst others Heidegger and Jaspers. The language of care and concern (*Sorge* and *Besorgen*), commission (*Auftrag*), resolution (*Entschlossenheit*), ambiguity and of course authenticity comes in for derisive critique. There is a brief mention, almost in passing, of Heidegger's notion of history, as cited in the *Letter on Humanism*. Adorno quotes Heidegger and then provides a devastating brief critical comment about the magical immediacy of the arrival of the human in its community with being. What for Adorno might result from an unceasing political and intellectual labour appears with Heidegger to occur simply by fiat: thus the human is. This, then, is the quotation from Heidegger, cited by Adorno:

Human being is not the lord of existence. Human being is the shepherd of being. In this 'less' human being loses nothing, but rather wins by reaching the truth of Being. He wins the essential power of the shepherd, whose worth consists in being called, by Being itself, into the trueness of its truth. This call comes as the throwing from which the thrownness of existence stems. In its essence, as being historical (*seinsgeschichtlichen Wesen*) human being is the existent whose being as ek-sistence consists in his living in the neighbourhood of Being. Human being is the neighbour of being.[39]

And this the comment by Adorno: 'Philosophical banality is generated when that magical participation in the absolute is ascribed to the general concept – a participation which puts the lie to that concept's conceivability.'[40] For Adorno the generality and simplicity of the claim renders it vacuous. If the absolute is to be thought it is, for Adorno, to be thought in conflict with and against the grain of any given simplicities or natural contours of language, whether everyday or sophisticated. The contrast of registers is of course deliberately startling.

For Heidegger, the *Nachbar*, the neighbour, is the nearby farmer, the *Bauer* who is *nah*. The combination of homely etymologies with a desanctified deployment of the Christian language of shepherds and keepers is hardly likely to recommend itself to Adorno's more sophisticated concern with the conceivability of the concept in current conditions. These notions of neighbourhood and shepherding for Adorno offer neither the insights of poetry nor the conceptuality of philosophy, but solely banality. The polemical verve of Adorno's critique is indisputable; its focus would be sharper, however, if the attention paid to the notion of authenticity were counter-balanced by an equal attention to Heidegger's notion of historicality, as here transformed into a notion about the history of being. The history of being for Heidegger is the arrival of a deepening crisis of destitution through the neglect of presentation in favour of what is presented. The history of being sets out the process in which there is or is not an arrival of an understanding and an appropriation of human historicality. Adorno does not here develop a discussion of this aspect of Heidegger's thinking and after this passing observation, the thinking of history fades back into the background. Even within the limits set out by the task of a critique of authenticity, Adorno misses the power of his own arguments. The antipathy between Heidegger's manner of descriptive imperatives and a retrieval of conceptuality could be sharpened. Heidegger is suspicious of a conceptuality which sets itself up in opposition to an already given order, and rather supposes that what there is must be conjured into revealing itself to an attentive composing thinking.[41] The virtue of Husserl's phenomenology as far as Heidegger is concerned is that it offers this possibility of revealing what is not already given, instead extracting what there is from its concealment in everyday taken-for-granted relations. Heidegger and Adorno thus share a suspicion about the adequacies of everyday understanding and what is given in uncritical or unreduced perception. The standoff between Adorno and Heidegger will be all the more marked once their contrasting responses to a limited availability of a diagnostic language and a lack of adequate conceptuality are set out.

Authenticity, *Eigentlichkeit*, is for the Heidegger of *Being and Time* an existential, a category distinctive of the kind of existence, which has given to it an understanding of being. It is thus never simply an experiential structure but one with cognitive and ontological preconditions and consequences, out of which understanding is projected. It is a question of appropriating and understanding this structure of preconditions given in advance of any particular experience and always in excess of the cognitive capacities of the bearer of that understanding. This is the structure of thrownness and throwing to which Heidegger refers in these lines from the *Letter on Humanism* and which elicits Adorno's mockery. However, it is also the structure of *hyperbole*, excess, and *elleipsis*, deficiency, discussed in the early Aristotle lectures, giving rise to the analysis first of ruination, *Ruinanz*, and then of fallenness, *Verfallen*, as necessary and not contingent features of the existence of human beings, modalities of existence no longer thought in accordance with Christianised notions of perfectibility. The caesura of the Hoelderlinian line can then be located within this structure of the thrown throwing, as its condition, when a third movement, a counter-movement, 'counter-rhythmic suspension', *Gegenwurf*, is added to the thrownness, *Geworfenheit*, and projection, *Entwurf*, of *Being and Time*.[42] These movements are to be understood not as some children's game but as a description of the spatio-temporal dimensions within which human being responds or fails to respond to the question of being, and something more like the Heraclitean image of children dicing with destiny begins to emerge.

This is a further challenge to the account in Kant's transcendental aesthetic of the basic structures of time and space, now thought in terms not of separable forms of time and spaces but of distinctive movements, combining time and space, in an arrival in the present as thrownness, projection out of a present, and contrary movement, in the present, in the counter-movement of the caesura. This provides a way into thinking different presentations of what is present. In *Being and Time* Heidegger theorises a retrieval of the past and the arrival of the future in a present, as conjoined conditions for a standstill, in a transformatory moment of insight into the nature of the movements of time and human understanding. Once these movements are highlighted, it becomes less obvious that Adorno can deploy the objection that Heidegger erases the movements of mediation and sublation at work in dialectical philosophy. Rather, Heidegger has taken up these movements and thought them differently, in response to the suspicion that dialectics were always at a standstill, always only capable of thinking what they had already resynthesised. At this point Adorno's and Heidegger's rather different responses to Kant's diagnoses of dialectical movement come into view. Adorno, by discussing Heidegger in the context of Jaspers's notions of existential philosophy and of limit conditions, aligns Heidegger's thinking more closely to a politics of individual self-affirmation than is quite accurate. For Heidegger, much of the point of his insistence on analysing Dasein is that it is not and cannot be immediately aligned to individual human existence. For Heidegger, human individuality emerges out of its interconnections with others, which may in some circumstances never permit the release of an individual into its own self-appropriated destiny. Dasein is thus a significant technical device which permits Heidegger to point out how unfamiliar humanity is to human beings, both collectively and individually. There is also an important dimension to Heidegger's class position, which disconnects him from the liberal politics of self-assertive individualism taken for granted in intel-lectual circles. For Heidegger, the question of community is much more: how does someone emerge from their communal background such as to be able to take up a relation to being, and accede to a decisiveness of thinking? It is not how to think com-munity from conjoined individuals. Adorno thus aligns Heidegger too closely both with Jaspers and with Sartre, whom Adorno so memorably denounces in his essay 'Commitment'.[43] Heidegger's differences with Sartre are of course equally well known, and he sets them out in some detail in *Letter on Humanism*. More significant here are Heidegger's differences with Jaspers.

Already in a review of Jaspers in 1919, Heidegger is taking issue with Jaspers' theory of worldviews, although with respect:

> Though Jaspers has only gathered up and depicted what 'is there', he has nonetheless gone beyond mere classification by bringing together in a new way what has already been available to us, and this must be evaluated positively as a real advance. However if it is to be capable of effectively stimulating and challenging contemporary philosophy, his method of mere observation must evolve into an 'infinite process' of radical questioning that always includes itself in its questions and preserves itself in them.[44]

These differences emerge more clearly in the course of the 1920s, but as with Heidegger's differences with Husserl, they become enmeshed in Heidegger's political adventure of the 1930s. Jaspers's critique of the third withheld section of division one of *Being and Time*, 'time and being', persuaded Heidegger to keep it back on publi-cation in 1927.[45] Jaspers also wrote the reference on Heidegger in 1947, declaring that Heidegger's non-interactive mode of lecturing and teaching was unsuitable in a context seeking to develop a new style of philosophising, free from any Nazi connec-tion. The question is: how might Adorno's critique of authenticity and Jaspers's cri-tique of the third section of part one of *Being and Time* be brought together to show how for Heidegger but not for Jaspers there is a questioning of a collective destiny, *Mitgegebenes, Geschichtlichkeit, Mitdasein*, in which the questions of politics, how to think collectivities, and questions of aesthetics, how to think receptivity, how to think local universals, how to think affectivity, might be recast.

The notion of authenticity, as deployed by Sartre and depicted by Adorno, is one which attaches to a romantic individualism and to individual identities. The one deployed by Heidegger in *Being and Time* attaches to Dasein not as an individual *Selbstsein* but as a generational and intergenerational transmission, one which is situ-ated between predecessors and descendants, ancestors and successors. Thus the gen-erational dimension of Dasein's authenticity goes missing in Adorno's account. This is especially odd since this notion of generational identity grounds the fatal decision to choose a hero as an intimation of another possible future. The notion of genera-tional being provides a location for thinking a relation between history and histori-cality and the moment of Dasein as *Mitsein*, being with, as *Mitdasein*, determinate existence alongside and coming into contact with other such existence, and a projec-tion into a survivable future. It is here that we can tie together the notions of histor-icality, *Geschichtlichkeit*, to be understood as condition of possibility for appropriating history; destiny, *Geschicklichkeit*; and aptitude, *Geschick*.[46] On this account, the manner in which to understand the notions of historicality and of authenticity is to think them together, to think them as replicating the movement of thrownness and projection; to locate them as displacing the concerns of aesthetics, with affectivity and receptivity on one side, and politics, as concerned with collectively constituted constraints on human understanding, on the other; to think instead in terms of trajectories of collective transformation. Such a thinking acquires a bad name when it is locked into the kind of transformations at work in Nazism, and the thought of trajectory, beyond good and evil as it is, requires some other thinking of normativity and of human flourishing in order to prevent it bringing with it the death of all human flourishing. For such a thinking, the value of human life and flourishing is to be argued, not taken for granted, and is to be hoped for, and worked for, not assumed as a necessary outcome of a preconstituted historical process. For the development of this thinking Benjamin's writings provide some significant cues and clues. These cues and clues, however, can be followed up only once the divided inheritance of Kant's thinking of imagination and art, of nature and the concept, as handed down through Heidegger's and Adorno's writings, is brought together again and relocated as a response to the new conditions of the coming century.

Notes

1 For Adorno, see M. Horkheimer and T. W. Adorno, *Dialectic of Enlightenment*, trans. J. Cumming (New York: Herder & Herder, 1972). For Heidegger, see the papers and observations gathered together in G. Neske and E. Kettering (eds), *Martin Heidegger and National Socialism: Questions and Answers*, trans. L. Harries (New York: Paragon, 1990).

2 See H. Arendt, *Eichmann in Jerusalem: The Banality of Evil* (New York: Viking, 1965).

3 See the analyses in 'The origin of the artwork' (1936), published in *Holzwege* 1951, trans. in A. Hofstader, *Poetry Language Thought* (New York: Harper & Row, 1971), pp. 15–87, subsequently referred to as PLT; and the protracted engagement with Hoelderlin, from the 1933–34 lectures on Hoelderlin's hymns, *Germanien* and *The Rhine*, published in the Gesamtausgabe (GA), (Frankfurt: Klostermann) as GA 39, to the 1941–2 lectures on *Andenken*, GA 52, extracts from which were published in *Erlaeuterungen zu Hoelderlins Dichtung* (Elucidations of Hoelderlin's Composing) 1949, 1951, and in GA 4, and in 1942 on the hymn, *The Ister*, GA 53. On the latter, see M. Froment-Meurice, *That is to Say: Heidegger's Poetics* (Stanford, CA: Stanford University Press, 1999). See also ch. 4, 'What is it to be human?' in J. Hodge, *Heidegger and Ethics* (London: Routledge, 1995), pp. 102–33.

4 I should like to take the opportunity here to thank Simon Malpas for a wonderfully rigorous reading of this paper, which has led to its immense improvement, and Ewa Plonowska Ziarek, who understood it even when it was still in a state of abyssal obscurity.

5 For the development of his analysis of the danger of technology and its contribution to a deepening nihilism in the Western world see the papers collected together in M. Heidegger, *The Question of Technology and Other Essays*, trans. W. Lovitt (New York: Harper & Row, 1977).

6 See Adorno, *The Jargon of Authenticity*, trans. K. Tarnowski and F. Will (London: Routledge & Kegan Paul, 1986), from Adorno, *Jargon der Eigentlichkeit: Zur deutschen Ideologie* (Frankfurt am Main: Suhrkamp, 1964), subsequently cited as JA and JE. *Negative Dialectics* was translated by E. B. Ashton (London: Routledge, 1973).

7 See G. Rose, *The Broken Middle* (Oxford: Blackwell, 1986). For the Hegelian background to this and indeed to Adorno's recasting of Kantian antinomy as dialectic of enlightenment see G. Rose, *Hegel contra Sociology* (London: Athlone, 1981).

8 The notion of antinomy here has a history going back to the writings of Kant, in his *Critique of Pure Reason* (1781, 1787), in which he analyses the antinomies of the understanding with respect to the deployment of concepts. Kant sets out an antinomy of practical reason in his *Critique of Practical Reason*, which concerns the different trajectories of an analysis of virtue and of happiness respectively. The argument considers the impossibility of deriving principles of virtue from considerations of happiness, and the indefensibility of supposing 'the maxim of virtue must be the efficient cause of happiness' (Ak. V. 113–14). There is a further deployment of the notion of antinomy with respect to judgement in the third critique, which will be averted to in what follows.

9 See T. W. Adorno, *Aesthetic Theory*, trans. R. Hullot-Kentor (London: Athlone, 1997), and for a careful analysis of it, C. Menke, *The Sovereignty of Art: Aesthetic Negativity in Adorno and Derrida* (Cambridge, MA: MIT Press, 1998).

10 See W. Benjamin, *Selected Writings, Volume Three, 1927–1934*, ed. M. W. Jennings, H. Eiland and G. Smith, trans. R. Livingstone *et al.* (Cambridge, MA: Harvard University Press, 1999), pp. 768–90.

11 For a recent account giving an overview of the different strands of French, German and North American discussion, see M. de Bestegui, *Heidegger and the Political* (London: Routledge, 1999).

12 This is the famous first sentence of *Negative Dialectics*.

13 This is the task is undertaken in *Being and Time*, trans. J. Macquarrie and E. Robinson (Oxford: Blackwell, 1964), where the notions of authenticity and historicality are introduced.

14 This breakthrough is already in place in the 1924 lecture to the Marburg Theological Society, *The Concept of Time*, trans. W. McNeill (Oxford: Blackwell, 1993).

15 *Jargon of Authenticity* works in a way as a prolegomena to a reading of *Negative Dialetics*, which presents an extended critique of Heidegger's account of being and of ontological difference. The issues are too complex for easy summary, and the dispute between Adorno and Heidegger will not here be pursued into this second text.

16 The implication here is that in the end Kant's distinction between a sensibility subordinated to understanding, in the first critique, and a sensibility conjoined with the imagination and not thus subordinated to the understanding, in the third critique, is not sustainable. For reflections on the arguments leading to such a disruptive outcome see my paper on Jean Luc Nancy's reading of Kant, 'Why aesthetics might be several', *Angelaki: Journal of the Theoretical Humanities*, 7:1 (Spring 2002), 53–66.

17 For Adorno on the delusions of positivism, see Adorno *et al.*, *The Positivist Dispute in German Sociology*, trans G. Adey and D. Frisby (London: Heinemann, 1976).

18 See M. Heidegger, *Kant and the Problem of Metaphysics*, 5th edn, trans. R. Taft (Bloomington: Indiana University Press, 1990). It is important to mark the difference between thinking in terms of concepts of time, its eternity or finitude, its limitlessness or its delimitation, which gives rise to antinomies, and a thinking of temporality, concerning the manner in which time makes itself evident to human understanding. The givenness of an intuition of time takes place in the workings of the imagination, which are thus revealed to be the condition of the possibility of time. Thus imagination as condition of time is understood to be temporality itself, as the mode of presentation of time. For a discussion of this reading in which Heidegger is criticised for losing sight of his own insight, and in

effect erasing ontological difference in turn, in affirming the sendings of being, see S. Zizek, *The Ticklish Subject: The Absent Centre of Political Ontology* (London: Verso, 1999), part 1, ch. 1.

19 On the emergence of the notion of oscillation in Heidegger's thinking, see my paper on Heidegger's thinking of time as movement, 'The genesis and structure of a thinking of multi-dimensional time', *Research in Phenomenology*, 21 (Autumn 1999), 119–40.

20 The word 'ellipsis' is retrieved by Heidegger from the texts of Aristotle in the course of the 1920–21 lectures on Aristotle, which he presented as an introduction to phenomenology in W. Broeker and K. Broecker-Oltmanns (eds), *Phaenomenologische Interpretation zu Aristoteles. Einfuhrung in die phaenomenologische Forschung*, GA 61 (Winter 1921–22) (Frankfurt: Klostermann, 1985).

21 See W. Benjamin, *One-Way Street and Other Writings*, trans. E. Jephcott and K. Shorter (London: NLB/Verso, 1979), p. 65 in Benjamin *Gesammelte Schriften*, ed. H. Schweppenhauser and R. Tiedemann (Frankfurt: Suhrkamp Verlag, 1974), WB GS IV.1. p. 107, referred to here as OWS.

22 W. Benjamin, *The Origin of German Tragic Drama*, trans. J. Osborne (London: NLB/Verso, 1977), WB GS I.1, pp. 203–427, subsequently referred to as OGTD.

23 OGTD p. 102, GS 1.1. 280. It is noteworthy that Benjamin here approvingly cites G. Lukács, *The Soul and its Forms*, trans. J. and N. Mander (London: Merlin Press, 1967).

24 See Adorno, *Aesthetic Theory*, p. 22.

25 M. Heidegger, *Letter on Humanism*, trans. F. A. Capuzzi, in W. McNeill, (ed.), *Martin Heidegger: Pathmarks* (Cambridge: Cambridge University Press, 1998), pp. 239–75.

26 Originally published in *Holzwege* (1950), this essay is a version of lectures given in Frankfurt in 1936. It is translated in PLT.

27 PLT pp. 39, 44, 44–5.

28 See Walter Benjamin's essay, 'On language in general and on the languages of human beings', in *One-Way Street*, pp. 107–23, WB GS II.1, pp. 140–57. For Benjamin there is no such ontological difference, as there is for Heidegger, grounding a distinction between systems of meaning at work in a natural order and those of human beings; all for Benjamin are merely moments in the unfolding of 'the unity of this movement of language' (p. 157). The privilege accorded by Heidegger to the notion of 'world' is unacceptable to Benjamin.

29 See English, PLT p. 71. The German reads: 'in dem die in der Geworfenheit ankommende Offenheit entworfen wird.'

30 See PLT p. 78 and then p. 77.

31 See Benjamin, OWS p. 95, WB GS IV.1, p. 138.

32 See Bloch *et al.*, *Aesthetics and Politics*, ed. R. Taylor (London: NLB/Verso, 1977), pp. 151–76. Apologising for Hungary's unique road to socialism and beyond takes on a rather different hue in the light of the role of Hungary in breaching the Berlin Wall in 1989.

33 The interview with Rudolf Augstein and Georg Wolff took place on 23 September, 1966, to be posthumously published, on 31 May 1976, in *Der Spiegel*, pp. 193–219. It appears in G. Neske and E. Kettering (eds), *Martin Heidegger and National Socialism: Questions and Answers*, trans. L. Harries (New York: Paragon, 1990).

34 See P. Lacoue-Labarthe, *Heidegger, Art and Politics: The Fiction of the Political* (Oxford: Blackwell, 1990).

35 Lacoue-Labarthe, *Heidegger*, p. 37.

36 For a discussion of this, see M. de Bestegui, *Heidegger and Politics* (London: Routledge, 1998).

37 Adorno's essay 'Cultural criticism and society' is translated in Samuel and Sherry Weber, *Prisms* (London: Neville Spearman, 1967); see *Prisms*, p. 34, German, p. 31.

38 See ch. 5, 'The caesura', in Lacoue-Labarthe, *Heidegger, Art and Politics*, which ends, 'This is unfortunately what Heidegger, who knew a good deal about the caesura (what else after all is the *Ereignis*?) and Heidegger alone can help us to understand, he who obstinately refused, however, to acknowledge Auschwitz as the caesura of our times' (p. 46).

39 For Heidegger's text, see McNeill (ed.), *Pathmarks*, pp. 260–1.

40 See Adorno, JE p. 46, JA p. 51.

41 On conjuration, see J. Derrida, *Specters of Marx: The State of the Debt, the Work of Mourning and the New International*, trans. P. Kamuf (London: Routledge, 1994).

42 See note 37 for the discussion of this in relation to Heidegger. See also Lacoue-Labarthe, *Typographies: Mimesis, Philosophy, Politics*, ed. C. Fynsk (Cambridge, MA: Harvard University Press, 1989), especially ch. 3, 'The caesura of the speculative'. In both books Lacoue-Labarthe cites Hoelderlin's definition of caesura as this counter-rhythmic suspension of alternation (p. 234). He notes the resonance on the status of Hoelderlin's lyric poetry between Heidegger and Benjamin's earlier analyses from perhaps 1914–15; see note appended to volume 2, of WB GS II.3 p. 921. Lacoue-Labarthe writes: 'If there is such a thing as an oeuvre of Hoelderlin, and if, as such, it culminates or finds its accomplishment at some point, then undeniably it does so in the lyric, however lacking in relevance such a category might be here. Heidegger it should be added is not the only one to insist rightly on this, and one can find exactly the same motif in the tradition (I am thinking, essentially, of Adorno and Peter Szondi) inaugurated by two well-known texts by Benjamin' (p. 211).

43 In Bloch *et al.*, *Aesthetics and Politics*, pp. 177–95.

44 See McNeill (ed.), *Pathmarks*, p. 37.

45 Jaspers's critique of the third section of the first part of *Being and Time* may have been on grounds of an inadequately thought-out relation between authenticity, as individual fate, and historicality, as collective destiny. It may have been in relation to an incipient biologism in Heidegger's writings, rehearsing Husserl's complaint that Heidegger in *Being and Time* was installing a regional ontology where he claimed to be doing fundamental ontology. Until some long-lost protocol of the discussion between Heidegger and Jaspers comes to light we cannot know. However, it may also be that the problem lies in the articulation of the relation of historicality to intentionality and of authenticity to the individuation of Dasein as *Selbstsein*. It is the notion of historicality which for Heidegger transposes the abstractions of Husserl's notion of intentionality into a system of localised meanings and connections, with specific linguistic registers such as give rise to the emergence of quite specific human beings with quite specific intellectual concerns. Appropriation, *Eigentlichkeit*, then would be the moment at which what is sent, the inheritance which is given, *Hingabe*, is taken up as an inheritance to be worked through, the *Aufgabe*, again deploying the term heavily invested by Kantian critique.

46 Tied into this etymological string is the further notion of *Geschlecht*, briefly invoked by Heidegger in *Being and Time*, which Derrida in a series of writings from the 1980s shows not just to be identifying human differences, between two or more sexes, but picking out differences based in blood ties and family relations. Derrida has four papers on Heidegger's notion of *Geschlecht*, three of them published and translated. '*Geschlecht*, sexual difference, ontological difference' (1983) is to be found in P. Kamuf (ed.), *A Derrida Reader: Between the Blinds* (Chicago: University of Chicago Press, 1994), pp. 380–402; '*Geschlecht* II: Heidegger's hand' in J. Sallis (ed.), *Deconstruction and Philosophy: The Texts of Jacques Derrida* (Chicago: University of Chicago Press, 1987), pp. 161–96;

and '*Geschlecht* IV: Heidegger's ear; philopolemology' (1989) in J. Sallis (ed.), *Reading Heidegger: Commemorations* (Bloomington: Indiana University Press, 1993), pp. 163–218. It is important to consider the very different resonances of a thinking of family resemblance and of sexual difference on the one hand, as philosophically domesticated notions, and of racial difference and blood ties, as politically supersensitive.

Index